Bonnie — thank you for the support!

~ Love + Liberation ~

ALSO BY JAN SMITOWICZ

ORANGE RAIN
REDWOOD FALLS

COMING SOON

KISS ME LIKE YOU MEAN IT: TRUE STORIES
STRONG HEARTS: THE LIBERATORS, VOL. 1
STRONG HEARTS FORWARD: THE LIBERATORS, VOL. 2

www.JanSmitowicz.com

REBEL
HELL

Disabled Vegan
Goes to Prison

a memoir

JAN
SMITOWICZ

Dedication

To Rachel: For sticking with me *during*.
To my amazing wife Andria: For sticking with me *since*, and forevermore.
To Mom and Jim: For sticking with me *always*.

Finally,
To the prison grounds' nonhuman visitors/residents: For helping to keep my spirit alive during even the direst times, and keeping my connection to the natural world not *completely* severed: the ground squirrels, rabbits, American kestrel, hawks, deer, frogs, praying mantises, raccoons, and cats. Thank you for being a tangible reminder of one reason I *had* to push through the suffering to maintain productivity in my creative endeavors.

"Our legal system may hide behind its rational interpretations of the law, but it is only to distract from the truth that the laws themselves are irrational and unjust. Like a mansion built upon quicksand, our legal system is doomed to sink under its own inhumanity."

-Romain Blavier, from a letter to the author

AUTHOR'S NOTE [feel free to skip]:
Why Self-Publishing?

Why self-publishing indeed, am I right?! Well, publicity is what gets books seen—publicity and marketing. When you're a nobody like me, even if you bust your tits and somehow do get published by a big swanky New York publisher, you *still* have to do the bulk of your own publicity. If I'm gonna do a majority of the legwork myself anyway, I might as well maintain 100% control of profits [if there even turn out to be any, that is] and content—in terms of what ends up in the book. I want my story to be nothing more and nothing less than *my story*, precisely as envisioned and executed. I'm not trying to **push the envelope** with my writing—I'm trying to **burn down the damn post office**! [Not literally, officer.] Self-publishing grants me that potential. My messages, and the activist-slash-rebellious stuff in my books, make the chance of landing a substantial publisher even more remote. And those things—the boundary-pushing and anti-political-correctness and shamelessness and dark humor [darker than the Marlboro Man's coffee—and his lung cancer], etc.—all of them are a *substantial purpose* of my writing! I'm simply not willing to betray the creative integrity and vision of my work. Not with this book; that's for damn sure. This one's too important—and honestly, in my humble opinion, too *unique* and *original* to sacrifice even a shred of its core essence. So then, I've decided to traverse the rocky path of self-publishing. To strike out on my own. Trailblazing the way to wherever it is I end up. Knowing, at the very least, that I did what felt right in my heart—for myself, for *you*, and for the craft itself. I believe, my Dear Beloved Readers, that you deserve to know my reasons.

So there you have it. Now what say we have some fun, search our souls [and the soul of *America*], and maybe even make a little fucking history together! How bout it?

~Jan~

FOREWORD

INTO THE PRISON VORTEX

Todd K. Shackelford, Ph.D.
Distinguished Professor and Chair
Department of Psychology
Oakland University
Rochester, Michigan

You are about to read [or so the book's author hopes] an extraordinary memoir by an extraordinary man. First, I'd like to briefly relay how I came to know Jan Smitowicz.

In my role as Distinguished Professor and Chair of Psychology at Oakland University [Rochester, Michigan], I have for the past several years organized an international two-day conference that brings together smart people from around the world to talk about a broad and unsettled area of work within my own field of evolutionary psychology. These conferences have featured the brightest minds in the social, behavioral, and life sciences, but also some of the most gifted fiction and non-fiction writers, both within and outside of academia. Our past conferences include "The Evolution of Violence," "The Evolution of Sexuality," and "The Evolution of Morality." Our most recent conference, held in the spring of 2016, addressed "The Evolution of Psychopathology." By the fall of 2015 I had locked in most of our panelists, but had yet to find a novelist that fit well with the conference theme, a novelist whose work incorporated elements of psychopathology.

Over the past several years I have become deeply interested in anti-natalism, despite having six children myself, and despite the fact that reproduction generates the grist for the mill of natural selection. In 2010, I read David Benatar's *Better Never to Have Been: The Harm of Coming into Existence* and, after some soul-searching, found his arguments deeply convincing and equally unsettling. Fast forward a few years to the fall of 2015. I stumbled upon a podcast featuring an interview with David Benatar. This particular episode of "The Species Barrier" featured three interviewees, each of whom was struggling in their own medium with issues of anti-natalism.* David Benatar provided an academic philosopher's perspective. The Norwegian rapper Mistro provided a musician's perspective on how one might address issues of anti-natalism. And then there was Jan. The podcast hosts had invited him on to offer a novelist's perspective—how might one incorporate social justice concerns, including anti-natalism, into the plot and characters of a novel?

Jan had recently published his debut novel *Orange Rain*. I understood from the interview that Jan incorporated anti-natalist ideas into the characters and plot in a book that sounded fascinating. I liked Jan's brutally honest but deeply empathic responses to the interviewers' questions. Within a few days I had purchased and read the novel. And what a novel! I knew Jan would be an ideal panelist for our upcoming conference—a novelist whose work incorporated themes of psychopathology into the plot and characters.

*www.thespeciesbarrier.podbean.com/e/the-species-barrier-35-antinatal/

Plus, I liked his edginess. Academics need more edginess in their lives—especially academics that attend fancy conferences.

I reached out to Jan and extended an invite. He leapt at the chance to join us, and I am so grateful for it: Jan's uniquely stylized perspective as a panelist helped make this one of our most enjoyable and stimulating conferences; moreover, his talk on anti-natalism and how he incorporates such important themes into his writing was a highlight of the conference! [Jan's stellar talk, as well as other panelists', are available at wwwp.oakland.edu/psychology/conference/]

When he visited Oakland University, Jan was adamant: If I liked *Orange Rain*, I'd *really* enjoy his prison memoir-in-progress. I was pleasantly surprised when he asked me to write the Foreword. Which you—Dear Reader, as Jan would say—are now [presumably] reading. After receiving the "Januscript," I devoured it in just a couple days. Not out of obligation, either—I simply couldn't put the book down!

It soon became clear that *Rebel Hell: Disabled Vegan Goes to Prison* is a stunning masterpiece. The content is certainly re-markable—a vegan, disabled young man's harrowing experien-ces during a two-year imprisonment in Illinois for trafficking marijuana. Also remarkable—in fact, singularly unique among the memoirs I have read—is Jan's unequaled stylistic panache; his beautifully crafted, outrageously candid, deeply empathic, and often uproariously funny narrative voice. He reveals the immense trauma of life in the "Prison Vortex" with incredible clarity. Even more substantial, however, is how he managed to engender the sense that I now know this man on a thorough and deeply personal level. I suffered when he suffered. Feared when he feared. And I was overjoyed when he triumphed.

Despite the dreadful circumstances, Jan somehow unearths humor in the very darkest places—and does so throughout. On many occasions, I found myself laughing right alongside him amid some of the most outrageously frustrating situations imaginable. His multifarious depictions of endless struggle against prison doctors hell-bent on decreasing or discontinuing his very necessary pain medications are equal parts hilarious and soul-withering. Oh—and then there are his disturbing, disgusting, but above all *entertaining* accounts of frequent physical-psychological degradation he was forced to endure with the . . . well, let's just say the *seedier* aspects of prison life. Leaving the narration of those sordid details to the man who must forever live with them.

Rebel Hell: Disabled Vegan Goes to Prison is a memoir—a *story*—like no other.

Todd Shackelford
October 2016
Rochester, Michigan

"My symbol for **hell** is something like the bureaucracy of a police state or the offices of a thoroughly nasty business concern."

-**C.S. Lewis**

PROLOGUE

HELL ON WHEELS

I.

We exit the "Rainbow Tunnel" and the Golden Gate Bridge flares into existence within our visual frame. Wispy morning fog lies in sheets across the exponential growth curves of bright red steel looping up to those iconic turrets. Lime-green hills rise and then roll off toward the coast on our right: the lovely Marin Headlands, painted with bright electric grass and clay-red rock clusters and sporadic tufts of lupine wildflowers in vivid lavender. The sparkling San Francisco Bay Area in full bloom. That sweet springtime melody ringing out from all directions. It's just past 7:00 a.m.—a time of day I adore yet almost never see; my sleeping patterns simply don't jive with early morning. I'm driving. Smoking an American Spirit cigarette and mindfully, even aggressively savoring the taste with every drag. The window's cracked just enough to flick off ash and exhale, emptying my lungs of smoke. Not many cigarettes left to enjoy for the foreseeable future—a length of time that might as well be *forever*.

A sidelong look at Rachel—my fiancée, best friend, and constant companion of three and a half years. She's staring out her window, eyes fixed on the same spot [which means anything that flits across her line of sight remains unregistered; it might as well be blank space]. The voluminous liquid clinging to her eyes indicates a kind of slow burn: a gut-level sorrow accumulated over extensive time. The sight pierces my heart with sadness. But I'm not crying. I sorta think I *can't* cry. Not now anyway. I've already begun constructing a thick, steel-reinforced concrete wall around my emotions, fiercely suppressing anything that manages to boil up to the surface.

The sun has risen in earnest now, its white-bright nuclear explosions flaring out in full view above the Berkeley Hills off to the left. Our tired, sleep-scrimmed gazes float east across the incandescent blueberry waters of the bay, its surface some 350 feet below us still as we're snaking down Highway 101. Down toward the bridge. The chilled brackish waters exist with perpetual full-contact *Hi-how-are-ya-nice-ta-see-you-again!* meetings— collisions—between pushy incoming ocean tides and westward-pressing freshwater from the complex, vein-like network of the San Joaquin and Sacramento Deltas that drain into the bay, their slow-gushing mouths many miles distant, farther even than Mt. Diablo's sun-blasted silhouette jutting up from the Hayward Fault and just visible through the morning's grayish-brown haze. The water seems flat from way up here. Flat and calm and expansive. Its mesmerizing blue unblemished save for the hyper-white staccato dashes winking into and then just as ephemerally out of existence with the waves, those liquid masses rising in a flash, curling inward on themselves, and then dropping back to the surface in an oh-so-brief but powerful crash, their meeting broadcast outward in a delicate breath of mist. Accompanied always by that immutable sound. A sound humans seem to know instinctually, in our blood, our very DNA, and why not? We can, after all, gaze into the all but boundless past and imagine our distant ancestors crawling from the primordial sea, those waves' aural constancy the *literal* soundtrack to our evolution.

Pressure, momentum, mass, force . . . physical constants that govern the interplay between separate entities, all merging to create a reality that is somehow both [1] easily predictable by the laws of nature; and [2] utterly startling, unexpected, amazing. Perspective alters everything—in a way similar to how particles act differently when observed.

Just like this.

This whole scene.

All of it altered by my chronologically distant perspective: truth is, more than half a *decade* has passed since the events I'm describing. I could pretend otherwise—but one of my most important goals for this memoir is ruthless honesty, no matter how painful it may [will] be. *Is.* Every single time I open this manuscript, just like every time I grabbed my yellow legal pad while incarcerated and held it before my face to write. Fucking *painful*.

I maneuver Rachel's beat-up old Honda Civic around the last descending curves and onto the bridge. Speaking of pain . . . I'm thinking how almost any part of the human experience can become pedestrian—or at least tolerable—via simple prosaic repetition. Can't it? Even horrifically shitty aspects of modern life, like debilitating physical pain. *My* pain.

See, on that searingly emotional early morning drive of ours—the gorgeous panoramic scenery unpurpling as post-dawn sunlight categorically brightens everything—I'm already hurting. Physically, that is, in addition to the ghastly parade of shorn emotions whirling cyclonically in my head. Hurting even though I already swallowed my standard morning dose of OxyContin [40 milligrams]! or OxyCodone Extended Release, you could also call it. For the typical humanoid, that amount of Oxy would result in nodding, slobbery heights of unimaginable euphoria. Forget *pain*! Unless you're experiencing catastrophic trauma-ish pain, like a protuberant broken bone, 40 mg of extended release Oxy is like Thor's hammer crashing down on a cantaloupe when it comes to vanquishing pain.

But not mine.

Of course not mine.[1]

Let's see . . . that morning, en route to San Francisco International Airport—May 18, 2010—I'd been suffering from that level of debilitating, disabling pain for over a year and a half. The very real prospect of being denied even a semblance of adequate pain medication while incarcerated is among the most terrifying worries out of the litany occupying my mind. Twisting my guts into stiff mangled coils of nauseous radiation.

Rachel and I speak very little. The last several months have been filled with endless discussion. This morning, our sorrow and the huge gravity of impending separation makes conversation feel pitiably insubstantial. I stick U2's *Achtung Baby* album into the CD player. Hoping to chase off the potent introspection facilitated at the moment by silence. Between our seats, my right hand grips her left. Hard.

---

[1] The meds obviously help to an extent, or I wouldn't be taking them—but more on this later. Much more; it's not a frivolity or marketing ploy that the word *Disabled* appears in this memoir's very [sub]title . . . sadly my condition is a dominant force in life, so it *has to* play a significant role in my story. Especially given the hideous, morally atrocious medical "care" I end up receiving.

I flick a glance over at Rachel and see her eyes flooded yet again—or maybe it's *yet still*—with tears. I'm crying now, too, but more from the beautiful song that's playing ["Zoo Station" [a song I've heard easily a hundred times, though it never walloped me with emotion quite like this]]. Her tears have nothing to do with the music. I know because U2 has never really affected her much. In one of our silent expressions that say *I love you*, I give her hand a quick tight squeeze. She returns the gesture and holds fast for several seconds. Then I swipe the volume knob with my index finger to mute the music. After taking a deep breath and a moment to gather my thoughts, I forcefully inject strength into my voice, hoping to project confidence. Unambiguous and utter certainty. "We will get through this, okay babe?" I said this as much to myself as to her.

She nods vaguely, averting her gaze from mine.

"We *will*, Rachel. Promise you." I bring her clasped hand to my face and caress my lips ever so delicately over the velvety flesh between her wrist and knuckles. Then kiss each of her fingers in turn.

Rikki's jealous. Our gorgeous, insanely affectionate American bulldog–pit bull mix has been sitting reservedly in the back seat the whole time. She knows something weird's afoot. Normally über excitable and amped to go on trips, she probably noticed that only *I* packed a bag. Plus the sweet girl's always been super clued-in to our emotions. Any time one or both of us exhibit despair, Rikki—without fail or false inference—would grow even more effusive and affectionate right away. Often to a degree you could easily label *pushy*, bulldozing her big goofball pittie head close as possible to our faces, moistening them with hot insistent swipes from her powerful tongue, pressing the side of her snout against our torsos or necks, staring imploringly and at length with those shocking glacial-blue eyes as if to say, *Okay Mama/Daddy, you can stop being sad, cuz RIKKI'S HERE AND SO EVERYTHING'S A-OKAY NOW!!* So she's come to grok our complicated sorrow, and she sticks her face between us and licks, whining low in her throat. Her affection game has been thrown outta whack the last few months—there's been enough generalized life despair floating around to fill an ontological/metaphysical stadium.

The full, dynamic character and nature of that imaginary stadium's contents will be thoroughly explored in the trajectory of time's arrow—warped and off-kilter though that trajectory may necessarily become.

Right now the only thing I'm trying to allow to matter is this drive, this final hour we three get to spend together. It's the last time I'll be with my fiancée for two years, except for a few guard-supervised visits. And . . . and Rikki . . . oh dear gawd, just *thinking* about it carves up my insides like a fish-gutting blade. Not only will I never get to see her, I won't even be able to *communicate* with her. At least Rachel and I can talk on the phone. Write letters back and forth. *Some* degree of contact. But with Rikki, nothing at all. To this day that realization sends dart-like pangs of hurt shooting into my heart, or soul, or whatever you want to call it. Perhaps saddest of all: *Rikki will not understand what happened.* One day I'm there, separated from her just a few hours a week and sleeping in the same bed every night, half the time spooning, half the time with her curled up in a tight fetal ball at my feet. Now I'm leaving, and I won't be back for *two fucking years.* How long will she remain expectant for my return? Will she eventually come to feel betrayed, abandoned? That possibility alone is enough to make me consider [yet again] fleeing the country to escape incarceration.

Rachel has been rock-solid for me. Her strength and courage are truly inspirational. I can't help but dwell on how all this is affecting her; this ceaseless nightmare on top of the weight of sorrow she/we already carry every day as hyper-aware and sensitive, conscience-driven citizens of planet Earth. As unrelenting voices for the silenced, tortured, nonhuman-animal billions, and the natural world as a whole.

When you go to prison, your loved ones are in many ways incarcerated as well. A close romantic partner most severely of all. Yet she's been really, really remarkably brave: not because this comes naturally or easily, but because it's *what I need.* Helping me navigate this treacherous psychological–emotional maze in ways uncountable. A maze very much like the Minotaur's labyrinth.

We pass through San Francisco—our old neighborhood whisking past as we ascend the streets alphabetically along 19th Avenue south of the park. After that, time seems to fold inward on itself and bring us the last 15 minutes to the airport in a blink, although that could just be memory's demolition-crew aspects: nothing worth remembering happened, and so it just *seems* as if time had passed within the space of moments, and only in retrospect.

Prison is like a black hole . . . so terribly dense and massive that it warps spacetime in dramatic, unpredictable ways—even from temporal distances [both before and after] that seem tremendous. This timewarping effect is among the biggest, most shocking, and most *definitely true* things I learn throughout my Prison Experience. A revelation, or rather a series of interconnected revelations, that present themselves over and over again, in ways staggeringly variable; revelations that not only *feel* real and right when instances of them happen, but which also hold up under the microscope of careful retrospective scrutiny.

We pull up to SFO's departures terminal's curb. Rachel's crying. Her capacity to love and to *care* appears boundless; I've yet to see anything that indicates otherwise. She's a woman with her emotions on speed dial, ready to be summoned at any time. And not at all in a bad way. She'll prove invaluable in helping me *feel things*—even amid times of multitudinous concurrent personal tragedy, when my psyche simply wants to shut down, go numb.

"I love you so so fucking much," Rachel says, striving for composure. "We'll be okay, right? We'll get through this."

"Of course. Together every step of the way. I love *you* so fucking much."

I'm not crying. I do get misty-eyed, hugging and kissing Rikki goodbye. But no open flow of tears like Rachel. There's a simple reason for this: *I've already said goodbye to them.* I've been saying goodbye to them every single day for the last two months. As I'll eventually learn during my Prison Experience, extended anticipation renders many events anticlimactic.

I fling my backpack over my shoulders and bend down to stretch my car-drive and pain-addled knees. Then wave and blow kisses and wave and blow kisses and wave to Rachel as she drives off. Within seconds she's out of sight and I'm alone. "Better get used to it," I tell myself out loud, unconcerned with the smattering of other people with their luggage and brief time away from loved ones and their smiles and their ignorance. They might as well be from another planet at this point. "Better get used to it, cuz you're *alone* now, in every way that really matters."

I'm almost able to convince myself that this fact is acceptable, that I can handle it.

Almost.

2.

The thread that unraveled my life was a black thread with yellow lines. It stretched horizontally across the upper-middle portion of America, beginning on San Francisco's Bay Bridge and ending just west of the George Washington Bridge, which leads into Manhattan [my destination]. This thread is about 2,900 miles long. It crosses 12 state lines. The thread is Interstate 80.

No, that's not quite accurate. I-80 was just the *physical* thread. What really led to the unraveling of my life was more *metaphysical*. Okay, there were two things, and both are basically different threads on the same shirt. Or maybe the same *thread*, but on different *sides* of the shirt. As you'll see, it's all very fucking complex and confusing to parse out the myriad factors involved. So I'll just make it simple and give you a *threadbare* explanation to get this bitch rolling.

Financial desperation: the foundation of this whole damn wild monolithic thing. Prosaic, I know—but the truth so often is. All of it originates in my not knowing how the hell I'd pay rent, even though I lived in a showerless, indoor-toiletless, *tiny* cabin in Mendocino County nowhere, 2.5 hours north of San Francisco. Didn't help that I was [and am] unquestionably disabled, but had been denied twice already for Social Security Disability. Managing to secure *food* only because I had an EBT card. Social Security Disability: the insurance policy that almost never pays off, even when your life gets in a wreck.

Lakota Indians had a warrior cry they'd shout before battling European colonizers: *Hoka Hey!* Which roughly means, "It's a good day to die!" When first offered this job, I thought it was a good day for that old life to die. My life of crippling financial anxiety, desperation, depression, selling off things I loved . . . Change was long, long overdue.

And that life was indeed about to die. Unfortunately, that death would cast me inexorably into hell.

I'm zipping along at precisely 2 mph above the speed limit on cruise control through western Illinois. Making fantastic time. This morning I was in western Nebraska. Now it's late afternoon, but I feel like I could easily drive for about ten more hours. My rented RV's fuel gauge hovers below the one-eighth mark. Time to take the next exit and refuel, maybe use one of my three empty Starbucks cups—which have been with me through about four states now—for some of that uniformly acrid and crappy gas station coffee, the sole purpose of which is functionality—*miles miles miles.* Sitting behind the wheel for as many interminable hours as I possibly can. Dusk approaches with a darkening of the overcast sky.

Then I spot a white car parked sideways on the wide, grassy median ahead. Heart leaps up into throat. I swallow thickly as eyes shoot down to the speedometer: 63 mph. Acceptable but foot still eases off the gas, natural reaction. Pass the highway patrol cruiser having leveled off to just over 60 mph. Avoiding eye contact with trooper and cruiser both. Big gas station to the left; I right-signal for freeway exit. Glance in side mirror—I think the trooper has pulled onto the highway. Hard to tell, though. There's another midsize white car behind me, obscuring view. I'm assuring myself, mantralike: *It's okay it's okay it's okay okay!* Just visiting family! Winter break. No sketchy cargo on board the RV. Besides, he'll surely just zip right on past!

Nonetheless, I drive with extreme caution and attentiveness: apply the brakes gently . . . ease down to a safe exit speed . . . make absolutely sure I'm planted smack-dab in the middle of the lane. Halfway down the exit ramp. But a white car's approaching from behind—*Shit!* Is it the cruiser, or just that civilian vehicle? Impossible to be sure from this distance via the side mirror [OBJECTS MAY BE CLOSER THAN THEY APPEAR].

Until the red and blue lights start flashing.

Okay. Okay okay *okay!* Ain't no thang, just a routine traffic stop. Deep breath. Maybe a brake light malfunctioned. Or gas lid's open. Something—because there's *no way* I committed a traffic violation. Gotta switch off the power to my crackling nerves. Eject all thoughts of cardboard boxes from my brain, expel them like projectile thoughtvomit. *What cardboard boxes? No idea what yer talkin about!*

The offramp splits into a pair of turn lanes with a stop sign at the bottom; straight ahead, across the perpendicular road, a towering steel windmill occupies the barren snow-brushed field there. I take one final drag from a half-finished cigarette and toss it into my makeshift ashtray: a repulsive stew, at the bottom of a Starbucks cup, formed by half a dozen butts marinating in an inch of filthy water. I flick the right turn signal on. Eeeeaase my RV onto the snowchoked shoulder. It's OKAY! I got this. It's nothing!! There's *nothing* illegal in the RV. No guns, no bricks of cocaine, no cardboard boxes filled with double-vacuum-sealed bags of marijuana, no stacks of Benjamins. I've handled cops in plenty of nerve-wracking situations before, and besides, this isn't sketchy because I've got no illegal cargo and so there's *nothing to be nervous about!* And I'm not nervous. Really, I'm not. Already talked myself down from the ledge of fatal anxiety.

The Trooper, parked behind me, climbs out of his Chevy Impala pulling a black stocking cap over his head. He approaches on my passenger side out of necessity—the RV jutted several feet into the [doublewide] lane, its tires on the other side pressed against a short, snowy embankment. My eyes are locked on the side mirror, watching him like a father who has stumbled into a NAMBLA convention with his young son. He slips in the snow and executes a sort of half-pirouette, arm flailing for balance. I stifle a guffaw.

I've rolled down the passenger side window by the time he arrives. I sit calmly in the driver's seat. I'm *sitting calmly* in the *driver's seat*. I really am sitting, and calm, in the driver's seat. It'll turn out to be a significant little detail. Now my brain has taken over, and I feel only a normal amount of nervousness. Same amount everyone feels during a highway traffic stop.

"Evenin," Trooper Marlow says. A scrawny little spitfuck with squinty green eyes. He lays an arm on the door through the open window. He's wearing black nylon biker gloves, the ones with Velcro straps above an exposed oval of skin. "Do you know why I pulled you over?"

"No, I really don't." Utter sincerity.

He glances up the exit ramp. Makes a vague gesture toward the top. "Ya crossed over the solid white line there when you were exitin onto th' shoulder."

I stare at him, incredulous. I'd been so careful. "Really?!"

"Yeahp. 'N that's kind of a big deal here in Illinois." He cites a legal statute. Or makes one up, who knows. I have a lot of personal experience and knowledge when it comes to police officers. While they were growing up, I'm fairly certain most were either bullies—the kids who'd harass and push you around for no reason, who'd bump into you hard as you carried a Cup O' Noodles, purposefully splashing its steaming hot water onto your chest—or they were themselves targets of vicious bullying. And they've compensated for it by clawing up a notch on the power hierarchy. Now they can harass others—legally! Somehow I'm positive Trooper Marlow is one of the latter. A wimpy scumbag who acts tough only because he can hide behind his badge if shit goes down.

"Oh wow," I tell him. "I'm really sorry about that. I didn't realize." At the time, I thought it was possible—however remotely—that I did indeed commit the egregious traffic offense cited. "I'm get'n a bit tired. I was just stoppin off to get some gas n coffee."

"That's ahright, lemme see your license and registration, please."

I must confess, my Dear Reader: I have this terrible [rational] fear that any time I reach for something during a traffic stop, I'll be shot dead like an unarmed black man in the streets. So there's some trepidation as I reach for my wallet, which is lying in a slot under the CD player. "This is a rental," I say, handing him my license. "So I don't know about the registration."

"How bout the rental agreement, you have that?"

"Yeah." I motion behind me. "Back there . . ."

"Grab that for me, if you would."

I move stiff-kneed to the dining table and pull the paperwork from a cupboard. Hand it to him and sit back in the driver's seat. He stares at the rental agreement for a moment.

And here's where the real weirdness starts.

"Okay, well I'm just gonna write you a warning. Please step back to my car with me, 'n we'll get that taken care of, kay?"

I hesitate—the hell's this about? I've been pulled over plenty of times and received numerous tickets [for traffic violations as well as simple fixits], but I've never once been asked to *get inside* a police cruiser while being written up. Never even heard of it—certainly not for a routine traffic stop! "Um." Confused, taken way off guard. "Is that normal?"

It seems *off* somehow, bigtime.

"Oh yeah, definitely!" he says far too cheerily, glancing back to see if I'm following.

His request may be strange and unsettling, but the more I hesitate, the more suspicious I'll seem. Just gotta remain calm. *No problemo.* Roll with the punches [not literally, one would hope]. I climb down from the RV and trudge back toward the cruiser. Knees cramped and burn-achy from the extended drive, nerves misfiring painfully. Cold wind whips my face. Fine beads of snow whirl around and bite into all exposed flesh. Maybe 30 degrees out. I'm wearing only a t-shirt and thin black sweater [VEGAN emblazoned in green across the chest], with navy-blue polyester gym pants. No underwear—I always remove my boxers on extreme drives. I'll do anything to shave off even a fraction of my constant discomfort.

Marlow and I approach the cruiser. I say, "Is it okay if I sit in front? I'm disabled, need to stretch my legs out."

"That's fine."

We get into the car. He peels off his douchey gloves and beanie. Begins scrawling on his clipboard's pad. "So where you headed?"

"Pittsburgh. Visiting family. And then friends in New York." Have to include New York in my supposed itinerary; the rental contract specifies that the RV will be returned just outside Manhattan. I actually do have tons of family in Pittsburgh; my maternal great-grandparents settled there after emigrating from Poland in the early 1900s. I've only met a handful of them though, and wasn't planning to go anywhere near the city on this trip.

"That's nice," Marlow says, focused on the "warning" ticket in his lap. Sounds like he couldn't care less if forced at gunpoint.

I attempt some chit-chat, as any normal humanoid would. "Yeah, my mom thought it'd be better to rent an RV. That way I wouldn't have to worry about finding motels. Any time I got tired I could just pull over in a rest area n take a nap."

"Oh yeah? Ahright."

"It's her Christmas present to me."

He will not look up! Even though it can't possibly be difficult to scribble a warning. Silence would feel awkward, though, and make me appear nervous. So I gaze around at the scenery instead, occasionally offering comment. It's amazing—I'm *still* not especially nervous. The windmill I noticed earlier stands a hundred yards ahead. Its giant single blade spins lazily, tracing arc after slow arc in the sky. The prior day, I drove past one of these windmill blades; it required the entire back end of a flatbed semi. I stared openmouthed. The thing was massive, taller and longer by far than my 28-foot RV. Never seen one that close up. To Marlow, I mention their shocking size. He replies with a caveman grunt.

"So," I say, "what's it like having an Illinois guy for president?"

"Oh, I dunno. Don't really pay much attention to stuff like that."

No surprise there—didn't much expect him to be a highly conscious individual of great social and political sensitivity. But of course. He is a dronelike pawn [or is it pawnlike drone?] for the rich, powerful white man's politically and economically charged laws. No reason to anticipate sophisticated critical thinking skills!

"Okay," he says, pulling his gloves back on. "Let's get you goin." He steps out of the car and I follow. Holy *shit*—am I really gonna get out of this?! No, I remind myself, it's not over yet; I suppress all inclinations toward relief and ecstasy. Marlow slips his dweebish beanie over his short black hair, like rolling a condom over a dickhead. "If I could get you t' sign this, you can be on your way." He proffers the mini-clipboard. We stand in front of his cruiser, between the two vehicles.

I take it and stare down for a few seconds; it's a gray sheet of paper resembling a traffic ticket. "So this is just a warning? I don't have to do anything else?"

"That's right." He has a tone of false deference that makes me want to wield the clipboard like a tomahawk and smash it across the bridge of his nose. "We don't really do verbal warnings anymore; everything's gotta be on paper."

[*Especially when the warning is just a bullshit ruse. Designed expressly to buy time.*]

"All right." I sign next to the X. He tears off a copy, hands it to me.

"Okay, mr. smitowicz, you have a nice evening."

Relief floods my body, threatening to burst the levees and manifest physically. *Cannot* allow that to happen. I'm almost free, almost through this dangerous minefield. I walk toward my rented steed. Reach the back end of the RV. But then Marlow's wimpy voice shatters my internal reverie.

"Hey, mind if I ask you a couple questions before you go?"

Looking back, I understand it all so clearly . . . this whole thing was a ruthless, psychologically calculated mindfuck; every single thing up till now was done only to *lower my defenses.*

Impressive. Slimy, but impressive. And I'll admit: my response here is the only real slipup I made. What follows still isn't justifiable or legal, but if I'd been just a quarter-inch higher on my toes, I might have avoided all of the madness that followed. Motioning to the RV, I say, "I really need to get back on the road. My, uh, my family's expecting me."

"It'll just take a second." He waves me over. In my mind, that's a command. I'm well aware of how reactionary, thuggish, and brutal cops can be. After all, I grew up in Los Angeles! Plus I've read dozens of the horrific police-encounter stories. Cops have both *power* and *credibility*—a combination as dangerous as a cobra who also spits venom. Able [and they know it] to get away with just about any-damn-thing they want. I consider refusing, turning around, and striding back toward the driver's seat. But I'm sure he'd just force me to return, and then I'd look suspicious for refusing, and it'd lower my chances of avoiding a search—which is now my primary concern. He also could apply one of their overused and beloved "pain-compliance holds" [read: *torture*, cloaked in fancy words that obfuscate the inherent trauma therein]. I don't want to risk that either, given my fragile bodily state. How fucked is it that cops purposefully instill guilt in us as a matter of course, whether we did anything wrong or not? Traumatizing often-innocent people simply because sometimes they deal with criminals! It's not acceptable. A completely unfair and abusable power dynamic. No big deal for me, though [or so I thought]. I can deflect a few questions from this witless ass-clown. I've lied and gotten away from overzealous cops many a time—an unavoidable facet of illegal activity-participation. In my head, I unleash a rebel yell: *Bring it on, asshole!*

I step toward Trooper Marlow. We're face-to-face now. He's positioned himself in a way that forces me to stand sideways relative to the cruiser, which ensures that his dashboard camera will depict us at an imperfect angle. I'm certain that this was no accident either. His questions besiege me in a discomfiting flurry; I can barely keep up. But my performance is quite marvelous, given the pressure-cooker circumstances. *Almost* flawless.

Marlow begins his in-*terror*-gation. "mr. smitowicz, are you traveling with any illegal contraband?"

I shake my head, scrunching my eyebrows—*My word, whatever do you mean?* "No."

"Cannabis?"

Isn't that just a more specific way of asking if I possess contraband? Staring right into his beady little eyes, I say, "No."

"Cocaine?"

I chuckle. "No."

"Methamphetamine?"

Okay, now he's just being redundant. "No."

"Heroin?"

"No."

"Guns, weapons, anything like that?"

"Nothing like that. I'm a law-abiding citizen." I can feel the million-dollar question looming, and sure enough—

"Do you mind if I search your vehicle?"

At long last, the only real reason for this bogus traffic stop is openly presented. Thankfully I'm confident and well prepared [or so I think]. "I *do* mind, actually. I believe in my constitutional right to privacy, so yes—I have a problem with it."

That should've been enough. Period!, end of story—Good day to you, citizen of this "free" nation, continue onward; you may pass, you may collect $15,000. Without "Reasonable and Articulable Suspicion," the police cannot legally search your person or property unless given express consent.

Also known as the Fourth Amendment. Which "prohibits unreasonable searches and seizures . . . [not] supported by probable cause." Just one problem though: the humanoids who're supposed to be upholding The Law oftentimes . . . well, uhhm . . . this might surprise you, but they often have *no compunction* about breaking their own damn laws! o, how the paradox stings! Like a hornet's ass-end to the eyeball. Like a stingray's barbed tail to the heart.

"Well," Marlow says, "I have reason to believe you may be trafficking narcotics."

Blinking, I tilt my head at him, stick a finger to my chin. "And why is that?"

He gestures to the highway. "I dunno if you're aware, but I-80 is a heavily trafficked corridor."

Wowww. Fucking *wow*! That's some ironclad probable cause: I was—GASP!—*driving on the interstate.*

"Officer, I have friends and relatives who've fought and died in wars to protect my freedoms as an American." Things are getting desperate. Time to dump some patriotic hoo-rah into this Podunk prick's mental slop-trough. "I believe in upholding those freedoms, and one of them is my right to privacy."

"Okay, I hear you, but I have reasonable suspicion. So I'm gonna go head and search your vehicle."

Now my internal response is potently visceral: helplessness and defeat, that awful duo, are gorging on my spirit and picking the bones clean. But I cannot give up. Can't forget what to do now. "Well, I just want it . . . you know, on the record that I *do not* consent to this search."

"That's fine, it's all on videotape," he says, leading me to the cruiser's backseat. Dude's awfully goddamn confident for someone standing on an ice-layered pond of legality so thin it's see-through. But of course, he knows things about this county's "Justice" system that I don't yet understand.

"Is it possible I could sit up front again?" I ask. The back seat's legroom is nonexistent.

"It'll just take a few minutes." He stuffs me into the back like one more sardine in a tin can.

A second cop car arrives. Really surprised I'm not freaking out. I'm in shock more than anything—numb. Uncomfortably numb. Officer Marlow and the new arrival [who is dangerously obese] mill around, waiting for something. Sitting on the seat beside me, there's a box of random equipment. I turn sideways and plop my legs over it. At this point I don't give a shit—and wouldn't even if you paid me. Legs already cramping badly, knees burning in a rhythmic throb, and no telling how long this shameful display of American "Justice" could take. Sitting sideways like this embeds a painful torque into my back. But at least it slightly reduces the omnipresent knee-hurt.

Several more cruisers, including a K-9 unit, arrive in rapid succession. The drug-sniffing dog is a beautiful German shepherd. Can't help but appreciate the irony: me, a vegan animal lover and rescuer, wrecked by an unwitting nonhuman dog-friend. Goddamn bastard cops! I can't really see what's happening anymore. A group of officers heads toward the front of the RV to enter and begin their illegal search. Of course—it was inevitable. Inevitable, as it turns out, from the moment I was pulled over. Actually, no—from the moment I drove past Trooper Marlow on the highway. But I'll learn all about that soon enough. The stupid, desperate, irrational part of my brain [which occupies most of my skull right now] tries to convince me of ludicrous possibilities.

Maybe they won't even find it!

Maybe they'll find it and, like good Christians, turn the other cheek.

Right. Becaue this whole charade was totally just for *practice*. As you can see, I've shifted seamlessly from numb shock to aggressive, almost perverted denial.

Within five minutes, half a dozen cops are sauntering toward Marlow's cruiser. Toward me. Arrest is imminent; it'll be the first time for me. Hell, not only never arrested, I've never even been inside a cop car. There've been troublesome situations—I got clobbered with a weeks' suspension during senior year of high school for drinking at a school function—but *nothing* like this! The pudgy cop, who was second on the scene, opens my door. "Step out of the vehicle, please."

Gingerly, with the crushing knowledge that this is the beginning of what will no doubt be the hardest stretch of my life, I comply. It doesn't feel like I'm simply exiting a car. It feels like I'm stepping across the threshold between one life and a terrifying and unfamiliar new one. And indeed—that's *exactly* what this is.

"mr. smitowicz," Tubby McFatterson says. "You are under arrest."

Shit! So I guess they did find the 53 pounds of medical-grade marijuana in the RV's bathroom.

ANYTHING YOU SAY **CAN** AND **WILL** BE USED AGAINST YOU.

PART 1

CAPTURE & ESCAPE

["OUR BONDS WILL NOT BE BROKEN"]

I.

"You have the right to remain silent," Tubby says. Another Officer cuffs my hands behind my back. It sends a lightning-jolt of pain crackling around in my lower spine. The others stand around, alert, in case I try to . . . escape? "Anything you say can and will be used against you in a court of law."

Don't you just love that part? A while after I realized I'm an anarchist, and I was questioning everything about the dominant culture we take for granted as givens, I thought about that part of the Miranda Rights, by itself. It rings unusually telling and truthful for the "Justice" System in its entirety. Surprisingly un-euphemistic. And when you extrapolate it out to our society as a whole, it's even more amazing. *Anything you say CAN and WILL be used against you* . . . We can examine that phrase and learn a lot about how to carry ourselves [especially if you're a social justice activist]. About how to tread lightly as members of this society, the most destructive and surveilled culture ever to exist in human history.[2] And for those of us in America—residents of the biggest incarcerator of any nation in the world.

"Do you understand?" asks the heart-attack-with-shoes after he finishes Mirandizing my ass.

I don't respond. Fuck them. I have a right to remain silent, right? They stuff me back inside the cruiser.

Someone takes off in the RV, and the cavalcade follows. I wonder if this is really the best thing they could be doing with their time. There must be women suffering abuse from their husbands, rednecks cooking meth, people burgling houses, all within 10 miles—you know, severe crimes that have actual victims? I'd love for them to find a single victim of mine. If there's no victim, why should it be illegal? I'll get into the real, *historical* reasons later.

We pull into a huge garage space. He leads me past the dusty RV and my heart plummets. The reality of my situation is gradually hitting me in intermittent waves of varying intensity. I just lost 53 pounds of incredible marijuana grown organically, hand-tended by peaceful, caring hippies in Mendocino County.[3] Instead of going to help people with medical conditions, or simply to make people happy, and expand their consciousness, it's gonna be burned in some fucking incinerator—wasted.

We're talking somewhere in the neighborhood of $150,000 to $200,000 worth of product. Product lost. No, not lost—*stolen*. Not to mention my own lost revenue; I was going to be paid $15,000 for this transport, which by itself is *twice* as much money as I've ever had in my life! But to dwell on this would kick open the door to usher self-destruction right on in. Have to compartmentalize it. Already I'm neck deep in shit, head tilted back, gasping for air.

---

[2] . . . says the guy writing a sensational, inflammatory, & borderline seditious book, ha! I'm not exactly a light-treader myself. But the important thing is that I know & understand the means used by those at the power hierarchy's very top— in America & otherwise—to stop people from effect-ively challenging the status quo [see, for example, the FBI assassination of Fred Hampton in his sleep; see, for example, the setup & 25-year incarceration of **innocent** Black Panther organizer Geronimo Pratt]. Also, I deliberately choose when & how to tread.

[3] Part of the "Emerald Triangle": three adjacent counties in far-northwestern California [Humboldt, Trinity, & Mendocino] where the local culture and economy is bedrocked by the production of marijuana in quantities that're literally unfathomable. One of the reasons I love Humboldt so much!

Marlow sticks me in a windowless ten-by-ten cell. A small steel bed's the only thing inside—if you could call it a bed. There's no mattress, no pad, nothing. Just cold steel. "We'll come back and get you in a lil bit." He shuts the door. I let out a wavering sigh, sitting down on the "bed." It's just as hard as it looks. But then, I'm gonna have to get used to miserable confined spaces. Oh gawd, I CAN'T THINK ABOUT THAT RIGHT NOW! Hard enough to ignore the persistent scorching vise-clamp in my knees.

I sit there, head in my hands. Trying not to be driven batshit crazy by the crushing psychological weight of the future's likelihood for unparalleled misery. Trying not to burst into sobs. Cold in here. The A/C is cranked [I'd rather crank some AC/DC]. I shudder. Still wearing just the polyester pants—no underwear—and a t-shirt and sweater.

Eventually—hard to measure time in a freezing room clouded by a fog of misery and fear, with nothing to do—the door opens and a different cop takes me to another room; this one smaller, with only a barren steel desk and two chairs. Uh-oh. It's interrogation time. I'm a radical social justice activist and I know how this works. They're gonna try to coerce me to snitch—to talk, to help them bust more people, adding feathers to their caps, so they can *advance their careers*. They're gonna try to play me against the person[s] who hired me. Play anything they can, really; this steel table may appear empty, but really it's overflowing with cards, a whole slew of em, with no cards *off* the table. Anything is fair game. After all, they're waging a Drug War here! I know what to expect. Know the game. But *they* don't know who I am or what I know. Let's just hope the interrogation doesn't include electric cables attached to my nipples and/or testicles, or waterboarding, or

OOPS! 'Scuse me. Pardon my slip-up, my slip-*away* from euphemisms. I meant to write, Let's just hope this doesn't include "Advanced Interrogation Tactics." Yeah. Those aren't legal in America, yet, are they? And, legal or not, they're not in use yet, right? Unless you're in some place like Guantanamo Bay, of course.

I psych myself up for what's coming. Raise my defenses against the impending inquisition-attack. Fuck these assholes. They've already taken SO goddamn much, and I only got pulled over a couple hours ago! The taking is just getting started. No more preventable taking! They won't get a shred of information they don't already have.

See, I got my political wings in the animal rights, anarchist, and radical environmental communities. Starting in earnest in late 2005 [about four years prior to this night], doing volunteer Hurricane Katrina relief work in New Orleans. Snitches—people who cooperate with the authorities to try and save their own asses, while betraying their fellow partner[s]-in-crime[s]—aren't just simply frowned upon in my political circles. They're *despised*. When radical activists provide information about their allies to the authorities, their betrayal is widely publicized, and these cowards are maligned, ostracized. Prisoner support groups and lists encourage others NOT to support them in any way.

Conversely, noncooperating defendants get flooded with things like:

[1] Encouraging letters of support and admiration

[2] Monetary donations for legal counsel, prison commissary, etc.

[3] Books [while/if incarcerated]

[4] And so on

These things often come from complete strangers!

But so now I have to deal with the inevitable interrogation—I'm just sitting there waiting for it. The only question is how exactly they'll present things, what tack they'll utilize. I'm thinking about the late Ed Abbey; controversial writer and naturalist and strident defender of all wilderness, especially his beloved American southwest. He wrote my unequivocally favorite novel, *The Monkey Wrench Gang*. A seminal and hilarious story of ecologically-motivated industrial sabotage. One of its lawbreaking main characters proclaims, "Nobody talks, everybody walks." Right now I'm trying really, really hard not to allow myself to think about the reality of my situation; the tremendous possibility that one particular person will *not* be walking.

They let me sit in there and stew in my fermenting anxiety for a while. Ten minutes? Fifteen? Who can say? Eventually, a young man walks in and sets down his phone and a stack of papers on the table. He looks like even more of a dweeb than Trooper Marlow. No way he's a day over 30. About 5'6" in shoes, 140 pounds. Close-cropped strawberry blonde hair. His face is pale, small, delicate-looking. I actually almost laugh out loud [lol]. *This* is the guy tasked with trying to pry information from me?! Jeez—give me some credit! I'm no snitch, but at least challenge me. Test my mettle, ya know?

"Hello, mr. smitowicz." Voice just as weak as he looks. He introduces himself and shakes my hand. Cuz, you know, we're like *buddies*! "I'm

Detective Grohen, one of three drug trafficking investigators for Illinois's District Attorney. We travel all over the country following leads. Right now my two partners are in Oregon working a sizeable bust."

Oh no. Oh gawd no. *Please* don't let these pricks go snooping around California, harassing my friends and family—people who're in no way involved with this! I'm thinking this is probably just a scare tactic; why would they travel all the way to Oregon for a state case?! But soon, through a dash of synchronicity, I'll find out it really is true.

"So. You're in quite a bit'a trouble here." He settles down into the chair across from me.

I nod, saying nothing.

"Possession of over 5,000 grams of cannabis with Intent to Deliver carries a penalty of 6 to 30 years in prison here in Illinois. *Trafficking* over 5,000 grams of cannabis carries 12 to 60 years. You're facing serious prison time, mr. smitowicz."

He's hoping to terrify me into cooperating, spouting these outrageous numbers. It's so transparent. I'm politically savvy enough to know that most people who *do* get convicted end up serving a tiny fraction of what they're charged with. On top of that, I'm confident I have a decent chance of beating this case altogether if I get a competent lawyer. In the initial stages, they charge you with every crime they possibly can. Like throwing prodigious gobs of shit at a wall, knowing at least some will stick.

But I'm not letting anything on; feigning utter obliviousness. I want to see exactly what they're gonna try. Playing my cards close to the chest. I affect grave concern, overwhelmed fear, staring down at my hands with brow furrowed. "Oh wow. Uh-huh."

He leans in closer, across the tabletop. Buying my ruse hook, line and sinker—on dry land! Grohen's gonna let me in on a secret, a way out, an alternative to serving 96 years in prison [haha]. Speaking quieter now: "But you know, it doesn't have to be that way."

I look up eagerly. I'm terrified, I'm desperate . . . Please help me, Mr. Police Man! "To be honest, jan, we don't care that much about prosecuting you." His sharp little green eyes bite at mine.[4] "It's clear to us that you're just caught in the middle, working for somebody else."

---

[4] And he's switched to my first name . . . we're cohorts now, buddies. Partners-in-*anti*-crime. He cares about me. He's concerned for my family, my life—this is *not* about him, about advancing his career. Of course not!

Now I'm staring at him. Waiting. Tell me more, friend, comrade; save me!

"What we really want is the people who *supplied* you, and the ones you're delivering to. They jammed you in the middle. They put all the risk on you, jan, and now they're just gonna let *you* take all the heat, aren't they?"

Now pitting me against them. Divide one, conquer all. He wants me feeling like a pawn. Wants me to hate everyone else involved. But I'm not a pawn. It's not like that. The person/s who hired me knew my fiercely desperate financial situation, and offered me a way out. They put enormous trust in me; I could've taken that $150,000-plus worth of product, sold it, and disappeared. Easily. They also knew I could get caught and snitch. But, aside from the political reasons discussed above, snitching is just plain wrong. Yes; believe it or not, I do have a strong sense of right and wrong. At this point in my life, I'm very concerned with doing what is morally justifiable, but not so concerned with what is *legal*. ILLEGAL ≠ WRONG, necessarily. LEGAL ≠ RIGHT, necessarily. To me, snitching is ethically fucked. If you choose to enter into an illegal partnership with someone, relationships of colossal mutual faith and trust are formed. If you get caught, the right thing to do is take the heat yourself—and do everything in your power to protect your partner/s. If you can't do the [prison] time, don't do the crime. That simple.

And it goes both ways. I trusted that *they* wouldn't talk if snagged. I just happened to be the one caught. Now it's MY burden to bear.[5]

Softly, Detective Grohen repeats: "Aren't they, jan?"

I screw up my face, as if growing pensive. As if realizing that I *have* been used as a mere pawn.

Several moments of silence while he lets his words sink in. Dude thinks he's slick. He really does. Know what else is slick? A nice healthy *turd*. In my book, he's only slick in his turdishness. And this is, after all, my book! "Our ultimate goal, jan," he says with heavy gravitas, "is to get you to complete your delivery."

Whoa. I must admit . . . I'm taken aback. Figured they'd just try to scare me, squeeze a little and assume I'd start squealing like an incensed toddler. But this, this is a curveball. Makes sense though; catching someone in the

---

[5] In time, I will come to understand that it's far more complicated than that, but my thinking at the time is very simple, reductive, & one-dimensional.

act of a quite-large drug deal is rather more damning legally than the word of a criminal snitch. Man. They're really looking to slam us hard; although the dumb pricks obviously haven't considered the possibility that I was just passing through! Bringing no crime or drugs whatsoever into their shitty little county.

"If you do that," Grohen says, dropping his voice, "You'll look really good in the eyes of the prosecution, and I'll be honest—there's a good chance you could *walk*, jan."

My eyes go wide. I'm shocked. I'm intrigued. I'm toying with him.

"But," he adds quickly, "if you ask to speak to a lawyer, the deal is off. This is your one chance. We could get things rolling right away. Just say the word, jan." He's riveted. He knows I'm gonna do it. He's like a nerdy teenager who just got told by the hottest girl in school that she'll take him behind the storage shed and show him her tits.

This sounds pretty fishy to me, though. Fishier than trout pussy. I can't consult an attorney before entering into an arrangement with the cops? Guessing this is because they know any decent lawyer would advise me against it. That s/he would tell me I could end up getting wrapped in an Interstate Conspiracy case [!] and get *even more* time. Yeah, the whole can't-ask-to-talk-to-a-lawyer-or-the-jig-is-up thing is sketchy as hell.

But I stare down at the table, and at my folded hands on top, pursing my lips, pretending to consider his proposal. In reality, my mind's already made up. It was made up long ago, before I even accepted the pot-muling job! "Uhhm," I say. "Well . . ."

He stares at me intensely. There's all kinds of weird shit happening on his face, like I can tell he knows his face is staring at me intensely, but he's trying to hide it, but he's failing, and knows he's failing, so he's got this twitching palsy-type thing going on. He's behind the storage shed with the hot girl. Her shirt is off, her bra is black and lacy, and she's unclasping it. *I am that girl.* I'm toying with him, and it's beautiful. Exquisite.

Finally I speak. "Yyyyyeah."

His mouth dips a little. Did he catch a peek of that sweet pink areola? "Yeah . . .?"

I stare him in the eyes. "Yeah . . . you can go **fuck yourself**. I want a goddamn lawyer."

He takes a breath. The shirt's back on, tits hidden away again; she—er, I—was just playing his ass like the chump he is. But he's pretending not to care. Like he didn't really even want to see the breasts anyway. Ha! "That's fine." He snatches up his papers and cell phone. "Doesn't make a difference to me." He hurries out and slams the door.

For the first time since before I spotted Trooper Marlow on the grassy median of Interstate 80, I smile.

2.

A different cop is driving me past miles of cornfields to the Henry County Jail, and I'm wondering just what level of hell my life will descend to in the coming months. But no. No! I cannot be doing that. It has to be just one day at a time. Any other way, I'll lose my shit and fall down a dark hole and never be able to claw my way out. Hell, even one *day* at a time might be too difficult to bear—one *moment* at a time is how I should approach this mess! Get through this moment, and worry about the next one when it comes.

Thank *Earth* I at least know our dogger [that's "dog-daughter"] Rikki is safe. She's with Rachel. I came dangerously close to bringing Rikki with me for company on this lonesome cross-country adventure. Which is now a TERRIFYING thought—anything could've happened if I brought her. They might've taken her to the local pound when I got arrested, where she could've been euthanized on the spot. Just thinking of it makes me queasy.

We arrive at the county jail. They stick me in a holding room to wait till they're ready to book me. There's a filthy bench and a shit-brown table with etchings in the hundreds. Bunch of swastikas, love-proclamations, ejaculating penises—the usual moronic garbage. Every time a Guard passes I ask to use the phone. *Soon*, they keep saying. Finally someone wheels it in on a dolly, cord stretching down the hallway and out of sight. I try my mom first, not expecting anything. Rarely does anyone at her house pick up the landline. The answering machine serves to weed out sales calls, wrong numbers, and anybody [almost everybody] Mom doesn't wanna talk to until she's ready and makes the call herself. It also provides Mom or my brother or sister time to actually find a phone. They're almost never resting in their respective cradles. Here's a sample message I'd leave—and probably in fact *have* left, numerous times, more or less verbatim:

Hey Mom, it's Jan . . . are you there? Please pick up.
Helllooooo . . . come on, pick up the phone. Please.
I know you're there because it's the afternoon and
you must be home from work by now. Find a phone!

Mom? Try checking Nicole's room. Or by your computer. Or on the piano. Come on, pick up please . . . Hello? Hellllloooooo-oo?! . . . anybody there? Please pick up! . . . Allright-fine-callmeback.

So it's no surprise that I'm unable to reach anyone there [though the lack of surprise does nothing to diminish further knot-tightening in my gut—I want to talk to my mother more than anyone else; my wonderful, caring, sweet, generous, indefatigably loving mother]. Next I try Jim, my stepdad. The robot-operator [RobOperator] informs me the call can't be completed. Rachel's phone, same result. I'm desperate for contact; suppressing a sob that wants to escape my body as badly as my body yearns to escape this jail. Lastly, I try my spermdad aka birth-father. It's the final number I'm able to retrieve from my manicked head. After several rings the bastard machine-voice RobOperator says Sorry, she's unable to connect the call.

BABYSHIT! She's not sorry. "She" is a goddamn machine! Incapable of regret. I'm enraged by the lack of consideration this ludicrous proposition represents, and so now I want to locate the precise individual who programmed this specific RobOperator and lock him inside a Port-o-Potty at 5:16 p.m. at a construction site and slowly fill the cabin with hornets, one by one by one.[6] I'd give him time to think about his crimes against me, and against humanity in general, resulting from his diabolical creation of such a frustrating and emotionally traumatic automated jail phone system. He'd also have time to beg for mercy. Which I would gleefully refuse while ushering the last few hornets into the Port-o-Potty-o-Death. There are times for mercy, and people who deserve it, but that shitbag isn't one of them. No mercy would I provide! Just more hornets.

Aside from this cathartic violent fantasy, it's starting to feel like I've been heaved off the end of a pier with a cinder block roped to my ankle. In my time of greatest need for a caring voice, for the slightest trickle of solace

---

[6] Why so specific RE: the time [5:16 p.m.], you ask? Simple reasons: [1] the port-o-potty will've had all day to accrue ample construction-worker-shit-&-piss—on their lunch break, having performed several hours of intense, bone-crushing manual labor, they'll no doubt require giant meals, preferably from a grease-hemorrhaging nearby Mexican restaurant; [2] assuming they punch those time cards right at 5:00 p.m., my chosen moment of asshole-RobOperator-programmer-shithouse-lockup ensures: [a] maximum shit & piss volume; [b] ideal "freshness" or ripeness of said shit & piss.

in this awful, psychotic, moronic, illegal, soul-wrenching, life-mayheming night, the comfort of the familiar in this vile, alien place, the fates have decided to abandon me. To make me cope with it all alone.

Maybe it's better that way. Maybe. But it damn sure doesn't feel good.

After banging my head on the table a few times, and tearing up and sniffling and then suppressing the whirlwind of emotions once more, I stand up and walk around. Examine my surroundings.

I can see into the booking room through the window in here, reflected through a different window down the hallway. One Guard stands behind the desk, digging through my backpack. I can understand why he would, though I dislike it. But then he removes one of my writing notebooks and flips through it, stopping to skim pages. My eyebrows draw down. Son of a bitch! The hell reason could he have for doing that, aside from pure nosy boredom? I wrack my brain to try and figure out if I wrote down anything incriminating. Don't think so—I'm not exactly a newbie when it comes to criminal actions and appropriate security protocol. The slightest jotted note might provide clues. That's why you should *never* write down plans about your crime[s], or anything remotely connected. Once again, this time all together: ANYTHING YOU SAY *CAN* AND *WILL* BE USED AGAINST YOU! This includes not just what you say with mouth or pen, but with your body language, too, as this fiasco will demonstrate soon enough.

Eventually I'm taken into the booking room and the process begins. The tall, pale Guard who was nosing through my stuff saunters in. They ask about my medical condition, and why I take OxyContin and Klonopin. I explain. It doesn't seem to satiate their apparent need to make themselves feel better about their own pathetic lives by trying to humiliate those over whom they hold power. They laugh about the number of different meds I have—Oxy, Klonopin, Cymbalta [which is an anti-depressant that can also help with chronic pain]—and talk shit.

"Man," Nosy says, "you got a whole pharmacy on you. Pretty fucked up, ain'tcha?"

"Yes, I am. Thank you."

After stripping naked in front of a Guard and taking the mandatory shower, he shoves a green vinyl mattress and some cosmetics at me, then we whisk down a series of doors and hallways, through a unit and into my new cell.

The Guard leaves. There's a lean young guy sitting on the bottom bunk, orange-sandaled feet resting on the dark cement floor. I toss my stuff on the ground and he glides over to greet me. "Wassup man? I'm james. They call me j.j. What they gotchu fo?"

"Say what?" He's extremely difficult to understand. Speaks in a rapid mushmouth. He repeats the question with exactly the same inscrutability, but hearing it again buys me the time needed to figure it out. I tell him my name—a little warily. Just like how in K-12 I hated introducing myself to people whose personalities I wasn't familiar with. You know, the whole "girly name" thing.

Sensational crimes can sometimes garner respect, so I don't bother holding back. While "Guilty Until Proven Innocent" is closer to the truth, and anybody in here could be a snitch, there's no denying the weed in my possession. I'm already coming to realize that my legal case rests entirely on demonstrating that it was an illegal search and seizure. "Haulin 53 pounds of weed," I say.

"Ooooh shit!" he cries, holding a hand over his grinning mouth. He gives me a spirited high-five, then hops up and hurries to the door. "Ey yo!" he yells. "New dude got popped wit fih'ty-three pounds'a weed!"

"Dayam!" I hear from several different voices and geolocations.

I stick my legal papers in the corner with my toothpaste and three-inch "anti-shank" toothbrush and a few small bars of soap. Then I heave the vinyl pad onto the top bunk's white metal. Only other thing in the room is a steel, seatless combination toilet-sink apparatus. It sits all of four feet from where the bottom-bunk occupant's face might rest while sleeping.

Moronically, I try hopping onto the top bunk straight from the floor, using both hands to lift myself. A typical brilliant Polack maneuver. My left knee slams into the bunk's steel edge with a thunderous **DUNK**! I fall off and stumble back. Pain excruciating, like getting kicked in the kneecap by a massive Danish rugby player named Rolff. "Oh, *fuck*!" I cry out, laughing and holding back sobs at the same time. I press myself against the wall, taking deep breaths, and then limp a few steps, trying to walk it off. Kneecap's numb. "Oh Jeezus that was retarded."

"Damn, dude," james says. "Ness time juss step up from my mattress!"

"Yeah, that woulda been the smart thing t'do."

And so ends the night.

Welcome to jail, jan. You can't get comfortable—so don't even bother trying.

3.

In the morning, the blinding fluorescent lights click on at 6:30 and james says they're calling my name for meds. Having NOTHING ELSE at the moment, I'll sop up some comfort from my pills. Better living through chemistry! The C.O. holds out a little plastic cup and I tilt all five pills onto my tongue. Swallow them. They lodge in my throat. I gag for a second, and then muscle them down the hatch, wincing at the acrid taste that lingers on my tongue. It's an unspeakable relief that they're providing my normal pain meds [from the supply I brought along with me]; I was pretty terrified they'd withhold the Oxy and Klonopin, since they're narcotics; but those are the only meds able to buff the razorliest edges from my pain. If I go an hour or so past my normal dosage time without them, it begins feeling like a studded vise is clenching and tightening on both knees in a thousand different places. Then the *burning* starts, and it somehow gets even worse. Lying down, standing up, sitting . . . position doesn't matter. It's all just varying degrees of hurt.

Here's a quick rundown; I'll be discussing pain and its treatment [or more often *non*-treatment] throughout this narrative.[7] So then:

My very first knee injury was a left meniscal tear after I awkwardly landed a front handspring-flip at the beach. This was on my 18th birthday in April 2003, a couple months before graduating high school. That's the nexus point. Since then, my life has been dominated by a ludicrous, devastating, and tragic sequence of false diagnoses, compounding and dog-piling injuries [which injuries were a result of [a] lazy and unconcerned and just plain shitty doctors, [b] a high pain tolerance, and [c] my fierce devotion to varsity tennis; I played the season's final half-dozen matches on that injured knee], inadequate medical testing to determine my exact condition, five [5!] total knee surgeries from 2003 to 2008 split three-two between left and right, respectively, and finally, the gradual development—then escalating severity—of chronic bilateral knee pain.

Obviously there's something catastrophically wrong with my body. I've seen more doctors than a Pharmaceutical Representative, specialist after specialist after specialist, and nobody can figure out precisely what the hell's going on.

---

[7] This one. This narrative here, the one you're per se reading at this very moment [& yet which I'm *writing* at this very moment for *me*, per se, on *my* timeline, one that is, per se again, completely different from yours—kinda weird in an onto-logical or existential sense, isn't it?].

Many things, though, do point to some kind of major nerve-damage-related disorder. That's the likely root of my pain, this pain that dominates my life and obliterates my concentration. Basically it comes down to this: the extensive mutilation resulting from all those injuries and tissue-slicing operations zapped my knees' nerves into a frenzied clusterfuck of haywire, spark-spurting, false-alarm-blaring lunacy. Now I'm in pain 24/7. Every waking moment a struggle to maintain sanity, to preserve some oblique semblance of a tolerable life. The struggle is constant. Variable only in its degree of intensity. All of that *even with* a medication dose and regimen strong enough to floor a heavyweight professional wrestler!

A little while after medications are handed out, they serve breakfast. I skip it because food will interfere with the meds' efficacy. Besides, how much could this Podunk county jail even have for a "strict" vegan? I lie in bed, deep in thought but even deeper in sorrow. Waiting anxiously for 9 a.m. That's when the phones begin operating. I want to continue my likely battle with the RobOperator ASAP. Must speak to a loved one! Rachel's gotta be borderline puke-sick with worry. Ach! just the thought makes *me* nauseous. But hey, at least I have my meds. Right?! That *should* feel like a consolation. I always know the very moment they begin to take effect. It starts with a sort of softening of the muscles and the psyche, tenseness easing a bit. Any pain that has gathered in my knees, as long as it hasn't already gotten über-bad, recedes to the back of my consciousness. A slight sense of relieving content may touch my mind. Luckily [if ANYTHING in this situation could be considered lucky], I take the stuff exclusively for pain, and never to get high. Otherwise, I'd be addicted instead of merely habituated. There's a massive difference.

After a few minutes short of forever, I look at the clock in the dayroom and see it's 9:10 a.m. Nobody's using the phone. I dash out and try Rachel and Mom again.

Same result as last night. I stand there and close my eyes and press my forehead against the cold, white-painted cement wall. Heart fluttering. Feels like I could pass out, or simply lose the will to live and crumble to the floor, dead. My lips move of their own accord; they're doing that twitchy thing where you know they want you to start weeping. I bite it back. I cannot allow myself to cry. *Cannot.* Again—and again out of sheer desperation—I call my stepdad Jim at his apartment. He and Mom are separated, mired in the complex process of divorce after almost 15 years of marriage. But he still treats me like a son. "**tHiS iS a coLLeCt CaLL**," the loathsome operator begins. I'm already giving up hope I'll be able to reach anyone this morning. Because in the context of all this madness it'd just . . . *make sense*. It's two hours earlier in California. Ring, ring, ring, ring. Nada.

But then I hear—holy shit, yehp!—I hear my stepdad's voice: "Hello?!" Mystified, as he should be. Probably wondering, you know, who the hell's calling him from jail at 7:15 a.m. in a state where he doesn't know anybody!

"Hey Jim!" I say in a rush of exhaled relief-air.

"Jan?! What's going on?"

I have to bite back tears yet again, tears that are just one small part of a veritable flood of emotions: joy at finally reaching someone, fear of his response, shame. "So," I'm finally able to croak, "I just wanted to let you know that I'm safe, but I'm . . . I'm in an Illinois county jail." My voice wavers and it's embarrassing on a base level because I'm an adult and a man and a criminal and I'm not supposed to cry, and it's worrisome on a less-base level because I don't want to demonstrate weakness to the other guys in here, knowing that's how people get fucked up in jail/prison.

"Jesus," he says. More shock in his voice than anger, thank Earth for small favors. I really don't need my dad's shame-heightening anger right now. "What are you doing in jail in Illinois?"

"I don't really think I should talk specifics about it right here, now."

"Okay." He knows that it's a good idea—we both heard the shitbag RobOperator say how all calls are subject to recording and monitoring.

"It's *so* damn comforting to hear your voice." Mine cracks on the second word, the italicized one. "I couldn't reach anybody last night."

"Yeah, I got several operator messages on my answering machine, and I wondered what the heck was going on."

"That's okay. I'm just really, really glad I could get ahold of you this morning." My voice cracks again. I'm coming dangerously close to crying, and there may already be some pooling action in the corners. "Just thought you should know where I am, but that also I'm safe." As if to reassure us both: "I'm safe. For some reason I can't seem to get ahold of Mom." I ask him to do me a huge favor and let her know what's going on, and to text Rachel as well.

"All right. So what's the deal, do you know what it's gonna take to get you out?"

Such a goddamn sweetheart, beneath his stern exterior! I'm so lucky he entered my life, taking me in as his own child. I'll forever be grateful.

"Supposedly I should be appearing before a Judge sometime this morning for a bond hearing, and then just go from there I guess."

"All right. I'll call your mother right now. Stay strong, Janno."

"I'll be fine, don't worry." Saying it as much for myself as for him. Eyes about to overflow with tears. "Love you."

"Love you too, buddy."

We hang up. I swipe at my eyes and glance around. There are only a couple other people in the dayroom. An overweight black dude sits atop one of the tables, feet resting on the bench-seat, staring up at the TV bolted to the wall in one corner near the ceiling. The morning news is on. A famous anchor, strikingly skinny compared to how bloated he used to be, speaks to hordes of people on the street in New York. A wave of intense surreality and disbelief slams into me. It's almost dizzying. *Manhattan*. If I hadn't been arrested yesterday, I'd be walking those very streets tonight, in unfathomable ecstasy, with more than double the money in my bank account/wallet than I've ever had to my name. There's something else surreal about the scene though . . . It feels like the television is broadcasting from another universe entirely. Not just because it's inaccessible to me, separated by Guards and bolted doors and some thousand miles, but also because I feel a definite—though as-yet-indeterminable—sense of bizarre unfamiliarity. This sense of the outside world's *otherness* is one I will come to know—via the long arc of time's arrow—as intimately as a longtime lover.

Four circular orange cafeteria-style tables are spread out in the middle of the dayroom, each bolted to the cement floor. An anorexically skinny white guy with a blanket cinched around his shoulders paces the room in what seem like endless circles [≈ 65 comprising a mile], staring down at the ground. His orange shower shoes go *clap . . . clap . . . clap*. He passes by the unit's sole shower, an alcove built into the wall between two cells. An opaque and almost semen-colored plastic curtain drapes from its silver rail. The two-man cells, nine of them in total—mechanically unlocked at 6:30 every morning and locked again at 10 p.m.—flare out across three sides of the trapezoidal dayroom/unit.

I finally manage to contact my mother sometime before lunch. After hearing from Jim, she learned that—before being able to receive calls—she had to open an account with the company that serves all Illinois county jails; the system is called Evercom.[8]

"*Mom!*" I cry, drawing out the vowel.

"Son! How are you? What thee helllll are you doing in Illinois, in jail?"

I struggle yet again to suppress the tears. In general, I tend to be a sensitive and emotional individual. And these current circumstances have cranked that emotionality up to 11. "I'm doing okay, Mom, considering. Trying t'stay strong."

"What did you do? Was it something to do with animal—"

"No Mom, no!" I blurt. She immediately assumed I got caught freeing mink at a fur "farm" or liberating animals from a "research" [read: torture] laboratory and smashing up the equipment or something; I unequivocally support such actions, but don't—physically *can't*—participate in them. She knows about the former, about my radical ideology. So her presumption had definite validity. "No Mom," I say. "Nothing like that." I hesitate for a moment, then decide to tell her. Set her mind at ease a little—she'll know drug-possession charges are much less serious than politically motivated crimes. "It involved weed, okay? That's all I'm gonna say right now."

A stretch of silence. She's known for a few years that I have a medical marijuana card; despite being a psychiatrist, she approves of this wholeheartedly. Knows that pot helps reduce the severity of my pain condition's worst secondary symptoms [anxiety and depression]. Both of which feed into pain and vice versa in an endless self-enhancing cycle. Like this:

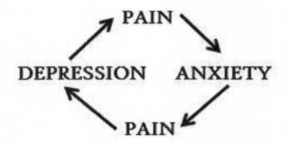

---

[8] In classic absurdist Polack fashion, she later tells me she thought the company was called "Ever Calm." As in, *You can relax now: you're in touch with your jailed loved one! Ever Calm.*© LOL!

Mom's probably assuming I got caught with nothing more than like a Ziplock bag. Personal-use amount. I'll let her continue thinking that for now. "Okay," she says.

"I should be having a court hearing within a few hours where they'll set my bond, so I'll know more then. But I . . . I just wanna get the hell outta here." Stupid voice warbling, dangerously close to breaking down here.

"We'll do what we can, all right honey?"

Sniffle. Gawd, gotta stop this crap! "Okay, thank you. Love you Mom."

Back in my cell, lying face-down on the top bunk. Mind just dashing madly. Zig-zagging with an Usain Bolt-like pace. I'm too shell shocked to read or concentrate on anything. Completely unable to utilize or even find some sort of useful distraction! I feel trapped, physically and mentally and every other way. This is *bad*.

When the Guards and inmate-workers deliver lunch trays, I manage to force down a couple slices of plain white bread and some mushy canned carrots. Talk to several other guys on the deck. A pattern begins to emerge. Of the 18 dudes here on I-block, at least 10 are here on drug cases, and *every single one* of those was pulled over and arrested on Interstate 80. Just like me. One guy got busted with 60 pounds of weed.

"Such bullshit," he tells me, shaking his head with anger-taut lips. "Cop said I was speeding. Man, I was goin 65 on cruise control." He punctuates this last with emphasis on each word. "Seriously!"

"Chh," blowing air through my teeth. "That's ridiculous." Based on personal experience, I doubt his veracity not the slightest. I delineate my own arrest. He empathizes; they used many of the same bogus tricks on him.

After the lunch trays are cleared, a Guard unlocks the glass entrance door and sticks his head in, hollering for me. Takes me out of the unit and leads the way through a different series of doors than last time, all of them the same faded turquoise.[9] Then we arrive at an ornately carved wooden door. "Putcher face against the wall 'n hands behind yer back." He cuffs me and then we enter the courtroom. I stare around in awe. It's lavish, as if we stepped through a portal to a different building altogether; everything

---

[9] It very much seems the lifeless color schemes inside jails & prisons are a deliberate part of the setup. Yet another way to crush our spirits—with dullness—stoking a slow burn in the soul's kindling. Thereby searing from out of us, as skin-layers after touching a flame too long, the will to resist any & all indignities heaped upon us.

looks brand new and spotless, gleaming, like every square inch has been scrubbed with a toothbrush. All the wood is walnut-colored, whittled with elaborate and elegant Victorian-esque flourishes. I stand before the Judge. Staring up at Honorable [sic] Judge Hamer—pronounced "hay-mer." He seems to be in his mid-50s, with salt-and-pepper-speckled chestnut hair and a leathery face etched with lines. His presence is marked by a stern severity that makes him look constipated. Needs to eat fewer [or rather *zero*] steaks and more leafy greens and fresh fruit. Methinks he's several shits a week short of clear- and level-headed enough to make decisions that invariably scorch havoc across lives uncountable.

Judge Hamer asks a short series of questions, reads the charges against me. I just stand there, hands cuffed behind my back, feeling awkward and stupid in my bright orange pants and shirt. After skimming through my papers for about ten seconds, he sets my bail.

At $250,000. Fucking *quarter-million dollars!* To be released from Illinois's jail system, you "only" have to pay 10 percent of your bail. So 25 goddamn *thousand* dollars just to go home! To be with my family and begin preparing our legal defense.

I'm rendered mute and dumb by the Judge's decision; it's a thunderclap-shock. Like a sonic boom that erupts without warning right overhead while you're walking in the forest. Here's a little perspective: my cellie james was convicted of diddling two very young children; he served two years in prison. Then, a few months ago, violated his parole conditions by walking past an elementary school. His bond was $50,000.

Let me get this straight then. For you *and* for me. Apparently, they'd rather have a convicted kiddie-diddler on the streets—one who violated his parole—than someone who was transporting flower trimmings?! My crime is apparently, per Hamer's logic [sic?], *five times* worse than james's? He could walk out of here for $5,000. But me, I'll only leave this jail if I come up with $25,000. Try to make sense of that one![10]

This is fucked. *I'm* fucked. The person/s who hired me for the whole pot-driving gig won't be able to help—suffice it to say I'm certain about this. And I have no idea if my parents will be able [or willing] to pay that price, especially when they find out precisely why I'm here! I could be

---

[10] If you do manage to make sense of it, please let me know. I'm serious. I truly can't fathom a sensible explanation for it. If you're magically able to formulate one, contact me. Really! My email is ██████████@gmail.com [*Ed.* [aka *author*] note: *address removed for a variety of what seem like obvious reasons*].

stuck in county jail until the trial, or whatever's going to happen. As you may know, the legal gears turn sllllooooooowwwwly in America, so I could be here for *months*. Just . . . waiting.

There are individuals in America, numbering in the tens of thousands, who've been sitting in county jail for months, even *a year or more*, simply because they can't afford bail. Men and women who haven't even been convicted of a crime! Their lives wasting away in these Gulags of Uselessness and Boredom. Separated from their friends and family. Jobs lost or, if they're *lucky*, on hold—their income, in any case, suspended indefinitely. Families suffering; struggling [even] more than usual because one of the parents has been *charged* with a crime. Many of these walking corpses shuffling around the dayrooms in county jails across the country will of course be found totally innocent—someday, at least. Whenever the gears of "Justice" [blood-streaked, rusted, and worn down from age and ceaseless motion—borderline-imperceptible though it may be—to a steely matte] manage to creak forward juuuust enough to reach them . . .

America: Land of the Free ©
[Some Conditions May Apply!]
[Offer Not Valid in All Locations]
[No Purchase Necessary—Though it Certainly Helps!]

I leave the courtroom in a daze. "Someone wants t'see you," the Guard says.

What the hell. I'm in trouble, aren't I? Things always seem to get worse precisely around the time I'm thinking *Hey, at least it won't get any worse!* The C.O. deposits me in a small room with a Plexiglas window. There's a speaker embedded at the bottom of the window, and a little slot under it; there's another, even smaller room on the other side. Two shit-brown steel folding chairs sit opposite one another. There's a metal toilet [no sink attachment] at the back of the inmate-room. I plop down onto the chair. Slouch at the waist and prop an elbow on my thigh. Covering my mouth with one palm, lost in thought, anxiety, terror.

Soon a heavyset guy in a gray suit enters the other room, sets down a briefcase. His cheekbones are hidden beneath a layer of pudge. Neat, close-cropped black hair, dashes of salt creeping in around the temples. He takes a seat before me, tucks his sheening black tie into the suit's coat. "Hello, mr. smitowicz." His tone comes off sounding both casual and business-ready. "I'm Bruce Carmen, a local attorney. In fact, I walked here—office is right up the street."

He unfurls his crisply ironed lawyer's pitch. Moved out here to raise his two kids away from the Big City. Utterly blown away when he discovered the number and rate of local drug cases [nearly all of them occurring, to confirm what I suspected after listening to my fellow arrestees, as a result of Interstate 80 traffic stops and search-and-seizures]. In time, this led Bruce to "become a sort of expert" on such cases. He cites some massive quantity of various drugs—x-thousand pounds—he claims to've effectively suppressed during his tenure as local defense attorney. "Suppression" of drugs seized by the cops is legalese meaning he convinced Judges that the evidence—aka illegal narcotics, here—was obtained via unjustifiable police activity. Fourth Amendment violations, in other words. If the Judge rules in favor of the drug-case-defendant, the evidence is ruled inadmissible, and so their attorney has thereby succeeded in "suppressing" it and the case is thrown out.

Bruce sounds *perfect* to me. Just the right kind of firepower I need, his intimate knowledge of Henry County's legal landscape a monumental ostensible benefit. He steps out into the hallway then and there to call my mom and fire his fastball pitch at her. Returning within just 90 seconds; she hired him on the spot!

Perhaps his apparent practice of lingering at the courthouse to solicit clients should've tipped us off. Maybe his eagerness to officially secure my business was a siren-like harbinger of something amiss. But I'm so frightened, and so alone [*overwhelmed* is a formidable *under*statement]. Nobody on my side with the slightest shred of power. Can you even imagine, Dear Reader, what it feels like to be staring down the double-barrel shotgun that is American "Justice"—those twin Black Holes of Death that could explode thunderously at any moment, blasting my life to tiny pieces? Our collective shock and fear are instrumental in Mom's decision to hire Bruce. Later, she'll deem him an "ambulance chaser." But it's easy to say these things now, with the crystalline knowledge provided by retrospect. By a remoteness in spacetime.

"So now," Bruce says. "Go head and tell me what happened. Don't hold back—you're my client now, so everything we discuss is confidential."

I can't stop the wide, giddy grin from spreading across my face. I'm not alone and helpless anymore. Trapped claustrophobically in felonious legal limbo. I have someone On My Side—and significantly, it's someone who knows this county and its particular legal mechanisms and players. Knows how to maneuver through all the absurd bureaucratic bullshit specific to this place. Now *I've* got some legal firepower! Being sans representation, without a legitimate advocate, is exquisite horror. Especially since I'm 2,000 miles from home in a place I've never been before, and *in jail there.* But now . . . the difference is astonishing. In just a few minutes I've gone from being utterly alone and powerless and hopeless in a constant daze of lethargic numb dejection to, well, whatever complex emotional amalgam constitutes the diametric opposite. It's liberating, powerful, a fat needle-shot of adrenaline banged straight into my heart.

Once I shake off my newfound, empowered fist-pumping confidence enough to concentrate, I lay out the whole story for Bruce—from the moment I saw Trooper Marlow's cruiser all the way through to my arrest. Providing abundant detail. Seems unbelievable to me, but it happened just last night. And I've already replayed every moment in my head a good 200 times; all of it is hauntingly fresh and recallable pretty much verbatim.

Bruce nods and *Uh-huhs* as I speak. When I describe how Marlow took me into his cruiser to write the "warning," Bruce shakes his head knowingly, lips pursed. Like he's heard it time and again. "D'you know what that was?"

"No, what?"

With heavy import: "He was buying time for the drug-sniffing dog to get there."

My body slinks way down in the steel chair. Mouth slack. Shaking my head. "Oh, man. That is messed up." But it makes so much sense! Marlow wasn't gonna stand in the snow for ten-plus minutes just to write a stupid [fake!] warning. Also, he undoubtedly wanted me right by the cameras, so he could find—post facto—something, *anything* about my mannerisms to use against me.[11]

He begins gathering his stuff. "Listen, I need to get some work done at the office, but I'll be back later this afternoon. Your mom has my office number and my personal cell number, so we'll be keeping in touch. I know it's boring, but hang tight, we're gonna get you out, okay?"

He leaves. His words—and far more importantly his being *my* lawyer now—have given me hope, but I'm once more feeling the crushing aloneness and impotence.

Back in my cell, I read an *Entertainment Weekly* that's floating around the unit. I can nearly hear myself getting dumber by the paragraph, but it's either that or go insane with boredom and depression; start bashing my skull into the endless dull stone walls and their soulkilling banality until my brains splatter from my head, just to escape this suffocating malaise. "Blank Walls, Blank Minds" is an anarchist slogan I really like and can identify with in here.

I know if I don't get bailed out by 5 p.m. today, Friday, I'll have to stay the whole weekend. Bails cannot be posted on weekends. I'm desperate to leave. Seems like the shell shock from having my financially spectacular illegal task thwarted by arrest has created this pernicious, relentless and unshakable *Gestalt* inside me. The near-trembling excitement I felt in anticipation of completing my job and receiving the dizzyingly massive [for me] payment of $15,000 was abruptly exterminated; but here in jail, there's no way for me to redirect the dregs of anxious energy still pulsating, quasarlike, in my head. That's the primary reason I won't stop feeling this profound ontological sickness until I'm released. Released and back home, where I can regroup and try to recover enough to face whatever terrors the future has in store. Doesn't help that I haven't spoken to Rachel in over 24 hours now; that may seem paltry, but in our intense three-year relationship, it's almost unprecedented. And these traumatic circumstances hugely amplify the effect. Despite concerted efforts to avoid it, I start obsessively dwelling on all the things I've lost. Like the financially stable future I was building for myself and Rachel and Rikki—something that would've taken many many years otherwise, given my health problems, my inability to

---

[11] This thought will prove more prescient than I could even imagine. And not just when it comes to Trooper Marlow, but for the Judge & Prosecution as well. All part of the stacked deck.

work any kind of normal job or hours. Rachel must be horrified for me right now. For our future. I stick my face in the scratchy gray blanket I've been using as a pillow [no actual pillows are provided] and begin to cry angry, bereft tears. Soon my face is drenched in hot moisture. Slimed with snot. Eyeballs burning, lids tired and achy. *How the hell will I ever get through this?*

Eventually I pull myself together and shuffle around the dayroom. Now the place is full of other inmates, and it's *loud*. Guys watch TV, do pushups and situps and tricep-dips; others play cards, and two are engaged in a chess duel. The default voice-level is a **SHOUT**. Even if the one they're talking to is right across the table. I return to bed.

I have a very active imagination, as any writer of absurdist and high-concept fiction should. But even that shuts down and closes shop when I'm miserable. I also can't bear to watch any mind-numbing television, or drag my eyes across the vacuous content of the magazines and books available in here, or hang around people with whom I have nothing meaningful in common. All these factors coalesce with the broader situation to form a festering miasma of intolerable boredom and depression that gnaws away at my spirit, my very will to live.

Somehow a couple hours pass. "So," I ask james at one point, "how is it here?" I'm trying to prepare myself for a potential stay of several days, Earth forbid.

He's been here for three months, opting to simply get some of his time served rather than get bonded out. "Iss koo," he answers. "De food pretty guh. I mean, not like McDonalze good, but decent. We get tacos tonight, e'ry Friday, cheeseburgers on Sa'day . . . you eat tacos?" he asks with an eager rising inflection—he's noticed something weird about my eating habits.

"What they got in em?" I say.

"Meat, cheese, lettuce, tomato."

"Nah."

He pounces. "Can I getchers?"

"Yeah, sure. I don't eat meat."

Dinner comes around 4 p.m. I eat the paltry shreds of iceberg lettuce and tomatoes, some canned fruit mix, and not much else. I'm a four-year vegan at this point, repulsed by the mere sight of animal products. I won't even eat, for example, the taco shells, because they have flesh-juices on them. Doesn't really matter though. My appetite is borderline nonexistent.

Shortly after dinner, a C.O. comes to get me. What the shit? I'm led back to the meeting room. Bruce is already sitting on the other side of the Plexiglas.

"Hey Bruce, what's goin on?" I sit down.

"You've got a bond reduction hearing in about . . ." He glances at his watch. "Ten minutes."

"Oh wow!" I cry. "Thought it was supposed to take like three days, minimum!"

He smiles, shrugs. "Pulled some strings."

We're back in front of Judge Hamer. Bruce requests a bond reduction. The Judge turns to a smug, boyish little man [*mannish* little *boy*?] standing off to the side; he looks like the legal system's Doogie Howser. Turns out this is the Prosecutor for my case; First Assistant State's Attorney Brian Kerr. The smarmy prick. "Mr. Kerr," Hamer says, "do you have any issues with this request?"

"Well," he says in a voice that sounds as gelded as he looks, "I'd be willing to accept a reduction, but I feel mr. smitowicz should be required first to surrender his passport to the court."

They want to ensure I don't flee the country after being released. Yes, yes, it's definitely acceptable! We agree to the condition and my bond is lowered to $150,000. Now I "only" need $15K to leave. And I need to get my passport sent here pronto . . . overnighted, UPS, FedEx, Falkor from *The Neverending Story*, whatever the hell it takes!

Back in the hallway, Bruce says he'll be back to talk in 45 minutes to an hour. The Officer will stick me in the meeting room to wait.

"Okay." But my stomach swirls. It's been about nine hours since this morning's meds, and the blade is starting to twist and dig. I just wanna splat myself facedown on something soft. Not sit in a steel goddamn chair!

The C.O. opens the door. I say, "I can't go back to the unit? I'm disabled, I—"

"You'll be ahright." He locks me inside and saunters off.

My anger flares like a jet of magma. There's a speaker on the wall by the door. I press the button. In a few seconds, the same Officer's voice: "What?"

I know he'll stop listening within just a couple seconds. "I need to lie down. Please."

Kch. "Then lie down. Plenny'a space in there!"

I turn and slam the chair against the wall with a loud metallic *clunk*. Stand there arms akimbo for a second. Then grab the chair and plop down, sighing. Fuck my life. Discomfort invades my knees immediately like a toothache. Imagine sitting in the back of a small two-door car with your feet resting on the seat, heels pressed against your butt—for five hours. That's the level of cramped achiness I *start* at. Every single day. After a few minutes, I stand and pace around, trying to ease the stiffness. Then, hardly aware what I'm doing, I storm over to the speaker and jam down the button with a thumb. Don't even give a shit anymore.

A response comes almost right away. "Shut up 'n stop pressin the goddamn button, fore I come in there 'n *make* you stop!"

Wow—kitty's got claws! Local high school football team must've lost last night, and I'm getting some residual fury. The cockface.

I sit for another ten minutes. Then I start feeling a pressure tightening in my guts. Uh-oh. No. Not now, please not now! Something wants out—and it's pressing its head against the portal of my anus. I look back at the steel, seatless toilet rim. It's splattered with urine. There's no toilet paper. *Of course* there's no toilet paper! That would be too easy, wouldn't it? Too sensible. And the C.O. already threatened to beat my ass if I pushed the button again.

I try to hold it in, but it's already prairie-doggin, and I've only been in here 20 minutes. Bruce won't be back for at least another 20 or 30. No way I can wait that long.

Screw it. Shit first, worry later. This is jail—no shame, no gain!

Since the rim's dotted with piss, I bust a squat. And yet still, when I squeeze out the turd, it plops heavily; toilet water splashes up onto my asshole and the underside of my scrotum. Repeat: my asshole and nutbag are wet . . . from toilet water. I'm actually surprised that Bruce doesn't return right then and look through the Plexiglas to see my bright orange pants around my ankles, legs quivering, balls dangling and dripping water.

The thought makes me laugh, now. If you're unable to laugh at your own shame and degradation, the terrorists have won.

I pull my pants back up and rise from the leg-trembling squat. Now my knees hurt too much to tolerate standing *or* sitting. Hell, what's a little floor scum compared to an unwiped ass? I lie on my stomach behind the steel chair, hands pillowed under my head; hopefully I can at least avoid getting filth on my face. The gray floor's like dense storm clouds. The hard cement presses nastily into my kneecaps.

Only a couple minutes pass before my butthole starts feeling slippery, itchy. Ah, *shit!* Even though it was a constipated plopper, guess I do need to wipe. Badly. The itchiness gets worse and worse. I can't well scratch it; we only receive clean pants and shirts once a week. That leaves me only one reasonable option [your definitions of reasonable, rational, normal, and a host of other things change very fast in jail].

I slide off my right sock and turn it inside out. Stick my hand inside, like a sock puppet. [What kind of sick-ass bastardly performance would entail *this*?!] Lying there on the floor, contorting like a worm, I try to wipe with just the heel, where it's gray and less likely to be noticed. I wipe a couple times and decide that's enough. Slip the sock back on my foot.

Hey, don't judge! If a Guard sees me with only one sock, he'll demand to know where it is. I'm stuck with these circumstances. Forced to do what I must to get by.

In a little bit, Bruce comes in. "Well," he says, sitting down across from me, "They've never done that before." Meaning the passport-stipulation. "Completely caught me off guard."

"I'm honored to be the first." Oozing sarcasm.

We discuss the best way to find my passport and get it sent here. Do I even know where it is? Well, probably either at my cabin in Mendocino County, or in some filing cabinet at my mom's house. Haven't used it since Jim and I went to Europe in 2002. Think think think. Okay—my [at the time] best friend Ryan lives at the cabin with me, but there's no cell phone service out there in the sticks. Could be a day or two before he goes into town and has reception. So it's gotta be Rachel. She lives an hour and a half south, but that's the best option. "My girlfriend Rachel can get it, *if* it's in NorCal," I tell Bruce. "Otherwise, prob'ly my mom."

He has me jot down a message for both of them, along with Rachel's contact info. After a moment's consideration, I list several places it could be at the cabin. Then finish with, *Tear the place apart if you have to! Thank you, love you SO MUCH.*

"Okay then," Bruce says. He steps out to call her, returning in just a couple minutes. "She's on her way to the cabin right now. Sounds like a wonderful girl."

I exhale several psi of tension. "Yeah, she is." Even though I'm in the worst situation of my life, I feel grateful right now. *Grateful* to have people out there who love me so much. And grateful my mom hired Bruce, who seems to Get Shit Done.

"Okay," he says. "All we can do now is wait. I'll be keeping in touch with Rachel and your mother. Maybe call her later tonight, see what's happening. Until then, just be strong, all right? The boredom's really the worst thing here."

He says that because he doesn't know the sock I'm wearing is streaked with feces.

I return to I-block a little less miserable; a bright gleam of hope shines within me, and it, you know, warms me up or something. Now I'm feeling kinda decent, with high hopes and the expectation that Rachel will overnight my passport first thing in the morning and it'll arrive early Monday. Only a couple [interminable] days to get through.

At around 8 p.m., I ring up my mom, hoping for good news. Here's the precise moment I start to learn just how dangerous HOPE can be amid the nightmarish bureaucratic clusterfuckery of the American "Justice" System. How very dangerous *hope* can be when you're staring in slack-jawed horror at the depthless, life-mangling, hyperdontic-with-fangs, ravenously insatiable maw of the Prison-Industrial Complex.[12] Soon—all too soon— it'll begin to feel, more and more, like *if I shit in one hand* and *stick my hopes in the other*, they'll end up filled with the same thing: **mounds of stinky shit.**

Mom answers the phone, voice warbly. She's crying. It immediately sends cracks rippling through my heart.

---

[12] [a] Which is a voracious gullet with an obvious & demonstrable human-flesh preference for **dark meat** rather than light. The Justice/Prison Systems [which are truly just two separate parts—connected & even *symbiotic*—of the same organism; I'd compare them to the shaft & the vibrating mechanism of an improbably large, rectal-tearing & rapey dildo], in other words, devour black lives to a far greater extent than they do everybody else *combined*. I'll return to this idea repeatedly throughout the memoir—because it's a monstrous ethical calamity, it's monumentally important, and also cuz the percentage of citizens who fully know & understand the extent of this national crisis is *criminally* [NPI] low.[b]

[b] NPI = No Pun Intended, FYI.[c]

[c] FYI = For Your Information. But you almost certainly already knew that, & TBH I already knew that you almost certainly already knew that, & hence this sub-subfootnote is almost certainly just another blatant literary technique I'm using to try to enhance the book-reading experience. In this case it's probably an attempt to *reflect*—through the very reading itself—the emotional & psychological effects of the American "Justice" System's complex & multifaceted assfuckery. Is this all a contrivance? Oh, most definitely. Is it pretentious? Maybe. But does it *work*?! THAT'S the important question. I very much hope it does indeed work. Very, very much.

"What's wrong?!"

"Sweetie, I'm so sorry—your passport is in Big Bear." She stifles the quaver in her voice, trying not to upset me even further. The same thing I've been trying to do for her.

My eyelids fall shut. Big Bear's a mountain town a few hours southeast of L.A., where my stepdad Jim has a house I lived in last winter. "Are you *sure*? Did Rachel tear through the cabin?"

"Yes. She and Ryan went through every square inch of the place, twice. It's not there. Then Jimmy overheard me talking about it and said he saw it in Big Bear when he was there last month. In the room where your stuff was."

My turn now to suppress tears. I clench my jaw, breathing heavily. Press my forehead against the white stone wall. Difficult to speak and even swallow, like somebody crammed that goddamn passport down my throat. Jimmy is my [then] 14-year-old brother. He's outrageously bright, with uncanny memory. If he's sure he saw it, then it's true. "Okay," I say, aiming to stay upbeat. "That's okay. Do you think you or Jim can go up there tomorrow or Sunday and get it?" No big deal really. In the grand scheme.

"Honey." Sniffling openly. "Big Bear's getting pounded by snowstorms right now. The roads are impassable. All roads up the mountain are closed. I'm so sorry."

Tears now run down my cheeks in silent dismay. "You gotta be fuckin kidding me."

"I'm so sorry honey," she says again.

The hope that was rising in me has been buried under a two-foot layer of fresh snow. But Mom is torn apart. I have to hide, as best I can, my misery; the chasmic emptiness filling my gut. She's already suffering undeservedly. Her kindness and generosity are nearly inexhaustible, but this should've never become her battle. I chose to take the risk. And yet now I've dragged *her* into this. Forced a tremendous unwarranted weight upon her shoulders. So it's my duty to reduce her distress in any and every way possible—that's the least I can do! I must convince her in no uncertain terms that I'm safe and capable of handling this.

Deep breath. *You can do this, jan.* "All right," I say. "That sucks, but I'm gonna be okay. You wouldn't've been able to send it out until tomorrow or Monday anyway! We'll just have to hope it clears up soon."

We talk a little while longer, both of us clearly trying to soften the blow of her awful news. She wants to know what it's like in here. I tell her it's not nearly as bad as I would've thought, and how almost all the other guys are very kind and helpful.

"Oh, that's so great! So you're not in danger of getting raped or anything?"

I chuckle; it's amazing, given the circumstances. I love how blunt and genuine our conversations are. A relationship we've really cultivated over the last few years. I think it's super healthy to have open, honest communication—maintaining a dose of sensitivity, of course—with loved ones. "No," I tell her. "It's not rapey at all. Only one person at a time in the shower. Besides, my cellmate may well prefer children over men."

"Oh my gawd, that's horrible!" Now she's the one laughing. "But I am glad for you."

"Yep. So please try not to worry about me. It's really mostly about getting through the mind-numbing boredom."

That night after 10 p.m., when the lights are cut off, james stands at our door hollering to guys in other cells. Shouting at nearly the top of his lungs to be heard. "EY YO BOS'N!"

"What up?"

"NUTHIN." Pause. "EY YO PISSBURGH!"

"What's goin on, james?" pittsburgh says.

A black guy named mike *loves* messing with my cellie. "james!" he screams. "Kill yoself."

"FUCK YOU, NIGGA!"

I try not to listen; can't help but hear anyway. Attempting hard to just focus my thoughts on Rachel. Her southward drive should be underway now. A six-ish hour trek from where she lives in Sonoma, a bit north of San Francisco, to Downey, which is part of the sprawling web of L.A. suburbs. I cannot wait to hear her sweet, loving voice.

"Hey james," mike says. "Spell 'nigger.'"

"N-dash-W-O-R-D," I whisper.

"N-I-G-G-A." james is half-white. Is this only half-acceptable?

"You a dumbass muhfucka, j.j."

"FUCK YOU, MIKE. KILL YOSELF. N-I-G-G-E-R."

"Yeah, thass right, fool. Spell 'couch.'"

He thinks for several seconds. "C-O-U-C-H."

"'Tomato.'"

james looks back at me. I spell it for him, and he turns to the door: "T-O-M-A-T-O."

mike cackles. "Quit get'n help from yo cellie, goofass nigga! You a stupid punk."

Now it's a shade more amusing than annoying. A bunch of guys on the deck are laughing.

"YOU STUPID!" james shouts. "LEAS' I DIN'T GET CAUGHT SELLIN *CRACK* LIKE YO DUMBASS!"

"I rather be *sellin* crack than playin wit lil *kids'* cracks!" mike fires back, without hesitation.

A chorus of *Ohhhhhhs* and guffawing erupt throughout the deck. james knows he got owned. "Fuck you, mike," he says meekly in defeat.

After an obnoxious, increasingly maddening half hour, james sings an out-of-tune lullaby before finally going to bed—still shouting loud enough for the whole deck to hear. Something about how Jesus loves all the little boys and girls, and He'll protect them from the devil as they go swimming in the river.[13]

4.

I wake up in the morning feeling like a giant sack of rotten garbage—physically and emotionally and every other which-a-way. My meds only dampen the lethargic shittiness.

I'm a tiny bit better after enjoying, from bed, one of mike's outrageous stories. He's riffing boisterously in the dayroom. "Man, I'm tellin ya. I use'ta be a fatass muhfucka. I'm talkin *nasty*, man! Weighed like fuckin 280 pounds. Now I'm like 190. Y'know that bitch from . . . damnit, uh . . . from Willie Wonka, the ho who eat that purple shit'n puff up like a big ole muhfuckin ball an' get rolled away? Thass what I looked like. All slobberin an' disgustin an' shit. But I *still* got all kinds'a hos!"

I spew gigglebursts with my eyes closed. Laughter really is the best medicine; especially when you're locked up.[14]

---

[13] [No, really. The convicted chomo [chomo = universal prison vernacular for *child molester*] actually does sing a lullaby on this subject.]
[14] Well, laughter & OxyContin.

After a "lunch" consisting of maybe 300 calories for me, I call Mom's landline. The operator does her spiel, then I hear, "*Baybeee!*" It's Rachel! she made it to L.A.! My heart soars, and I mean absolutely SOARS.

We haven't talked in 48 hours—each one, each hour, a jail-elasticized contortion of spacetime. She expresses volumes in that one-word greeting. A picture may say a thousand words, but so can *inflection*. I'm spectacularly happy to hear her sweet and velvetishly low-pitched voice, and feel even crazier about her than before. Literally benumbed by my overwhelming love. Something in my head chooses that moment to chime in: **I have to marry this woman**, it says.

We've discussed it obliquely in the past, but I've long been hesitant, ambivalent. For a host of reasons [e.g., I hate the idea of using our Straight Privilege to get married when gay people still aren't allowed to in most states.[15] It's the same feeling I'd've had if I were alive in the early 1960s, and used my White Skin Privilege to vote when blacks couldn't. Rachel and I are huge LGBTQ advocates; homophobia enrages us.]

Immediately upon hearing her voice, tears flood my eyes. I must seem to you like a total crybaby! But unless you've been through it yourself, you can't understand how desperate and traumatic and emotional these last few days have been. Transforming me—in the split second Trooper Marlow decided to conjure a fabricated traffic violation and pull me over—from uncontainably thrilled and hopeful about my future into . . . well, into whatever husk of an excuse for living I now have.

"Baby, I'm so fucking sorry," Rachel tells me. "How are you?"

"I'm . . . I'm hangin in there. Miss you s-o m-much." My voice cracks.

"I know baby. I've felt so awful since the moment your mom texted me with 'Jan's in jail.'"

"Can you believe this shit about Big Bear? It's just my luck."

"Completely fucking awful," she says. "But it's gonna be okay, sweetheart. Me and your mom and Jim are all here for you, and we're gonna do

---

[15] [a] At the time of that phone call—late January, 2010—a pitiful mere 5 *states* [HOLY FUCKING SHIT!! see below] had legalized same-sex marriage: Massachusetts, Connecticut, Iowa, Vermont, New Hampshire.

 [b] WOW! I'm writing this amid the final draft edits, & simply *cannot believe* that, just 6 years ago, there were only 5 states w/ marriage equality! Shit blows my mind! Seeing as how—since the ruling on *Obergefell v. Hodges* in June 2015—all 50 U.S. states have at least been **supposed** to grant same-sex marriages, Kim Davis & her vile ilk notwithstanding.

everything we can. I'll stand by you no matter what happens. No matter what. Okay?"

Tears are streaming down my face. Now I'm just trying not to flat-out sob. I feel surrounded by love, and it's so very comforting in this dark hole. "Thank you, baby. You're the best. I love you so much."

We talk until the RobOperator bitch informs us our 30 minutes is up. Apparently, she [Rachel, not the operator] started heading for L.A. at three a.m. Drove straight through the night, over seven hours total because of morning traffic. I can't believe her loving dedication. I've done myriad acts of incredible endurance-driving, but we're different in that regard. Any time she's behind the wheel for more than 20 or 30 minutes, her eyelids grow leaden, and she verges on passing out. This makes her late night trek even more impressive. Uplifting. Shows how badly she wanted to get to Mom's and help us out. Whatta gal!

Stress and depression in massive amounts are expelled from my spirit, just by talking to my wonderful partner. I spend much of the remaining day in bed. Staring at the wall. I yearn tragically for Rachel and our pit bull Rikki. Thinking of all the happy memories we've made—Rikki's adorable goofiness as she chased balls at the beach, hiking all around the S.F. Bay Area, skinny-dipping in Mendocino's Eel River, countless road trips all around California . . . so many spectacular memories.

In the afternoon, james says, "Ey jan. You eat cheeseburgers?"

"Nah man. I don't eat *any* meat."

Pause. An alien concept that requires a moment to unpack. "Thass, uh, unhealthy man. You gotta eat meat."

Christ, I don't want to get into this right now. "It's actually healthier."

"Nuh-uh!"

"Trust me, man, there are plenty of studies you can look at. It's healthier—that's a fact."

"You eat chicken?"

"Nope. No meat."

"Fish patty?"

"No. *No meat.*" Can't blame him for being unaware though; he's from Kiwanee, 15 miles up the road, a town of a few thousand. Probably never met a vegetarian—let alone a *vegan!*—in his entire life.

"We got fish sanwich tuhmorrow. Can I gitchers?"

Sigh. "Yeah, fer sure."

Later, in the dayroom, I'm semi-watching several guys play cards. Masturbation comes up. "james says it's *forbidden* in his room," I mention offhandedly [no pun intended [NPI]].

Several of the guys scoff at the absurd proposition. mike throws down a spade and looks up at me. "You ferreal?"

"That's what he told me."

He looks at james, then laughs derisively. "Man, you gotta be fuckin kid'n me!" Shakes his head. "Tryin d' tell another grownass man he cain't pull his muhfuckin shit! It ain't *yo* room nigga, it's *bof* uh y'alls. An' I *know* james be whackin it!"

"No I ain't!" james cries defensively.

"Fuck outta here, nigga." He tosses down a card with a light *smack*. "You tryin d' tell me yo ass take *half hour* shits?"

We laugh our asses off. james shakes his head, avoiding all eye contact.

"j.j.," mike says, "don't be tryin d' pull that shit." He looks at me. "jan—fam—you do whatever you wan'. Don' be let'n this chomo-ass boy say you cain't do somethin. Anytime I feelin bad I juss go in that room, put the blanket up over th' window, an' play wit myself for awhile. Then I feel better!" He shakes his head again. All of us [except for james] are cracking up. "This nigga tryin'da tell people they cain't play wit theyselves. Thass *crazy*."

I talk to Rachel and my mom several times throughout the day. Big Bear continues getting slammed with snow. I suggest that we try to convince a friendly neighbor, who has a copy of the key, to mail my passport here if the roads don't open soon. But Mom dashes the idea immediately. "The mail's not even being picked up or delivered! *Everything* is shut down."

Goddamn! What a perfect time for my luck to embark on the worst losing streak EVER.

That night, james announces he'll be sleeping on the empty top bunk in boston's room so they can play checkers. Obviously convinced I'm going to masturbate one way or another after what mike said. Even if james is in the cell. This isn't true—haven't sunk *that* low [yet]. But hell, I'll take the peace and quiet; that excites me even more than the chance to jerk off in privacy! He bids me goodnight with, "Juss don' git anything on the walls er my stuff er nuthin."

Christ, what does he imagine I'm planning?! Does he view our world from the absurdly over-the-top, gross-for-the-mere-sake-of-grossness perspective of a Chuck Palahniuk novel? Such a weird hangup to have in jail!

But don't think for a second I didn't take advantage of the opportunity! Like I say—or rather write—elsewhere, it's Nature's Anti-Depressant. The All-Natural and Organic GMO-Free Sleep Aid. It takes several minutes, wherein I rub and squeeze and jiggle-joggle my flaccid dick, to get hard; misery and jail are less-than-great aphrodisiacs. Takes me longer than usual to finish, as well. Maybe seven or eight minutes. I'm a quickie, I know! But I'm good at getting women off, too [allegedly [sometimes]]. And even better at getting myself off. I've got the *moves*.

5.

After breakfast, james drags his vinyl mattress back into our cell. "You clean up 'n e'rythin, right?"

"Dude, I didn't even jerk off."

In actuality though, I did jerk off. Remember? I just wrote about it like two paragraphs ago!

A bit later, I call Mom and she immediately shouts, "GREAT NEWS!"

"What?!" I cry. "What is it?"

Apparently Bruce pulled some more strings [if he were tugging these threads from the same sweater, that thing'd be nothing but a ball of yarn by now]; because of the unusual circumstances, he managed to set up a meeting with Judge Hamer and the Prosecutor. We'll try to persuade them to let me bond out and go home without having to get the passport here beforehand. Amazing! Mom and Rachel and my siblings and Jim and I are joyous, brimming with anxious hope.

It's time now for me to broach the subject, since it may soon be possible. "If Bruce gets them to allow it . . ." Gawd, it's so difficult to come right out and ask! "Are you and Jim . . . are you guys gonna be willing, and able, to bail me out?" I feel lower than a mudgrub. Ashamed to be dumping this on them.

"Uh-huh," Mom says. "Why wouldn't we?"

"Well, I committed the crime that got me here!"[16] This is only part of the truth, since America's draconian drug laws and broken Justice System and overzealous, lawbreaking cops are also among the reasons I'm here. But it's crucial she knows I take at least some responsibility.

"I know you did, but . . ." She doesn't have to finish. As long as she's financially able, she'll help me. It's just the way she ticks. Her generous,

---

[16] Jesus, jan, whose side are you on? Why try talking her out of it?!

forgiving nature. Like taking me to the hospital if I were seriously ill. Such a tremendous person; only at my very best do I deserve such wonderful parents.

That Sunday stretches out like freshly spat gum stuck to your shoe. The only books here are unreadable: terrible pulp science fiction or fantasy novels and religious garbage. They squeak a rickety library cart from unit to unit every other Sunday; it came a week ago, so I'm shit outta luck. I watch some TV. Until the NFL games come on, and almost everyone gathers before the spectacle like frigid Neanderthals around a nighttime fire. Shouts and screams and hysterical nonvocal utterances soon erupt and then continue unabated for several hours. It's deafening—no exaggeration. Anxiety-inducing. I retreat to my cell and alternate between the dual inanities of *Entertainment Weekly* and staring at the wall. Usually my vivid imagination could sustain me for hours, but my brain has largely shut down in here.

The remaining half-day drags on f o r e v v v e r r r r r r r. It's because of our meeting with Judge Hamer in the morning, and the subsequent possibility of posting bond without first submitting my stupid snowbound passport. I could leave tomorrow if they agree to the altered proposition! How could I *not* be obsessively anxious, hence elongating each individual minute, no matter the resulting malicious effects on my psyche?

The only interesting thing all day comes after all the football lunacy; another wild story from mike. He's entertaining the dayroom and I over-hear, again from in bed. He's practically shouting. "Ey yo fam, I 'member this thing that happened when I'uz like 12." He speaks with electrifying animation. Arms waving, pacing back and forth twitchily, gesturing with his hands. "I was wearin a, gawdamnit a Simpsons shirt, one'a them 'Ay Carumba!' shirts. Wen up t'my older sister who was like 15 'n bumped in'da her wit my big'ole fat ass. Y'know, one'a them hipcheck things? Her ass went *flyin* t' the groun, nigga. An' then . . . then gawdamnit I'uz laughin like a muhfucka, 'n she pulled out a can'a MACE 'n spray me *all over the fuckin face*! Shit hurt like a *muhfucka*, fam. I was wipin out my eyes 'n cryin an' shit, 'n she juss *laughin*, nigga. So I got a can'a pop, uh uh muhfuckin Coke in the 'luminum can, an' straight *smashed* that shit on the side'a her head." Guys are laughing uproariously, myself included. "Pop sprayin e'rywhere, all over th' livin room, she was screamin, my face all red an' puffed up 'n shit. It was wild, dawg."

6.

Monday morning. Today is either *the* day, or just another day; and if it's not *the* day, if Hamer and the Prosecutor don't let me bond out, there's no telling how long I could be stuck here in limbo—consuming starvation-level calories, meds on the verge of running out. My nerves flare out in spastic, sparkler-esque crackling before I'm even fully awake. I take a shower after they dole out meds. My first one since the rushed, mandatory, Guard-supervised spritzing on Thursday night during the intake process. Cleanliness is pleasant after several days of feeling too shitty to care.

I talk to Mom and Rachel. The Big Bear Blizzard-Job, storm of the half-fucking-century, is finally blowing over. It dumped *six feet* of snow over the weekend. Roads still buried; a couple days or more till they'll open. Please, Earth: please let them release me if I agree to mail the passport once it's accessible! I'm a mess. Stomach twisted into a clenching, knotted mess. I just wanna get the damn thing over with, one way or another. Tom Petty was right—the waiting really is the hardest part.

Again: I could be released *today* if Hamer grants our request. Home and in Rachel's arms with Rikki beside us by tonight! If denied, it'd easily be another five days, even a week. The difference feels cavernous right now.

Mom went to Bank of America this morning and convinced a manager to let her transfer $20,000 to my account [ensuring I'd have enough to bond out and get a flight home], overdrafting her account in the process. She wasn't allowed to transfer such a large amount online, which is how she usually helps my pathetic, disabled, broke ass. I could never say it enough: WHATTA LADY!

I have a feeling that you may once again be questioning my intestinal fortitude. And rightfully so! What's another few days or a week there in Henry County Jail? As I discussed earlier—many people wallow in county jail for months, sometimes even a year-plus, unable to afford bail, waiting powerlessly for an eventual trial with nobody advocating for them other than their court-appointed, overworked, often ill-prepared public defender [whom we jailbirds call "Public Pretenders"]. Well, guess what? Looking back, I'm willing to admit I *was* acting weak! But try to understand there are factors making it especially rough for me. Like my disability; it's difficult to get through a regular day on the *outside* given the severity of my chronic pain. And I have access to none of my usual distractions and other helpful things in here. I'm even more thoroughly at the mercy of my physical-mental state. Then there are the pestilent circus acrobats looping madly through my skull: *What if I'd done _____ differently when Marlow pulled me over? Or I should've never taken this job in the first place! What was I thinking?!*

All these myriad factors coagulate into a rotten cesspool of overall fuckiness [that's fucked-up suckiness]. And so it is that I head into the courtroom, for whatever reason not cuffed this time, with numbing fear and a leaden, nauseating weight in my gut.

And yet . . . somehow . . .

Bruce persuades them to let me bond out now! Due to the extenuating circumstances—the passport's physical unavailability, my having a low flight-risk given that I'm disabled, and this is my first ever arrest and felony charge—Hamer agrees to let me leave if I'll sign a statement vowing to get my passport here within one week. No exceptions. If I fail, they'll issue a warrant for my arrest. I gleefully sign the agreement. My entire body feels continuously on the verge of seizure-like joy-tremors.

Bruce meets me in the Shitsock Room before I'm returned to the unit. "You're an absolute wizard," I say, grinning with elation. "Thank you so much!"

He shrugs with a modest little smile. "I do the best I can for my clients, that's all."

"No way. You pulled off *two* miracles, far as I'm concerned."

I gather my meager possessions right away back in the unit. Then, per the advice of a veteran county jail resident, push the speaker button by the dayroom's exit door. "Yeah?" It's a gruff voice; a familiar one. Oh Christ— the same guy who told me to shut up or he'd come and *make* me shut up, which necessitated the Shitsock Incident!

"Hi, I just received permission to bond out from Judge Hamer and the money's ready so I'd like to post bail. Name is jan smitowicz."

"Hold on." Long period of unbearable silence. During which I imagine multitudinous ghastly scenarios: judge changed his mind . . . or forgot to file/sign the papers . . . or it'll take a day or more to process them . . . or there's no record of my being booked in the first place, and so I can't bond out and so I'll be stuck here forever, et al. [I've heard about myriad bizarre fuckeroos; almost nothing would surprise me by now.]

As if to validate these fears, my card doesn't work. The Officer tried it twice. Leaning against the speaker, sweating, verging on total meltdown, I confirm that he used the right card. And he did. Nope! not working.

OH WAIT—*there it goes!* It worked, I'm good to go! They got their $15,000 [yes, I realize the painfully exquisite irony that this is the *exact* amount I'd've earned from the muling job if not for my illegal capture]. I'm even more elated than I would've imagined. So elated that it's like I'm not even facing many years in prison—a mandatory minimum of SIX if convicted—and like I'm *not* facing an uphill legal battle . . .

Because, right now, all I can think is *FUCK ALL THAT, I'M GOIN HOME!* And my mind's deadset on reaching L.A. *tonight.* Despite the local airport's tiny size. Determined to get the hell out of this vile, gawdforsaken county/state. The sooner I make it home, the sooner I can begin processing all that's happened. Start preparing for the intense battle and everything else to come. And also to heal my psyche from the trauma of being caught, being illegally pulled over and illegally searched-and-seized and arrested. The trauma inherent in transitioning away from a secure financial future with splendid possibilities and toward the certain impending horrorshow.

I get everything completely ready, going so far as to fold my mattress and stick it in the corner. I spend the last hour before dinner simply pacing the dayroom. Staring down at the stormcloudish cement. I can't read, can't concentrate on anything but GETTING OUTTA HERE.

Finally, around 4:15, a Guard walks in and calls, "smitowicz?" I hurry over. "Yer leavin, grab yer shit."

I proclaim some quick gratitude and farewells to the other guys. Then snatch up my mattress. "Stay free!" I shout, gliding out the door. The Officer leads me through a network of hallways and locked doors to the booking room. Have to sign some papers before my departure. I'm jittery, sweating. I switch from the orange prison clothes back into my blue nylon pants, black shirt, and black, green-lettered VEGAN hoodie. Somebody hands over my backpack and a Guard takes me out. Through the grimy little chicken-wired window in the back door, I see it's snowing heavily; a sheening white downpour. She unlocks and opens the thick steel door.

A massive grin sweeps across my face. Threatening to crack my heavily chapped lips [usually I slather them with hemp balm ten to fifteen times per diem, but of course now I've had nothing for five days]. I jet out the door while it's still swinging open and escape the building's walls; the sense of *erupting* from that stuffy nightmarish box out into the great wide open that extends pretty much to infinity is like a cosmic-scale orgasm, a tremendous supernovic release. I'm outside now in the dense, veiling snowfall. Seems I can *hear* the ever-so-gentle hum as a thousand white flakes drift down through the frigid evening air and press into the pavement. No adjectival superlatives could convey the intensity of my liberation and ecstasy. I tilt my face skyward, so the falling snowflakes drop onto my cheeks and lips and glasses and into my mouth.

Pure glory.

There's a black-checkered yellow van sitting at the parking lot's far end; Rachel set up an airport cab ride for me. I jog toward it, another grin yanking my lips wide. My knees cry out: *Hey asshole, take it easy, wouldja?!*

But I can't take it easy. Not right now. It's a big wondrous world out here, and at the moment I'm graced with a rare . . . *fullness of gratitude* to be alive and experiencing it. Life's worth living—through all its senseless hardships and cruelty and pain—so long as I can still feel awe before the world's marvelous wonders. I'm confident I can face the future, both immediate and eventual, with dignity and my head up high. Nothing can break my spirit!

7.

At tiny Quad Cities Airport, I stride to the nearest counter, which happens to be American Airlines. I'm locked inside get-home-tonight-no-matter-what mode. And I do indeed score a ticket that'll put me in L.A. tonight, with a transfer in Denver.

After passing through security, I enter the airport's sole terminal. Use a payphone and dial Mom's landline. Rachel answers. "Baby? Are you out?!" So much hopeful expectation and concern in that voice.

"Yes! I'm at the airport. I'm coming home, baby—and I'm gonna make it tonight! I'll hit LAX around eleven. Will you pick me up? And bring Rikki?"

"Of course! I can't *wait* to see you."

I'm sure. Even despite her having no idea what I'm planning to do later, at Mom's house. "Ditto."

I step off the plane many hours later at LAX, legs jellyish, knees burning with the acute pain caused by extended positional similarity. Everything feels and looks . . . *surreal* somehow, like I've traveled not through time and space but through *dimension*. I've been to LAX dozens of times; every shuttered store, all the dark kiosks, even the terminal's carpets and tile flooring, it all looks familiar. But there's also a nearly indefinable sense of otherness. A bizarre mental coloration to the world that might best be described as the opposite of déjà vu, also known as *jamais vu.* "Never seen" rather than "Already seen." The complex feeling of being in a recognizable place that nonetheless seems eerily unfamiliar. This, I can now write with confidence, is a strange side effect of incarceration and its many attendant psychological-emotional stressors. The sensation remains huddled in some corridor of my brain for quite a while. But it's quickly relegated from the forefront by rabid excitement.

My heart races as I powerwalk through the airport and then exit the air-conditioned terminal into a *whoosh* of warmly enveloping air, effluvious as always with jet, diesel, and gasoline exhaust. But right now this noxious mixture of airport-exclusive fumes is just fine. I stand out near the curb. Jonesing for a cigarette. Cars and shuttles and buses hurtle wildly across lanes, inside the pickup-zone and out. People bustle around with suitcases clasped at their sides, or wheeling luggage behind them, or in front on stacked flatbed carts. LAX is always popping; it's merely degrees of hurried madness. I wait. Rake my teeth over chapped lips. Scan the incoming cars, head darting around like Stevie Wonder on crack, for Rachel's forest-green Honda Civic. License plate proudly boasting **LUVTOFU.**

Then I see her car. Hundred yards ahead! She's staring right at me, with Rikki's big blocky pit bull head clearly visible in the backseat. Something inside me bursts, something I'd been damming with a substantial mental wall; a flood of jumbled emotions nearly flattens me in its torrent. Relief. Ecstasy. *Wholeness.* So many things. She screeches to a halt and cranks the e-brake and leaps from the car, slamming herself into my arms. "So glad you're back," she's able to murmur, faced pressed against mine. Her tears moisten my ear and cheek. Rikki's going apeshit in the backseat, her entire butt wagging: *Daddy's back OHMYGAWD!!*

"You're tellin me." We kiss, fiercely. Then I grip her hand. "Now let's get the hell outta here!"

It truly is the first time I've ever been happy to smell LAX's cloying stench. I can't wait to get home and simply lie down. Been a difficult and exhausting day. Hard to believe that—just this afternoon!—I was in *jail* some 2,000 miles away. I slump in the passenger seat. Rikki's smothering me with love, huff-puffing wildly, licking my face between gleeful high-pitched whines. I turn backward and draw her tightly to my chest. "My baby!" I rub her velvety-furred head, scratch her ears, plant smooches on her adorable wet nose and the soft, whiskered skin beneath it. Rachel plops into the driver's seat and we take off.

"Ohhhh my GAWD," I say. "It's indescribably amazing to be outta that hellhole and back in California!"

"I'm sure." She rubs my thigh and then clutches a hand. I grab her American Spirit cigarettes. So nice to light it up and take that first drag and slowly exhale the white smoke out my cracked window. We merge onto the 105 East; now it's really feeling like my journey's almost over. Glorious.

"L.A.'s never looked so beautiful." I hold the cigarette in my left hand and roll down the window, stick my head way out. The mild late-night winter air rushes past my face, through my short hair, and I unleash a barbaric *YAWP!* of unbridled joy. Then I kiss Rachel.

"Happy?" she says. Smiling, glancing over at me frequently. It's like we've been apart for months, rather than just eight days.

I roll the window back up and look at her. Grinning like a madman. "Just a tad." I lunge over and kiss her soft cheek. Use my fingers to gently turn her face toward me. We kiss for several seconds; she keeps an eye-slit trained on the road. Then I sit back and shout, "Let's get some goddamn rock 'n roll goin in here!" I turn on the CD player and AC/DC comes on— the staccato opening guitar of "For Those About to Rock [We Salute You]." They're her favorite band, her obsession. Angus's riff portends some badass rockage. I crank the volume.

We rock out the final 20 minutes to Downey. There are, amazingly, few other cars on the freeway. Rachel's not aware our lives will soon change in ways unimaginably drastic. Hell, *I'm* not even fully aware.

Once we get home, I wake my mom and greet her two adorable, ecstatic beagle girls, Whimsy and Snoopy. Mom hugs me fiercely, without a single critical word. She knows it's the last thing I need right now. My younger brother and sister are at Jim's place nearby. I'll see them tomorrow.

Rachel and I sit on the porch swing. Both puffing on a cigarette. We don't usually smoke this much, but it's hard to care about anything other than *feeling better* after all that's happened. Wispy smoke-snakes curl upward from the tip and disappear into the night's darkness. Smoking helps settle my jagged nerves. Takes my mind off the knee pain, if only for a few minutes.

I take another drag and fidget, stretching out my cramped and caustic knees. We make smalltalk; there's a moment of contented silence. Then I say, "Thank you so much for everything you did while I was in there." I grip her hands in mine. "Rushing up to Mendo to look for my passport, driving down here so you could help my mom and talk to me, calling my doctors to reschedule appointments, calling the jail, getting the taxi there for me—all of it would've overwhelmed my mom to the breaking point. I'm not exaggerating: she couldn't have done it. You were my anchor; you could'a broken down any time on the phone, but you didn't. You stayed strong for me. Encouraged me, kept me from buggin out."

She stares into my eyes and I stare into hers. They're a lovely, dark hazel-ish brown. I continue speaking. "Now, I've been thinking about this for a while, but all you did convinced me it was the right thing. That you deserve it." Still clutching her hands, I rapidly drop to one knee before her and say, "Rachel, will you marry me?"

She nods immediately, grinning like it'll crack her face if she's not careful. I rise up and we kiss. She tells me how joyous and thankful she is without saying a word, telling me with her mouth and tongue and arms, our connection spoken wordlessly and yet so clear.

"I love you so much, Jan." She holds my face in her hands. Leans over and kisses me once more. Then I rejoin her on the swing and we're just sitting there, hands entwined on her lap.

I change tack after a happy wordless minute. "Hey. I honestly don't think I'll spend another day in jail. Seriously. This case is a fucking slam dunk. Textbook illegal search and seizure—I'm gonna walk."

She doesn't respond for several seconds. Looking down. Then she says, "Either way, I want you to know that no matter what happens, I'll stand beside you every step of the way. All right? Me, you, Rikki—nobody could ever take away what we have . . .

"Our bonds will not be broken."

INTER-MISSION 1A

NOTES & OTHER RANDOMLINGS

I.

POLICE REPORT EXCERPTS

On 01/21/10 at approximately 5:13 p.m., I, Trooper Beau Marlow #5872, was on stationary patrol in the median crossover of Interstate 80...I observed an eastbound...white motor home traveling, at what appeared to be a rate of speed slower than the posted speed limit of 65 miles per hour [mph], near the above stated cross over. As the white motor home **[hereafter 'WMH' to save my precious fingers]** passed my location, I observed that the driver drastically decreased the WMH's speed as I could see the WMH's brake lights activated. I also observed the front of the WMH lower to the ground due to the decrease in speed. The driver of the WMH also immediately activated the right turn signal of the WMH. I left my position in the median crossover and began driving eastbound on Interstate 80. I observed the WMH take the exit ramp from Interstate 80 eastbound to Illinois Route 82. I observed the WMH cross the solid white fog line **[false]** located on the south side of the roadway of the ramp by a distance I approximated to be 18 inches for approximately 4 seconds **[I approximate this to be utter bullshit]**, committing the Illinois Vehicle Code [IVC] violation of improper lane usage. I pulled in behind the WMH, activated my emergency lights, and effected **[*sic*?]** a traffic stop on the

WMH...and made contact with the male driver and sole occupant. The driver was swaying from side to side and was visibly trembling [**Yes—he really, ACTUALLY FUCKING SAID THIS, here and on the witness stand. I'll get into it more in Inter-Mission 1B; for now, I'll just say this: No further comment? No field sobriety test for what** *obviously* **sounds like the behavior of someone** *obviously* **intoxicated out of their fuckin skull?!**]. I introduced myself/department [?] and requested the driver's license of the driver [**redundancy** *sic*—**he just said I was the sole occupant, so who else's driver's license would he request other than the driver's license of the driver??**]. The driver asked me how I was doing; I advised [**sic?**] the driver that I was good. I noticed that the front compartment of the WMH had a [**sic**] numerous food items, coffee cups, and trash items in it. I also noticed an odor of air-freshener emanating from the WMH. The driver asked me if there was a reason that I pulled him over; I advised [**sic?**] the driver that there was a reason for him [**non-gerund** *sic*] being stopped....smitowicz's hand was visibly shaking as he handed me his driver's license. I requested that smitowicz produce the registration to the WMH...smitowicz walked to the rear of the WMH, and then returned with the rental agreement to the WHM [**redundancy not necessarily** *sic*, **but at the very least it is indicative of a true moron; a truly serious moron**] . smitowicz's hand was again visibly trembling as he handed me the requested rental agreement...

smitowicz and I returned [**huh?**] to my squad car where smitowicz was seated in the front, passenger side seat of my squad car. smitowicz advised me that he was disabled and that it hurt for him to sit in cramped spaces. I observed that smitowicz's breathing appeared deep and labored as I could hear him breathing and I observed his chest rising and falling dramatically with every breath he took. smitowicz was also looking all around him in a very nervous fashion. I ran a routine computer check of smitowicz's driver's license. smitowicz licked his lips constantly and could not seem to sit still in his seat [**Didn't you literally** *just* **make note of my stated discomfort within cramped spaces?**]. smitowicz was constantly swallowing. smitowicz then asked about the Wind Turbines [**reason for capitalization unknown**] in a field on the south side of Interstate 80 in Geneseo which were visible from our location. I sent Trooper Jared Steen #5556 of the Illinois State Police [ISP] District 7 a message via my in-car computer asking him to immediately assist me with the traffic stop [**WHY?! Oh yeah—the whole warning's a bullshit ruse**]. smitowicz described his fascination with the Wind Turbines. The registration to the WMH returned as valid through Nevada. smitowicz popped his neck with his right hand and began rubbing the back of his neck...I asked smitowicz if he was on vacation; smitowicz responded that he was going to visit family and friends in Pennsylvania and New York. I observed that smitowicz's face was twitching [**lol! you're starting to grasp at straws here, dude; not to mention *seriously* stretching your believability**]. smitowicz also continued rubbing his face and was still moving around nervously in his seat [**see above**]....I began writing smitowicz's written warning. smitowicz lifted his glasses and rubbed his nose. smitowicz cleared his throat and patted his chest [**wtf??**]. smitowicz asked me how I like living in Illinois; I advised him that Illinois is cold [**thanks for the "advisement"**]. smitowicz advised me that he was born in DeKalb [**sic; I was born in Anaheim, CA, and I actually "advised" him that my *dad* was born in DeKalb**].

And so on.

****

jan is awesome and brave, courageous!
His appearance in court, outrageous!
-Mom

****

The jumble below is a QR code for which you can download a free app on your smartphone [if you don't already have one; really easy, just google it]. Scan this and it'll direct you to a video of Mom and I messing around during the hour prior to turning myself in at Henry County Jail. [I used www.goqr.me]

Or just go here:
https://www.youtube.com/watch?v=Az07Z90j-Tk&feature=youtu.be

****

This is the first missive I receive in prison from my little brother Jimmy, who was 15 at the time—

I saw the movie of you blowing bubbles with mom [*see above*]. **I nearly cried. It was so beautiful.** ☺

Tomorrow with band we're going on a field trip to Knott's Berry Farm. An unholy cesspool of long lines, mass regurgitation, and capitalism.

You should use that in a book.
[*Ed. note: and so it is done!*]

. . . P.S. If the seal is broken, Dad read this letter, this mission has been compromised. Destroy this letter.
Or use it for rolling paper.
On second thought, nevermind. That's what got you into this.
Miss you.

Jimmy, 6/13/2010

INTER-MISSION 1B

Motion to Suppress [the *Truth!*] Hearing

What can I write? Obviously we lost the Hearing. Cause, you know, this is a *prison* memoir and all—not a court-win memoir! Two facets of the hearing stand out for me: [1] *I actually thought we had a good chance of winning*, despite aaaallll I already knew about the American "Justice" System; [2] I wasn't the only one who thought our chances were pretty good—the Prosecution clearly felt that way too, because the first plea deal they offered me was a mere *six months' sentence*, plus a hefty fine. The State would've never issued such a relatively timid, sweetheart deal if they were confident they'd win [after all, just like cops benefit from arrests, certain people involved in court cases are **incentivized** to produce guilty pleas; this is an inherent, unwavering aspect of the Criminal Justice System that creates massive [I'd even argue *criminal*] conflicts of interest. It's so clear to me; clear, and clearly unjust/ undemocratic. I'll address this issue and its repercussions in detail shortly]. We obviously chose not to accept the first offer. Primarily because Mom and I maintained hope that, in some dim recessed alleyway of potential futures, I might finish my post-graduate work and become a teacher. This still felt like a possibility way back then in spring 2010. Physically doable. But a felony conviction on my record would make it impossible. Plus we were so certain [gawd knows why] I'd get a fair shot in court—which would've been a slam dunk for me, bad knees and all! Apparently, the suffocating pressure and stressfulness of the entire situation made me forget or disregard *everything I knew* about American Justice. One of those instances where, consciously or not, you think you're somehow exempt from easily predictable realities. Our hopefulness, and the seemingly obvious paucity of evidence against me, gave us too much confidence. So we turned down that six-month offer to instead bank on escaping with my clean record intact.

Such fools we were! If it weren't for this memoir, I'd have nothing but regrets about our choice. The choice that created unquantifiable suffering and cost me almost two years, instead of six months at most [cut in half for good behavior . . . plus the Stateville Nightmare might not've ever even happened—I could've ended up serving the entirety of that little baby-bit in County!] Yes indeed, this memoir is *everything*: the payoff from our dizzying investment of money and time and misery and opportunities lost; the nexus point around which everything swirls; the final subtraction-via-addition, subtracting all my lingering remorse by adding this story to the world's vault of creativity and sociopolitical importance. It's the **only thing** that could transform my merciless Prison Experience into a worthwhile roadblock.

The Hearing was a veritable ass-rape of justice. Must I even address it in detail? No, hell no, it's all too infuriating—so I'll just provide a rapid-fire account of the salient parts. Call it, I don't know, *Scenes from One Tiny Specific Incident Among Centuries of Shameful Injustice*. Or something.

Scenes from One Tiny Specific Incident Among Centuries of Shameful Injustice [Or Something]

FLASH

I'm back in the lavish courtroom, but this time wearing a dress shirt and slacks instead of my orange jail uniform. Mom's sitting on one of the polished oak benches behind the boroquely carved wood partition that swings open into the courtroom floor proper. Bruce and I sit at one table, with the dweebish prosecutor twat, First Assistant State's Attorney Brian Kerr, at the other. Prosecutor Kerr—smooth- and baby-faced [and -dicked, almost certainly]—looks like he's playing grownup in his slightly too-big suit [as opposed to Bruce, who has a well-fitting suit but slightly too-big body, heh heh]. Trooper Beau *snicker* Marlow's also here, sitting #douchebagily back in the gallery, on the side opposite my mom. No surprise there—he fucking knows what he fucking did, and damn well fucking knows *my mom* knows what he fucking did: the nonexistent traffic violation he used as an excuse to pull me over, then as coercion to get me inside his patrol car, buying time for the drug-sniffing canine's transit, and so he could later analyze the video and concoct a veritable litany of bogus reasons for post facto justification of his illegal-unconstitutional-big-brotherish searching of my vehicle and despicable thug-like theft of my property . . . Bruce nicely summed up the whole case's charade-like nature amid a long email that came between my bonding out and this Hearing:

> *The worst part of the stop was Marlow's statement that he had a basis for detaining Jan after Jan rejected consent to search because I-80 is a known drug trafficking corridor.* **If that were a valid basis for detaining a traffic stop subject, then the cops could stop and search everyone.**

[In other words, my arresting officer *straight-up told me* his justification for initiating a vehicle-search, and that reason was a cut-and-dry violation of the **spirit** *and* **letter** of the Fourth Amendment—but then later he made up a bunch of shit about my supposed nervousness that was innately difficult to prove or disprove; all the intricate details of which were admittedly quite shrewd given what an obvious fucking moron Marlow is.] Ugh— don't even get me started on the heinous-anus excrement he extracted from his rectal cavity [aka *brain*] and splattered all through his police report! A document that, if I hadn't known it was legitimate, I'd've been certain was a masterwork of satirical mindfuckery by one of my close friends, or the most unparalleled piece of absurdist brilliance in *The Onion*'s history, a scorching-caustic satire of appropriate police procedure, cop stupidity, and hyperbolic-to-the-point-of-

This is pretty good, but just a little too ridiculous—maybe tone down the over-the-top stuff by about 20% and it'll be GOLD!
~Onion Ed.

-level-embellishment.

Truly, we're talking about what'd be—IF it weren't presented as a true, honest account of what really happened—a satirical tour de force the likes of which maybe haven't been seen since Oscar freakin Wilde![17]

The Hearing gets started and it seems to me like Bruce is putting on an absolute rockstar performance, dropping seemingly inarguable logic like he's carpet-bombing the whole damn room! "A hundred times zero is still zero," he says multiple times—referring to Trooper Beau's extensive list of my "suspicious activity."

FLASH

Trooper Beau Marlow's on the ~~witless~~ witness stand.

<u>CLAIM:</u>
When I approached the defendant's vehicle, he was standing between the driver and passenger's seat, swaying from side to side and trembling.

<u>FACT:</u>
LOL. Are you, sir, *actually fuckin kidding me*?! Like, is this an **actual joke**? That's the only way it'd make sense or work. In reality, I was sitting in the driver's seat calmly. OF COURSE. I've got nerves of steel—it's not like this was the first time I ever committed a crime, or even the first time I got pulled over with an illegal amount of weed in my vehicle! When my Dad #2, Jim, saw the police dashcam's video of the pull-over and arrest— and keep in mind he's extremely critical, in general and of his kids in particular [especially amid a scenario in which, oh I don't know, he and Mom paid $15,000 to bond me out of jail!]; if anyone in the world were to watch that video and react honestly, he, more than any other person, would easily find problematic suspiciousness in my demeanor and behavior—and yet he *didn't*. Didn't point out a myriad of ways that I exhibited extreme nervousness; the kind of severe, tangible anxiety typified here more than anywhere else by this particular outlandish claim from Marlow. No, in

---

[17] If you think *I'm* being hyperbolic, just remember: Beau's police report claimed that, when he first approached the fabled White Motor Home [WMH], I was "swaying from side to side and was visibly trembling." NOTHING I could ever write about that ludicrousness could possibly be considered hyperbolic when compared with the police report's heap of WOW! HOLY CHRIST THAT'S A LOAD OF SHIT! hyperbole. Seriously! That halfwit cunt puts the *total cock* in *total bullshit concoction*.

actuality, what Jim said after viewing the police tape was, *How the hell were you acting so calm?! You deserve an Academy Award, Jan. Wow!* I couldn't believe he responded that way. Thought for certain that he'd perceive a huge amount of suspicion in my actions. But nope!

Back to Marlow's statement—under oath, no less: I was "Standing between [the seats], swaying from side to side and trembling." And yet Marlow didn't say a goddamn *word* about this when it allegedly happened. Nor at any other time during the traffic stop. The first time it ever came up was in the police report he concocted at some point after the cavalcade of officers transported me and my RV to the station. Don't you think that, if an officer pulled someone over and the driver was acting *that weird and fucked up*, they just might . . . I don't know . . . DO A FIELD SOBRIETY TEST?!? Or at the very least *acknowledge* it? Say, "Sir, could you please have a seat?" SOMETHING?

This claim just defies any and every bit of common sense, police protocol, believability, and so on. Can you imagine how hard my jaw dropped when I read that shit in the very first police report [which unfortunately I was unable to secure for reproduction here]? It never failed to produce uproarious laughter in me and anyone to whom I described it, in prison and In the World.

As Mom brilliantly pointed out in an email to Bruce:

I read the police report and as a psychiatrist (not as a mother) it was blatantly apparent that he was lying!!! When someone is so nervous as to appear how he described Jan (I.e. twitching, sweating, shaking, or whatever he said), they are NOT capable of chatty small talk. It really has to be one or the other to be believable—Jan was either chatty and relaxed or he was obviously physiologically responding to stress. You just can't have it both ways! [Ed. note: Well-played, Mom. Well-played indeed.]

CLAIM:
There was a takeout salad sitting on the passenger seat that I noticed had a particular smell coming from it. I could tell it was very old, as if the defendant was in a huge hurry and didn't have time to stop and eat. The salad was visibly...uhm...for lack of a better word, it was visibly rotting.

FACT:

My head hurts. *That's* a fact. I'd bought the salad from Subway literally no more than 45 minutes before getting pulled over. I was eating it little by little while driving. It's obvious now that, with trafficking cases, cops try to justify their illegal searches after the fact by holding up certain little details about either [1] the defendants' behavior, especially as it relates to nervousness/fear and the like—it serves them so well that such things are highly subjective, not to mention anxiety's a *normal* response to interacting with cops, whether you're guilty of a crime or not!—and [2] aspects of the defendants' vehicle's interior. These two things were the entire house of cards the prosecution built its "case" around.

CLAIM:

As I stood outside the vehicle's passenger window, I detected a strong smell of scented airspray, as if the defendant had just sprayed the air, trying to hide something from me.

FACT:

I did indeed have a can of air freshener, but this was because—at that point in time—I'd smoke a cigarette now and then while driving long distances because it helped me stay awake and alert, and smoking in my rented RV was expressly prohibited. So I didn't want the smell of cigarettes to linger. On top of that, the canister was back in the RV's kitchen sink, 10 feet behind the driver's seat. The last time I could've possibly used the spray was 45-plus minutes prior, when I stopped at Subway. I'd smoked two or three cigarettes since then, including one that I was halfway through, and which was *still lit*, when Marlow came up to the vehicle. There's no chance any smell of the organic, orange-based Trader Joe's air freshener remained after 45 minutes, several cigarettes, and driving with the window rolled halfway down. Again—a post facto attempt to prove that he had *tangible, demonstrable* evidence for suspicion. A cop can't—or rather, **isn't legally justified in**—pulling someone over and searching their vehicle just because. They're *supposed to* have actual evidence that's truly convincing, tangible, inarguable, defensible, etc.

Luckily—for the career-advancement of cops, lawyers, judges, and for the Justice System and Prison-Industrial Complex in general—that's just not how it plays out in reality . . .

FLASH

Let's just break it down and analyze this shit for a second . . .

What is the truly greater evil: delivering 53 pounds of flower buds [which just for the record = a few beer cases' weight], or the crimes—*committed by the very people tasked with upholding our laws*—of cops' lying on the witness stand [i.e. perjury], and the willful disregard of the Fourth Amendment to the Constitution by judges? Which crime has more victims? Which crime has a worse effect on society? Cops and judges know they can get away with violating the law. The System is rigged, plain and simple.

So then, why should anybody inherently respect the law when the very people in charge aren't respecting the law?! As defense attorney Tim Lohraff so eloquently put it, echoing my sentiments above, ". . . [Cops] will testify in court and lie—which is perjury. So you have a cop committing a greater felony to convict a lesser felony" [quoted in *Drug Crazy*].

The fact that, on a surface level, our legal system *appears* democratic is integral to maintaining the whole illusory charade. [Obviously there are plenty of fascist governments wherein the legal system is far worse than ours, but they generally don't try to pretend they're fair.] In America, the System's pushers—drug connotations very intentional—have conned most citizens into believing we have this egalitarian, exemplary legal system. It requires personal experience and/or research [imagine that!] to glimpse the truth. I believe this fully: If all the best minds of a generation gathered together and deliberately tried constructing a legal system that seems democratic, but is in actuality more pernicious, heartless, senseless, and unjust than the American one, they would fail spectacularly.

FLASH

Now it's time for the prosecution to makes its "case." ← I use quotes not because of the pun, for once, but because it was hardly a case at all; Prosecutor Brian Kerr literally relies on NOTHING ELSE aside from the cop's "testimony" [see above] and the dashcam video, which supposedly shows terrible anxiety and sketchy suspiciousness on my part [also see above: Mom's psychological assessment, and Jim's disbelief and praise of my apparent calmness]. The farcical lunacy somehow—against all odds—manages to continue unabated. Kerr tries to display the video from his laptop onto a pull-down projector screen near the witness stand. But it's not working. Something is wrong with the projector, just like the video's audio magically vanished right before the drug-sniffing dog arrived! So Judge Hamer simply watches the video on Kerr's laptop . . . with the cords only long enough to bring it within five feet . . . and the audio that does still exist is messed up, to the point where Bruce and I, sitting 15 feet away, can barely even hear it. *This* is what the judge is basing my future on?! Bloody fucking madness! [Why am I surprised? why in the world should I be surprised by now?]

FLASH

I'm back home in Mendocino County and trying to enjoy life as much as possible. Though I'm failing spectacularly. It's been about two weeks now since the Motion to Suppress the Evidence Hearing [though it was much more like a Motion to Suppress the *Truth*; I know, I've already said this literally word-for-word, including in this Inter-Mission's very title—but certain things bear or even *demand* repeating]. We're just waiting to hear from Bruce about Judge Hamer's verdict. And every day my anxiety grows more and more. A wretched all-consuming **Dread** that started in my gut and now seems to permeate through, like, each and every one of the forty-trillion [40,000,000,000,000] cells in my body. That's of course a ridiculous statement, because why would **Dread**, an emotional sentiment, possibly be inside my actual cells? The logistics are improbable at best. EXCEPT! . . . except I think that's *really how it feels*! Waiting to learn whether logic and decency and constitutional adherence and Bruce's terrific arguments have somehow convinced Hamer to go ahead and grant the Motion to Suppress and symbolically dump the prosecution's "case" into the fucking sewer— the only proper place for it, the one place it belongs . . . that waiting period creates invasive prolonged symptoms like gut-clenched terror, annihilated concentration, trouble sleeping, a maddening and ceaseless psychological fixation that renders *impossible* the enjoyment of anything-and-boy-I-sure-do-mean-fucking-anything [including *actual* fucking! [with Rachel, not with my Mendo cabin-roommate Ryan [necessarily]]]. A speedfreak-like restlessness that makes me wanna blow my goddamn brains out with a .38 magnum or hell maybe even two of em one in each hand barrels pressed against my ears just to make sure the brain that facilitates these feelings is obliterated, increased pain → anxiety → pain → depression → pain, smoking even more cigarettes and weed because I don't give a shit about moderation anymore, and so on . . . yeah, it does indeed FEEL like these facets of **Dread** exist in 40,000,000,000,000 distinct places throughout my body. Who knows; I'm not a scientist! Didn't even perform up to my usual standards in freshman high school Biology, and that was like over a decade ago! So hell, maybe **The Dread** *is* permeating every one of my body's cells.

I mean . . . now that I've run through all that ↑↑↑ shit . . . I'm starting to consider the possibility that human emotion, especially *my* human emotion, is so overwhelmingly powerful and dramatic and sometimes like in this case just totally *pestilential* that maybe the cell-permeating thing IS possible. **The Dread** is so goddamn intense during this limbo-week that perhaps it's able to defy the very Laws of Nature.

Yeah, yeah definitely; the concept's growing on me. Emotions—for humans and other animals alike, human supremacist-enculturation not-withstanding—are already nebulous and metaphysical in a lot of ways. So why the hell not? Certain-feelings-manifesting-themselves-on-a-cellular-level is nifty, rock solid symbolic linguistic expression. In my opinion. Words alone aren't always sufficient to express the magnitude of some things, and emotions are undoubtedly one of them; something I'm trying to demonstrate in tangible practice with this memoir. I see no compelling reason not to suggest, then, that hyperbolic language vis-à-vis my cellular **Dread** need not be limited to the symbolic—that some emotions are so inexpressibly consumptive that, for all intents and purposes, symbolism becomes reality . . . hyperbole becomes understatement. When trying to render the inexpressible in ways that feel adequate and immediate and *real*, I ask again: why the hell not?

As a writer, words are just about all I have. Might as well utilize them to maximum effect. Even if it comes off as over-the-top, absurd. Given the degree of ludicrous absurdity that permeate the Prison Vortex, I'd much rather overstate my case than express it weakly, without a gravitas comm-ensurate to such utterly preposterous circumstances! If I fly too close to the sun in this #Januscript, I can at least take solace in knowing I did my goddamndest to reveal and even mimic the insane, farcical illogic and—dare I say it? [I do, I do]—the apparent logistical/scientific/ metaphysical *impossibility* of the Prison Vortex's somehow legitimate essence!

Anyway, I'm running errands nearby in the little town of Willits when I finally learn the judge's decision. I'm inside the local natural foods store staring at organic vegetables in a kind of **Dread**-daze and my phone rings and it's Jim. I'm wondering now if Mom convinced Jim to deliver the news because she just straight-up didn't have the heart to be the one to tell me. How you holdin up? Jim asks me. Okay I guess. Your mother got an email from Bruce—that's your lawyer's name, right?—a little while ago. Oh gawd, I say, and my heart begins thumping. Did we lose the Motion? Yeah, Jim says. Sorry buddy. Ughhhhhhh, I moan. Unable to form actual words, spirit doing its plummeting act that I'll become ever more familiar with. Then Jim delivers the knockout, seeming to make sure his voice only subtly indicates the horrific gravity of the information: Bruce said the prosecution has offered a new plea deal of seven years.

Now my heart seems to just . . .

just . . .

-STOP-

What?! I cry. Starting to wander the aisles in an aimless shuffle. It was *six months* before how'd it get all the way to *seven years?!* [I shouldn't have to even ask the question . . . we lost the Motion to Suppress [the Truth], so of course the State OFFICIALLY has the upper hand now. It already had the upper hand, the stacked deck in its favor, as I've tried to convey. But to go from six months to seven *years?* Such a staggering leap! And it really, in my opinion more than anything else, proves that the prosecution *knew* it had a pitiful case.

↓↓↓↓↓↓↓↓ **REALLY IMPORTANT!!** ↓↓↓↓↓↓↓↓

This is emblematic of probably the biggest, most irreparable problem with America's "Justice" System: Certain outcomes facilitate the advancement of political careers! Simply put, judges and prosecutors are literally *rewarded* for landing convictions. Given America's general Tough on Crime ideology, careers in or arising from the legal system advance mainly on the strength of their conviction record. Rather than, say, based on experience alone. This ever-so-predictably-and-*no-fuckin-duh!* fosters bias. A despicable and unjust *lean* toward guilty verdicts and harsh sentencing. In an actual fair system, there'd be NO HINT WHATSOEVER of built-in reward or political gain for securing convictions. But as it currently works, everyone involved in the "Justice" System except defense lawyers inherently benefit from landing guilty verdicts or scoring plea deals. Think of it as generally analogous to traffic cops' having monthly ticket quotas. They don't result in overzealous and/or inappropriate ticketing in *all* cases. But they most certainly *encourage* an implicit predisposition toward meting out tickets in 50-50 scenarios, when it could go either way. The only element judges and everyone else involved in court cases should be concerned with is a fair examination of provable facts. A laser-fine focus on impartial analysis, without ever *ever* shunning objectivity in favor of a particular result.

That's the best explanation for why, before the Motion to Suppress, they offered the now-unbelievable sweetheart deal of six months. The prosecution knew its case against me was shit; that it'd be relying entirely on proving the search and seizure was constitutionally justifiable. They knew the Motion to Suppress Hearing may well've allowed me to walk free. But they were yearning for that *guilty* plea—given the aforementioned benefits—and so extended me a ridiculously low offer. Knowing what I do now, I obviously should've flung myself onto the six-month deal. And I would have—had I been privy to a mere inkling of an idea that my plea deal would skyrocket if we lost the Motion! Irrespective of that permanent felony on my record. Of course, *now* this all seems so simple and easy-peasy. Hindsight etc.

There in the natural foods store, I'm trying to compose myself. To not physically crumble onto the market floor, sobbing. *How . . .* I say. *How'd it go from six months to* seven *years?!* But I already know the answer to that. Jim tries to comfort me: Bruce says with good time you'll probably only serve about three years. But even that is utterly unthinkable. Three fuckin years; *36 months.* I expected to get a year, maaaybe two. Oh christ. Oh man this is BAD. Quickly I thank Jim and hang up and rush outside as the full weight no that's wrong not even the full weight yet but just some of the crushing weight of this news wallops me and I have to collapse on a picnic bench just outside the entrance so I don't fall down jelly-legged, and there I slump now shaking and jam my face into my hands and start sobbing openly ostentatiously not caring just needing to let it flow sitting there in full view of customers walking in and out and loading their vehicles with groceries and no doubt staring at me some uncomfortable some saddened some probably amused remember this is American humans we're talking about but I don't give a shit I just hunch there trembling for real trembling not like Marlow-trembling i.e. not at all and sobbing terrified even more somehow than the last week so much **Dread** now not even gonna try and express it but merely sit there weeping and shaking and overcome by the horrorshow my life has descended into all because of one desperate poor choice on my part resulting from my disability and the System's failure to help me even though I needed it so badly needed and yes deserved it too all the injustice and corrupt malignant bullshit of this society now come crashing down like a bunker-buster to wreak havoc on my dumb stupid shitbag life.

I tried to express the intensity of **Dread** I felt during those few-ish weeks in limbo as we waited to hear back from Judge Hamer. Much of that **Dread** remains after hearing the news, although of course it's shifted to a different focal point [i.e. prison]. And increased tremendously—as unthinkable as that may seem, especially given the number of pages/words it took me to approach an accurate representation of how I felt *before* Hamer's dismissal of the Motion to Suppress. The merciless firestorm continues raging inside me; a conflagration that incinerates every part of my mind and heart its fury-flurry reaches. But now, in addition to **The Dread**, my mental state's moved from fear-marginally-dampened-by-the-possibility-of-winning to outright misery . . . to hopelessness, fatalistic terror, ferocious rage at the blatant injustice, and then the powerlessness engendered by *that* . . . [as mentioned, I already knew the "Justice" System was a corrupt load of dogshit, yet it was an abstract awareness; knowing something's wrong and unfair is one thing—actually having firsthand *experience* of that injustice's malicious effects is a whole nother beast altogether! I imagine there exist solid parallels here between my despising culturewide institutional racism and misogyny as a white man compared to actually *being* a black person or woman or etc. Like, hell—I know with every fiber of my being on a cellular level that getting into a legit fight with Brock Lesner would be terrible and unfair and so on . . . but that knowledge is absolute nothingness compared to what it'd feel like laying in a hospital bed all stitched and stapled up, big purple bruises developing all over, eyes swollen shut, concussed and bru- talized, with my body—and no doubt at times my vocal cords, if they even still worked—screaming in agony despite both heavy sedation and an IV morphine drip set at maximum levels. This latter is a solid analogy of my before-and-after emotional state, too]. This stupendously dramatic psy- chological transition happens very quickly within me. After that stretch of shocked public weeping outside the natural foods store, the emotional numbness that is my normal go-to response for all overwhelming personal tragedies is utterly unable to set up camp—my complex agony and horror are too strong, swatting aside with great ease any attempts to compart- mentalize or subdue or even trick myself into reducing them. They are the Real Deal. They're here to stay for a long, long time.

My next court date is scheduled for mid-May; about seven weeks down the line. I have definite suicidal feelings throughout the period. Actually, I've had them since like the moment I was arrested, but they're coming at a feverish pace and fervor now like never before. I'm also—no joke—*very seriously* considering the possibility of fleeing the country. Henry County of course still has my passport. So I'd have to find a way to travel under the radar, by unconventional means. Flying is an obvious non-option. I don't personally have [and couldn't procure through reasonable means] the kinda money that'd be required to charter a private plane and hire someone to illegally transport me across the Atlantic. Mexico, or better yet, South America, seem like the best potentialities; the farther away from the U.S. I end up the better, naturally. Maybe I could sneak across the border on foot into Tijuana and then get a bus or driver to shuttle me south? Or perhaps go to a shipyard—along the American West Coast or in Mexico—and bribe someone to stow me away on like a garment transport vessel heading to Guatemala or Honduras? Or maybe Canada; I have friends and allies there, so maybe I could cross the border somewhere in the wilderness and pay someone to pick me up? Then again, perhaps I needn't leave the country at all! Being a kind of autodidactic student of the radical animal and earth liberation movements, I've read numerous accounts of animal liberators and/or political arsonists et al. acquiring fake identification and living "underground." In fact, I'm a casual acquaintance of one dude who did just that; he was wanted for freeing several thousand mink from fur farms and managed to stay "on the run" and out of custody for something like seven years. So I talk to people. Explore and consider the options. But there's one huge particular issue that pretty much obliterates any chances to make any of these work: my knees. The disability, the severe constant pain, and resulting necessity to take narcotic pain meds every day. I could plan it so that I'd depart immediately after filling a prescription, but that'd only give me 30 days to make it to wherever and find a way to procure a reliable supply of the meds I need to do anything away from bed. No, it's just not even remotely realistic . . . between my lack of money and my disability, there's just no way. I have no choice but to stand tall and face this nightmare the best I can. Do my time and be done with it instead of essentially courting a lifelong target on my back.

Three years though . . . and that's the best-case scenario [so it seems at the time] . . . *36 goddamn months!* In prison—me! with my complex health issues that render me all but unable to defend myself . . . it's absolutely fuckin terrifying.

Rachel and I try our best to enjoy the remaining couple months we have together. I spend very little time at the cabin in Mendo, since it has no cell phone reception or internet. Most of the time I stay with her in Marin County half an hour north of San Francisco. We take several roadtrips in the time between my bonding out and my incarceration. She and Rikki and I; through Yosemite to Mono Lake and Death Valley and then Southern California to see my family one last time; to rain-sodden but still gorgeous and magical Humboldt for the scraps of ancient redwoods protected in State and National Parks; and then many frequent day trips to our favorite places in the greater S.F. Bay Area, like Point Reyes National Seashore in remote western Marin, Big Basin Redwoods State Park in the Santa Cruz Mountains south of S.F., Año Nuevo State Park on the coast a bit north of Santa Cruz, with its lovely wetlands and shorelines and sand dunes and magnificent elephant seals, coastal drives along the edge of Sonoma and Mendocino Counties, and Montgomery Woods State Park, a small but glorious pocket of oldgrowth redwoods in central Mendo.

Mom and I have been corresponding with Bruce via email and phone about my options over the course of this downtime. After all, a plea deal is just that: a deal you make with the State in an effort to secure the best outcome for yourself among numerous shitty potential outcomes. Bruce thinks there's a better alternative; he has a massive hardon for an eventual *appeal* that could see me walk away—with no felony on my record and not another day in jail. His preferred course of action is that we do a "stipulated bench trial"; this entails an incourt admission that, if tried, the State would be able to convict me of Possession with Intent. Then the judge'd sentence me then and there, in all likelihood to the minimum of 12 years, and we'd file an appeal to the original Motion to Suppress. It's basically just a way to fast track an official sentence in order to appeal ASAP. The appeal process entails a [supposed] random selection of three members from Henry County's district's five assigned appellate court judges; we'd have to get at least two of the three judges to rule in my favor for the sentence to be overturned. That's where it gets super tricky. According to Bruce, among the five potential judges are the following: two [2] conservatives who will almost certainly rule against me; two [2] more liberal-minded judges who would likely rule in my favor; and the final one [1] potential judge is right up the middle, and could go either way. If I happened to "draw" both of the liberal judges I'd almost definitely win the appeal and go home sans felony. But then, of course, there's the flipside—I could end up with both conservatives and the strength of our appeal case would be borderline irrelevant [the fact that Bruce can make these predictions with confidence is unsettling; shouldn't the *appellate court judges* be at least close to immune from ideological bias and hence rule solely based on the case's facts and our appeal's sturdiness?! It's yet further tangible evidence that the American Justice System is *not* just].

After a huge amount of careful thought and discussion and weighing of my options, Mom and Rachel and I all agree that the very real risk—and maybe even, given the legal tomfuckery we've now seen firsthand, the *likelihood*—of losing an appeal and having to swallow a fucking 12-year sentence instead of plea-dealing for seven years is just too great a risk. Too much of a difference in prison time.

I should provide a quick rundown of these numbers, because they aren't necessarily stone-set. They don't reflect the actual amount of time you'll end up serving and so can easily become confusing. This'll really put things in perspective even more. There are five different "Classes" of felony in Illinois—in the order of most to least severe, it's X and then 1 through 4. The 12-year sentence I'd get with a stipulated bench trial would be categorized as a Class X. This automatically entails serving *85 percent* of your sentence. You also *cannot* receive goodtime credit; you're disqualified from shaving time off your sentence by going to school or entering a drug treatment program while incarcerated. So if I chose the appeal route and lost, I'd be looking at a little over *10 years'* imprisonment in reality. That's a lot. A whole goddamn lot. Alternatively, the 7-year offer involves pleading guilty to "just" a Class 1 felony. Which means I'd only serve 50 percent of those 7 years [every felony classification aside from X gets your actual prison term cut in half]; plus I *would* be eligible to earn goodtime. I could in theory serve as little as 2.5ish years—but 3.5 at the absolute most. This obviously makes the plea deal seem like an even more clearcut choice. I can at least imagine serving 3ish years. But *10* fuckin years? A DECADE?! Utterly and completely unthinkable. I'd end up in a max joint. Or more likely, I'd kill myself before it ever got that far—if I were unable to flee the country or disappear underground.

One last note. About that whole Class X thing . . . Per the Illinois Department of Corrections [sic] website, "Class X sentences are reserved for the most violent offenses [Murder, Armed Robbery, Sexual Assault,

Drug Trafficking [emphasis added]].”[18] I wonder if anyone even considers how moronic and just plain silly it is to include my muling a few boxes of flower buds in even the same *universe* as rape and murder and child molestation? In what world does it make iota-sense to lump traffickers in with the “most violent offenders”?! I’ll tell you: only in the insane assbackwards world of the American “Justice” System and its War on Drugs. Where the literally stupefying-ludicrous has become commonplace; believable only because it’s true. If just a handful of these things were chucked into one of my novels, I’d *SNAP!* lose any and all suspension of disbelief I’d managed to cultivate.

So it’s looking like that plea deal’s the way to go. Even still . . . *three years!* Starting shortly after my 25th bday, the prime of life—at least in the context of my pathetic crippled ass. The whole thing is just straight-up dumbfounding. Then, seemingly out of thin air, and just a few weeks prior to my next court date of May 20, an extraordinary—and extraordinarily bizarre—situation presents itself. Something I’d never even heard of in real life. All of my reading, all my studies of social movement-histories and political prisoners, and still I’d never once considered or encountered anything like this. Bruce hits us with an email saying that the judge and prosecution might be willing to lower my plea deal to 4 years—so 2 years’ imprisonment, in actuality—

[*WHAT?! Yes yes fuckin hell yes!*]

—**IF we paid an additional “fine” of $25,000-$35,000**!

. . . .

[*WHAT?! What the actual fuck?!?*]

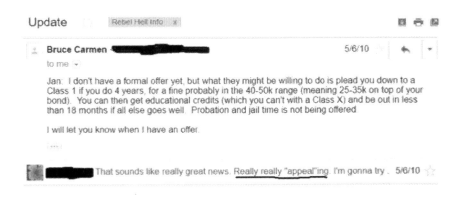

Except for Bruce, nobody with whom I've talked about this—and I've told a *lotta* goddamn people in the 7 years since it happened—has ever heard of such a deal either. Not one single person. And that includes more than a couple lawyer friends and ex-convicts! When I express my shock and disbelief to Bruce, he's totally nonchalant. "I've actually seen it numerous times," he tells us [yeah, I bet you have, given the disgusting and blatant corruption of your shitty cornpone garbage-ass county!]. "In fact, I had a client who was caught with several kilos [!] of cocaine and was able to walk, without serving any prison time, by paying $70,000 [!!!]." Dude! You're a friggin lawyer! Acting waaaay too nonplussed about this crooked undemocratic madness; far too nonplussed—can't you at least *pretend* to be, like, just a little bit . . . PLUSSED? I mean, *Holy shit*, right? I've thought about this extensively; I can predict the most likely response from bootlickers and #*Yessirs* and "Blue Lives Matter" types. You know the type. People who might defend this "fine" offer with something to the effect of, *People get hit with fines in court every day! Haven't you seen like the start of a DVD or—hell, you're in your 30s, right?—a VHS tape with that longass warning from the FBI about not copying and distributing the movie or you could receive up to a year in jail AND/OR A FINE OF UP TO $5,000 or whatever?!*

. . . Yyyehp, yes of course I have. On DVD *and* VHS, yes indeed. But this just feels different. And I'm quite sure I know why it feels different: BECAUSE IT *IS* DIFFERENT! They already levied a fine. The plea deal has from the beginning included a substantial fine—which I mentioned earlier, before the Motion Hearing, when the offer was six months. When I wrote that it was a hefty fine, boy o boy did I mean it! These sick fucks are essentially enacting some kinda bizarro-world's modern iteration of debtor's prison. Viz., they're hitting me with nearly *$180,000*—that's-right-no-typo-it-really-is-180-thousand-dollars—in "fines and court fees and lab testing and drug enforcement" [see payment-summary image below]. That latter part is the biggest aspect that really twists my nips. Both financially and ideologically . . . it's the principle. I don't understand it one damn iota, but on the "fine"-summation sheet they later give me, I'm being charged $135,000 for "Drug Enforcement." This is apparently their esti-mation of my 53 pounds' street value. Which they're charging me. For the weed. Charging *me*, for *my* weed. The weed that they *took*! All I can think to say is a simple WHAT?! You profiled me—"Heading east on Interstate 80 through a heavily trafficked corridor with western license plates"—then pulled me over on a 100 percent fabricated traffic violation, detained me for both an unjustifiable reason and length of time, based solely on a non-legally-defensible hunch; you probably tampered with the dashcam's audio so you could openly instruct the drug dog to signal [on the wrong side of the RV, no less]; you performed an illegal search and seizure and stole my goddamn flower-bud drugs, AND THEN YOU HAVE THE FUCKING GALL TO *CHARGE ME* FOR THE VALUE OF THAT WEED?! My heavens! It's like a meter-maid stealing your Ferrari and leaving a ticket in its place for the car's sticker price.

No, this is way different than a fine that might accompany prison time. This offer to reduce the plea deal from 7 years to 4 years if we pay $25,000-$35,000 on top of the $15,000 already spent bonding me out of jail . . .

IT'S A GODDAMN LEGAL [sic?] <u>SHAKEDOWN</u>.

Straight-up. Plain and simple, end of story. A shakedown.

```
10/25/13 13:23:11  GAL/JIMS 8.0   PRTDUE        PAYMENT STATUS INFORMATION

   Case number     2010CF000021D 001

   Litigant        ████████████

   Agency          County Crm & Juv

   Due date        11/18/2013

                        Due         Paid        Balance
   Fine             40,000.00    40,000.00          .00
   Clerk             1,605.00       420.00      1,185.00
   State's Atty         30.00          .00         30.00
   Court                50.00          .00         50.00
   Automation           10.00          .00         10.00
   Judicial Security    25.00          .00         25.00
   Drug Enforcement 135,000.00         .00    135,000.00
   Document Storage     10.00          .00         10.00
   Drug Crime Lab       90.00          .00         90.00
   Mandatory Drug Fee 1,975.00         .00      1,975.00
   Trauma Center       100.00          .00        100.00
   DNA Identification  200.00          .00        200.00
   Child Advocacy Fee    5.00          .00          5.00
   Total           179,100.00    40,420.00    138,680.00
```

*If they think they're ever, EVER getting even a fraction of that sum, they can go do some deep squats on a long, fat dildo, and hence . . . well . . . literally **get fucked**.*

Know what else? They were from the get-go fully aware of my disability's nature and extent. I made damn sure of it, because it was an extenuating factor from a variety of angles. It produced inherently greater-than-usual desperation and fear on our part for my physical health and safety/well-being. And I think they took advantage of that fact; knowing my family was financially well-off, and would want me to be as safe as possible given my limitations. Even so, for a while my parents weren't sure whether or not they'd pay the "fine." But eventually Mom decided that, given said disability and my suffering and need for adequate medical attention, she wanted to do everything in her power to ensure I'd end up at a minimum-security joint. So in the end, they forked over another $25k to that putrid county. It still cracks my heart every time I think about the gangrenous injustice. Staggering. And I don't think I'll ever stop feeling guilt that my parents [under extreme emotional duress, I should add] shelled out such an absurd sum of money just so I'd have a lesser chance of experiencing serious harm. That guilt . . . their money and heartache . . . just a few more elements that make this memoir so crucial—that necessitate my *rebel yell* from *rebel hell*.

In the end, the whole legal charade detailed in this Inter-Mission comes down to the following simple little rhyme. Another self-coined phrase I really like, as did all the other inmates I shared it with . . .

COPS LIE
JUDGES BUY
WE FRY

PART 2

WELCOME TO MY NIGHTMARE

["The Word *Why* Does Not Exist Here"]

I'm sick. So, so damn sick.

Sitting here on this freezing steel toilet, a filthy toilet that hasn't been cleaned in easily half a year, stainless steel that is most certainly *not* stainless, its bowl covered in brown and yellowish splotches; there's not even a hyphen-sized glimpse of silver lining down inside. I know it's sometime in the afternoon because lunch came a while ago, but that's all I know. I'm planted on the toilet yet again. Squirting hot, painful diarrhea. Already—it's no later than mid-afternoon and *already*—I've lost track of today's shitcount. Lost track after about seven. Yehp, that's right, I've had to shit at least seven times today! and I've been awake fewer hours than that! By now, it's often just liquid, like I'm horse-pissing from my anus in scorching jets. Ass hole raw and enflamed.

I'm so goddamn sick. My chin rests between the palms of my cheek-cupping hands as I sit, just sit, and wait to see if I'm done shitting for long enough to justify collapsing from the toilet and into bed three feet away. I scratch my head, my dark-blonde-stubbled head that I buzzcut about six [?] days ago in Henry County Jail the night before getting transported here to Stateville—a maximum-security prison with a separate Receiving area where convicts wait to be "processed" and then, eventually, shipped to an appropriate longterm prison. The head's itching maddeningly; both from dandruff and from having not showered for the past six [seven?] days. It's so itchy that, if I can't stop focusing on it obsessively, it seems like I'll literally go insane. My finger-nails are overgrown now to almost baglady-levels; it's been three weeks since I was able to trim them. If I stick an index finger nail-first atop my scalp and drag it down to my forehead, the fingernail comes away stuffed with a yellowish-white pâté of dead-skin flakes.

I am being walloped fullforce and head-on with a violent detoxification. One that is dangerously severe; a predictable result of my medications' precipitous forced dose-plunge. This is literally life-threatening negligence by health care. You're *NEVER* supposed to drop a patient's benzodiazepine [a class of anti-anxiety meds—Klonopin, in my case] milligrammage by more than half at once if they've been on it for any length of time. That alone is terrible enough. But it is standard psychiatric practice, as any competent doctor in the field will tell you.[19] But when I got here, they instantaneously dropped my Klonopin dose by *two-thirds*. One potential risk of such a steep and immediate drop is that I could have a seizure at any moment.

What I better do is I better simply not have a seizure in the first place, because *nothing will be done about it*. We're completely alone in the cell, me and craig. So I need to just try to not-have a seizure. That's the best plan.

And then there's my face! It's beginning to itch as much as the dandruff head, as if tireless bugs are crawling with their tiny legs *skrik-skrik-skrik* all over my face's lower half. I haven't shaved in over a week now—no razors currently available—and so crazed ferocious hair is sprouting all over my cheeks and neck and chin, with little cactus-needle blonde hairs pricking stiffly now into my lips and even my tongue.

CONFESSION: I kinda want to die. No, wrong . . . I really want to. I really *really* want to die. This is it. This is more than I can handle. I'm dehydrated. Haven't slept for more than two consecutive hours in four days. I've been shitting ten to fifteen times a day. Eaten maybe 800 calories

---

[19] Trust me, this I know for sure [my mom's been a psychiatrist for over 20 years].

total in the last five days. Shedding pounds at a truly perilous rate.[20] They warned me about this place; guys who'd been here before, with whom I shared the cellblock during my second, two-week stint in Henry County Jail, they tried to describe the Stateville Receiving process. But nothing could ever prepare you for this. NOTHING.

And I want to die.

I beg the gawd I don't believe in to *Please gawd please fucking kill me.* Smack me with a fatal heart attack. A terminal seizure. Doesn't matter: I cannot handle this anymore! I'm a strong person and I've been through a lot and I can deal with a lot. This, though, this is too damn much. Kill me gawd. Please just kill me. I don't care anymore. So very ready to die.

If I could kill myself—if I could kill myself RIGHT NOW—I would, with not the slightest twitch of hesitation.

How did I get here? Not just to this geographical place, but also mentally, psychologically: How'd I get here this fast? I was feeling so strong! Ready to face anything with my head up high. Prepared to tolerate any amount of shit flung my way. I really believed these things, really truly did. So how did I descend into such darkness, such soulcrushing despondency, so damn fast?

How did I get here?

Well . . . I arrived physically about a week ago. On a van from County Jail; Henry County, where they arrested me. Where I "caught my case." I spent two weeks there, waiting for the bimonthly Stateville transport, and things were okay and I felt confident, tough, prepared to smash through all troubles. But now I'm here and it's a whole new universe. A nightmare of the darkest, scariest, most disturbing kind.

Welcome to my nightmare.

-Thursday-

The very moment we arrived at Stateville, I knew my time there would entail unfathomable gruesomeness and suffering. That's precisely what I'd been told; seeing it in person merely confirmed the warnings.

Six humanoids came in the van from Henry County Jail: two Guards and four inmates. I sat in the very back row with an elderly guy named

---

[20] In the end I'll have lost **19 pounds in 27 days**. Dropping from 183 lbs. to 164— more than two pounds every three days—for just under a MONTH.

ken. The drive from Henry County Jail to Stateville Correctional Center took a couple hours. I'd spent two largely uneventful weeks in County after signing the plea deal. Two weeks indoors, with not even a glimpse of the outside world; after that, I quite enjoyed the drive. Staring out at the landscape, the trees and cornfields, the clouds and blue sky, provided an immense spirit-lift.

Our hands were cuffed in front of us for the drive. Ankles cuffed as well, so we had to move in short shufflesteps. I had a difficult time simply getting into the van. Had to stick my hands on the seat and hop, pulling myself up. Thankfully I received a dose of kindness from a fellow prisoner; he knew about my knees, and ceded his aisle seat to me so I could stretch out.

As we drove east on I-80 [a surreal experience, to say the least], ken told me his story. He had balding, short white hair with a dash of pepper. Age: 68. Bespectacled. His wife was slowly, painfully dying of cancer. Morphine barely touched her pain, a tunneling kind that bore all the way into her bones. But then she discovered marijuana helped immensely with it. Far more than did any pharmaceutical cocktail. It also eased her chemo-nausea, brought back some of her appetite.

They'd been married for 43 years. ken felt compelled [obligated, even] to acquire good, strong, medical-grade marijuana to ease her agony; all he could find in their suburban Pennsylvania town was weak gutterweed.

So ken flew out to San Francisco and rented a car. Acquired a proper medical cannabis recommendation. Then he went to several dispensaries in the Bay Area and accrued two pounds of marijuana. Enough for at least a year—to provide relief until her inevitable, imminent death, in other words. ken stuck the large Ziploc bags of pot into a briefcase in his trunk. He struck out for home. For his dying wife in Pennsylvania.[21]

His route was identical to mine: Interstate 80, which officially begins on S.F.'s Bay Bridge. He made it over the Sierra Nevada Mountains via Donner Pass and through California. Made it through Nevada, where his two pounds had suddenly gone from a misdemeanor to a felonious amount. He made it through Utah and Wyoming and Nebraska and Iowa [just like

---

[21] Anybody who thinks marijuana shouldn't be legalized—or AT THE VERY LEAST decriminalized—should think about ken & his wife, should carefully consider their example; if this doesn't change their minds, they need to take a long walk off a short plank in the middle of the ocean. They're heartless assholes with no place in a civilized, rational, sane society.

I did on my muling gig], all states with varying levels of draconian possession laws. For the sake of perspective: If I'd been popped in Wyoming,
I'd've been facing *five to ten years'* imprisonment. Granted, I did have 26.5
times [!] more cannabis than he did. On not-nearly-as-laudable a mission.
Immediately after passing through Davenport in Iowa, he crossed a bridge
over the mighty Mississippi River and into Illinois. Then—also just like
me—he unwittingly made a catastrophic mistake.

He entered Henry County on Interstate 80.

Driving on I-80, you're in Henry County a mere 27ish miles. Tragically
though, in 2010 A.D., that 27 miles was patrolled by two State Troopers
whose *sole job* was to pull people over and find drugs. I'm not making this
up. I heard it from too many local residents, including my lawyer Bruce,
and witnessed it firsthand: both times Mom and I flew out there, we stayed
at the Best Western in Geneseo. Literally within sight of the spot where I
was pulled over. Both times, I'd stand on the grass right beside the hotel to
smoke cigarettes. And both those times, I watched at least one pulled-over
vehicle getting ransacked by multiple Officers, drug-sniffing dog in tow.

ken's arrest story is even more blatant than my own. Which is no easy
task—congrats, Henry County Troopers! Where would we all be without
you, devoting the bulk of your working lives to stealing people's flower
buds and then giving perjurious testimony to get them imprisoned for it?
You are frontline warriors on the battlefield for America's soul! Dedicated
soldiers in the war on medicinal flowers. Your selfless contributions to
safety and justice are truly inexpressible. I only hope that, some day, you
receive everything you deserve for all your staggering achievements. One
can dream, right?

After ken was pulled over, that particular Trooper sped past him and,
one after the other, stopped *three other cars*. Then visited them one-by-one.
Ain't that some shit? When the Trooper approached ken's car, he claimed
to've "smelled something funny" as he drove in ken's wake. ← Read that
sentence again; really let it sink in and percolate through the ole noggin.
Dude needs to get on *Ripley's Believe it or Not!* posthaste. He's got the nose
of a damn bloodhound on steroids—ken's two pounds of Ziplocked weed
were in a closed briefcase in his trunk. That there's an otherworldly sense
of smell, *amiright*?!

The evidence of Henry-County-tomfuckery has mounted to absolute
Andean heights.

A queasiness radiates through my guts immediately upon our entrance to Stateville's compound. That's by far the best word for it: COMPOUND. Its entire perimeter circumscribed by three chainlink fences staggered ten feet apart, each with five feet [in width and height] of mangley looping razorwire clustered at the base and spilling from the top. This looks like something straight out of the *Saw* movies. We're talking what's gotta be miles upon miles of jagged steel. All felons convicted in Illinois's northern half spend at least ten days being "processed" here, no matter how minor and nonviolent our crime/s. This place is the *apotheosis* of prisons; people all across the country know about its infamously terrible conditions. The climactic prison riot and escape sequence in *Natural Born Killers* [1994] was filmed there—that should give you a hint of its fundamental nature.

The van pulls up to a building near the entrance and we four inmates shuffle inside. Right off the bat, we're visually gob- and eye-smacked: the cavernous interior resembles a warehouse, one that got gutted and then stuffed with a sprawling grid of several dozen "bullpens." Massive holding cells, each enclosed by ceiling-high fences of blue crisscrossing metal, each filled with 30-foot-long concrete benchslabs in rows uncountable. A Guard orders us to stand with our foreheads pressed against the nearest bullpen's blue metal. ken turns around; a whiteshirted Lieutenant is loitering over by a table where several Guards sit. Some are picking at Styrofoam takeout containers of food. Others play cards. "Sir," ken calls out meekly, "can I please use the restroom?"

"Turn the fuck around ole man," the Lieutenant barks. A caustic disgust sours his gruff voice. Like he's guttering himself simply by responding; like ken's a repugnant "lower" life form—a potato bug maybe, or some other ick-factoring creepy-crawly.

ken turns right the fuck back around. Forlorn. My heart breaks, and simultaneously kicks up a notch as fear-adrenaline floods my veins. I catch ken's eye and shake my head, lips pressed together in a sad flat line. Trying to comfort the poor elderly guy: *I'm sorry, buddy. We will get through this.* Prison's kinda like the military, I imagine, in the sense that our dangerous pressure cooker environment can produce powerfully cohesive bonds in just a few moments.

A giant black Correctional Officer yanks off our hand- and ankle-cuffs. Per his booming instruction, we scurry into the nearest bullpen. An inmate worker hands out paperbag lunches. Lay's potato chips [4 oz.] and a sandwich with bread even more white than my fishbelly-pale asscheeks, a slice of cheese resembling curdled Band-Aids, and the most revolting bologna I've seen in my life. I'll soon learn this is referred to as "slickmeat." It's a pinkish-brown color, with gruesome splotches of red and white and gray. Yes, gray. Damn thing looks positively diseased.[22] Someone describes it perfectly: "Shit don' even look *real*. Looks like somethin from one'a those plastic Fisher-Price kitchen sets." Nail on the head. We also get a grade-school-sized carton of cow's skim milk, which I trade for another bag of chips. I unload the despicable meatslab and cheese on someone else. Eat my two bags of Lay's. Then I squeeze the slices of bread into dense balls and eat those.

Soon we're moved from the cage to join, at the expansive room's far end, a line of guys who came from disparate County Jails. A doublewide door stands open at the front of the line. We inch forward. Like cows and pigs being led to slaughterhouse-bound transport trucks . . . except animals are invariably innocent, and we won't be getting our throats slashed and flesh eaten.[23] Only our souls will be slaughtered here. First up after passing through the doors is Personal Property, where workers sit behind a couple tables. I have nothing. Except the $124 remaining "on my books" from County. As we walk onward to the Clothing Station, ken looks bereft. I ask him what's wrong.

"They made me turn in my wedding ring." He's rubbing the pale band of skin at the base of his ring finger. "You're not allowed to have anything with raised patterns, because you could use it to cut someone. But mine didn't even have any! It had our names engraved, but they were sunk into the ring, not raised!" He's verging on tears. My heart aches even more for him. "jan, I've been wearing that ring for *43 years*. Since the day we got married."

I stare at him gapejawed. "You haven't taken it off even a single day?"

---

[22] And probably *is*!—like much animal flesh, since about 99% of meat comes [out of economic necessity] from factory farms, where abhorrent overcrowding, terrible nutrition, & filthy conditions contribute to stratospheric animal sickness levels.

[23] Unlike those nonhuman animals, we actually did something wrong, to get here. But or at least illegal, to end up here! [Unless we were wrongfully convicted, but you know what I mean—unless you *don't* know what I mean; if that's the case, email me & I'll explain to you in better detail what I mean.] My email is ████████@gmail.com [*Ed. note: address once more removed for a litany of what seem like obvious reasons*]

"Not once. My wife's gonna have a heart attack when she gets it in the mail. No explanation, nothing. Just a package with one of the rings we've been wearing for 43 years straight." Big fat tears stand out now in his blue eyes.

All I can do is shake my head in disbelief. Almost crying myself. "I'm sorry, ken. That's just beyond awful."

And yet the senseless humiliation and madness has barely begun.

At the Clothing Station, we're told to line up alongside about 20 other inmates, shoulders almost touching, backs pressed against the frigid white-brick wall. Three Guards are spread out across the line. One of them barks orders. We have to strip naked, tossing our clothes down before us.

"bootcampers" are inmates who work for the prison; well-behaved guys from over in the maximum-security section, employed here in Receiving. bootcampers scuttle down the line, plucking up all our clothes and canvas shoes—aka "Karate Joes"—and throwing them in gray plastic trash bins.

"NOW!" roars one of the three large and muscular Officers who lord over the Clothing Station. "LISTEN RRREEAL CAREFUL, CUZ YER ONLY GONNA WANNA DO THIS HERE PART ONCE. FUCKIN TRUST ME." He is reminiscent of R. Lee Ermey—Gunnery Sergeant Hartman from director-auteur Stanley Kubrick's *Full Metal Jacket* [1987]. "NOW RAISE YOUR ARMS AAALLL THE WAY UP 'N WIGGLE YER FINGERS." The twenty of us, lined up tight, obey in silence. "OPEN YER MOUTHS 'N STICK OUTCHER TONGUES . . . OKAY. RUN A FINGER BETWEEN YOUR TEETH 'N GUMS, ALL THE WAY AROUND ON THE BOTTOM. AHRIGHT. NOW THE TOP." All three Guards stare back and forth at this line of naked manflesh. Scanning for evidence of contraband, such as bulging orifices or appendages. "GRAB YER LOWER LIP 'N PULL IT DOWN . . . RAISE YER UPPER LIP WITH YER FINGERS SO IT TOUCHES YER NOSE." He pauses. They're scanning, glaring. "KAY. LIFT UP YER NUTSACKS . . . NOW JUST YER DICKS . . . NOW TURN AROUND AND FACE THE WALL.

"FIRST, LIFT YER LEFT LEG SO I KIN SEE YER FEET . . . NOW WIGGLE YER TOES. SAME THING WITH TH' RIGHT FOOT. AHRIGHT—HERE COMES THE FUN PART." He stops again. Fierce, dark little eyes beading up and down the line. Voice totally emotionless; he's done this five days a week for gawd knows how many years. Like a proctologist without the psychologically bolstering effect of knowing at least you're helping to prevent or treat illness. While this experience must be pedestrian to the Guards, it's traumatic for me and surely many others— given its inherently humiliating and degrading nature. It strips bare [so to speak] fundamental notions of privacy, dignity, and bodily autonomy, to name a few.

The beefy Officer continues his deadpan and authoritative instructional onslaught. "Y'ALL SURE BETTER GET THIS RIGHT TH' FIRST TIME. TRUST ME." That's the second time he's implored us to give our trust. "BEND OVER, SPREAD YER ASS CHEEKS, AN' COUGH AT THE COUN'A THREE."

We comply.

Yeah, there's no way I'm the only man who feels violated by strip-searches. There seem to be axiomatic and deepseated differences between the ways strip-searches affect us versus how they affect them, the Officers. For many/most of us, the experience produces a litany of feelings, ranging from mild discomfort to demoralizing humiliation . . .

But for the Officers, *it's just another Thursday.*

This example feeds perfectly into one of my main theses arising from the knowledge I gain in prison—or throughout this book's narrative arc, if you will. The Prison System is masterfully good at creating situations and even entire *institutions* that are fueled by a central facet of the Bureaucrazy; one of its most crucial mechanisms, without which the Bureaucratic Model would fall apart, collapse under the terrible weight of its own inhumanity. This apparatus is the **division—the impenetrable severance—between those individuals *working for* the Institution and the individuals being *worked on* by it**. In prison, this translates to the absolute necessity of total disconnect between

STAFF |||&||| inmates

Obviously this disconnect is not and cannot be physical in prison. Staff members, those working *for* the Machine, must "take care of" the inmates, those being worked on *by* the Machine.[24] So rather than being corporeal,

---

[24] The only way the disconnect could become physical too is if industrial civilization lasts long enough to where prisons can be fully operated by actual machines [it won't last long enough]. With any Staff currently required to interact with prisoners replaced by robots. Luckily, industrialism will collapse due

the stark separation here is more existential and psychological. Consider the sequence last narrated. Our being strip-searched . . . all the way down to the space between toes and inside the mouths and beneath penises and scrotums and of course right at the stretched-open anuses . . . thoroughly searched, and not just once but again and again, anytime we have visitors, anytime we move locations [searched on departure *and* arrival], and so on. Now think about how this and so many other redundant and/or senseless procedures are required—and how all of them encapsulate and epitomize numerous elements, like: [1] a clear dichotomy of power that is *meant* to be felt; [2] situations that humiliate/degrade/dehumanize us, yet have been rendered mundane and all but unaffecting for the Staff—habituation, and surely in many cases willful psychological-emotional suppression, having purposefully created this mechanistic sense of detachment in them; [3] the circumstantial engendering of *hopelessness* in every one of us as individual human beings, whereas [4] Staff members personally benefit from and are implicitly encouraged to . . . *not* care about our suffering, *not* think about how it feels for us to endure so much trauma, *not* think of us as individual human beings [and if they can't help but do so, they must never forget that we chose to break the law and so deserve whatever happens], and perhaps most importantly, simply *not think about any of this at all if possible!*

I very much hope that you'll keep this stuff in the back of your mind going forward [perhaps referring back to it as needed—maybe you could like highlight these page numbers or whatever]. Starting again when the actual narrative resumes in a few paragraphs, and then continuing literally beyond the book's ending [read: indefinitely; see Inter-Mission 1B's "fine," debtor's prison, a permanent felony record, and so on]. You will see this functional and inherent disconnect between us and Them so many times throughout the entire story; I hope that, now, you'll be able to instantly recognize this dynamic in its multitudinous iterations—notice and then also *understand* how the cuntish behavior of specific Guards or Lieutenants or Doctors or other Staff isn't nearly as significant as are the institutional mechanisms that facilitate and encourage such behavior.

The American Prison System is a sterling paradigm of this. *Set up* to intentionally provide bureaucrats little to no knowledge of the anguish produced by their decisions, their blind allegiance to nonsensical rules. A

---

to ecological excess & population overshoot well before technology ever makes possible such a frightening, [even-more-] dystopic reality.

System designed with layer upon layer of redtaped insulation; protecting everyone who works inside from facing [or *feeling!*] responsibility if anyone suffers extreme trauma—or even gets killed—as a result of said rules and decisions. So then ultimately, the Bureaucratic Model both encourages and facilitates the elimination of culpability for *everyone* operating therein. Allowing any and all of them to pass the buck onto someone else in some other department continuously, for an endless length of time if necessary. Built-in cyclical abdication of fault, guilt, and consequences for anyone and everyone. <u>Forever</u>.

What horrifying, wicked genius! How could such an enduring societal stalwart appear so benign—and *necessary*—yet in reality be so astoundingly pernicious and wretched, facilitating even good, kindhearted individuals to enact policies and regulations with absolutely monstrous consequences for undeserving humans?! [Also, I'd be a real piece of shit if I didn't at least mention nonhuman life and the biosphere as a whole . . . the most ultra-innocent of all . . . and how the Bureaucratic Model resigns them to an *even worse fate* than it does people!] But here's the thing: it's NOT necessary, my Dear Reader. It's merely an institutional design that allows for the relatively easy governance and control of human beings in massive, endless hordes. That's right—I'm laying blame at the feet of rampant human overpopulation for the Bureaucrazy as well! And not without ample justification. I mean, yah of course we've already waayyyyyy overshot this planet's carrying capacity—which is not to say we should find another planet to inhabit, as that's not only ludicrously undoable, but also a heinous pile of moronic thoughtfeces; how about fixing the [only] goddamn planet we already have, instead of resigning ourselves to buttfucking the place to death with pollution and then starting the process all over again somewhere else [and again, that's IF it were even possible, and once more all together yes everyone even you all way in the back, IT'S NOT FUCKING POSSIBLE, SO JUST STOP. OKAY?-GOOD-THANKS!]—so, given the overall stupidity of the human species, the Bureaucrazy is probably here to stay until we get our population down down way down to a sensible pleasant number that accounts for the fact that we're not the Chosen Ones or Gawd's Children or All That Matters but rather a single bloated selfish disgustingly overabundant species on a planet of 10,000,000 yes ten million different ones, all each and every one special and ecologically important some more or less than others but all with just as much right to be here no screw that more of a right to be here than us, cuz we're just a whole damn stupid ass shitload of Clever Hairless Apes [not Wise, just Clever, much too clever for anyone's good], and my wife and I are childfree and I already got vasectomized at age 25 right before my incarceration began so I'm not in a glass house and can go ahead and throw stones and so I'll make it ever-so-simple even though I know my Dear Readers are hella smart definitely above average [Love You! ☺] but still just in case here are 4 simple suggestions-or-maybe-more-like-pleadings:

[1] If you have 0 kids and you/your partner don't really want to have any, then DON'T! Be cautious, but if you do get pregnant, there's NO SHAME in abortion!

[2] If you have 0 kids but want 1+, be some poor child's absolute *hero* and ADOPT! There are 415,000 children in U.S. foster care today.

[3] If you already have 1+ kid/s, STOP! Want more? Be some poor child's absolute *hero* and ADOPT! There are 415,000 children in U.S. foster care today.

[4] If you have functioning sperm, aka *semen-demons*, stop them! Be like all the cool kids—and also like me—and get vasectomized! Planned Parenthood performed mine on a sliding scale of $0-$400 [≈ cost of 1 abortion!], and since jan = unemployable cripple, mine cost *zero* $s. Awesome! They're so great, I love them! Thank you Dr. Heller!!

I met with him first and he wanted to know my reasons because I was "so young" and might change my mind.[25] So I hit him with only about 60 seconds of the ∞ish seconds for which I could've listed reasons, and he was like, Okay—you've obviously put a lotta thought into it and sound confidant, sooooo let's get you prepped! And the hardest part of the procedure was a slight tugging pain that lasted ≈ 3 seconds—yet I've never been more satisfied with any of my personal actions. It's the best thing I've ever done for myself, and for the planet, and for my female partners [given that our society places a sickening amount of the pregnancy-burden on women; this is total bullshit, and more men need to step up and take this proactive measure, thereby removing some of that shitty, inappropriate weight from off of women's shoulders like the decent partners I'm certain many of you are].

. . . .

---

[25] Isn't it just a big ole hoot that society almost never gives an iota of a shit when, say, a 21-year-old woman *has a baby*, and yet it's difficult in most places for a *30-year-old woman* to get sterilized?! HAHAHAHAHA . . . HAHA . . . oy . . . stop it, 'Murica, yer logick's showing!

Oops! sorry, went into Ramblemode again, but *c'est la* ME; and hey, sometimes tangents can reveal important information. Even so, I'm sorry my Dear Beloved Reader, please forgive me!

So then. I know my analysis of Bureaucrazy was . . . well . . . crazy, but it'll make more sense all the time as you flip/swipe through the pages and my hypothesis's evidence builds and builds into a veritable skyscraper of stacked experiential proof. My whole entire summation may've seemed deceptive in its simplicity. But the more you see, and hopefully *feel*, the more sense it'll make. In any case [NPI—haha, that pun works really well, as this stuff applies to literally almost *any case*] . . . these specific elements of the Bureaucratic Model I've been discussing are a definite focal point, one from which so so many variations on the System's madness are able to *shoot out from* and also be *held together by*, like the hub of a bicycle wheel and its flaring metal spokes.

Simply put, it's clear to me now:

American prisons represent the quintessential modern ideation of the Bureaucrazy.

They demonstrate what the Bureaucratic Machine looks like when functioning to its maximum effect. Taking people [mostly black] who are—when you root out and toss away the dogma and stereotypes and rhetoric—guilty of little more than petty crimes, and then forcing us to endure psychological, emotional, and often physical anguish and trauma. Not to rehabilitate or "cure" us, but primarily to satisfy certain demands of industrialism and capitalism. I.e. cheap [basically *slave*] labor, and political career-advancement in a massive range of fields. Preparing those with *some* power to move into positions of *even greater* power. Thereby keeping the Machine cycling smoothly and at an ever-quickening pace, without malfunction or surcease. Everybody [that matters to industrial capitalism] wins!

When at last the horrible stripsearch sequence mercifully ends, boot-campers come up to each of us and request our shoe and clothing size. I tell the dude 12 or 11.5 and Large. He drops a pair of 11s at my feet, along with an insanely baggy bright-yellow XXL jumpsuit. The crotch sags a good foot below my already-saggy nutbag. Sitting inside one of the Karate Joe canvas shoes is a thick bar of white "State Soap."

We move on; single file, cold and nude, through this weird closet sized room with a powerful blacklight on either side. They're almost *nuclearish*, radiating an indigo shade across our flesh to reveal any lice, crabs, or bedbugs. Next, we're allotted three minutes to shower. I stick my glasses into one shoe and enter the spacious, tiled, partitionless room. Spraynozzles positioned every four feet. We have to remain barefoot. No choice, no shower shoes to protect against fungi and infectious bacteria here at world class Stateville. Since I'm not wearing my glasses, luckily, anything over three feet away is heavily blurred—other genitals, for instance. Or guys glancing at *my* cock and snickering. Or pointing. Laughing boisterously, making a scene, perhaps even uttering the dreaded word "babycock." Let it happen; I just don't wanna know about it!

Good thing I don't have a hardon . . . that'd just be *weird*. After a couple minutes of rapid sudsing, an inmate with obvious mental disabilities expresses what most are no doubt thinking. *"There's too many DICKS in here!"* he cries in a highpitched, whiny voice. It's funny as hell; many of us burst out laughing. "I'm get'n *outta here!*" he declares. *"There's TOO MANY DICKS IN HERE!"* He throws on his jumpsuit and exits the showers. A Guard tries directing him to the next station. "There were too many *dicks* in there!"

"Yeah, I know there was," the Guard says, ushering him leftward. "Now go *that* way, getcher ID picture taken." inmate too-many-dicks turns right—back toward the showers. "No, other way!" inmate too-many-dicks heads to the left diagonally, toward the Nurse's Station. "No, goddamnit!" the C.O. says. He grabs too-many-dicks's arm and leads him to the ID area.

"There were too many *dicks* in there!" he laments one last time. Then finally sits on the stool for his photo. Despite my amusement with this sequence, I'm also legitimately panged with an acute sadness for him; he's gonna have a rough time in prison. Constantly subjected to laughter and mockery for his mental faculties.

I step into my jumpsuit, which is loosey-goosey in every spot. Absurdly loose. I'm once again joined up with ken in line. They snap photos for our ID cards. We're electronically fingerprinted at the next station. "Jesus," ken says, bending over. He presses down on his right shoe's toes, revealing a full two inches of extra, empty space. "I asked for a 9; they gave me a 12!"

"Goddamn." Shaking my head, I think for a moment. "Well hey, would it help t' downgrade a full size?"

"*Anything* less than a 12 would help." Quickly and discreetly, we switch shoes. The 12s are only a tad big on me, as opposed to flopping like clown shoes on ken.

Arrows painted in bright orange onto the dark cement floor lead me to the next stop. It's like a cubicle, except with nine-foot stone walls. I take a seat and hand my paperwork to the heavyset guy sitting opposite me at the wooden desk. He's wearing a Chicago Bears pullover sweater and Cubs baseball cap. And wearing also a peculiar distinguishing look of smarmy false entitlement, one I'm already beginning to suspect is the exclusive domain of prickish, low level prison officials. His attitude strongly reinforces this concept. "So, whatta y' in here fer?" Weathered bluegray eyes scanning my paperwork.

"I copped out to Possession of Cannabis with Intent to Deliver."[26]

He rolls his eyes. Sure didn't take much to piss him off! "*Copped out,*" he says, voice oozing with smegma-thick snideness. "Okay. So wha'chu actually *do?*"

A moment's hesitation. "Got caught transporting 53 pounds."

"Okay then! Very good. When yer not in jail, whatta y'do?"

"What do you mean?" It's a genuine [and legitimate] question. Does he mean for money, leisure, or what? *Whatta y'do?* is pretty vague.

He stares at me blankly for several seconds and then chuffs air from his nostrils. His face is pudgy and hideous. "You *deaf* er somethin?"

I cock my head, truly baffled. What's with this fucker?!

"Ooookay," he says, looking down and breathing deeply. "Lemme try this another way. D'ya have anybody on the outside?"

"Yeah—fiancée, Mom, stepdad, brother, sister . . ."

"Fuck it!" He signs the page with a list of all the intake stations I need to visit. Shoves it back into my hand. "I'uz tryin'd help ya, but I guess ya don't wannit. Move on d' Station 17."

I blink, totally mindfucked. The hell just *happened?* No clue what I did wrong. I move on in an angry daze of confusion.

After standing with my back against the wall for a couple minutes, I'm summoned into another cubicle. It's the psychiatrist. He seems friendly—an avuncular air, gray beard and goldrimmed glasses. I say, "My mom's a psychiatrist."

"Oh," sounding interested, "where does she practice?"

---

[26] "Copped out" = pled guilty

"Out in California. She's getting pretty good, too . . . you know, from all the practice." I chuckle. He smiles wryly. "That's where I'm from. She works at a couple boarding-care facilities in Southern California."

"That's nice. So I see you were taking some pretty serious medications on the outside and in County Jail. Just so you know, it's not their policy to prescribe narcotic pain medications here. So I'm telling you right now, you won't be getting the OxyContin. Also, you're on a pretty high dose of Klonopin."

My heart's a clenching fist hammering against my ribcage. I try to remain calm. "But those are the dosages prescribed by my chronic pain specialist, who's been seeing me for over six months." I'm borderline panicking. Really, *really* don't wanna detox—especially in this hellhole—from two years of [unfortunately necessary] daily pain meds.

"Doctor," I plead, "Why can't they just give me the meds I brought here with me from County?"

His jaw dips open. "You brought narcotic pain medications here?"

I give him a sidelong stare. "Well yeah, wasn't gonna leave em behind! Last I saw, one of the C.O.s from Henry County had the bottles in a paper bag. Why?!"

The Doctor shakes his head. "There's a good chance they're all gone now. Some of these Guards are just as bad as the inmates!"

I slump back in my seat. "That's just wonderful."

This Doctor actually seems to have a touch of compassion: "I believe you do have serious pain, so I don't want you to go through this without any help. I'm prescribing Trazadone, 150 milligrams at night. That should at least help you sleep." He begins jotting on his prescription pad. "I'll also give you one milligram of Klonopin, twice a day."

Fan-fucking-tastic! I feel queasy. During my two weeks in Henry County Jail, I was taking six milligrams per diem. This helped the time pass much faster, as I slept some 14 hours a day. But now the dose is being precipitously severed by two-thirds. That is not good; in fact, it's straight-up *dangerous*. I could have a seizure. And I'll have even less pain relief and sleep aide than if "only" my Oxy was eliminated.

In other words, I'll be locked in a cell 24 hours a day for at least ten days—maybe way more—and I'll be detoxing from OxyContin *and* Klonopin. This will be truly HELLACIOUS. Far beyond my worst nightmare.

Now I'm even more dazed. A storm cloud of dread shadows my every move, and soon, a sickness-tornado will suck me up into its ferocious interior. I shuffle off to the next station for an eye exam.

Are they really gonna make me detox in this fucking place? They act like I was scoring heroin on the streets! All this stuff was prescribed, by my one and only pain doctor.

After they check my eyes, I head to the Nurse's Station. Explain my complex health problems to a kindlooking Nurse in pink scrubs. She sends me across the warehouse-like room to the Doctor's Station and I collapse onto a bench. Knees are killing me. And this is a mere prelude, a fractional whisper of the misery to come.

A Nurse calls my name. My heart seems to perform a pirouette, because she's holding a familiar paper bag. "We managed to track down your meds."

I sigh deeply with relief. For some senseless reason I'm hoping the presence of my outside meds will actually benefit me somehow. Guess I'm not yet aware just how thoroughly sick this place's bureaucratic mechanizations are. Also, how insanely ridiculous is it that I'm *surprised* some dipshit C.O. didn't steal the medications to get high on or sell? She sets down the bag 15 feet away, on the reception area's counter. Then walks off.

I'm all alone. Literally no one in sight. I should rush up and grab the bag and take out the two med bottles, jam them into my sock. Or at least dump as many pills as I can into my shoes. But I'm frozen; can't move. I'm too scared. I'd receive a savage wooden baton beatdown from the Guards if caught.

How badly I'll end up wishing, amid the interminable days and nights to come, that I'd at least *tried* to get them. Replaying the scene over and over in my mind, convincing myself I could've gotten away with it. But I'm too demoralized to even make an attempt. Pitiful.

After a minute [hating myself], the Doctor summons me into the examination room. An overweight Indian with a very heavy accent enters. Instructs me to sit on the exam table with its butcher paper. I explain my physical condition. My disability. Pleading for compassion, for some semblance of treatment.

He doesn't want to give me *any* medication beyond what the Psychiatrist prescribed. "You gotta be kidding me!" I say.

"You're not on the outside anymore, are you? You're in prison." He speaks so fast and mushmouthed. Hard to understand.

"Okay. But they gave me these meds in County. And I brought them here with me. It's not like the prison has to spend any money, I'll be gone before they run out!"

He takes out the orange plastic bottles from the paper bag, the one I should've fuckin raided when I had the chance. Gives them a quick once-over. He holds up the jar of OxyContin. "See, I cannot give you this such thing. Is narcotic medication. It is banned."

"It's what?"

"Banned. *Banned.*"

"Okay, fine. Can't you at least give me *something* in its place so I don't have to suffer through excruciating pain the whole time?"

Nope! They have Tramadol—a low-level opioid similar I'd say to Vicodin—but not for me. It's only given out after injuries. So fuckin what that the nature of my condition is such that it *always* feels as if I'm acutely injured! No bullshit here, no exaggeration: this is just as cruel as feeding me 500 calories a day when I need at least 2,000. JUST as cruel.

I drag myself from the room nearly trembling in anger, trembling in sheer terror of the hellish purgatory I'm being thrust into. This is unconscionably inhumane. This is quite literally torture via medical neglect.

Other stuff happens to complete the intake process, but I'm hardly aware. Mind numbed and hazy from the impending horrorshow. They draw blood. I'm corralled into another bluefenced bullpen, this one about the same size as your average living room—with 50+ men jammed inside. I find good ole ken. He shakes his head at me, shellshocked. "Man, this'll be rough. I was warned, but this is *terrifying*. Beyond belief."

I tell him about my experience. Then blurt, "Why the hell are we here? This is like a SUPERMAX! Why would completely nonviolent offenders be brought here? Why can't we just go straight from county to prison?"

ken halts my not-quite-rhetorical questions with an upraised hand, palm-out. "Hey. Listen. The word *why* does not exist here."

I stare at him. Speechless; stomach rolling. It's among the most painfully sagacious statements I've heard, ever, about anything.

We're herded back to the bullpen-warehouse by the entrance. After at least 30 more minutes of sitting on the backless concrete benches, packed so tightly that our thighs and shoulders push against flesh on either side. Then they corral us into a different bullpen, this time in alphabetical order; then into yet another, where they hand out our shiny new photo ID cards. We are told to memorize their number as soon as possible. Throughout our prison residency, all identification and information will be filtered via that inmate number. It's official; our processing is underway. Transformed in one afternoon from human beings into mere alphanumerical codes.

Then it's time to wait further. Time seems to melt, oozing into a fetid stew of bubbling torture. At least for me. An hour passes, surely, followed by at least one more. Knees grow more and more cramped . . . then begin to burn as if consumed by a caustic, flaring chemical fire . . . back feels like I've been pickaxing boulders all day. No amount of stretching or rubbing can even mitigate them. I start sweating, heart pounding despite the long, near-motionless period. Anxiety; internal hurricane; the exquisite torment of an extended low-level panic, forcibly suppressed by necessity: can't display any signs of weakness! This is BAD.

And I ain't seen nothin yet. It'll only get worse, with a nadir nowhere in sight.

They pass out plastic dinner trays. The main item is a stifflooking bun covered in what can only be described as *slop*: a slimy grayish liquid with small hunks of gray meat. Like dollarstore dog food no animal lover would force on their canine companions. I eat a few bites of mushy canned carrots and cold, stiff tater tots.

After another warped stretch of who-knows-how-long, we line up to receive a wad of bedding and a paper bag. Then we're directed in a single-file row down a very long central hallway. Officers bark out convoluted directions and then get disproportionately angry when we mess up in a confused jumble of bodies and baggy jumpsuits and floppy shoes.

This place is a human factory farm. Horrifically cruel, cramped. We've become much like animals—units to be processed, and little to nothing more. [Yet we're still living in wild luxury compared to 99 percent of nonhuman animals, and we're not butchered for our flesh; NO human suffers like animals do every single day!]

Each "Gallery," A to Z, forks off from the central hallway; they're comprised of three levels with ten bluedoored cells on each. ken and I both end up way at the end in Gallery R. We yearn to be chance cellmates. Otherwise, there's a great possibility something awful will happen to one or both of us at our cellmates' hands. We could be stuck with a serial rapist, a murderer. Somebody with a 20-year bit and nothing to lose.

Unfortunately, ken's placed two cells down from me. Second floor in the middle. We climb the stairs. He trips halfway up, falling to his knees on the slatted blue metal. Goddamn clown shoes! I halt and rush to help him up, certain we'll be yelled at and even beaten for stopping. But luckily the Guard in our gallery says nothing.

We shuffle past the other second-floor cells. Each one has a small barred window; a stream of black faces stare out. "Good luck," I tell ken as I stop at Cell 204 and he continues down the line. An ID card sits in my new cell's window, which identifies the occupant as john-something-Greek. The door slides open mechanically.

I step inside. The door *whirrs* shut with an ominous reverberating clang.

I will exit this cell once—ONCE—in the next two weeks.

john greets me from his bottom bunk. We shake hands. I set down my paper bag, toss my bedding onto the top bunk, and climb up. Exhausted, rundown, and so very sore. "Goddamn!" I cry. "The fuck's wrong with this mattress?"

"Pretty lumpy, huh?"

That's a gross understatement. The mattress's sides are elevated nearly a foot higher than the rest, while its middle-half has almost no stuffing at all. I can actually feel the hard and unforgiving steel underneath. And yes, it's lumpy: like lying on myriad discs of unevenly shaped clay, with hardly any give. It's impossible to get remotely comfortable.

john and I start chatting and find we have a mutual love of classic rock; especially, for him, Pink Floyd and Led Zeppelin. Two of my favorites.

The cell's features are obscured in dimness. The only illumination right now comes from outside the cell—fluorescent overhead lights that blare 24 hours a day, flooding in through the barred window above a tiny steel desk in the corner, with its round steel seat welded to the table. The whole room is smaller than a moderate walk-in closet. Cement floor extremely dingy; it quite obviously hasn't received a thorough cleaning [read: disinfection] in months. Same thing goes for the sink-toilet combo, which is one steel unit just like in County, sitting three feet from the bottom bunk. It's *filthy.*

I'm able to pass out before long—amazing, given the maddeningly uncomfortable mattress. Pure exhaustion. I'm worn ragged from the day's marathonic activities, and from the constant humiliation and fear and confusion.

I awake a few hours later to a cacophony; someone's banging out a beat on their door and freestyle-rapping. "Christ," I croak, groggy. "That's just awful!"

"That's our neighbor! Does 'at shit for like three or four hours every day."

". . ."

Soon a couple Officers, their large and jangly keyrings providing echolocation, start moving through the gallery to drop off paper bags. This unleashes a veritable ruckus. When it's your time to leave Stateville, an Officer sticks a bag outside the cell with your name and prison-destination written in Sharpie. john, as he suspected, receives a bag. He's ecstatic. Even though they're sending him to a high-medium-security joint called Illinois River. That's what this place does, although I don't quite know it yet—after two weeks [hell, two days!], you're THRILLED to be leaving, no matter where it is you're headed. Turns out anything's better than this American Gitmo.

Breakfast arrives. At first I'm baffled, assuming I must've fallen asleep without realizing—it feels like the middle of the night! john sets me straight: breakfast is delivered at 1:30 a.m. "What?!" I cry. "Why the fuck does breakfast come in the middle of the night?"

[*The word* why *does not exist here.*]

"Dunno, man. It's crazy."

Below the cell's barred window—flush with the tiny slice of corner table—there's a rectangular wooden panel. This is called the "chuckhole." When meals are served, a C.O. steps down the line of cells, unlocking and opening the chuckholes. A bootcamper follows in the Officer's tracks with a wide, tall cartful of trays. Chucking two through each wooden hole.

This "morning," we receive Styrofoam trays with two lukewarm little pancakes, a glob of grits, a packet of imitation maple syrup [high fructose corn syrup and brown food coloring], and cartons of juice and skim milk [4 oz. each]. I polish off the "orange drink" in a few gulps. Manage to swallow three or four bites of the cardboardish pancakes with some syrup. I try the tepid grits; they're flavorless. Textured like blended sandpaper and tap water. I can barely choke them down even with syrup mixed in. "Ey john, I'm vegan. Want my milk?"

He's silent for a moment. "Maybe. Just leave it on the table." He packs his few papers and a change of boxers into his paper bag and throws on his yellow jumpsuit.

About 20 minutes after dropping off the quasifood, bootcampers return to collect finished trays—which we jam into the chuckhole—and the Guard slams the little panels shut. And I mean *slams*, a loud wooden clunk that reverberates against the gallery walls, destroying any and all efforts to sleep through this mad, senseless middle-night "breakfast." I'm positive the Guards bang shut our chuckholes as loud as they can on purpose—specifically because it sabotages sleep.

"Hey," john says, "I'm too amped up to lay down anymore, so you can move to the bottom if you want."

"Sweet, thank you!" I lower myself from the decrepit mattress of wildly improbable lumpiness. Feeling sorry for whoever comes in here next and has to sleep up there, though also very grateful for the timing. Now I'll claim the bottom bunk and my next cellie will have to suffer the top.[27] The lower mattress seems relatively flatter and more uniform. Still some weird grooves and plateaus to contend with, but they're minor compared to the goddamn badlands up top! At least that's what I think then.

"Ahright," john says a little later; he's sitting at the table, jittery as hell and so very anxious for the move to legit-prison. "I'm'a drink that other milk." He does. Within 15 minutes, around 3 a.m., it starts churning his guts. "Oh man. Here we go! Gotta take a shit."

"No problem, bro." I roll onto my side, facing the wall. This is what passes for privacy in a two man cell!

"Man," john says when at last he's depleted of juicy, stomach-clenching diarrhea, "I was *pissing* out my asshole!"

It's been 20 hours since I last received pain meds. Knees're cramping bigtime, with an occasional flareup of fiery pain, but the detox hasn't yet begun in earnest. Even more great stuff I can look forward to! So many wonderful things waiting, in my future's shadowy recesses, to pounce like those facehugger things from *Aliens*. Ample looming dread for my brain to manically cycle through during the interminable sleepless nights to come.

A Guard calls out: time fer those'a us that got bags to leave. "All right john," I say. "Stay free once you get out. Good luck!"

"You too, jan the man." We bump fists. The cell door slides open and john steps out. Nearly crackling with excitement in his oversized bananaic jumpsuit. Then the door clanks shut and he's gone.

And I'm all alone in the dim, filthsmeared hellbox.

---

[27] Unless he threatens to kick the shit outta me if I don't let him have the bottom bunk, which I see as a major possibility; I have to forcibly eject these thoughts from my head. One moment at a time—I'll deal [somehow] with whatever horrors come, but I gotta try to avoid worrying until they *do* come.

-Friday-

is without question the loneliest day in my life to that point. I'm woken at about eight a.m. by a few hollow dinks on the cell door. "mr. smitowicz?" a nasally male voice calls. "I'm here with your medication, please bring something to drink."

I drag myself from bed and grab the juice carton I've been filling with clouded sink water. Stagger to the door. Through its window I see a short bald man. He slips a tiny envelope through the minute gap alongside my door. I tip the two meager pills into my palm. Klonopin and Celexa and nothing else, oh my. This will get very ugly very soon.

He watches me swallow the pills and then bustles onward. I return to bed, surprised my knees aren't already screaming [though my back is stiff as a board from the weird sinewave-like mattress]. I lie faceup, staring into the void. Wondering how the hell I'll get through this. The detoxification process will begin at some point today; that's in addition to the nearly unadulterated pain. I'm expecting unprecedented sickness to invade my guts at any time—with not even so much as a Tums for succor.

There's nothing to help pass the time in here. I'm depressed and too lethargic for any exercise. Worried, also, about burning calories. Based on the "food" so far, I'll no doubt begin dipping into my body's fat reserves very soon. I deliberately packed on 20 pounds in the month leading up to my incarceration—knowing it'd likely take some time to figure out how to acquire sufficient vegan food on the inside. But those 20 pounds will be eaten away far more rapidly than anticipated in here. Need to conserve my energy and avoid sacrificing calories in every possible way.

The cell's only reading material is a Gideon's Bible and a brown paper bag stuffed with religious literature. Stacks and stacks of pamphlets that won't provide more than a few minutes' reprieve—and that's *if* my atheism can even stomach them. No way to write, either. I could scribble in the margins of my information packet [which includes a page titled WHAT TO DO IF YOU ARE SEXUALLY ASSAULTED], but I don't have a pen or pencil. Some long-gone occupant fashioned a deck of cards from several dozen milk cartons. Ingenious, though sadly useless for me. No idea how to play solitaire or any other one-person game.

According to the impressive hand-drawn calendar—glued to the wall with toothpaste—I won't have access to the fenced dogrun "Yard" until tomorrow. And no shower for five days. That's right: Stateville provides shower access once a week. The interim should be great fun, given my severe dandruff and consequent itchy scalp.

My thoughts turn to Rachel. For the first time since we said goodbye at S.F. International, I'm beginning to *really* yearn for her. An actual physical sensation, clamping on my chest and wrenching my guts. I start to tear up. I'd give anything just to snuggle with her on this lumpy mattress right now. Ten years off my life? Gladly. A finger? Take em all. My testicles? Grab a knife! The brown blanket they gave me is ancient, dotted with numerous holes. It's bunched against my chest like a football. A small fabric-comma trails out from the wadded mass. I grab this loose bit and clutch it hard, eyes closed. Pretending it's her hand. Tears slide down my cheeks, tickle my nose. A few of them meander into my lips' downturned edges and deliver their hot, salty taste. "Love you baby," I mutter, voice quivering. "I miss you so much." A whimpery little blip occurs from my throat. I grip the blanket

[*her hand*]

even tighter. Imagination working with such desperation that the loose fabric legitimately starts feeling like her hand. In all its unique intricacy. "Please don't give up on me, darling. We'll get through this. Together. *I need your strength.*" A depleted moan; a wet sniffle. This is the only true privacy I've had in over two weeks. And I damn well know the value of a good cry. So finally I let myself submit to this rotten despair. To just . . . let go. Sob into my pillow and groan and weep unfettered, shedding tear after tear until my eyes ache like sore muscles, face soaked, lips and chin slimed with mucus. Even after I'm all cried out, still I cling to Rachel's hand; fingers stiff and achy from clutching hard for who-knows-how-long.

Lunch arrives—at 9:30 a.m. [!] A cold fishcorpse-patty, stiff-dry white bread, limp iceberg lettuce, peas. I set the tray aside. No appetite; plus, any food sitting in my stomach will interfere with whatever minute effects the Klonopin may have. Shockingly, I'm still not in bad pain yet. Just the normal woke-up-a-while-ago amount. Perhaps my brain has erected some defense mechanisms to help me manage a little easier.

I sift through the religious literature [more like SHITerature!] stuffed into a paper bag. There's a massive tome called "Free On the Inside." I skim through it. The basic premise: Even if you're incarcerated, you can still soar on the Mighty Wings of Freedom if you have the love of Jesus Christ in your heart.

What a crock! Isn't it funny, and highly telling, how religion preys [NPI: no pun intended] on people stuck in perilous and/or vulnerable situations—e.g. prisoners, the terminally ill, and drug addicts—to obtain converts? You could counter by saying it's an attempt to help those people. Sure, in some cases. But it's also unquestionably a slick tactic to recruit new blood into their cult of ancient superstitions. I think it's pretty devious and twisted how they focus their energy on weak and susceptible people who're already looking for a crutch. And it's especially egregious to push religion on children; parents and others who frighten malleable-minded kids with threats of hell and eternal damnation is straightup child abuse if you think about it. Independent thought, though . . . not exactly something encouraged by religion.

I flip to the book's opening pages and read through the frequently asked questions [FAQ]. Here's just one of them: *Is there a way out of addiction [drinking, drugs, sex, gambling, homosexuality]?* As my eyes hit that last word, I cry out "Oh my gawd!"

Lip curled with revulsion, I heave the fat book across my cell, pages fluttering like the wings of a dying bird as he plummets from flight, and it thumps against the door with a hollow reverberation. "Goddamn scumbag shitheads!" The question's implications are vile, unconscionable. Not to mention utterly preposterous. As if human [homo]sexuality were a *disease*, like drug addiction!

Stop reading this—right now, this instant—if you think I'm wrong. Put this book down and embark on a personal journey for some common sense and compassion; you may want to start the quest by prying your bigoted, peabrained head from your fat ass.

Consider: People will never crave, say, heroin . . . *unless they've already tried it.* Not addiction-type cravings, anyway. But droves of young boys and girls feel same-sex attraction long before having any sexual encounter. It's literally not possible—by definition!—to be addicted to something you've never even tried. Period, end of story. This fundamental and sadly prevalent ignorance is pretty goddamn intolerant for people who claim to be followers of Christ—you know, the Prince of PEACE?! This kind of thinking is precisely what leads to the routine oppression of LGBTQ individuals. Remaining silent when confronted with such extreme bigotry is a tacit approval of hate, and the violence it often breeds.

This occurrence serves to heighten my already extreme aversion to the barrage of conversion attempts I'll no doubt have to fend off in prison.

The rest of the day is a dim, lonesome blur. Time is becoming somehow elastic, like saltwater taffy. A phenomenon that'll only increase the longer I'm imprisoned. After hurling that moronic book into the cell door, I lie there in a miserable stupor for hours. Thinking how amazing it'd be just to have Rikki here; to feel her warm, comforting body as she cuddles up close and I curl my arm around her downyhaired chest. In my wonderful, monastic little cabin in Mendocino, I fell asleep every night spooning her like that. She preferred lying at my feet—but was always happy to snuggle with me until I fell asleep.

I emerge from the daydream to find I'm crying again. This is rough, man. And I haven't even started detoxing yet!

To my surprise, I only shit a couple times that first full day. And they're solid. No diarrhea yet. Opiates tend to plug you up; yet even when my condition had become so bad I needed strong, daily painkillers, I was still shitting once or twice a day. Testament to the digestive healthfulness of a vegan diet. But now that I've been forced off adequate meds, a powerful diarrhea-surge is imminent. Could take a couple days to begin. Either way, this is NOT a safe place to detox from opiates and benzos.

Sometime in the evening, my cell neighbor starts banging his chuckhole and rapping again. Loud, obnoxious noise makes me have terrible anxiety. And his freestyling's a severe auditory violation. Then an awful thought pops into my head: What if I get a CELLIE like that? I'd go batshit crazy, start smashing my head into the stone walls just to escape it. Or try to drown him in the toilet. Something. I don't even want to give the idea breathing room in my skull right now.

I find out soon enough. Must be late evening, because new people start filtering into the gallery. The noise and commotion kicks into high gear. Dudes shout from their cells. Many of the new arrivals already know people here; they're from the same neighborhood and/or gang. What kind of life is that, where numerous people from a single circle of friends—from the same family, even—are in prison at the same time? Recidivism is a bitch; one that bitchslaps over HALF the convicts in Illinois! [Estimates vary, but it's definitely over 50 percent.]

Finally my door slides open with its mechanical buzz, and a mellow looking white guy steps in. He's about my age. *Please* don't be some kinda Nazi asshole! Being interesting wouldn't hurt, either. We shake hands and introduce ourselves. His name's craig. Tall and skinny like me, but with dark eyes and hair [buzzcut, like mine]. He sets his stuff under the table and climbs onto the top bunk. "Man I'm fuckin exhausted," he sighs. "That intake—Jeezus *Christ* this mattress is lumpy!"

"Yeah, it's pretty bad, huh? So what're you in for?"

He pounds on the mattress in a futile effort to lessen its discomfort; thing's about six months beyond salvageable. "Retail Theft."

"Ha. Same as my last cellie."

craig took a plea deal and will serve one year. "I'm a heroin addict," he says. Simple factual statement, no shame or compunction. I admire that. "Stole shit to resell and feed the monkey." He's got a deep, warm voice.

"How long you been doin it?"

"Psh. Like ten years, off'n on. Mostly on. It's a fuckin beast, man. Don't even try the shit if you haven't already. I been t' so many rehabs I lost count. Just can't kick the shit."

"That's . . . awful. Sorry to hear it. I've been takin Oxy for over two years for my messed up knees. But they're cutting me off here, so I'm'a start detoxing any time now. Pretty fuckin terrified."

"Yeah, Oxy is heavy shit. Basically the same withdrawals as heroin."

I want to mention the massive difference between shooting heroin and eating pills for a legit medical condition, but I hold my tongue. Don't want to rock the boat before we get to know each other. He could be a lunatic. Convicts are often masterful at hiding their real selves.

craig explains how he managed to support his $200-a-day habit. He'd enter stores like Walgreens wearing a backpack and simply load it up. Sticking to small but expensive items, like aspirin and other over-the-counter medications, fancy razors, vitamins . . . things that provided the most buck for their bang. Then he went to specific "A-rab" markets or liquor stores and sold the loot for about 20 percent of retail value.[28] craig says it was an even better scam for the store owners [who knew exactly

---

[28] Middle Easterners are almost universally referred to as "A-rabs" in Illinois prisons. This is one of those slang terms that could be a Chicago thing, or a prison

what was happening]. They sent these stolen products to the manufacturer and received a refund—thereby making some 80 percent profit. This was apparently such a widespread phenomenon in Chicago that sometimes craig'd encounter a *line* of fidgety, sunken-cheeked junkies fencing their stolen wares. Eventually, though, the cops caught on and busted these stores. It was a big sensational news story. One place made *15 million dollars* in a single year doing this.

Now that—THAT is how you grift!

"Holy shit!" I cry. Never heard of anything like it. I enjoy learning about the furtive underworld of drugs and criminal activity. It's endlessly fascinating—whole entire continents lying just beneath the surface of everyday life, which you could walk right by and never know it.

We begin telling jokes to lighten the mood and slay a little time. Hopefully ward off some misery from this desperate situation we've been flung into. The first one he tells is a hilarious prison joke ending with the line, "Ohhhh no, you're NOT gonna like Thursdays!"

I clap my hands and laugh uproariously.

"Like that?"

"Hell yeah, that's epic!" It's already obvious that I'm lucky to've landed craig as a cellie.

We stay up until breakfast [though *midnight snack* would be more apt]: cold grits that've been sitting out so long they've congealed—you can jab a plastic fork into them and lift up a single rectangular block—bread [not toast, just bread] with jelly packets, and pineapple juice. I swallow the stale bread and drink the miniscule juice carton, which contains a pitiful mere ten percent actual juice. After they collect our trays, I finally submit to my unpleasant Trazadone-induced grogginess and go to sleep.

I wake up shortly before the Nurse arrives with morning meds, feeling heavily dazed and nebulous. Although at least I feel better than yesterday morning; the previous night's Trazadone gave me a monstrous, throbbing headache that lingered several hours. For some reason, it also gave me a monstrous, throbbing boner! I really wish the Doctor had just prescribed a goddamn tiny bit more Klonopin instead; it'd help me sleep better, with no side effects, and also slightly diminish my pain.

---

thing—or both. Given that I've only lived outside California while incarcerated in Illinois, it's impossible for me to know which. This linguistic/sociocultural puzzle intrigues me.

[111]

Maybe I'll fill out a request slip and send it to the Psychiatrist.

-Saturday-

Each day   c
         r
           a
             a
               a
                 w
                   l
                     s

The food is nasty without exception, and somehow manages, despite wild improbability, to reach new levels of culinary horror on a regular basis. The portions are always teensy. In County, recidivist-felons referred to the Stateville trays as *Lunchables*. Now I understand how very apt that moniker is.

I start detoxing today, my second full day inside the cell. It begins with painful stomach cramps and violent jets of diarrhea—pissing out my asshole, as my first cellie john said. I'm so damn embarrassed having to ask craig to face away on, like, an hourly basis. Often even more. "Dude, stop worrying about it," he insists with kindhearted sincerity. "I've been through worse, I know what it's like. Just gotta make it through a few days, and then it gets easier n easier. Okay?"

His words mean a lot to me, and I'm so very grateful. I could've been stuck with a dumbass sophomoric dipshit of a cellie, one who mocked me every time I had the squirts. Instead I scored a guy who's been through the exact same fundamental process! Different only in the degree of severity.

Sometime in the hazy middle of that first sickday, craig's taking a nap. A gassy swirling bubbles in my guts; the prelude to a fart. I lift my ass off the bed to allow some room for escape. I push.

A hot wet blast explodes from my ass. *Oh, SHIT!* Please don't let that be what I think it was. Gingerly, I slide from the bed and stand, legs spread. Trying to keep my boxers from coming into contact with my ass. I rrrrrrip the Velcro line running from neck to crotch on my yellow jumpsuit, pull everything down, and sit on the cold steel toilet. Staring down at my white, state-issued boxers—one of just *two* pairs they provide for our entire stay— in utter dismay. The back end is covered in a flattened-softball-splotch of yellowish-brown diarrhea. It was a goddamn #SHARTBLAST! I clamp shut my eyes and my jaw. This is too much. How many rapidfire indignities can one person handle?

I do not want craig to find out about this—let alone wake up and see me standing naked with diarrhea-splattered boxers in hand! Believe it or not, I do have a shame limit [the boundaries of which will be expanding on a continuous basis throughout my prison stay]. So I'm being as surreptitious as possible. After finishing on the toilet, I ball up the ruined boxers in a tight wad—goopy yellowish parts on the inside—and stuff them at the bottom of the dirty clothes bag john left behind. Then tightly roll the paper bag closed and stick it in the corner behind the toilet-sink unit. I sure as hell won't wash the #beshitted underwear in the sink. I'll just have to wear my lone remaining pair of clean boxers until Wednesday. Only another five days! That's shower day; I can take the beshitted drawers with me to wash.

Until then, I must be ever-vigilant and avoid soiling myself again.

The chuckhole clunks open for "lunch" and we get two cold and stale corn tortillas, some chickencorpse salad-type thing, a threebite scoop of canned carrots with the mushiness of babyshit, and potato slices. "Jesus," craig monotones. "Potatoes're inedible."

I try mine. He's right: so undercooked they're almost crunchy. "Dude. How hard is it to cook a potato?"

craig's frowning, shaking his head forlornly. "This place is worse than I remember. Way worse."

This is his second incarceration. Last time he also got popped for Retail Theft to support his smack habit. How will another prison bit do him any good? He won't receive tools or treatment to help him stay clean. He doesn't need punishment. He needs *rehabilitation*. If anything, prison could make his addiction worse!

Dinner's more of the same. Noneatable potatoes, absurdly undercooked. Except now they're shredded instead of sliced. "Hey craig—I bet they scavenged all the potatoes left in the trays from lunch and just put em through a shredder. 'They'll eat em eventually, keep sendin em back! It's only a matter'a time till they get hungry enough.'"

He laughs, but there's no joy in it. An empty sound. Like knocking on a hollow, dead tree.

Tomorrow, Sunday, is my wonderful mother's 50th birthday. I won't be able to wish her a happy one. The senseless bureaucratic workings of prison leave so much unnecessary suffering in its wake. This is a concept that, back then in Stateville, I was just barely beginning to make surface-scratches at, but which would prove in time to have seemingly depthless significance and ramifications.

craig and I discuss movies, and find that we have similar tastes. He's a huge movie buff with an incredible memory. He even knows all my obscure favorites, stuff like *Midnight Run* [1988] starring Robert De Niro. Having craig here, this wretched situation is almost tolerable—almost. Sometimes. Now if only I weren't shitting diarrhea 10+ times a day, my asshole chafed raw and pulsing like a sore tooth.

I sit at the desk and write a request slip to the Psychiatrist, explaining how the Trazadone isn't much helping me sleep, and the side effects are terrible [e.g. I'm so dizzy every morning that I almost fall over, vision churning, heart pounding]. I ask to be taken off Trazadone and to receive a little more Klonopin instead. I also include a plea for Immodium AD or something like it for my savage bowel-mayhem. Hand the slip to a passing Guard.

From up in bed, craig sees the fat wad of dismay splattered across my face. "Hey man," he says, staring at me, "wanna borrow a writeout?" This is a stamped envelope you buy from Commissary; it's the only way we can send mail. "To write your girl or whatever?"

"I don't have any paper. Or even anything to write with!"

Henry County allows you to bring nothing along. But other facilities have different rules. He brought seven stamped envelopes from County Jail. "I have some writeouts with paper inside em," craig says. "And a pencil, down there in my folder by your feet."

"You sure?" Don't wanna feel like I'm imposing.

He holds my gaze for a moment. "I'm offering one—take it if you want it."

I smile. "Thanks man, means a lot to me."

Later that evening when craig's napping, I grab the writeout and little four-inch pencil from his bag and write a letter to Rachel. Filling the unlined paper from corner to corner, front and back. Trying to keep it upbeat for her. I do mention the medication debacle and my detoxing, but also add that the pain isn't nearly as bad as I anticipated.

[*It'll get there jan, don't you worry!*]

I describe how badly I'm yearning for her; how I spent a long time yesterday clamped onto my blanket, imagining she was here with me. I ask her to wish my mom a happy belated birthday. And I talk about craig—

the letter's only aspect I don't have to contort and manipulate into sounding more positive than I feel—and how lucky we are to be cellies. How he's comforting me through the detox process. By the letter's end, I'm sniffling, #tearpools accrued in my eyes.

Late that night, though not as late as breakfast, craig and I discuss music. It's another thing we share: fierce love and extensive knowledge of classic rock. Pink Floyd, the Stones, Zeppelin, AC/DC, Creedence, U2, Neil Young—a few of the artists we both dig. Providing conversational fodder for many hours. Each other is all we have to pass the long, mindnumbingly dull, madness-inducing hours. We want to avoid at all costs fraternizing in silence with our inner thoughts. We're both dueling some vicious demons [primarily the mercurial, leaden guilt of the pain we've caused our loved ones]. We'll have ample time to work through the mental anguish and guilt, to hopefully find a semblance of redemption, forgiveness. But Stateville is not the place or time. Already miserable enough here; all that really matters right now is pure survival, overcoming this ordeal with our sanity intact.

Eventually, sometime after "breakfast," we go to sleep. I have one of the craziest, most vivid dreams of my life. Must be at least partly because my REM-brain is "waking up" without the downers it's so accustomed to. In the dream, I've become a successful writer. I meet and hang with the beautiful lead singer of a [nonexistent] band I love. Her name's Lizzy; she loves *my* work too. We experience a bunch of wild, screwed up stuff. In the end, Lizzy overdoses on a new synthetic drug called "Jaz." I rush her to the hospital and she survives.

I wake up not long before meds come, and I'm feeling the intense joy, sorrow, and excitement to be alive that I felt in the dream. This lingers for hours. I love when strong emotions from a dream carry over into waking life. The dream would make an amazing short story, and I vow to write it as soon as possible.

I'm finally detoxing in earnest. It's been four days [≈96 hours] since my last opioid-dose. Symptoms: extremely low energy—so low it's difficult to *move*, to even sit up in bed; diarrhea eight to ten times throughout the day; the visegrips have begun their savage clamping act around my knees; and I have NO appetite. The day's total caloric intake consists of an orange drink, a blueberry biscuit, and about one cup of peas, corn, and stewed tomatoes. That's it!

"Don't worry," craig insists. "It's been, what, four days since you had pain meds? Tomorrow or the next day you should be a lot better."

My erratic sleep only compounds the problems. I'm "lucky" to get a couple consecutive hours. Then I'm woken by one thing or another: the wooden CLUNK of the chuckholes as they're [intentionally] slammed shut by Officers, the mad zoomonkey yammering of other inmates, the doorkicking and horrible rapping of our neighbor, the cacophonous flush of our toilet, which sounds like a giant fire hose on full blast and lasts for about five seconds, or the cell's fluorescent overhead lights that blare on every four hours for count, and stay on for twenty to thirty minutes. All that piled atop the lack of meds—which help me sleep.

One of the names we hear guys yelling a lot is "thumbprint." craig and I have a good laugh over that one, and begin to make fun of all the absurd nicknames people have, hyperbolizing them:

"Hey dental exam," craig yells through the crack in the door. "What up, joe?"

"Yo belly button lint," I say. "Whatchu doin fam?"

"Ey yo blood draw? Where that nigga chuckhole at?"

"chafed scrotum! You heard from yeast infection yet? That muhfucka crazy!"

But seriously. Here's a realistic sample of things we'd hear, accounting for directional acoustics and slurred, mushmouthed and/or indecipherable speech:

Ey thuuuumbprint!

What up, joe?

We got donut tonight!

You seen duh bon foo goin back
South Side dis nooty?

Yeeah so nooskie fo sheen.

Kill yoself!

??????????

Yeeeeah, that bitch ain't
been us too footy non bit nigga.
On er'ythang!

?????????

On my mama, joe!

On ER'y-muhfuckin-thang!

t-bone! You know dat
bitch kool-aid fuck down
on fo tenant up will
hat mitch pill d'rgee?

. . . . . Yeeeah!

Fuck diznookie, but oh Cicero plan boo-boo dirge.

. . . Kill yoself.

Etcetera. And this happens even at two a.m. when we're trying to sleep! It gets louder, more ubiquitous, when the meal carts are rolled in and sit downstairs by the entrance—always just *sitting there* for 15 or 20 minutes, growing cold, the trays getting not-passed-out for no determinable reason. The nearconstant noise wears more and more heavily on our frayed nerves. [I'm already on edge relentlessly from the sudden plummet in Klonopin— it feels like my skin-organ is trying to crawl off my body in *one piece.* Benzo-withdrawal is torturous, even worse to me than opiate-withdrawal.] And then it gets worse. The most wretched and prodigious stretch of diarrhea seems to've peaked; but on the same day, my sleeping abilities are utterly shattered.

My Trazadone and #meagerdose-Klonopin arrive each evening around five or six p.m.[29]

That night, as predicted, I sleep for an hour or two, then wake up and lie there uncomfortably for hours upon hours. I sample numerous different positions—all the usual greatest hits, and then I delve deep into the weird experimental B-sides: tucked in a tight pencil-straight line into the main

---

[29] This in & of itself is absolutely senseless/moronic/ridiculous. The Trazadone is a *sleeping medication.* Why the FUCK are they passing out sleeping meds at 5 or 6 in the evening? I'm tellin ya, even if I do manage to fall asleep atop the raging hardon caused by the Traz, I won't *stay* asleep. The best I'll get is a couple-hour nap. Which then makes it *even harder* to sleep during actual nighttime sleeping hours. I truly think—& craig 100% agrees—that the *purpose* of Stateville is to BREAK OUR SPIRITS. Plain & simple. How else to account for things like breakfast at 1:30 a.m., blaring fluorescent lights for count every 4 hours [what're we gonna do—flush ourselves down the vagina-sized opening in the toilet??], & all the other lunatic practices here?

halfpipe-shaped indentation running up the mattress's center; lying atop the high plateau on the outer edge [which is too hard and hence painful for my kneecaps]; shoving the mattress up against the wall so most of it flops over me and half my body's inside the notch and the other half sort of dangles off the outside edge; even flipping the mattress over to try the underside . . .

None of it works. That's another thing about a sudden dramatic benzo drop—it's damn near impossible to get even a little comfortable, since your entire hyperdrive nervous system is tweaked with more sensitivity than the male glans. And this mattress would be uncomfortable if I were on my *normal* medication regiment.

Speaking of penis heads, I also try Nature's Sleeping Pill. Blow my load into a wad of toilet paper, flush it down the obstreperous toilet [don't worry, craig's passed out up there—I made sure]. Feels great in this hideous environment where any positive sensations are near-nonexistent. But still I can't sleep. Eventually I hear the metallic clanking as "breakfast" trays arrive, and the chuckholes begin to squeakbang open. craig wakes for breakfast and we eat our #jellybread and juice. I give him my grits, which are once again solidified into a single cold globule. This morning the grits have a strange grayish tint. I think of *Oliver Twist*, and how, if Charles Dickens could see Stateville, he may well've abandoned whatever project he was on and write a novel taking place here. "Looks like gruel," I say.

"It's *gruel* and unusual punishment," craig fires back. We cackle. That feels good too; so basically, laughter and ejaculation are the only good sensations I've discovered thus far.

craig hops up on his #elbowy mattress and goes back to sleep and still I lie awake. I'm fully conscious for 3 a.m. count. Then beyond. Finally, I try something completely different. Lying on my stomach with my head at the bed's foot, utilizing the gallery's 24/7 fluorescent lights that dimly illuminate the cell's front third via our window, I start the short story based on that crazy-vivid-happy dream I had last night [or was it the night before? time continues to bleed like a bad watercolor]. Right away I realize it's unspeakably difficult to write every sentence and even word; there've only been maybe ten other times in the last *two years* I've even attempted to write without pain meds. Because—like many sufferers of pervasively severe chronic pain—it invades my every thought, obliterates any chance for extended concentration. The shit is truly #Vikingish. Slash-and-burn-esque. Pillaging-plundering my brain.

At least back in 2007 when this non-injury-related pain first began manifesting itself, I was in a good writing environment! I'd lie on the couch at our San Francisco apartment, staring out the big living room window at trees pincushioning Twin Peaks, or the wonderfully colorful houses in our Outer Sunset beach-neighborhood. And since we were on the third floor, and the avenues ascend eastward, I could see clearly for dozens of blocks, each street a little higher in elevation than the one in front of it [moving west-to-east away from me]. This house baby blue, that one cheddar orange, this one bright pink, that one purple and lime.

But there are no colors in here. These cells are the total *absence* of color. Even the door—bright blue on the outside—has a gray interior. I wanna bash my face into the wall until it's widely bloodsplattered, just so there can be some life in here. Say it again: blank walls, blank minds. Don't underestimate dullness's effect on the human psyche! I'm considering doing it, the headbashing. Seriously. In addition to adorning the walls with some lovely bright red, it might knock me unconscious. Then at least I could fucking *sleep*.

It must be after four a.m. now, and I don't feel tired AT ALL. It's driving me batshit. I stare at the speaker on the wall between my bed and the #sinktoilet. With its little silver button for emergencies. I've heard stories; that you're likely to bleed out before anyone responds. Yet still I consider trying it. The Indian Doctor told me to push the call button if I became unbearably distressed. But I gleaned on the very first day that nobody working at this nuthouse gives a flying fuck at a soaring donut for any of us, young or old, sick or well. Pushing that button will only piss them off.

I run through song lyrics in my head, just trying to relax in the most comfortable [no—*least uncomfortable*] position. Mentally sift through all my favorite bands and name their every album along with the year it was released, then every song, in order, on each one.

I'm fidgety in extremis. Feet wanting to tap and bounce interminably. When you're medsick, detoxing, the attendant sleeping-difficulty only compounds the other awful symptoms. At least I'm not going insane with cravings, I guess. But just because it could be worse doesn't mean it's okay, or ethically acceptable, that I'm forced to endure this. If you fall and break a leg, you won't experience less pain just by thinking about somebody with two broken legs. That oh-so-clichéd outlook of relative suffering is often moronic. "Health Care is a Right, Not a Privilege"—that's what it claims in our information packet. But in prison, "health care" mostly just means keeping you alive. Not healthy, or even marginally comfortable if you have a serious medical condition. Just not-dying. But we're considered wards of the state; they shouldn't incarcerate us if they're unwilling to provide even the simplest, cheapest form of medical succor. We're still goddamn human beings. This is still America.

I finally slip into a light sleep after six a.m. count.

And then, of course, I'm forced up after a couple measly hours by the med-Nurse. craig's awake now too. I tell him, "Y'know you fart a lot in your sleep?"

"Do I?"

"Yeah, it's funny as hell. They're often *ménage à trois* farts."

"The hell's that mean?"

"They come in threes."

He takes a moment to review what I said. Then he bursts out laughing.

-Tuesday-

is the day we start getting truly stircrazy [I've been in the cell six days, craig four]. "Dude," I tell him at some point, "I was awake last night all the way through till after lunch. Or this morning, whatever. Seriously considered pushing that emergency button. I was just fuckin miserable man, hurting so damn bad."

"Don't do it," craig insists. "If it gets that bad again, don't push the button. Wake me up first and we'll talk and at least try to take your mind off it."

I'm touched again by his kindheartedness. Given my radical politics and compassionate, openminded nature, it's been many years since I held the common misconception of junkie-as-soulless-monster. Never hurts to have a concrete reminder though. His offer is one a longtime friend would make. Only we just met. "Thanks, craig. That means a lot to me."

"Don't mention it."

"Just did."

Dinner brings an atrocity that's somehow even more repulsive than the dogfood-slop ["I *love* that slop!"]. craig recognizes it from his previous bit. It's known, with infamy, as the "Cock in the Sock," a sausage resembling someone's titanic, flaccid gray dick. Not only that, it's wrapped in clear plastic that has to be rolled off like a condom. Cock in the Sock. Jeezus everlovin Christ! craig struggles to choke down the sausage, even though he's been complaining about stomach-groaning hunger for several hours. I eat a few limp iceberg lettuce leaves and carrotmush and two slices of plain white bread. Luckily [??] my appetite remains absent. Otherwise I'd be famished, tormented by intense and nonstop hunger pangs—hell, craig's eating all his food, plus all the meat and eggs he can stomach from my trays, and yet *still* he's hungry!

Later that afternoon, the Trazadone clobbers me into unconsciousness, but once again I'm awoken after only a couple hours when two guys burst into spontaneous, shouting babble between cells. That's it for me—I'm awake for hours. Just like last night. This unfailing sleep-disruption is a strange and oblique form of torture, yet it's torturous nonetheless. I'm lying there, uncomfortable hurting FUCK! trying to sleep, gawd oh gawd oh shit goddamn why can't I *sleep*? mind racing. When will I get the hell outta here? Why*fuck* did I have to get caught? Why are the humanoids who're running this place such discombobulatingly improbably inept sadistic utter fucktards?

[*The word* why *does not exist here.*]

Knees and back are slaying me. I'm tellin you, it's *bad*. The sonofabitching kneevise tightens, twisting harder and harder clamping tighter every single minute wrenching enflamed acidburn pain AAAAHHHHH FUCK! All made that much worse by my evergrowing inability to sleep.

Sometimes I'll begin drifting off amid a magical stretch of total quietus. But then my own dumb stupid head will sabotage everything. Random thoughts partycrashing my mind, rendering me wide-eyed-awake. These invasive thoughts are like some drunk idiot barging into the room when the party's over and I'm about to pass out: "HEY MAN, WHAT'S UP?! LET'S *TALK*!!"

Yeah, sure, I'll try a stand-and-pace-the-cell routine. But that gets old faster than a mayfly; just four normal-sized steps take me from toilet to cell door. I sit down on the table's pizza-sized stool complete a few puzzles somebody left behind, locating words amid jumbled letters. It's intolerably brainless. Crossword puzzles could be nice; they require actual mental effort, and so'd be a temporary distraction. But there aren't any, of course. They'd be a form of grace. Of [minor] succor. Can't be having that!

Doesn't matter anyway. Before long, the knees're wailing a manic pipe organ fugue—something loud and aggressive, like maybe Boëllmann's Toccata [*Suite gothique*, 1895]—and I have to lie back down. I've determined that my mattress's least intolerable area is the halfpipe-shape running up the middle. Now I experiment with different configurations of sheet-blanket-jumpsuit: [1] Tattered, thin brown blanket as pillow, wearing my yellow jumpsuit for warmth [the cell's always frigid], sheet on top; [2] Wadded jumpsuit as pillow, sheet and blanket on top for warmth; [3] Etcetera etcetera etcet-etc. Nothing, NOTHING provides reprieve. Each has advantages and disadvantages that cancel each other out. In the end, all of them equal misery.

Now, too, my head's beginning to itch like a bastard—and lemme tell you, bastards itch like a *motherfucker*! Been a full week since I showered. A week! Not since all the way back in County, which seems like months ago. This is officially the longest I've ever gone without a shower. By two days! And for my prior record, I was in New Orleans doing post-Katrina relief work, which was like this entire other world wherein showering was a distant, and distantly low, priority. My dandruffy scalp no longer feels like a mere irritant; now it's more like something *alive*, a thousand microscopic insect legs, prickling along and scraping, poking with buzzing persistence. I scratch and scratch and scratch. This only makes it *raw* and itchy.

Finally, I decide to take a "birdbath" in the sink. Not a fullbody wash, I'm too drained and pained for that; but at least I can wash my prickly scalp. This is sometime in the middle of the night, that's all I know.[30] I strip down to my boxers and get started. Water eases from the faucet in a short weak arc—like a playground's drinking fountain—rather than flowing straight down with any meaningful pressure. Two buttons sit next to the faucet. Cold and hot. Push one, and you're graced with five seconds of lazy flow. They're purposefully designed this way so inmates can't leave the water on to flood their cells—same reason the toilet can only be flushed once every few minutes. Stripped to my boxers, I press the hot water button, splashing cupped handfuls onto my head. Water trails down my

---

[30] Earlier, craig & I were discussing how time has *ceased to exist* in a tangible sense. We see no sunsets or sunrises—or ANY sky, for that matter. *Any* natural light. No matter what

/time/

it is, the amount of light filtering into our cell, & its fluorescent character, remains identical. Time manifests itself strictly as a series of events . . . meds, lunch, dinner, meds, & breakfast, with count every 4 hours. Then on a larger scale, the only way that time even *matters* is in regards to the crucial occurrences we're eagerly awaiting. I.e. Wednesday: showers; Thursday: razors; Saturday: Yard; __day: physicals; __day: leaving this hellhole.

neck and back. I have to alternate between hot and cold because, after using *hot* three consecutive times, the water becomes scalding. Unusable.

I finish and collapse back in bed. That maddening scritchy-itchiness has greatly diminished. It's relaxing.

BUT I STILL CAN'T SLEEP!

To be clear, all my sleeping difficulties primarily stem from the detox process; the noise and the horrific mattress et al. are just secondary issues. I honestly don't know how much longer this can continue—getting four hours of sleep in a 24-hour period—before I lose my shit [and not in the way I lost my shit all over my underwear]. I haven't heard back, nor will I ever, it turns out [shocker!], from Dr. Corcoran. Still maintaining hope for some Immodium to ease the diarrhea. That would be tremendous—because I'm continuing to shit liquidly about eight or ten times a day. Apparently I misjudged the Doctor's compassion—or it only extended so far. Apparently, he doesn't need to know how the new medication is working for me. Apparently—oh, nevermind. Fuck em all sideways.

As if agreeing, craig farts in his sleep. One big rip, a smaller one, and then a babylike *pip*. I laugh out loud [lol]. Thank Earth for humor. Without it, I really honestly don't think I could make it through this fucking gulag.

Once again, I'm awake all night. After meds, I tell craig about my miserable night, once again. "Can't take it anymore, dude. It's unbearable."

"It'll be all right, bro. Can't last much longer. It *can't*! You've been detoxing for, what, four or five days? You'll be good in another day or two."

I'm pretty sure that's what he said yesterday.

-Wednesday-

"Let me ask you a question," craig intones at some point, affecting the mannerisms of a salesman. "Do you enjoy inmates bangin on their doors 'n slamming their chuckholes 'n screaming to each other 'n doing the most gawdawful freestyle rapping, to the point where it sounds like the world's biggest loudest fuckin monkey house? Well then, you're gonna LOVE every day at Stateville!"

Giggling, I try one. "Let me ask you a question. Do you enjoy sleeping on the most lumpy, uncomfortable mattress imaginable, one that feels like it's been stuffed with the bones of dead inmates, with your head lying in a festering swamp of bedbugs 'n lice and the urine 'n feces 'n semen 'n smegma of a thousand convicts, to the point where your head feels like it's been doused in acid and set ablaze? Well then, you're gonna LOVE every night at Stateville!"

Beloved Reader: perhaps it seems like we're having great fun, and so how bad could it be? But I assure you, we laughed because we *had* to, lest we "bug up," lose our shit. This really is an environment where you can lose your grip on sanity, and we'll see it [or rather hear it] happen firsthand.

My appetite's finally, slowly rearing its head. This is good and bad. Good because it means I'm at least approaching an end to my detox-sickness; bad because now I'll have hungerpangs on top of everything else.

I appear to be losing a frightful amount of weight. On the wall opposite our beds, five feet above the toilet, there's a dingy, scratched-up mirror. You can barely see anything in it. Mostly just shapes. But that's enough. I stand with one foot on my bed and one foot on the toilet's rim [half-expecting that foot to slip, splashing calfdeep into the filthy shitter's water—it would fit right in with the larger patterns taking shape here]. I lift my shirt. Facing the mirror sidelong. My chest actually sticks out farther than my stomach, which seems to've lost every trace of fat. The pectoral and bicep muscles that looked decent when I left County have shrunk. A lot. So the fact that my chest *still* extends farther out than my stomach is even more disturbing. "I'm wasting away, man."

"Yeah, this place is rough."

At about five p.m. a Guard reaches our cell . . . SHOWER TIME!! We glide out, towels in hand. Following the C.O. upstairs to the third floor, then way down to its far end. Two shower stalls are built into the wall side-by-side. craig steps into the farther one—then I notice a giant water-pond has accumulated right outside the first stall. I remove my clothes a couple meters back so they don't get wet. Leaving my canvas Karate Joe shoes on [they're laceless, since we could use laces to make various dangerous [read: awesome] things, like a personal noose for my highly vaunted third-floor dive] in an attempt to avoid slopping the vile bacteria-laden water onto my feet.

This hope gets drowned the moment I step inside. *Literally* drowned: Several inches of cloudy water have accrued on the shower floor like a stagnant bog. This filth reaches up past ankle-level; milkily obfuscating my canvas shoes, putrescent used water soaking through the fabric to engulf both feet. My lips warp in disgusted horror. Guard clangs the door shut. Its bottom half is a solid, rusted panel, the top half steel-barred. Christ—even the damn shower is a cell!

Flattened Styrofoam boxes float in the lukewarm, germridden water. Other inmates used them to keep their bare feet from touching the floor. A great idea—at some point! But now they're irrelevant, and my feet're submerged in the grotesque #filthwater. I'm admittedly a half-retard in matters technical and mechanical, yet even I can plainly see what's wrong. The shower design is senselessly, unfathomably moronic: *the drain doesn't lie on the floor*, like in every single other shower I've ever seen. Instead, it's built into the back wall, *several inches off the ground*. Hence, it only starts draining once the water level rises above three or so inches. Wow. Just *wow*! I try heaving water into the drain by using my feet like paddles, but all I manage to do is spread the muck.

Hold on though. The shower's abominable grossness is not sufficiently terrible by itself to fit in with the rest of Stateville. It therefore shouldn't surprise anyone when I discover the shower has precisely two settings: On and Off. Pressure's decent, but the water becomes scalding hot within seconds. I'm talkin *painful*. I can't even stay directly under it; forced to stand off to the side, cup my hands under the spray, and then splash it over my body. It's like taking a birdbath in the goddamn shower! Can't help but laugh [because it feels *slightly* better than weeping]. This—this place—is overflowing, so to speak, with incessant, psyche-withering lunacy. It's pathological.

To vent some rage, I begin SCREAMING Metallica's song "Creeping Death," which craig and I were singing earlier. Screaming its #killragey chorus over and over, screaming so hard and loud my voice develops that weird grinding husk that leaves your throat raw and achy.

I keep thinking this nightmare couldn't possibly intensify any further. Surely its feverpitch has peaked, and soon it'll cool down so I can take a breath and relax a little. But it *does not* let up. I think it's the wallmounted shower drain that finally convinces me: this place is **intentionally designed** to grind us down and break us apart, piece by piece. Physically, mentally, emotionally, all of it, everything that makes a man a human being. And it's working. It's fuckin working.

No! No, goddamnit . . . I can't allow it. Cannot cannot CANNOT allow it to break me! That'd only solidify my submission to the "Justice" System, to the Prison-Industrial Complex, and to this place itself. A submission that'd feel far too much like a tacit approval of their dehum-anizing madness. That's not me. I do not approve, and must not approve. Cannot let these scumbag bastards with their scumbag System defeat me; I cannot let them win. It'd demonstrate—to them, to me, to everyone—that the System is omnipotent. Fully capable of destroying even its most caustic, strident ideological enemies with pitifully short-lived and feeble rebellion.

Mom predicted my psychological descent to this very place. She told me the Guards'd be savages, how they'd try to wrench away my humanity. I believed her, and she was right. I tried to prepare for it—and thought I was prepared, I really did—but like I wrote before, *nothing* can prepare you for this. Nothing except having actually experienced it already. And even then, even if you've done it before, it's *still* monstrous. Just look at craig.

I'm done showering after only five minutes. Not just done, but very much wanting to leave; my skin is lobsterish from the ferociously hot water, and I've had enough. But I can't leave—the showercell door is locked. So I just stand there air-drying, then towel-drying, waiting for the C.O. to release me from this putrid rank foul motherfucking bog of festering bacteria and fungi and piss and bungjuice and nutbag-hair and maybe semen and smegma and other assorted bodily #manfilth. Several minutes pass. I'm getting cold. Still ankledeep in the appalling water. Finally the Guard arrives to escort us back to our cell.

He unlocks my cage. "Hurry up 'n get dressed," he says, and then deftly punts my jumpsuit and boxers toward the pooled water by the shower. They land right squarely on the exact spot I successfully managed to avoid. Smackdab in the middle of the water. It's truly *Curb Your Enthusiasm*-esque in its painfully exquisite antiperfection.

I step into my white boxers. Same ones I've already been wearing for five days—I was apparently so frazzled that I forgot to wash them [also forgot, like the stupid #headfucked idiot I am, to bring the shartblasted-pair]. Unsurprisingly, it's only now, after already exiting the shower, that I notice the "clean" pair is poo-streaked as well. Not to a calamitous degree, like the first ones and their legit Jackson Pollockian-layer of outblown fecal material [thanks, detox diarrhea! thanks, cocksucking Stateville Doctor!]. This is a milder stain. As if someone got a dollop of auburn paint on their wrist and swiped it clean on my boxers' ass-end. But I'll have to continue wearing them for many days. Awesome. I shake my head, pulling my now-wet yellow jumpsuit back on. Carry the drenched, quagmire-tainted shoes at my side as we return to our accommodations. Eyes dog us hungrily from every cell's window. Eyes almost exclusively set within brown faces. It's crazy; watching a couple inmates pass back and forth every 20 minutes is entertaining enough to keep guys planted near their windows. Another sign of the crushing monotony here.

My jumpsuit is soaked from that damn Guard's Sportscenter-highlight-worthy kick. The entire torso in back and on one side, soaked. I lay it down on my bed. Then notice something for the first time and can't help but chuckle in dismay. It's so perfect!—*my jumpsuit also has a shitstain.* An eggshaped mark that looks chocolatey. The shartblast of destruction must have splattered my old boxers and then seeped through before I could remove them. An accident proving to be even more terrible than initially thought, vis-á-vis its ostensibly proliferating series of nasty repercussions. Ones that continue revealing themselves anew even a week after the fact! Will the shartblast's vile tendrils *ever* taper to an end? or will I stagger through the entire rest of my life, continuously discovering new shitstains, all of them stemming from that single, oh-so-brief shartblast event?! Please, oh dear gawd please that I may be spared from such a cruel and gruesome fate! Again . . . Larry David. *Curb Your Enthusiasm* on a bad LSD trip. I only have one jumpsuit, and the fabric is thick. There's no way to wash out the stain. I'm stuck with it.

Later in the evening, luce, our freestyling neighbor, calls out an offer: six Ibuprofen for a writeout. I jump up and call, "Hey, I'll take it!" through the door.

craig only has a few writeouts left. But he knows how much I've been suffering. "Ey looch! My cellie wants those pills. Don't try'n play us though. Send your line over."

"Aight, ho'd on."

This is my first true introduction to the mindboggling resourcefulness of prisoners. Somehow luce has figured out how to open his cell door's chuckhole, which is locked *from the outside.* He then sticks his arm out and tosses his "fishing line," able to pass things back and forth between the two cells in either direction. Something plops onto the cement right by our cell. craig sticks his fingers under the door and grasps the line, pulling it inside. I gingerly drop down to my hands and knees. The floor's filthy—carrot shreds, bits of cheese, bread crumbs, flakes of pastries and frosting, dirt, dustbunnies, mysterious clumps and hunks of DK-DWK [Don't Know, Don't Wanna Know]. Now I can see luce's line; it's a thick string, the last few outer inches looped over a tube of toothpaste for throwing.

"You got it?" luce calls. "Now pull at th' string. Go slow."

craig eases it under the door, inch by inch. Turns out these fishing lines are created by tearing a bedsheet into many strips, then tightly winding and knotting them all together. A makeshift rope! I'm blown away by the creative ingenuity—not to mention the hours upon hours it must've taken to construct. luce's gotta have at least an entire bedsheet invested in this one line alone.

As craig pulls, an object slides into our cell: the cardboard backend of a legal pad, with six Ibuprofen resting upon it. "Oh hell yeah," I say. "Thanks looch!"

"Really hope it helps," craig says.

"I think it will." My spirit soars, and I'm feeling better than I have in days. This is as powerful a sign as any that I'm woefully desperate; to be thrilled by the acquisition of mere Ibuprofen! Two weeks ago I could've swallowed TEN and felt no relief. Felt nothing at all, except maybe a stomach ache. The vise is clamping hard. Thank Earth for this development—my misery is such that a few weak OTC pills seem like a goddamn windfall. I take two 400mg Ibuprofen, fiercely hoping they help, even just a tiny bit. At this point that alone would be glorious. "Thank you craig. Really appreciate it, bro."

"No worries. Hope they help!"

At his urging, craig and I figure out the lyrics to the sweepingly emotive Pink Floyd masterpiece, "Comfortably Numb." We sing it together, lying in our separate beds, and by the last verse, we're belting it at the tops of our lungs. Chills ripple up and down my spine, and then flare out into fullbody tinglies. The song is so powerful and gorgeous. Even sung a cappella by two mediocre voices. Already I miss my beloved music so damn much.

craig then suggests we kill some time—give this dreary hellhole a little life—by scrawling lyrics on the walls. I use our pencil nubbin to scribble the first chorus from "Time," also by Pink Floyd [far-and-away my favorite band], onto the wall opposite our bunk. Its emotionally flooring message assumes an even greater meaning in this wretched, timewarping, soulsucking place.

The pencil stops working as craig writes a line from The Doors; its lead core cracks near the tip, which then rolls off. "I'll fix it this time," craig says. He sits at the table and gnaws at the wood. Trying to expose the tip again. Splintered wooden flecks cling to his lips and gums; he spits and sputters them out.

"Lookit this," I say. "We're forced to act like *beavers* just to have somethin to write with!"

We take a few turns scrawling more lyrics. Soon, incredibly, the visegrip starts easing up! I'm also getting a little drowsy. "*Wow,*" I say. "I think the pills're actually helping!" Before long, I fall asleep. Probably around nine p.m.

I awake when the gallery's breakfast-rustling begins. "Man, can't believe I slept straight through like that! Musta been over three hours, don't you think?"

craig's sitting at the desk. "More like four, dude. Great sign! You're getting better'n better every day."

"And see, those meds from luce did help! Thanks again."

"Glad to help." Then he rips a big fart that vibrates against the desk's metal seat. I giggle. Goddamn!—laughter is pure distilled happiness; thank Earth for it, and for craig.

Breakfast: juice and bran flake cereal, but no milk. Fine by me! Being vegan, the breast milk from a sick and suffering cow disgusts me. But several guys are pissed. "Where's are milks?!" someone cries from the first floor. Right away we can tell it's our old friend shitmouth.

"Ain' got no milk today," a bootcamper says meekly.

"WHAT?!" shitmouth roars. "Cereal witout milk? BREAKFISS witout MILK?" He bellows unintelligibly for several minutes. Eventually, after a failed attempt to incite a riot, he calms down, resigned to his milkless fate.

An hour or so after breakfast—middle of the night, in other words—my knees are growing badly cramped again. craig and I were playing the "Six Degrees of Kevin Bacon" game. But now the knees are screaming too loud for anything to sufficiently distract me. It's gonna be, I already know it, yet *another* fucking night of sleepless in Stateville. I'm wide awake, and hurting bad. "Fuck it," I cry. "I'm pushing the intercom button." They need to give me a shot of Ativan, or morphine, or some goddamn thing! *Any* goddamn thing![31] I press the silver button, which is a few feet diagonally up from my bed. Wait ten seconds. Twenty. Nothing happens.

"See," craig says. "Stupid thing ain't even hooked up! All for show."

I push it again, then taptaptap thrice in rapid succession. Out of frustration mostly. I collapse back into bed. Suddenly the intercom emits

---

[31] Silly jan—you *still* haven't fully internalized the ugly truth: THEY ***DON'T*** *FUCKING CARE!*

a crackling noise, and then a bored, monotone voice from a black female: "What is your emergency?"

I bolt up and stick my face right by the speaker. "Yeah I have a severe chronic pain condition in my knees I've had five knee surgeries." Spitting the words fast before she can cut me off. "The Doctor told me if it got really really bad to page you on the intercom, and well I'm in excruciating pain and haven't hardly slept at all in four nights and so I was just—"

"sir, do you know where you are?" Her voice oozes heartless irritation. So much that I want to strangle this bitch, and every other bastardly gatekeeper at this gulag.

"Yes, I do know where I am. An Illinois Department of Corrections facility, and I'm supposed to be provided with medical care. The Doctor *told* me—"

"You really think we have a Doctor here 24 hours a day, just wait'n aroun all night for sick people?"

"No, I don't." Building up an incensed lather. "But are there not Nurses down there right now? Do you not have *Nurses* here 24/7?"

"Yes. But this is not a hospital, sir. We don't have Nurses go runnin aroun all night to people's cells whenever they want somethin."

"Oh, that's okay!" I'm speaking now with my own twinge of bitter sarcasm, talking down to her like the asshole moron she is. "I am capable of walking down all by myself; the Nurses don't have to come runnin to me—I do still have legs!"

Guess she didn't enjoy getting the bitchy sarcasm turned on her: the intercom clicks off, dead. She's gone.

"Fucking *cunt*!" I yell, slamming my fist against the speaker.[32] I consider pushing the button over and over again, just to irritate her. Maybe start screaming *HAALP, MY CELLIE'S KILLING ME!!* or something. craig's chuckling. I glare at him. "Glad my pain and suffering brings you joy."

"Nah man, it's just so ridiculous 'n fucked up. Such an uppity bitch! And the things you said were hilarious. Whole thing was just hilarious. What a cunt."

---

[32] Flatten those feminist hackles, please. She's a cunt. Just a word. If it'd been a guy, I'd happily call him a cunt [as I did Marlow et al.]. These Bad Words are nothing more than ways to express extreme frustration & anger—completely detached from their etymological meaning. Words are just words. *Intention*, and the person speaking, matter infinitely more. You'll see me exhibit plenty of stark & even risky anti-misogyny in due time.

"That's what I said."

"They're sick. I think you gotta be gushin blood or dyin for them t' even consider doin somethin."

He helps me move on—not get over it, just lessen the agitation—from my fury by satirizing the total absurdity. "Hey," he says, "there's shit and blood and jizz all over the walls in here. My mattress is covered in urine and feces from a previous occupant. Floor's flooded with two inches'a piss n toilet water! 'Sir, what do you think this is, a five-star *hotel* with maid service?'"

Laughing, I try one. "Hi, there's a dead body in here! Looks like he was stabbed 30 or 40 times by his old cellie. Blood everywhere. Pretty sure the corpse has been here for a while. It's startin t' rot. Smells really, really bad, and maggots are squirming all over the dead body! 'Sir, what do you think this is, a mortuary? Do you really expect us to have morticians here 24 hours a day to run around pickin up all the dead bodies?!'"

We're in stitches. A smile is a precious gem in this hellhole. Laughter doubly so.

Ah, craig, you truly kept me from going temp-insane [you, along with my inner strength and indefatigable sense of humor]. Thank you brother. I strongly hope you're safe and happy—wherever you are. Stay clean, stay *free*. And Shine On, You Crazy Diamond!

Yep, it is indeed another agonizing sleepless night. Pain pain pain, of course . . . thoughts racing . . . profound, #abyssian despair at the seemingly boundless litany of challenges, both current and impending . . . pain pain and sure, why not? more pain . . . throbbing, churning, fiery pain . . . extreme foot-twitching restlessness . . . ceaseless tossing and turning, which soon turns into gutclenching, borderline-hyperventilating anxiety. I masturbate. Does nothing to help me sleep. Its pleasure dulled by my frantic yearning: for relief, for sleep, for a cigarette, for *anything at all* to provide even the briefest succor. A little later—after three a.m. count's halfhour-activation of every cell's blazing fluorescent overhead lights, which're automatic and unchangeable for the duration of count—I jerk off *again*. ANYTHING for a few priceless moments of escape.

That's when it happens: for the first real legitimate time since beginning my incarceration just under three weeks ago, a blind consumptive fury slams into me head-on. This is an altogether different sort of rage than I'm used to. I've always had temper issues [thanks, Dad]. I've long underwent fits of turnip-faced anger; but after I was arrested, and even more so after the abortive charade of preposterous injustice officially known as our Motion to Suppress hearing, I started experiencing this unprecedented, uniquely severe and grim and relentless flavor of rage. It's uncontrollable, overwhelming, even distressing in its ferocity. And it often arrives with disturbingly vicious and violent fantasies—which are out of character. Before my arrest, I was a generally peaceful individual, even at my angriest. Violence and gore actually made me uncomfortable.

So tonight, when this new rage comes on, it only furthers my already substantial distress. I'm just lying there in bed. Yearning for sleep. Then suddenly it hits me fullforce, creating savage angst and *Gestalt* and *je ne sais quoi* and other things best quantified by non-English words; these feelings have nowhere to go, no outlet, so they just fester inside me like the stagnant water in that first shower stall. Like gangrene of the **soul**. Bottle suppress bottle suppress bottle and suppress, that's all I can do with this rage. I'd like to have a solid, unfettered sobbing session. But I can't. All external signs of weakness must be summarily executed. I tend to cry pretty easily—but do you think I can allow myself that luxury, *ever*, in prison? Not a chance.

Here's where the violent fantasies come in. Because I'd also *really* enjoy murdering the "Doctor." More than anything else right now, really, I want to murder that scumwad in brutally creative and barbaric ways—and *not* with something as impersonal and unimaginative as a gun or even a knife. No, I wanna strangle the life from him with my bare hands while at the same time heaving a knee into his testicles 25 or 30 times, so that he suffers the ungawdly pain of ferocious bluntfury-trauma to the groin as he simul-taneously experiences the sheer terror of suffocation and imminent death. Or maybe I'd knock him down with a blow to the head from a garden rake—not the flimsy kind either, I'm talkin the ones with sturdy steel tines used for like raking horseshit—and then kick him with steeltoed boots in the stomach, the spine, the head [which is already bleeding from several puncture wounds via the raketines, and looks like an unpeeled russet potato you've stuck a fork into to see if it's done cooking], the face, and the soft flesh of his inner thighs, kick kick kick kickety kick kick 60 or 70 times, until, shrieking so hard his larynx ruptures blood and fleshbits exploding from his mouth and into my grinning lunatic face, he dies, snuffed out by contusions and shock and massive boy I do mean *massive* internal bleeding. No mercy. Even if he were screaming for mercy I would give none, would not stop kicking him with my nonleather vegan boots or kneeing his balls until two minutes after he stopped breathing or hell maybe even more.

If I'm unable to murder him personally, I'd be sad, but as long as he dies, I could bring myself—eventually—to accept it. Maybe he'll get habañero-based hot sauce in his eyes, and as he's clawing around the sink, he'll accidentally switch the garbage disposal on and somehow slip and his arm will plunge down into the drain and it'll shred his fingers and hand and he'll be stuck and when his hand is sufficiently shredded the blades'll go to work on his forearm, and meanwhile his eyes are scorching-agony, and his wife is screaming in horror right nearby, but she can't do anything to help him because she's handcuffed to the radiator for some kind of freaky sex game. And he bleeds out after half his arm is eaten up by the garbage disposal [an apt phrase here], and dies with the knowledge that his poor wife could've saved him if he weren't such a perverted misogynistic sexfiend, and he dies praying for it to stop, *pleading* for help from the gawd that it turns out doesn't even exist—which he learns right after dying, that there's no gawd, and then he suffers the agony of that knowledge for three to four minutes, and then his consciousness goes eternally blank.

These are my thoughts, lying in bed. That is my exquisite rage. Is it any wonder that prison chews up humans and spits out monsters? American prisons sure do seem like a brigade of brainless heartless sociopaths running an insane asylum. We're *all* crazy—inmates, Guards, Administrators, Wardens, politicians and citizens who support this shit, members of the Prison Bureaucrazy—it's just that *they* happen to hold the keys, *they* are on the other side of the walls and doors. May every "tough-on-crime" politician contract syphilis from the hookers and/or gigalos they're fucking out of boredom with their ugly spouses, and may it slowly work its dark magic on them until it destroys their brains [if their brains can be considered reasonably functional in the first place] and makes their peckers and/or clits break off in their hand while they're masturbating to weird, ethically questionable fetish porn.

Do you see it, my Dear Beloved Reader? Do you? I'm too pained and drained, in every sense of both words, to step up onto my soapbox—which normally entails those nifty attendant soapbox images that, if I'm being honest, are an obvious literary contrivance that pretty much scream "postmodern." So then, given my current state, the following Soapbox Moment will not include the usual climb. Thus:

Do you see what's happening, Dear Beloved Reader? This place—which is merely an epitomized version of all U.S. prisons—is doing the *diametric opposite* of what our culture expects out of prisons. Their whole purpose is supposed to be crime deterrence. Right? But that's blatant fucking bullshit once you see how things really are. In reality, in America, prisons are gawd-awful at preventing crime; they're about 90 percent punitive and, at most, ten percent rehabilitative.

That's why recidivism rates are so high.

How high? That's a complex question to answer; I don't wanna take up much space trying to delineate exact numbers, because when they're as high as they are, even a broad range is sufficient, and adequately demonstrates the point. Sometimes recidivism is defined as a return to crime. Other times it corresponds only with *rearrest*, not reconviction [which is what I find most important]. Problem is, statistics on the former are easy to find, and the latter extremely difficult. So all I can really do is say that rearrest rates are very very high—somewhere between 50 and 75 percent—and encourage you to further research the issue if you're interested.[33]

In any case [NPI], at least the *reasons* are clear. The American "Justice" System and Prison-Industrial Complex foster a *culture of hatred* toward all authority. The Officers treat us like subhumans, like dogshit-scrapings. Rehabilitative programs are few and far between. In the corporate capitalist Land of the Free, money rules above all else. And there's no money in rehab! Wrecking lives over nonviolent "crimes" is STAGGERINGLY lucrative—for prisons and their service industries, for every level of law enforcement, for courts and judges and prosecutors and other attorneys and on and on.

It pays—literally—when people return to prison. So it shouldn't surprise anyone that these Systems often seem *designed* to foster recidivism [more on this later]. You do your time, paying your "debt to society," and you emerge, as if from a dark cave into the blazing sun, trying to readjust your vision, only to learn society gives not a glancing fuck about you. Atop that, you find there's now an irascible target on your back; you're now a Convicted Felon. Any governmental assistance—welfare, disability, food

---

[33] Info gleaned from several places, mainly the National Institute of Justice at: www.nij.gov/topics/corrections/recidivism/pages/welcome.aspx [site accessed 4/9/16].

stamps, etc.—is now either impossible [by law] to receive, or even more difficult than it already was. That felony-record target on your back makes it even harder to find a place to live, and erects further barriers between you and legitimate legal employment. No wonder so many people resume a criminal lifestyle!

The System's rigged. It really is that simple, for all its complexity . . . just like with corporate and governmental positions, it's a Revolving Door.

These thoughts weigh heavily on my exhausted [but not sleepy!] mind. I try working on the Lizzy-dreamstory, but only manage adding a few tepid sentences to the whopping halfpage-total I've produced amid several attempts. Can't focus. It's the pain and depression, but I'm also feeling overwhelmed by the whole situation's twisted lunacy—from the illegalization of marijuana almost a century ago [a law rooted in racism and false pretenses, which I'll primer at some point] to America's *criminal* health care and related insurance industries, from my getting pulled over on a fabricated traffic violation all the way to this cell, and the entire parade of absurdity and assplowing in between.

I can't lie here anymore. Restless ennui seems underacknowledged as a form of psychological discord; they can be as bad or at times even worse than traditional anhedonia. For me, malaise and depression are often inseparable—which is why I coined and regularly use the term *#deprestless*. Sleeping, craig farts twice. I roll out of bed and stand up with a groan, legs nearly buckling. In huge letters on the wall above the desk, I write:

WELCOME TO REBEL HELL

That's right, I've already decided to eventually write a memoir of my Prison Experience, and not only that, already have the main title! All the way back in mid-2010. I glance around; our dim cell's getting penciled up nicely! And with actual thoughtprovoking things, unlike the garbage prior occupants have tagged: swastikas [Nazi punks need to fuck off and DIE!], dumbass ignorant gang symbols, nigger-this and nigger-that, and perhaps worst of all, I LOVE JEHOVAH! in several spots.

I'm awake all night. Again, all the way from midnight snack through to morning meds. This makes *four* in a row. I cannot handle it anymore. Absolutely cannot. I've *still* got diarrhea, shitting some half-dozen times a day. Still experiencing the awful bouts of skin-trying-to-unhinge-from-my-body discomfort. Still in nearly ceaseless psychological and physical agony. How can I possibly cope for another week or more?!

Suddenly it hits me. An idea for how I might finally end this hellacious stretch of sleeplessness. It's risky; an extreme rule-violation that could— no, *would*—result in extra time added to my prison sentence. But it could also be well worth the risk. I'm far beyond casual desperation at this point, willing to try anything just for a chance to simply reduce the torment. My heart thumps at the possibility [and its horrifying potential repercussions].

-Thursday-

morning, at long last, reveals itself with the med-Nurse's arrival. She slips my mini envelope through the doorcrack. I tip the pills into my hand. Then quickly, with just the slightest movement, tilt that hand downward to dump the meds at my feet. I faketoss them onto my tongue and sip water from my reused juice carton, its cardboard soggy against my lips like wet newspaper. The Nurse moves on down the line. I pluck both pills off the ground, swallowing my Celexa. The Klonopin I stash in an empty bran-flake cereal container from this morning.

craig awakes with a yawn and a fart. I need to make sure he's okay with my plan. Sometimes the mere sight of drug use can bring his heroin jones rushing back, or launch him into the despair pit over some of the terrible things he's done to acquire smack. "Nother beautiful morning in paradise, eh?" I'm sitting at the table now, looking up at him.

"Ha. Yeah, really." He rubs the sleep from his eyes, sitting up.

"Sorry for this, but I gotta ask—would it bother you if I snorted my Klonopin?"

"Psh," he says, waving it off, "not at all, dude. Do whatcha gotta do." And it really is that simple: I'm doing what I have to do. Desperate times call for desperate etceteras.

"Thanks craig. Cuz I didn't sleep a wink, again, all last night after breakfast. I can't take that shit anymore. Need the meds ta hit harder. I *need* a decent block of rest."

"Totally understand. Go for it."

I decide to wait till after 9:30 a.m. lunch. Falling asleep last night was made even more difficult than usual by my returning appetite; shitty, no question, though it is a good sign, indicative of improving health. Problem is—given the miniscule foodportions *and* my veganism—I'm getting an average of maaaybe 800 calories per day. Luckily, this morning we receive an only half-repulsive lunch [starvers can't be choosers]. I eat canned corn mixed with reconstituted mashed potatoes.

After allowing these meager rations to digest a bit, I grab my tiny blue Klonopin and place it on the desk's circular metal seat. craig and I have been sharing a small stick of deodorant. Its flat plastic lid looks perfect for crushing pills into a fine powder. I begin rocking the lid back and forth over my Klonopin. Super careful to avoid any errant movements, which could eject pieces from underneath the cap. When it's almost fully crushed, I delicately sift through the pile and locate those minute bits that've yet to powderize. Then I finish em off. First phase complete.

This whole time, we're listening for the jangling keys of an Officer on deck. I'm terrified of getting caught. Certainly. But I'm far, far more terrified of having yet another night like the last four! Fairly confident there's no Guard right now in our gallery, I tear a strip of yellow paper from my release-date form [such delightful irony] and roll it tightly to create a short straw. I use my ID card as people use razorblades. Scrimming the powder into a mound, sculpting a several-inch line. That little pill yielded a surprising amount of powder! My heart races. I've tried snorting [pills and nothing more] like twice in my life.

Just then, sitting on the floor and hunkered over the stoolseat, about to place the straw in my nostril, I hear clinking keys and stop dead. Guard on deck! But where? Downstairs? On our floor? "Ey craig you hear that?"

He's lying in bed, lost in his own painworld. "Not sure. Don't think so."

I lean back down. The key sound is gone. Probably my crackling nerves just overreacting. Or maybe a Guard popped in for a quick glance. I ease the paper straw into my right nostril and press the opposite side closed and sniff hard, moving up the line, watching the fine powder disappear. Seems to take forever. My nostril burns. I suck hard, trying to finish with one last pull. Then it's all gone. "Hoo-*rah*," I say, sitting up with squinted eyes. An unpleasant chemical twang stings my nasal cavity, but no surprise there. It's abnormal to inhale pharmaceuticals. Plus, the couple times I've snorted something was years ago, and primarily for the novelty factor.

After completing that rigmarole, I eat a few Ibuprofen and the giant horsepill Trazadone that I set aside last night, hoping now for as much pain relief and sleep as possible.

And it works! I lie down, and remember hardly any sleep-struggle. Next thing I know, I'm waking up, and feel amazingly refreshed. Figuring I got maybe four hours of sleep, which would be the most consecutively in like five days. craig soon wakes up at the gallery's dinnercart rumblings. That means it's about four p.m.—I slept for nearly *six hours*! I'm beyond thrilled. I stand up and pace the cell, try some kneebends and other stretches, and tell craig the good news.

"Yeah," he says, "you look a lot better. Better rested, more energy. Less pale."

"More good signs, right?"

"Great fuckin signs, buddy! You're get'n better and better."

I've been at Stateville for exactly seven days now. An entire week; hard to believe. All day, we yearn for a summons to Health Care. You must get a physical examination before leaving. And apparently it's among the final steps, an indicator that you'll be moving on shortly thereafter. If we get our physicals today, we could leave tomorrow! and for sure by Monday.

Even so, things are *still* becoming more and more unbearable. My detox-sickness is abating, but at the same time other aspects are worsening. You can only acclimate so much to a wretched place like this; the isolation and claustrophobia and stircraziness builds. I haven't shaved in well over a week; neck itches ferociously, and the little whitish-blonde cactoid hairs around my mouth feel increasingly like toothbrush bristles jabbing my lips and tongue. It's constant. More maddening and invasive with each new day.

Every time a Guard steps into our gallery, we stop whatevering to listen with baited breath. Dying to hear people called for physicals. Even if it's not us! Call *somebody*. So then at least we know things're happening . . . there's actual movement, people leaving. craig informs me that, last night, not a single person received a bag. Some 90 dudes here in R-Gallery, and zero departures. Murmured rumors have cropped up: Stateville Receiving is way behind schedule. Illinois's zealous brand of the "War on Drugs" is overburdening its System. Facilities statewide are at full capacity—despite having several dozen state prisons. We could be stuck here not for the typical 10 to 14 days, but for *20 or 30*. A concept literally unfathomable. We cannot allow ourselves to project so far ahead. HAVE TO think about—and get through—just one day at a time. Mayhap even less!

Our desperation for a Doctor to grab our nuts and say *Cough* are dashed as the afternoon wanes. "Fuck!" craig shouts after three p.m. count, which signals the end of Business Hours. "Shit!" He sits at the table doodling.

The pencil is now shorter than my pinky. Our sole writing implement, dwindled down to nothingness. I'm starting to feel like Geoffrey Rush in the arresting movie *Quills* [2000], about writing's redemptive power in a place of horrid isolation. "This is rough, bro," craig says.

"'Tis indeed. But you seem extra down today."

He shakes his head. Face drawn, sagging from the tangible gravity of regret. "Just thinkin about all the times I fucked up. All the people I've hurt." He turns to look at me in bed, eyes pooling with tears. They take on the thousand-yard stare. "My parents hate me, dude. Haven't even talked to them in like four or five months." He tells me about a trust fund they set up for him; fully $60,000 that he managed to acquire, and then blow on drugs in a mere *two months*. "Wasn't just the trust fund, either. I've done all kinds'a messed up stuff, man. Took their credit cards 'n spent thousands of dollars. Stole jewelry and fenced it. Literally can't even remember all the things I did. Fucked em over bad." He looks up at me again with wet, haunted eyes. "When you're in the grip of that addiction, you'll do *anything* to score. Pure survival—like you're gonna die if you don't get that shit into your veins."

I almost shudder. His words and their gravitas utterly chilling.

"The number'a times I fucked up is just beyond belief. Dunno if I can pick myself up again. Don't even know—"

"Ey thumbprint!" somebody calls.

craig rolls his eyes. "Don't even know if I *deserve* to get up. I literally can't see a future for myself. When I try to imagine a future, it's just . . . blank."

A pained silence descends for several minutes. We're both gutwrenched by the hurtful things we've done to people we love.

After a while, he tells me about Cook County Jail, which serves all of Chicago. It houses a staggering 12,000+ inmates, more than any other American jail. It's infested with gangs. Fights erupt constantly. craig saw people smoking weed, dropping ecstasy, even shooting heroin and smoking crack! He witnessed multiple stabbings on his most recent, four-month adventure there. Dudes would tear jagged metal strips off the light fixtures, then grind down the edges into fine sharp steel until eventually they'd have what amounted to a two-foot fucking *sword*.

"Hooooly shit!" I cry. "That's crazy. Thank Earth I didn't end up there. I could not make it through that kinda shit!"

We lie in bed quietly for a stretch. Dinner arrives. craig opens the plastic tray and stares down into it. Holding still for several seconds, just staring. No affect. Then he looks away, shaking his head with a sigh. "Your favorite!" He hands my tray over.

"I *love* this slop!" I say, quoting my single-day cellie john. It's the infamous biscuit-and-slop meal. I eat the pineapple chunks and potatoes. "At least we got real fruit."

"Yeah," he says absentmindedly. He takes a nibble of the dogvomit-looking slop. Then he sits back. Runs a hand through his bristly black hair. "Man, *I* can't even eat this shit." He's losing weight too—and don't forget, he often eats double corpsemeat portions!

When meds come I'm able to pull another successful sleight of hand, stowing them away for later ingestion by methods both oral and nasal. I'm thrilled; this is an example of what it means to be an anarchist. A rebel. If the System in which you're forced to live makes no sense—if its operating principles work poorly for your unique needs—*try to find a better way.* And, if you can avoid getting caught, DO IT! That's my philosophy, practiced at all possible times.[34]

craig tells me how he met his off-and-on girlfriend of eight years. I describe meeting and courting Rachel, a very sweet and poignant story. "I thought she was so cool. Too cool for me, and hot—way out of my league!"

During my Stateville time, the L.A. Lakers are playing the Boston Celtics in the 2010 NBA Finals. I grew up in Los Angeles, and used to be obsessed with playing and watching basketball; the Lakers have always been "my team." I stopped watching basketball in 2003 when I went to college. But I still maintain some residual nostalgic affection. In County Jail for two weeks before Stateville, I watched a couple Lakers' playoff games. But now I haven't seen any of the Finals. I'm really hoping to escape this place in time to watch at least *one* game.

---

[34] Check out Tom Robbins's extraordinary novel *Still Life With Woodpecker* [1980]. One of his main characters—the fieryhaired, dynamite-enamored Bernard Mickey Wrangle [aka "The Woodpecker"]—explains the difference between an outlaw & a criminal. It's genius: "If you're honest, you sooner or later have to confront your values," Wrangle says. "Then you're forced to separate what is right from what is merely legal. This puts you metaphysically on the run. America is full of metaphysical outlaws. I've simply gone one step farther." There's a reason I have the book cover's woodpecker tattooed on my right bicep!

Without our unbelievably numerous commonalities and near-identical senses of humor, craig and I would've tried to drown ourselves in the grimy toilet bowl long ago. Even so, we agreed a couple days back that, if there were a Suicide Button, we'd be unable to resist pushing it. Just so the crushing misery would stop.

For days, I've carried on an elaborate halfjoke that, when [or if] we leave the cell for Yard, I'll instead sprint up to the top floor and climb the rail and swandive down, faceplanting on the concrete three stories below. craig discourages me—but also maintains that it'd be wiser to tie a sheet around my neck, knot it to the railing, and *then* jump off. So at least I'd suffocate if my neck didn't break. "No way," I told him. "That'd give the Guards time to stop me, or hoist me back up before I died. If I do it, I'm goin for *broke*. Literally!"

"Friday"

comes with the ennui now familiar to us. craig exes *Thursday* off the wall's pencildrawn calendar; specific days are becoming more like abstract onto-logical concepts than real-seeming things. Another one has passed. But what's that even mean, really? We have no clue when we're leaving . . . could be mid-next week, could be in a week, or two, or even more. "Hell," craig says, "we could get lost in the shuffle and forgotten—stay here for months!"

He's sitting at the table, feet propped on my bed. Wearing just boxers and a t-shirt. His boxers are extra-extra-extra-extra-Large [4XL!], even though *XL* would be big on him; the paper bag of sundries they give you during intake is a total crapshoot. Not even an attempt to provide clothes based on your actual size. craig's 4XLs are absurdly loose. Oftentimes he'll stand and they'll drop straight down to his ankles if he forgets to hold them up. He tried tearing a strip from his bedsheet to fashion a crude belt at one point, but failed. Due to all this, I'm averting my eyes—his large pink ballsack is plainly visible. Really plainly—teste-satchel looking like a fat glob of unfurled brains—to the point where it's difficult to *not* stare. But when he theorizes about getting erased from the system and stuck here indefinitely, my gaze whips right up to him. Terror bubbling inside me. His huge nutbag occupies my stare's periphery. I train my eyes on his. "The fuck you talkin bout?"

"Think about it, dude. Hundreds 'n hundreds'a people moving in and out every week. You know how crazy things are down there. You know how stupid these motherfuckers are. Our paperwork could get accidentally tossed in a trashcan, or sit in the bottom of some goddamn pile nobody knows about!"

"craig, you're scaring me." The possibilities race through my mind, and I see it, I see how easily it could indeed happen. All it'd take is one spiteful or absentminded or idiotic person to disappear our records. Then we're nobodies. We're fucked. No phone access; our only recourse would be to mail desperate letters. But they'd take many days to actually get sent out. And then somebody on the outside would have to exert VAST amounts of time and energy into breaking through the red tape, the Bureau*crazy*.

Did the Nurse slip me some LSD? I'm growing scarily paranoid.

"We could be stuck in here for weeks." craig throws up his hands. "*Months!*" He stares at me with wide-eyed fear, #Jupiterian gravity. He's just as withered by the thought as I am. "What the fuck would we do? Write request slips? Push the intercom button? We saw how *that* worked!"

Yep, and I never heard a thing from Dr. Corcoran, the Psychiatrist who fooled me into thinking he gave a shit. I wrote him long ago to say the Trazadone was having awful side effects, and asking for something to ease my diarrhea. But nothing resulted. Not a single goddamn word.

"What could we do?" craig continues, more and more animated. Did he get the bad acid too? "Letters to our people? Have em call? It'd take weeks for anything to get done, at least." He's echoing my own terrorthoughts precisely. "Hell, they could even stop taking our mail! We'd be completely cut off from The World![35] *What would we do?* Ask for help every time a C.O. passes by? Yeah right! They don't give a shit about us."

He's borderline panicking. A cold feardrip is leaking in the pit of my gut. I lick my chapped lips and it makes a dry clicking sound. Like striking flint for a DIY campfire. "All right craig, you're seriously freakin me out. Stop. Please stop."

"But don't you see how it could happen?!"

"YES, and it's terrifying. That's why I want—no, *need*—you to stop, because I do see how easily it could happen in this psychotic-ass dungeon. It won't happen *won't-won't-won't!* It could but it won't, okay?"

He shrugs; his expression says, Let's hope so! . . . but who knows?

---

[35] "The World" = prison vernacular for everything outside prison. Mirroring in slang, unintentionally, the bizarre ways prison feels like a parallel universe.

luce starts kicking his door and shouting bad rap. *"Bitches ain't shit, y'all hos needa suck my dick, y'all muhfuckas ain't shit, suckmahdick!"*

craig and I glance away from each other. He lets loose a mighty sigh, and luckily seems to've calmed down a bit.

"I'd just kill myself," I say. "I could not handle it."

He nods slowly. Staring at me in total agreement.

My stomach aches incessantly for food. "Hunger pangs" doesn't convey its heaviness. Makes it sound like a thing that comes and goes, in short bursts. It doesn't express the *constant*, leaden weight of true hunger. A hunger that seldom leaves my consciousness; that our meager rations only temporarily stave off the worst of. Nineteen pounds in 27 days—that's how much weight I'll end up losing from County through Stateville to prison. Shrinking from 183 pounds to 164. *Nineteen pounds in 27 days!* The Stateville Diet. The *Starvation* Diet. Imagine the kind of hunger entailed in losing that much weight that fast. Despite being sedentary almost the entire time!

I actually look forward to meals now. These paltry and disgusting cold meals.

I'm sure of one thing: There's no higher power above to help me get through this. Unless we're talking about craig, up in the top bunk. I can't rely on anyone but myself and my own *inner* strength to survive longterm. This is Rebel Hell. But if I let it conquer me and destroy my amazing spirit, they've won. Simply cannot allow that to happen. No matter how intense the struggle—or how violently the sharp- and manytoothed monster in the abyss yanks at my feet—I must claw up up UP, until I manage to break free. The planet desperately needs human rebels on her side. Which is also the side of [real] justice, compassion, sanity, *life*. The planet and all her myriad creatures. Including us.

I haven't shaved for nine days now, the longest stretch in my adult life. Face hideously unkempt and nasty. Neck the worst of all. Covered in sharp whiskers, poking and scraping, itching almost as much as my scalp in full dandruffed antiglory. And I already talked about the hairs surrounding my mouth; how their jabbing cactoid-action is painful and aggravating. The lip-follicle equivalent of nails on a chalkboard. When a Guard walks by in the evening, I ask him when we'll get razors. "No telling," he says. "We're all out right now."

Out. As if they're a rare commodity. Jeezus.

At night, I'm again able to dump my meds on the ground and squirrel them away for later. I tried to fashion makeshift earplugs one night from tightly wadded bits of moist toilet paper. It was disastrous. They blocked very little noise—15 decibels, tops. Not only that, the toilet paper got stuck deep in my ears a couple times and proved feistily difficult to extract.

craig and I agree to stay up together until after "breakfast" tonight—so that neither of us will be ripped awake by mealtimes' bustle and noise. But we've exhausted so many subjects. You can only be stuffed in a cell with someone 24 hours a day for so long before even your most kindred spirit becomes tedious. Then you have to *work* to keep one another distracted. "Tell me a story," I say.

He chuckles. "So I'm, what, here for your entertainment?"

"Of course! We need to entertain each other, so we don't lose our damn minds!"

"Good point." A pause. "What kinda story?"

"Whatever. A drug story. A *happy* drug story."

He ponders for a few moments. "I outran the cops once when I was driving on acid."

"Holy shit! Nice!" He tells me the story, and it's a great one indeed. But then I just grow depressed again. Remembering the huge timelength for which I'll be deprived of wild fun, in all its forms.

"Saturday"

morning, when a Guard calls the second floor for Yard, craig hustles out of bed and throws his jumpsuit on. He's stircrazy from being so pent up. Yearning for fresh air, and to escape the cell. I am too, but the "Yard" sounds pitiful—a small concrete block extending out from the gallery's far side, the whole thing encased in chainlink fence [even overhead]. And I'm just depressed and hurting too much to bother. The door whirs open and craig leaves and then it slides shut and I'm truly alone for the first time in over a week. I consider jerking off, given the sudden privacy. Yet I can't summon the energy. Besides, it's not like I've had any trouble rubbing em out. Just gotta do it when craig's asleep. Then again, I even did it once when he was awake—not just awake, but sitting at the desk six feet in front of me! He was reading a loaned copy of Penthouse that luce sent via his line. That's right; craig was *reading* a Penthouse while I masturbated! If that doesn't perfectly encapsulate Stateville's mindbending weirdness, well . . . hopefully other things I've written encapsulate its mindbending weirdness. I have no idea when that happened, the incident that could technically be considered sexual harassment on my part. Time is becoming more and more

disjointed\\

the longer we stay in this hole.

craig returns from "Yard" a mere 15 minutes later. Good thing I felt too miserable to coerce my dead flaccid prick into a pleatherish semi-erect state! He could've walked in on me with my cock in hand. [Wait—allow me to clarify: He could've walked in when my cock was in *my* hand, not with my cock in *his* hand!] I ask how it went.

"Okay. Really didn't have a chance to do much. Saw your buddy ken out there."

My eyes go wide, heart leaps. "How is he?!"

"He's doin okay. Asked if you were all right." Suddenly he becomes animated. "Dude, they haven't been giving him his heart medication!"

Slackjawed, I stare. "You kidding me?"

"Can you believe that shit?"

I shake my head, flummoxed. "How can they *do* that? These people are goddamn psychopaths. Like real, actual psychopaths. Seriously! This place is a lawsuit waiting to happen."

I'll repeat that phrase so many times over the course of my incarceration. Yet it takes months for me to realize the underlying reason these things don't become successful lawsuits.[36] Prison administrators—those working inside a facility, and the ones in state capitols' DOC offices—are extremely shrewd. Their Doctors are no doubt instructed to provide only the cheapest, lowest level of care. They only hire "Yes-Men." Company Men and Women who toe the line. This doesn't just save the Bureaucrazy money. It also protects them from lawsuits. So long as they do *something* [even the barest minimum], if they're taken to court, they can just whip out medical records. "Look, we did what we could!" Then it's our word against theirs. convicts vs. Doctors. Take a wild guess who the Judge and/or jury will

---

[36] People *do* sue the IDOC [Illinois Department of Corrections [sic]] frequently, but rarely do inmates actually win.

believe! Same fundamental principle as cops lying on the stand, as Trooper Beau [snicker] Marlow did with me.

Money talks. No, money *screams*—and since Lady Justice is blindfolded, her *hearing* is fantastic! If she is indeed blind, it's that much easier to hear money talking. People charged with felonies aren't just fucked in the courtroom. If they go to prison, they're fucked in the Doctor's office, too. With impunity. And you know why? *Because it's cheaper.* Really is that simple. The Doctors and their DOC employers [read: corporate masters] know they can get away with almost any amount of neglect.

This is a fairly straightforward revelation. Can't believe it took months for me to fully grasp its extent. All I can hope is that, by demonstrating tangible evidence to support my claims, I'll raise awareness, creating some tiny chinks in their vast and many-layered armor. With sufficiently multi-faceted, ferocious resistance, they *can* be destroyed.

I must maintain that belief.

Otherwise justice—REAL JUSTICE—will *never* exist in America. This rotten System cannot be reformed. Only destroyed, burned to the ground; and then, using the ashes for fertilizer, it can be replaced with something sensible, humane, and based on rehabilitation—NOT profit.

Can you, too, hear the naysayers? *It doesn't matter if it makes sense or not, this is* reality, *so just shut up and get over it!* Don't you see though, my Dear Reader, that this is also, in so very many ways, the precise logic of the "free" world? Fact: There's not a single rational, adequate reason marijuana should be illegal—not when you know the complete story [rather than the misleading sound bites spoon-fed to the masses en masse by pop culture and the mainstream media]. *But it's the law! Doesn't matter if it makes sense or not!* I suppose it also doesn't matter that this particular law is rooted in antiquated, blatantly false information from 80+ years ago? Because that's a fact, too.[37]

---

[37] Quick history primer: Harry Anslinger was the Federal Bureau of Narcotics' Acting Commissioner for some three decades, starting in 1930. In 1935, he proclaimed marijuana was a drug "as hellish as heroin," assuming a feverish personal mission to make it illegal, on top of its demonization. He went against all scientific and medical research, acting contrary to the Assistant Surgeon General's & the American Medical Association's advice, among others; the principle "evidence"

Transcendentalist Henry David Thoreau composed his most famous works in the mid-1800s. Yet they are radical even by *today's* standards. That's how ridiculously visionary he was. In his seminal essay "Civil Disobedience," he wrote: "Unjust laws exist; shall we be content to obey them, or shall we endeavor to amend them, and obey them until we have succeeded, or shall we transgress them at once?" To me, that single sentence exquisitely delineates the precarious behavioral/ideological dilemmas of living with a "Justice" System like America's.

I'm betting you can guess *my* preference of the three choices offered by Thoreau!

"Sunday"

in the early morning hours, we experience up close what it's like when a guy totally loses his shit—"bugging up," as it's called. This dude returns from a parole board meeting; he must've gotten terrible news. "Iiiiiiit's mah birthday!" he cries, loudly enough to echo into the gallery's every corner. His voice is feminine. Pitched high. Is he being purposefully obnoxious, or's that just his normal tone? "Anybody wanna send me a writeout for mah birthday??"

"O'fer fucksake," I mutter. As if it wasn't already difficult enough for me to sleep!

"How bout a snack?" That same ridiculous squealing yell. "It's mah birthday! Somebody please wish me a happy birthday . . . Come on, pleeeeeeease?!"

I run both hands through my bristly hair. "This is too much." craig hasn't spoken, though I know he's awake.

"WAKE UP, everybody! *Iiiit's mah birthday!* Come on, I'm stuck in here on my BIRTHDAY. Someone gimme a snack!"

"Ignore im," craig finally croaks.

---

he supplied to Congress all came from *newspaper clippings*, & *all of them* from the notoriously reactionary & oft-fabricated papers of Yellow Journalism kingpin & all-around scumwad bastard, William Randolph Hearst. The early to mid-20th century's equivalent of modern tabloids, basically. THAT is how marijuana became illegal. Now it's deeply entrenched, & few politicians have the guts to take it on. It's also worth noting that Anslinger went to Geneva in 1936, hoping he'd be able to convince the League of Nations to issue a global ban on weed. *All 26 member nations* rejected his pleas! In the mid-1930s, no less; that should tell you something. [Info gleaned from various sources, but mostly *Drug Crazy* by Mike Gray.]

"Ahright fine, if nobody's gonna do it, guess I have to. *Happy birthday to me, happy birthday tooooo me!*"

"Dear gawd!" I cry, unleashing a sigh that crescendos into a loud groan. "Please stop. Please just stop."

"He'll get tired and shuddup soon," craig says. "Just chill."

But he doesn't stop. "I'm stuck in prison on my birthday!" Continuing unabated for at least half an hour. "I'm so *saaaaad*." Repeating, over and over, his [admittedly memorable] shout: "Iiiiit's mah *birthday!*" Then he imitates an obstreperous, crying baby: "*WAH! WAAH! WAAAAAH!!*"

"You gotta be kidding me," I say. Crazed with frustration. Grinding my teeth. Face hot as hell [temperature-wise, not aesthetically].

He carries on fake-wailing for several minutes. Then again reminds us that *Iiiiit's his birthday!* sounding ever more desperate and pathetic. Like so many times throughout my prison bit, I tell myself that at least it can't get worse—and then it immediately gets worse. He starts impersonating a blaring alarm clock. "*EH!, EH!, EH!, EH!* WAKE UP EV'RYONE—IT'S MAH *BIRTHDAY!*"

"Dude, I want to murder this dipshit." My jaw aches from teeth-clenching so hard. "Not even kidding." I'm trying to ignore him, but it's impossible. craig and I can't even maintain a conversation. We have to just lie there, besieged by the madness.

"EH!, EH!, EH!, EH!, EH!"

I jump up and rush to the door in a blind, sizzling rage. "HEY!" I roar through the crack. My voice caroms around the gallery, distorting as it fades. "EY, you inconsiderate asshole!" He drops quiet. No doubt hoping I'll converse. "Try that shit when you get to the fuckin *joint*, okay?! See what happens! Happy birthday—now shuthefuckup, y'dig?" Simple but true; he'd get shit-stomped without these lockdown-cells' protection, and knows it.

That was my first- and last-ditch effort. I'm done. Shaking my head, I shuffle back to bed and collapse facedown. He still hasn't said anything— but it's not a peaceful silence. Each moment *draaags* with it the weight of knowing he'll reboot any second.

Yet—miraculously—he doesn't. After carrying on for upwards of an *hour*, with some of the absolute most obnoxious noise pollution, he's done.

"Hooo-ly shit," craig says in awe. "It actually worked!"

"For now."

"Nah man, I think he's done."

"Seriously wanted to strangle that douchenozzle."

I'm perplexed by craig's apparent lack of annoyance. Then he explains before I have the chance to ask. "Dude was *buggin up*. It happens, man. Totally outta his fuckin mind. Prob'ly won't even remember half'a what he said later on!"

I go quiet for a moment. Considering his evaluation from my nuanced writer's perspective. Then I say, "Seriously, you think so?"

"Know so, jan my man. Guy's prolly been here for months, like luce. Or the Parole Board just gave im real bad news. So he straight-on *lost it* for a while—bugged up. It's this place, bro! This fuckin place."

Oh wow. Wow! Now I understand, and I'm confident craig's spot-on. That's what happened. Yehp, I can totally see it . . . *this place*. This absolute gulag. I'm feeling more sorry than homicidal now for the guy. Hell, that could be one of us in a week—or less!—if we don't get our physicals. It's a goddamn scary thought; that almost *anybody* could lose their shit and bug up from the endless stressors, lapsing into a fuguelike state. It's sobering, to put it mildly. When finally I respond to craig, my voice is weak, hushed. "Shit dude. That's actually really sad. And terrifying."

Even more frightening, in an immediate sense: I asked a Nurse about physicals earlier. He said they're a week to 10 days behind. Which means we could be stuck here for some *17 to 24* days in all, rather than the standard 10 to 14. Before we're shipped onward into prison's comforting arms, will one—or *both*—of us bug up, too?

Stateville Receiving: a Kafka-lover's wet dream. A prison that makes Nabokov's facility in *Invitation to a Beheading* seem like a perfectly sensible place.

"*Man*," craig says later that morning after lunch, sitting at the desk, "this is rough."

The way he's seated—facing me, with both feet stretched out to rest on my bed—his large, saggy pink nutbag wails its presence from inside those ludicrous 4XL boxers. "Yeah," I say, "it's really rough."

He stares up at the calendar toothpasted to the wall. I try not to glance at his bulbous scrotum. I swear I don't want to; that first accidental glimpse was gross, floppy, and weird-looking enough! But it's like a gnarly potato-ish growth on someone's neck: you don't necessarily want to look, but it's hard not to sneaka-peek. "Hmmm," he says. For a moment I'm sure he caught my eyes in the wrong place, because he takes a second to adjust his boxers. "This is your eleventh day here. My tenth. Even if they *are* a week behind, we should still get our physicals tomorrow or Tuesday."

I can't fathom another five days here, let alone a week or more! My diarrhea's almost run its course; but now, instead of shitting all the time, I'm *hungry* all the time. Soon my ribs will be jutting—no exaggeration. This is the lightest and skinniest I've been since mid-2002, the summer between my junior and senior years of high school—when I was exercising and playing tennis every day, running a seven-minute mile. "Sure hope so," I tell craig. "Don't know how much longer I can take this."

"We'll make it, bro. No choice."

I didn't swallow my Klonopin this morning. I normally do, garnering at least an iota's relief from the unrelenting pain. But this time I stashed it in my plastic cereal box, hoping to traverse the day without. If successful, tonight I can have *two*. And then be graced with a terrific night's sleep if lucky. Maybe a whole four or five hours! [dare I hope?]

We spend the remaining afternoon and night wallowing in unrealized hope. Like having blueballs of the *spirit*. We're both lacking the emotional and mental energy to play wordgames or tell stories. I don't anticipate a razor anywhere near my near-future [a razor for shaving, not suicide—although the latter grows more attractive every single day, for us both]. My face's cactoid-hairs are stabbing my mouth with increasing ferocity, and into my tender, desiccation-cracked lips.

SCREW THIS—I can't take it anymore. If they won't provide basic hygienic instruments, I've gotta at least try something on my own [get this: craig hasn't had a toothbrush this whole time; his sundries-bag simply didn't contain one [though it did have those fabulous and fashionable 4XL boxers!]]. Sadly, my technical ingenuity is paltry at best; in my first do-it-yourself attempt to shave, I pull the staple from my information packet, straighten it out, and, with a sharp pointed tip, scrape hard back and forth over the furry white caterpillar hunched across my philtrum.[38] This does nothing but rake the skin raw. Hurting both my flesh and—because it was such a stupid idea—my pride like a bastard. [And as we've established, *bastards* hurt like a *motherfucker*.]

---

[38] That indentation between your nose & upper lip; *philtrum* is Latin for "lower nose." Don't try to say you only learned lunatic-slang & grotesque personal details while reading this!

Seems like there's no other option . . . the hairs ambushing my mouth need to be removed *manually*. As in, using my fingers and nails. I've never done this before. No idea if it'll work; I've never even approached this level of crazed discomfort! I snag a spot above my lip, clutching [hopefully, at least!] lots of hair between my index finger and thumbnail. I pinch down, hard. Deep breath in. Deep breath out. Okay.

I tear my fingers away fast, violently. Exquisite pain erupts in a white-hot flash that leaves me trembling, teeth clamped, eyes watering; it's like squeezing fullforce at a subcutaneous zit that fails to pop. I examine my finger. A few pitiful hairs cling to the skin—tiny white commas of hair. Fantastic. Well, at least I know *some* hairs will come off. Unfortunately each pluck produces the facial equivalent of a throbbing toothache. I try to avoid thinking about how it'll no doubt take dozens of yanks to extricate a sufficient quantity of hair. One tug yields maybe five, at best. Sometimes none.

I stop for a minute when craig hops down to take a piss. This time his 4XL boxers slide all the way to the floor; he finishes peeing with his taut ass cheeks fully exposed. We laugh. "Don't even give a shit anymore," he says. "It's like we've known each other our entire lives."

"Yeah, seriously!" A swath of flesh above my lip pulses. "I feel like you're my best friend in the world. Granted, yer the only person I have contact with right now, but you know what I mean . . ."

He flushes the cacophonous toilet, which sounds as catastrophic as the mountainous vacuum cleaner from *Spaceballs* [1987] ingurgitating Earth's oceans. "Totally," craig says. "Yep!" He pulls his boxers back up, and then rips a fart so tremendous it very well might've caused the ass end's fabric to flutter backwards, rippling away from his skin. I titter. He flashes a wry thumbs-up. Then, with a comedic roar, heaves himself up to the top bunk and slams down.

I spend the next couple hours yanking out facial hair with brute force, time-outing when the needlejab-pain grows too acute or my fingers too numb. Eventually, it feels like I've plucked a majority of the most aggravating hairs. So I stop. It wasn't pretty and it damn sure wasn't easy, but it worked. Somewhat.

When evening meds arrive, I'm able to stash the Trazadone [thank Earth]. But my knees have become unbearable. I swallow the Klonopin to ease some pain and soothe my mind. I'm still saving the other one to honk later; I do not wanna try snorting two pills—one is unpleasant enough. I'll do it later tonight, after breakfast.

We burn through the night hours [well, *smolder* through would be more accurate] by sharing halfhearted stories and reminiscing about early '90s wrestling; yet another commonality—we both grew up watching WWF. He tells me a fascinating yarn about going to a club, where a bunch of people were drinking samplesized Scope mouthwash bottles filled with GHB.[39] At some point he blacked out and got his ass kicked. Woke up the next morning covered in blood, lying in a random hotel tub. He emerged from the bathroom to find several people snorting coke, none of whom he'd previously met.

"Damn, that's nuts!" I say. "My wildest stories are tame compared to every one'a yours."

"Psh," he says, shaking his head with regret, shame. "You can have em, man. I'm sick'a that life."

After what seems like another eternal evening,

//time, more disjointed-blurred-slippery every day// breakfast arrives. I eat jellybread, quaff an orange drink. The Styrofoam trays also contain one of the strangest foods we've ever encountered. So apparently, one of the facilities in Illinois operates a full-fledged turkey slaughterhouse; my soul weeps just thinking about it [PLEASE don't let me be sent there!]. Convicts massacring turkeys—as if the poor sweet birds weren't brutalized enough when "regular" people run those death camps! Due to the costcutting element of interprison food production, most state prisons' meat products are turkey-based, so we can at least deduce that much about this particular delicacy. Thin, orangish-brown strips the width of three fingers, with strange grooves and divots running along their surface.

"Oh my gawd," craig says. He picks one up, turning it in his hand. "Looks like tire tread!"

"Prob'ly *is* tire tread."

After he chokes down as much of the baked rubber roadtrash as he can, we sing "Comfortably Numb." It's become our nightly ritual. Sung each

---

[39] Gamma Hydroxybutyrate, aka the date rape drug, which has also been used recreationally at clubs & raves; it's a central nervous system depressant, a sedative. Drug information frequently gleaned from Erowid.com, a great source for tons of info on pretty much any recreational drug in use.

time with ever more passion and gusto, it has morphed into a lifeline that helps secure our clutching grasp at some remote semblance of remaining emotionality. This time during the chorus, I nearly #joyweep at the words' and melody's transcendent beauty. Despite our sorrowful condition.

Eventually, it's quiet enough that I should be able to sleep soundly— especially with a little chemical aid. I plop down on the floor next to the stool and grab my snorting straw. Crush up the Klonopin and sculpt the powder into a long thin line. Then it's a *Honk!* and a *blach!* and a *hoo-ahh!* Another delightful FUCK YOU to the System that's denied me anything even nominally approaching adequate meds for my condition. Thanks to this recent Rebel-Yell-regiment, I've finally strung together some decent consecutive nights' sleep. This makes the detoxification process much less harsh on my body. And it hinders my pain's ability to fully flex its brutish #Schwarzeneggerian muscles. I inhale hard through my snorting-nostril and swallow a gob of cringingly bitter snot. As usual, my nose feels icy and numb.

At some point later, a bootcamper is sweeping on our floor. Absent-mindedly singing. It's soulful and melodic; he has fantastic range, and can even do that impressive voicewarble-thing. I hurry to the door and call out, "Right on brother, keep singin!"

I'm watching him through the crack. He turns around and strolls over, wearing a lovely smile. Is it just me, or do black guys with nice smiles have the *best* nice smiles?

"You sound awesome, keep it up!" I say. "That straight-up fills my soul—I'm dead inside, I need that shit!"

He chuckles. "Thanks, mah dude." Then he moves on, continuing to sweep. No longer singing.

He must not've realized how totally serious I was.

"Monday"

morning now, or so the calendar tells us. We're once more *yearning* to be called for physicals—even though our rational minds know the over-whelming likelihood is that it won't happen. Each passing hour further dashes both our spirits. "Come on C.O.," craig yells at the door. "On these PHYSICALS! I'm ready to have my nuts grabbed!"

"Just send the Doctor up here," I cry. "I'll gladly stick my balls out the chuckhole for im!"

But no. We get to stick our genitals through zero holes today—we don't get called for physicals. In fact, nobody gets called from the entire gallery! "Jesus Christ," craig says. He paces the cell—our Fourstep Shuffle. Hands locked behind his head in helpless exasperation. "You realize we could be here another *week*?"

I don't want to think about it. Cannot fathom another week of this miserable indignity. And, though I've written this several times before, it bears repeating: I cannot and should not think so far into the future.

Being in this kinda place gives me even greater respect for individuals who've been persecuted primarily for their influential political beliefs— some of whom are *definitely* innocent, and many who're *probably* innocent. People like Leonard "Crow Dog" Peltier, American Indian Movement member and prisoner of the State since the early 1970s; he was locked up, on the basis of evidence that was questionable at best, for allegedly killing two Federal agents who instigated a huge firefight-standoff on the Lakota Sioux reservation in Pine Ridge, South Dakota. And Mumia Abu-Jamal, a black Philadelphia journalist and vocal supporter of the Black Panthers and MOVE. Framed for killing a police officer, he's been incarcerated for over 30 years. And yet Mumia continues to speak and write, inspiring *multiple generations* to fight the power structures that surround us. Then of course Nelson Mandela—one of my biggest heroes. He spent 27 years in prison for his major role in the African National Congress, which anti-apartheid "terrorist" organization he cofounded [he also helped create its MILI-TARY WING, *Umkhonte we Sizwe*—"Spear of the Nation"—though, unsurprisingly, that little tidbit has largely been airbrushed from common historical instruction; Americans seem to love glossing over the fact that many of our political warrior-heroes utilized or at least supported tactical violence to help achieve justice]. If those people, and so many more, could face such pulverizing repression and still effect social change, I damn well better maintain relevance while serving my two measly years![40]

---

[40] RE: Peltier—watch *Incident at Oglala: The Leonard Peltier Story*, a spectacular documentary available on YouTube as of 5/1/16. Even better, listen to *In a Pig's Eye: Reflections on the Police State, Repression, and Native America*, a live talk by Ward Churchill, available from AKpress.org or YouTube.

RE: Mumia—see *All Things Censored, Volume 1*, his fantastic, eye-opening spokenword compilation.

RE: Mandela—in 2002 I had the dizzying honor of seeing him speak in person! He gave the closing address at that year's International AIDS Conference in Barcelona, Spain [Jim, Dad #2, is an AIDS specialist, so we went to Europe for

Evening rolls around, signaling that yet another day has passed without physicals. "Fuck, man," craig says, nearly in tears. "I can't take this. We gotta get out of here!"

"I know, craig. I know."

We're feeling, acutely *feeling*, the utter nonexistence of personal agency. The only thing rivaling this fierce degree of helplessness for craig is his heroin addiction. How fucked is that? I'm here because of flower buds, and craig for thieving a couple hundred dollars' merchandise from a multi-billion dollar corporation. Yet here we are, on 24-hour lockdown, in a place that differs from supermax-prisons in name only.

That night, not a single person on our wing receives a bag—no one leaves. Just how long will we stay in this hellhole?

"Tuesday"

afternoon, every *minute* clamps down on us with tremendous force, as if the ether's transmitting a deep-ocean pressure. PHYSICALS, we think constantly, telepathy unnecessary to read one another's minds. *Physicals today, PLEASE!* Each minute that ticks by without any summonses is a bayonet plunged into our hearts. By dinner we realize it's not happening, once again. craig is enraged. But me—I'm clobbered by a legit panic-attack. "Dude," I say from my body-punishing mattress on its white concrete slab, "I can't take this anymore!"

"I know man, it sucks balls."

"No. I can't take it! I'm losing my mind bro, I have to get outta here." Speaking faster and faster. Despair and fury swelling with each sentence. "I was just tryin t'make a better life for me 'n Rachel 'n Rikki. I'm fuckin sick of struggling to just get by every single month, just to eat and keep a roof. I should be on disability! I should've never been in the desperate situation that got me trafficking in the first place, but the cocksuckers at Social Security don't know what the goddamn *fuck* they're doing." I'm weeping now, but I don't give a damn. "And then this beautiful opportunity comes along, a job I could actually *do*, and feel good about—takin dank-ass organic weed to the east coast, stuff that'd help sick people feel better, and reduce their dependence on nasty poisonous animal-tested pharmaceuticals, and help others just *get high* if they wanna get high.

---

that & other Euro-adventures]. Mandela's memoir *Long Walk to Freedom* [1995] should be required high school reading.

They're goddamn flower trimmings! they're like so incredibly mellow and minor, specially compared to how toxic and dangerous alcohol is, why'm I getting locked up over fuckin *flower trimmings*? Yeah they're illegal, but they shouldn't be. Weed's only illegal cuz of racist misinformed antiquated laws from like almost a century ago that make *no sense* in a society that's intelligent and 'free.' Which of course it's not, but it could at least live up to those claims once in a while! Maybe it's politically too difficult to overturn the drug laws—well okay, fine then, but they at least shouldn't enforce them so motherfuckin aggressively, to the point where cops will commit *perjury* and judges'll ignore the constitution to throw down a conviction! If I hadn't gotten assfucked in court so hard the back of my *throat* hurt, I'd be financially independent by now! Writing every day, volunteering 'n shit. Instead I'm in PRISON, and my parents spent over *50,000 fuckin dollars* on my pathetic crippled ass. And then also WHY THE FUCK are we *here*, at Stateville? We're nonviolent offenders! didn't hurt a single person in any way! Why're we here, in this cruel, disgusting fuckin cesspool that's just like *bursting* with dehumanizing inhumanity?"

I'm sobbing now. Having maintained control only long enough to spit out my words. The floodwaters have risen throughout my entire stay, and but now the levee I constructed has collapsed into rubble. craig's been lying up above in silence, listening like a true friend—seeming not the least bit judgmental or irritated. It's amazing how I don't even feel embarrassed; just outta my mind. Overcome.

Hey, what right do you have to complain? some will say. *You broke the law! so now you have to suffer the consequences.*

But that is such a foolish, oversimplified, politically naïve outlook. Think about who's constructing laws: politicians, whose campaigns are largely funded by the fabulously wealthy. As a result, lawmakers don't truly serve average citizens, but rather the corporations and donors that help them get elected and reelected. Of course, there are obvious things that should be illegal as long as industrial civilization exists [which hopefully, for the sake of all life on Earth, won't be much longer]. Stuff like rape, burglary, battery, murder. But should we really be imprisoning people for victimless crimes?! After all, incarceration has abominable rehabilitative success here. Many people emerge worse than they were before. The amazing activist, writer, onetime political prisoner, and retired University of California, Santa Cruz professor Angela Davis has been active in numerous issues for over four decades, including prison rights; she cofounded the organization Critical Resistance, which aims to abolish the Prison-Industrial Complex. In *Angela Davis: An Autobiography*, she wrote, "Jails and prisons are *designed* to break human beings, to convert the population into specimens in a zoo—obedient to our keepers, but dangerous to each other" [emphasis added].

Given all this, it seems to me like prisons should be reserved only for the dangerous and violent. With some alternate punishment—can you say *Community service?!*—or rehabilitation of some sort for nonviolent and/or victimless offenders. But that won't happen without major social upheaval. Maybe even revolution. Because prison is Big Business, and economy *über alles* dominates American policy. The words *In God We Trust* are printed on US currency [though remember, that only started in 1957]. But that's backwards, a total perversion of reality . . .

In God We Trust shouldn't be printed on money— *In MONEY We Trust* should be printed on <u>bibles</u>!

After I'm cried out, craig finally speaks, sotto voce to help soothe me. "I know how you feel, buddy." His simple caring ear—allowing me to vent, and openly weep, without making me feel like a wimp—is indescribably meaningful. "Just hang on. We'll get through this, jan."

"I know. No choice, we have to! I just can't stand lying around with nothing to do, nothing to read or even listen to except our fellow monkeys in this zoo, screeching and bangin on their cages."

"Seriously. Fuck this nuthouse, and the people running it."

"Thanks for listening." Snivel. Snotwipe. "Really, really appreciate it, craig."

"Course. Each other's all we got in the world right now. And believe me, I understand. Cried a couple times myself."

I'm still sniffling a little. But the floodwater has receded, leaving only a bathtub-ring of moisture. All those feelings remain inside me; I managed to vent the accumulated pressure, though. Feeling much less depressed [for now at least]. Hard to believe how strong our friendship's grown in a mere eleven days. Again—these intense, fiery circumstances have acted like a kiln on soft clay vessels, creating near-unparalleled unity. What ridiculous fortune that we ended up cellies!

The day leaks by, a frigid dribbling stew of shared sorrow. After dinner, I fortuitously pull another [literal] sleight of hand, saving my pills for a more appropriate hour. No one got called for a physical today. Once *again*. "Man!" craig says. "This gets worse and worse by the hour. They must be *really* far behind."

"Morons," I mutter dispiritedly. "The prisons wouldn't be so damn overcrowded if they'd stop lockin people up for nonviolent drug offenses. And bullshit like Retail Theft. Should be community service or something, not fuckin *years* in prison!"

That night, Officers actually deliver a few bags, brown paper crinkling in their hands. It's been so slow we're legitimately stunned. craig and I, like a pair of clownish fools, find ourselves hoping we'll somehow get bags. Such senseless folly—and sad, so very sad and pathetic—on top of being dangerous to our already-fragile psyches. You don't receive your bag until two or three days after physical exams . . . minimum!

So when a bag is plopped down outside our cell, we shoot each other a look, faces complexly drawn with confusion. "Fuck was 'at?" I say. craig leaps down off his bunk and rushes to the door. Stares through the window, unmoving. "Dude!" I cry. "*What is it?*" I'm sitting up in bed tensely. Eyes lasered on his back; breath a fat hard lump lodged in my throat.

He monotones, "Holy shit."

"WHAT?"

With affectless initial disbelief: "You got a bag, bro." Then—incredulousness blasted apart by the shocking but undeniable apparent reality—"*You got a fuckin BAG!*"

My heart seems to seize up, a paralyzed rock in my chest. "Don't kid me like that, craig. That ain't fuckin cool." Such a joke would be for him uncharacteristic, but even so, that seems like the only possibility.

He steps away from the door, motioning theatrically. "Come see for yourself!"

No, my heart is still functional—cuz it's positively thrashing now. This has to be another of Stateville's cruel fuckups. *Has to.* But I nonetheless snatch my glasses from the desk and jam them onto my face. Step forward next to craig and peer out the door's peephole, nearly trembling. My whole body, every pore every *cell*, thrumming with a feral, crackling electricity.

A brown paper bag lays right outside our cell. Sharpied on it in big distinct letters: **JAN SMITOWICZ M23514**

My mouth sags open; O O O P E N way wide, as if airlifted from a twist-ridden mystery/thriller movie and dropped to land straight onto my face. Stomach feels like it's trampolining deftly, swiftly up and down atop my Adam's apple. I manage to force out a breathless *"Noway."* Tongue swipes across my lips, mouth like burlap. "It's gotta . . . gotta be a mistake."

craig's grin spans from ear to ear. "You're OUTTA HERE, brother!" He holds up a hand and I push forward a perfunctory highfive with no enthusiasm. Still don't believe it. Really don't. It's just not possib . . . No, there's no way, *right?* but lookit the bag right outside sitting right there! could it seriously could it *possibly* be?

"How could this . . . be? How." My forehead's like a map of the Rockies. "Physicals . . . !"

"Must be so overcrowded they're just sending people on without em!"

"No way." But now I'm beginning, with extreme caution, to consider allowing myself to believe it. Or at least to *hope* it's true. This could very well be catastrophically naïve, here in this special kind of once-in-a-lifetime nightmare madhouse—maybe I'll go down and get strip-searched and but only then will they realize they've made a mistake—would that not fit exquisitely well with every.single.thing we've seen here thus far?

Now though, pretty much in an instant, I'm internalizing and accepting the stark reality of what I see before my eyes. The bag's right there with my name and ID number on it. A mistake of such staggering magnitude *does* seem improbable . . . screw it, I'll allow myself to believe. Almost have no choice; body seeming to step in and decide, no matter what my mind is screaming. *Omygawd it's true I'm leaving this hellhole. Leaving TOMORROW MORNING!* The feelings're railroading into me fullforce now, acceptance strengthening within, and my fearful paranoia—no matter how legitimate—cannot slow this veritable freight train. I actually have to bend over at the waist and lean forward, forearms propped on my thighs, to avoid literally collapsing. I snatch deep breaths with every inhalation. Almost hyperventilating. Wide-eyed. I unleash a lunatic's wordless scream, and then cry, *"I'm getting the fuck outta here!!"*

craig goes to clasp my hand, still grinning, but I smush the potential handshake to oblivion with a heaving bearhug. craig laughs. Looking so happy you'd think *he* was the one leaving. His thrilled joy for me demonstrates such beautiful human decency. Proof of a damn good friend and person, that's for sure. This man—craig andrew l___—how well does his complex personality and behavior jive with your junkie stereotypes?

"How's it feel, my brother?!" he asks.

"Aaahhhh," I exhale, running a hand through my greazy hair. We're still standing by the door. "Un-fuckin-real. Impossible! Getting a bag *before* my physical?!" I don't yet know where I'm headed—the bag's prison-ID number is obfuscated by a fold. But I don't really give a shit right now; just to know I'm escaping this place is sheer unfettered ecstasy.

Eventually, a Guard shoves my paper bag through the chuckhole. **K17** is scrawled under my name. We hurriedly pore through the list of prisons and their corresponding alphanumeric codes that somebody wrote out and toothpasted onto the wall. **K17** refers to a facility called Jacksonville—a minimum-security joint. *Minimum!* Thank Earth for that; there's really no good reason to send me somewhere worse—but *reason* doesn't exactly run rampant here, does it?!

It's highly telling that I'm more concerned with *How far away?* than *What security level?* my prison happens to be. The cramped bus ride will be hellacious, excruciating pain; I've been terrified this whole time they'd ship me off to a facility in far-southern Illinois, some eight hours distant. Luckily, craig assures me it's no more than three hours to Jacksonville. Relief fills me up like a presurgical pharmaceutical-cocktail injection.

I flash craig a grin. "Scuse me for a sec." Then I turn away and emit a series of barbaric *YAWP*s, screaming with unalloyed joy. I hop around and pound on the door and repeatedly kick the toilet-sink console [its thin metal reverberating cacophonously], hollering the whole time—sometimes words, sometimes just unintelligible glee compressed into dense sound-balls and ejected from my lungs like concussion grenades.

After calming down from the lunatic celebration, I snort a Klonopin and swallow my Trazadone, hoping to sleep for at least a couple hours. Tomorrow's gonna be a loooooooooooooong day. We exit our cells at 4:30 a.m., but don't board the buses until about eight. Such endless absurdity! I expect allday suffering, and so I'm trying to prepare accordingly.

I sleep for a couple Trazzed-out hours. craig rouses me when it's time to leave. I stick the few meager pages I wrote on that dreamstory in my paper bag; I'm either wearing or holding the sum total of my worldly possessions. It could be liberating under the right circumstances, but here and now it feels like enslavement. Because I'm forced to rely on the prison for every basic need.

craig and I say our final goodbyes. We've discussed his coming to California for a visit, and we plan to write each other from prison [Rachel serving as go-between], but who knows? In my heart, I doubt I'll ever see him again. We embrace one last time for several seconds. "Good luck bro," he says. That beautiful grin plastered again on his face. Totally genuine. "You'll do fine."

"Thanks, craig. You'll prob'ly be leaving tomorrow or the next day! Thank you for helping me get through this."

"We helped each other."

I nod. "Yeah. We did." A Guard arrives outside the dungeonbox we've shared essentially unbroken for eleven days. "I hope you land a minimum, too." The door slides open. Now that the moment's finally, *finally* here, part of me is sad—how spectacularly improbable!—to be leaving craig. "Good luck, brother," I say, and step out of the cell. No matter what the outgoing process is like, no matter how agonizing the bus ride, I'm fucking *done* with Stateville! Or at the long tunnel's end, anyway. All other thoughts are absent from my head.

Walking toward the stairs, I glance back and see good ole ken traipsing along in his big floppy shoes. I give him a huge smile and nod. His face is covered in long white whiskers. Eyes painted with a sickly, my-mother-just-got-assaulted-in-front-of-me glaze. Already thin when we arrived, he's now positively gaunt.

Downstairs by the gallery's exit, we're instructed to stand with our backs against the wall and keep quiet. "Hey man!" I whisper to ken. "How you doin, buddy?"

He shakes his head, eyebrows raised and eyes closed. "I tell ya, no matter how much detailed descriptions you get of this place beforehand, *nothing* can prepare you for the reality of it." I wish you all the best in the world, ken. Thanks for showing me kindness and sanity at a time when I needed those more than anything else. Shine On, You Crazy Diamond!

Once everybody's gathered, they lead us down the long central hallway and into the cavernous strip-search room. I'm not eager to have my poo-stained undies and babycock—puny when it's flaccid, at least—visible to 50 other guys. The C.O. has me strip naked and then he sifts through my clothes. When he's done [no commentary on the stains, thank you sir!], he makes me enact the same ritual as when I arrived. Including the everpopular closer, in which I bend over and spread my ass cheeks so he can look at my flared anus. In makes *no* sense to strip-search at every point of transfer; I think the process is done at least in part to humiliate, to further #subhumanize.

There's a reason some 36 languages have the adjective "Kafka-esque." Stateville epitomizes that reason.

They shuffle us inexplicably through some halfdozen bullpens, each of us crammed shoulder-to-shoulder and thigh-to-thigh, and sitting on long cement slabs with no back support. We're kept in each bullpen for 20 to 60 minutes. My back aches, and both knees are painclenched and burning caustically. I'm dreading the bus ride ever more. I know my body, and so can tell you right now: it'll be like getting my teeth drilled sans Novocain [which I've experienced].

This level and kind of pain—my kind—creates periods that're like . . . like an hourglass lying on its side. Where time ceases to mean anything because every moment is fractured by suffering, and the cessation thereof is an abstract concept with an end unseeable.

After some threeish hours, they finally herd the several hundred of us leaving just today [!] into lines alongside four giant buses, each one farting sooty fumes as they idle with their diesel engines' characteristic chubbing rhythm. Inside, a Guard leads each inmate one-by-one to a seat, cuffs his ankles, and then cuffs his already-cuffed hands to one of two long chains running up the interior's length, one chain between each side's inmate-pairs. This modified jumbo-bus is an imposing beast. All side windows have been covered by mounted blacksteel panels, so it's dim inside. I believe the panels serve two purposes: [1] they prohibit us from seeing out and, say, making obscene gestures at passing motorists; [2] much more importantly, civilians are now unable to see *inside*. Wouldn't want people looking at the human beings in these Department of Corrections [sic] buses! with our faces and emotions—*tragic* emotions—plainly visible and easily interpretable. Yes, some of us have done horrible things, "and it's an important way to look at [us]," as environmentalist author Derrick Jensen writes in his fabulous book *The Culture of Make Believe*. But, he argues, it's also crucial that people *do* see our faces; crucial that you "enter into particular relationships with these particular men who have these particular backgrounds and have committed these particular crimes, for which they are paying their own particular prices." In other words, for you to see us as dynamic *individuals*; to recognize that we all live amid unjust societal Systems. And under the right [or wrong] circumstances of desperation, our roles could easily be reversed—I could be driving next to a DOC monstrosity with *you* sitting hunched and miserable behind those black-steel panels.

Do you think policymakers, both inside and out of the Prison-Industrial Complex, want you to consider such things? Or would they prefer that you remain unaware; able to pleasantly avoid confronting the difficult—nay, *shattering*—ethical implications of their System and its innate racism and inhumanity? These are not rhetorical filler questions. Navalgazing hypotheticals. Not at all. No, these are some of the most important and immediate [anthropocentric] civil rights concerns in modern America. They deserve painstaking consideration; their repercussions *demand* those in charge be held accountable for their heinous crimes, which often match or exceed the vast majority of prisoners'. Like the Pennsylvania judge who raked in over a million dollars selling defendants to prison. Astoundingly, he was actually convicted, and actually received a substantial prison term—30 years [still got off easy given all the lives he ripped apart, and I guarantee he won't serve three decades, but nonetheless . . .] Some crimes by those in power are so obviously egregious—and so publicly excoriated—that a fat sentence kinda had to be doled. It helps maintain the *illusion* of justice; for all the cops that murder unarmed black men and get acquitted of all charges, the occasional example must be made. The exceptions that prove the rule.[41]

Anyway, the bus's stuffy air is cloyed by sweat, grimed body odors and human heat. Some 80 inmates are packed in like sardines—a clichéd comparison, yes, but also entirely fitting [so to speak!]—I've never personally witnessed human bodies *actually* stuffed any more sardinelike than this. Each one of us occupies a blue plastic seat that would better suit Kindergarteners, every pair so mushed together it's like we're trying to cram into selfies. The aisle is all of three feet wide; only traversable in a sideways shuffle.

Scuffing my shoes along the black plastic floor, I move up the bus. It takes a mere halfsecond glance at the interior's layout to realize I'll be doubly fucked—no, exponentially more fucked—if I'm jammed into a non-aisle seat. Each successive row of chairs is only separated by a meager *couple feet*. Which means even the shortest of shorties will have their knees and

---

[41] "Judge Sentenced for Selling Kids into For-Profit Prison"; *Blue Nation Review*: http://bluenationreview.com/judge-sentenced-selling-kids-profit-prison/ [accessed 5/2/16]

tibias crammed against the seatback in front of them. And I'm no shorty at six feet tall. If the Guard forces me to occupy an inner seat, thereby disallowing a chance to stretch my legs into the aisle, it'll be game over. Not just torturous pain—that's unavoidable on a several-hour bus ride, even if I'm sitting in back on the floor!—but overwhelming, intolerable agony. I'd unquestionably have a panic attack and start freaking out, screaming, crying, begging for mercy.

It really is that bad. Whether you believe me or not, it's the absolute truth.

And so . . . knowing what you do about my random fortune thus far, can you guess what happens? The Guard, OF COURSE, tries to place me in a window seat. Panic hurtles at me, teeth bared and ready to attack. I can hardly breathe. Sweat breaks out across my body. "Uh," I force, heart beginning to heave madly in my chest. I cannot allow this. Having an unfettered panic attack in front of these guys, some of whom are also headed for Jacksonville, would reveal severe weakness, and potentially sabotage my longterm safety. I plead in rapid desperation: "Officer, I have really fucked up legs I've had five knee surgeries I *really* needa stretchem can I please *please* have the outer seat?! it's seriously an emergency, if—"

"Got a Doctor's note?" he monotones. Staring at me. Impatiently, I think, though his eyes're obfuscated behind sunglasses.

Oh, shitkickin-bastard! No, o gawd please no! I feel sweat dampening my armpits, my head and back and groin; heart races like I just mainlined crystal meth. My teeth clench together uncontrollably. "I don't. But—"

"Then ya don't *need* to sit on the outside. You *want* to."

No, no, that's not the case at all. But I understand what this is. Almost immediately I understand, thank Earth, before any of my explosive fury can manifest itself: it's a test. The Guard actually does believe me; but he expects resistance, and instead wants me submitting to his authority— wants me to admit he's correct, that I don't officially NEED [per Doctor's orders] the aisle seat. So I trust my gut and, in this instance, acquiesce to the power hierarchy. "Yeah," I say. "You're right. But it'd *really* help. So if you could please just let me . . ." Christ; it doesn't matter, I gauged the situation wrong and he's gonna deny my pleas. I can feel my body flooding with terror and panic, adrenalized blood palpably gushing through my veins.

But amazingly—against all odds—the Officer grants my frantic request! I'm rendered speechless in gratitude for his tiny [though *massively* helpful] gesture of humanity. I take the aisle seat with such relief and relative joy that you'd think the guy'd delivered me news of a gubernatorial pardon! For one, this demonstrates the minutial severity of my pain; these kinds of changes, which might seem like throwaway concessions, feel in actuality like goddamn windfalls of fortune! Secondly, it's a tangible representation of the absurd, even pitiful ubiquity with which my condition pervades every last little detail of my existence. It's preposterous. Depressing. Then again, the joyous reprieve I felt in securing this aisle seat *is* a solid indication that I am, at times anyway, maintaining the appropriate, moment-by-moment perspective on getting through this whole nightmare. Which I think is crucial—as I've written elsewhere.

The Guard cuffs my hands to the chain running at hip level between me and my seatmate, then moves onward. Get this: if you have to piss [or, Earth forbid, take a shit] during transport, you summon an Officer; if he's feeling magnanimous, he'll escort you to the back of the bus. A sloshing pissbucket—literally just a deep plastic cylinder—sits back there, and that's our "toilet" for the entire trip's length! Can you even imagine? Straightup Third World shit right there. And this goes for every single bus; whether you're a lucky SOB traveling just a couple hours, or you're headed waaaay down south to Shawnee or Vienna Correctional [sic] Center; either of which would entail at least six hours' total driving time! Just *try* imagining 360 minutes in this cloistered monstrosity with nothing to piss or shit in but an excrement-accumulating bucket.

After we're all cuffed and stuffed tight, we embark on the two-hour drive to a medium-security prison called Logan—the state's centrally located transfer point.[42] All four of these massive buses—which are being escorted by two state trooper vehicles and two motorcycle cops—reconvene at Logan. Then we're loaded onto smaller buses that fan out in every direction, sending everyone to their new prison homes. We exit Stateville. It's over; totally over, thank Earth!

OVER! O HELL YES *THE STATEVILLE NIGHTMARE IS OVER!!!*

One nightmare over. One challenge down. Only ≈xoo,yxx,zyz,xxx more to go.

I stare down at my cuffed hands. Cuffed ankles. I've now truly become just another faceless convict. It's official and complete—I'm *in* the prison

---

[42] In the eventual course of my incarceration's bizarre & savage trajectory, I actually return to Logan Correctional [sic] Center for an extended stay!

system, branded a felon for life. Some antiprison activists maintain that, in many ways, *every* felony conviction represents a life sentence.[43] On the bright [ish] side, I should be spending the remainder of my incarceration in Jacksonville, barring some terrible disciplinary violation. Either way, it'll be just a few more hours of this physical hell. Then I can go borderline comatose facedown in bed for the next several days to recover.

The bus [more like convict clown car—ConClownCar!] driver's playing rap "music" on the radio. Total aural garbage: celebrating violence, relentless consumerism, and misogyny. We've driven all of a hundred yards, but already my knees're cramping up again, a predicator of the burning #viseclamp. *You can do this*, I mantra internally, *You can you can you CAN! Be strong—just a few more hours*. I've become so used to pain that sometimes I can mostly ignore it; ignore the endless "background" levels, anyway. Unless I'm doing something that requires extended concentration. But here's the rub: *so many* circumstances cause overwhelming flareups. Also, I don't need a wheelchair or cane [though I did spend three months in a wheelchair during my sophomore year of college, when I'd developed the multitudinous bilateral meniscal damage necessitating my third and fourth surgeries that summer]. Because the pain isn't orthopedic or structural, and hasn't been since 2007. Point being, my disability is sadly *invisible*. Only blatantly manifesting itself inside; in my knees' haywire nerves and in my head—i.e. neuropathy. Which invisibility makes living with it even more difficult. Sympathy and appropriate consideration that much harder to come by. And I'm sure, to a dreadful degree, that the difficulty will increase dramatically in prison.

Pain is a half-ton gorilla on my back, his mighty arms clutching me in a deathgrip. Will I ever escape his stifling grasp—will medicine find a way to cure or even just mitigate severe chronic nerve pain disorders? Or will I have to tolerate this my whole *life*? On this day as I leave Stateville, I've "only" had this level of pervasive pain for about three years, and I already sometimes feel I'd be better off dead.[44] How will I ever withstand several potential *decades* of this madness?

---

[43] See, e.g., an article about post-prison job prospects here: https://thinkprogress.org/for-almost-everyone-going-to-prison-is-a-life-sentence-for-your-job-prospects-bf81d5408ac3#.aor1a3enz [accessed 5/5/16].

[44] I already felt that way, and that was all the way back in 2010! Now—as I'm finalizing the edits on this #Januscript—I've been dealing w/ the ubiquitous 24/7/365 pain for some 9+ awful years! And, since that day on the bus, my pain's

I close my eyes to try and escape; escape the detestable music, the pain, the stinky unventilated air. Then suddenly it's like a movie projector has been switched on in my head: I'm out at Gold's Bluff Beach in a flash, one of our most beloved places in the Humboldt/North Coast region. It's in Praire Creek Redwoods State Park; down a long winding dirt road through the redwoods—so wonderfully remote and often deserted, half an hour from the closest middle-of-nowhere gas station. I turn away from the horizon-spanning Pacific to find I'm back with Rachel and Rikki! my bare feet sploshing on the wet, hardpacked sand with each languid step; every so often, a dying wave embraces my feet in its chilly delicate touch, rolling past in a final crawl for the tideline—before which there's an unevenly snaking band; a swath of loose, darkened sand, sprinkled with shells, flecks of wood, and strands of orangish-brown kelp that squish under my feet, slimy but also pleasant. Rachel looks gorgeous. Her wavy, shoulderlength chestnut hair flicking in the ocean breeze's occasional soft whoosh. Brown eyes gleam-shimmering under the cloudless sky. She's grinning her big toothy sweet joygrin. I can see her cheeks' ever-so-lightly dashed freckles; she glances at me with pure adoration and I snatch the vision into my memory, fastening it there like a medal. Then I spill my attention onto our dogger [that's *dog-daughter*, if you don't recall] Rikki. I pick up and heave smoothened batonlike hunks of driftwood. Watching her bound gaily after them. Paws scuffing through the moist sand as she skids to a halt. Rachel and I laugh and laugh. I've got a huge goofy smile arcing across the middle half of my face. This is unfettered bliss. A *real* heaven.

But I'm only able to hang onto this beautiful mindfilm for so long. Intrusive thoughts soon materialize, a sky full of storm clouds darkening the scene, and then—just as suddenly as the vision appeared in my head— it blurs and then fractures like a dropped sheet of glass and disappears. Now my thoughts are being tugged in the opposite direction. I begin dwelling on how I won't see Rikki for almost two years. Nor Rachel, except for a few days of surveilled, super-low-contact visits a couple times a year, if we're lucky. My heart cracks anew. Is there a certain limited quantity of emotional pain a person can withstand in their lifetimes—especially one as attuned to their feelings as I—before simply shutting down, benumbing themselves to the world? It feels like I'm already approaching this after

---

become *even more severe* . . . with a commensurate linear increase in my depression & feelings of Better-off-dead. Boo-fucking-hoo, woe is me, etc. ad nauseum.

Stateville's nightmare-indignities. As I wrote in my debut novel *Orange Rain*, published in paperback by independent, progressive Trébol Press in 2014: "[Main character Max Wright] keeps wondering how the human body can take so much trauma, so much shit, and stay intact. Stay functional."

The bus ride sees yet more bodily trauma heaped upon my mountainous lifesum; a relentless onslaught of pain pain painpain. Invading my mind like Berserker Vikings; occupying it like American military bases posted up worldwide. Even when I extend my legs all the way out, they're still cramped and churning as with, say, battery acid. I yearn for OxyContin— or Vicodin, Klonopin, anything . . . even alcohol [which I detest]—for respite from this misery, no matter how brief. I clamp my eyes shut and continue mantring the hopeful confidence-boost of my internal dialogue. Trying not to break down into tears.

I'm surprised when we arrive at Logan; as I wrote before, time's felt like an hourglass on its side. Our sardine can busfleet-quartet eases in among a looong row of others. I'm so stunned by the sight that my pain recedes for a moment, mind simply unable to comprehend the massive throng of new inmates heading to prison—on this one single day, in this one single state, several *dozen* buses fill the expansive parking lot! All of their idling diesel engines combine to flood the area with noxious fumes.

Witnessing that the parking lot's almost as jammed with buses as those buses are jammed with *people* serves as a tangible reminder of America's incarceration rates. We [well not we, but rather the political systems we've been forced to live with] imprison more people than *any other nation on the planet*. Both per capita and in total. We must also remember and, whenever possible, tell everyone the worst part: America's flabbergasting, repulsive, and utterly fucking pathological rate of incarcerating black people, which is an unequivocal moral catastrophe . . .

I'll parse it all out with extensive details very soon in the next Inter-Mission. For now though, I'll just point this out: while blacks make up 15 percent of Illinois's general population, they comprise about *58 percent* of its incarcerated population. These numbers are more or less consistent with national trends—at least to the extent of blacks' astoundingly disproportionate rate of imprisonment compared to their civilian population.

STAGGERING is the word that comes to mind. Every time I think about the numbers, no matter how long it's been since I internalized them . . . STAGGERING.

Given all this—none of which is opinion, but rather factual statements backed by widely available statistics if you care to look—I think it's time to drop a pipebomb-quote. In *The Culture of Make Believe*, Derrick Jensen [who provided the blurb for this book's front cover] writes, "Our judicial and penal systems form a massive interlocking set of racist and terrorist organizations, [the latter of which] is defined, remember, as one that deters through terror."

America's endless Company Line is how we're "The Greatest Country in the World." Its prison numbers clash discordantly with that claim; yet still that Line is spewed, Tourette's-like, by American politicians and the mainstream media. If this country is so damn spectacular, why are massive throngs of people locked up? Imprisoned at rates *and* sheer numbers that're unprecedented? Why do so many people commit serious crimes [as defined by those in power]? Keep in mind, lots and lots of criminal behavior is rooted in despair, in thorough dissatisfaction—with poverty, with one's living conditions, with economic opportunities or lack thereof, with the status quo; dissatisfaction with a combination of these, or with something else altogether. The question remains: *Why are so many people so unhappy, willing to engage in activities that risk incarceration, if America's so great?*

We're a Prison Nation. Through and through. So it makes sense that one of this book's central theses is that those of us living within the confines of industrial civilization are *all* prisoners, to varying degrees. Bound by laws that often infringe on our personal birthright-freedoms; bound by the chains of financial bondage, forced to work and pay money to simply *exist*—what else could rents or mortgages [aka shelter] be considered?

Of course, there are levels of freedom, and prisoners have some of the lowest. Perhaps the only individuals below us in America are sex slaves, and then—way, way farther below, at the *very* very bottom—nonhuman animals trapped inside fleshfarms, vivisection laboratories, fur "farms," circuses, rodeos, zoos, and the like. They committed no crime—except the crime [?!?!?] of being born nonhuman.

Soon we're unloaded in groups and led to the smaller, retired school buses that will transport us to final prison destinations. I'm lined up outside one of these. A Guard standing at the wheezy pneumatic-hinged door checks our IDs to make sure we're in the right place. The weather has changed a great deal since I was last outside. On Henry County Jail's back steps with Mom almost a month ago. It's well over 80 degrees now, so humid it feels like you could grab a handful of air and toss it around like a steaming baked potato. When I'm halfway to the front [or halfway *from* the front, if you're a pessimist], the Guard makes a shocking realization: there's a guy here who isn't supposed to be here; and I don't mean at this specific bus—*he was never supposed to have left Stateville!* After everything we've gone through, all the procedures and processing and hours of waiting and hours of driving, the poor bastard's simply sent back . . .

A last reminder of the madness I've [hopefully!!] left behind for good.

Once on the bus, I ask a Guard how far it is to Jacksonville. He says three hours. I sigh, clenching my eyes shut and again trying not to burst into tears. You gotta be kidding me! craig was certain it'd only be about an hour. Was he mistaken? or are we taking a circuitous route to drop guys off at other prisons first? or is the Guard just plain old tormenting me? In any case, I have zero control. Better to try and zone out. Helps that the bus isn't close to full—I'm able to set my heels on the seat across from mine, taking some of the stabby deep-sea pressure off my knees. I work to again unhinge my consciousness. Stare out the window at passing farmland and trees and cars.

After less than one hour, we exit the highway and approach Jacksonville Correctional [sic] Center. "Three hours" my asshole! This is my first concrete sense that Officers will do psychologically malicious things for the sheer hell of it. To break the monotony of their pathetic jobs, in which they're essentially babysitting grown men. I'll become all too familiar with this nasty Guard-inmate dynamic in the ensuing months.

We stare at the facility, at its squat redbrick buildings, tall double fences topped with neat coils of razor wire, half a dozen beige Guard towers standing sentinel. As the Officer uncuffs me, I say, "Wow, that was the fastest three hours ever!"

"Amazing, innit?"

Fuck you, dipshit—hope you die a slow and relentlessly agonizing death.

We stagger out of the bus. Squinting against the unadulterated sunlight. Sweat breaks out sheening off flesh almost instantly. I despise humidity—

accustomed to a lifetime of pleasant, coastal California weather. I'm yearning to reach my bed and crash the hell out. I won't feel the full relief of
arriving at a proper livable prison until I'm settled in at least somewhat.

In yet another crushing and senseless bureaucratic incidentalism, I find
out that we won't receive our new state-issued wardrobe until tomorrow.
Which means even more time in these filthy fucking clothes—in the poo-
streaked boxers I've been wearing for some 12 [!] days; in the obnoxious
florescent-yellow jumpsuit that stands out like egg yolk in a vegan's fried
rice, made that much worse by the big ovular brown stain on its ass. Such
a fabulous way to begin residence here! *Ey, y'know that new dude on the wing
with the glasses?*

The one 'at shit himself? Yeah . . .

Ugh! The endless proliferating shittiness!

We're led through a series of procedures: intake [cue strip-search], a
primer on inmate rules delivered in the Gymnasium, a short Nurse-visit
in Health Care, lunch. Just a whole lotta bullshit to further my misery.
After Stateville, we look and feel like friggin war refugees. Here's what I
looked like immediately upon arrival at Jacksonville:

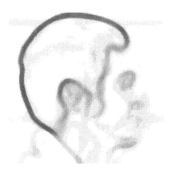

Well . . . that's a pretty accurate depiction of my *mental* state anyway. This
is the actual picture—the only known surviving photo of me in prison
except for one taken the day before my release, which I think is like a
couple decades down the line from here:

The prison grounds look gorgeous—though this is really just another function of how I've spent the last month, since Jacksonville's quite plain. However, it has a few nice features, like the several-acre grass field within the circle formed by all the buildings; a cluster of plants growing right beside the Health Care Unit's gravel walkway, each sprouting dozens of vivid, handsized orange flowers—their bold peachcream color almost incandescent after my month of gray dullness. Also, there are several rabbits relaxing in the shade beneath some bushes near the Gym. I flash a grin: rabbits live here! Nonhuman *life*! I worried of not even *glimpsing* animals my whole incarceration, an awful proposition. The rabbit-based negation of that alone provides a lift to my spirits.

I look up at the sky again. Mesmerized by its color and by a few scattered clouds. I'm overwhelmed with a sense of grandeur similar to how I feel standing, say, at the edge of Glacier Point in Yosemite National Park, staring out at Half Dome and El Capitan and Yosemite Falls, or when I'm perched on the rocks at Aguereberry Point above Death Valley, gazing through the softening distance across that infamous desert basin at the Black Mountains, at the picturesque landscape of roiling folds and troughs and hills in every shade and texture of dirt, sand, mineral. If this is "all" it takes—a month of lockdown—for me to be engulfed in glorious awe at the mere sight of clouds and blue sky and a few flowers, I can't begin to fathom what it'll be like after 23 months here!

It's kinda funny [-sad, not -haha]; for the last couple years, I've been telling Rachel I'd likely end up in prison someday because of my radical earth and animal liberation politics. I just figured it'd be for a truly worthwhile crime. Like freeing caged mink at a fur farm or spiking oldgrowth trees, something in that vein.

But here I am, stuck with this vile shitsack-stupid reality. I made my choices. Now I must deal with the fallout.

After an interminable period of approximately a dozen hours [and I mean a *Baker's* dozen], we at last receive our bed assignments. I'll be in 3-House, the middle of the crescent formed by Jacksonville's five housing units. It's straight across the central grass field from the Chow Hall. I enter the unit with a few other haggard newbies. It took 27 days [and 19 pounds of body weight], but I've finally arrived at my new home! At what should be my residence for the remaining 23ish months. Now I just have to determine how to best maximize the time, while staying true to my principles. It's simple: I *must* find a way to maintain my spirit, my compassion and humanity and indefatigable rebelliousness, throughout this experience. I cannot allow them to take away that which makes me special, that which makes me . . . ME!

. . . .

. . . .

. . . .

. . . And finally, I have to determine the best ways to hopefully [I guess?] ward off the desire to kill myself.

INTER-MISSION 2

SEEING ≈ BELIEVING
[I HOPE]

The following pages feature a hypervisual look at the total number of black and nonblack individuals who were locked up—*just in Illinois alone*—around the time of my own imprisonment. KEEP IN MIND that the visual below is *not* adjusted for comparative population. It's just the total numbers; Illinois's entire civilian population is comprised of about 73.5% whites and just 15.1% blacks.

Each x = one [1] white resident
Each and every single O = one [1] black resident

Allow me to hammer home the point right quick: *every single one [1] of the* tiny little marks below symbolizes an individual human being incarcerated in Illinois, each of them with their own unique set of personality traits, life experiences, stories, heartbreaks, lovers, friends, family, opinions, dreams, goals, aspirations, creative ideas [well, maybe not everyone has this last, but point taken?], and so on. Naturally, one of these marks denotes yours truly—me, your humble author. I have no idea which particular **x**-symbol among the 14,137 of them signifies me, and that's **kinda the point**! At least I think it is . . . [Total #s noted on the other end]

```
xxxxxxxxxxxxxxxxxxxxxxxxxxxxxxxxxxxxxxxxxxxxxxxxxxxxxxxxxxxxxxxxxxxxxxxxxxxxxxxxxx
xxxxxxxxxxxxxxxxxxxxxxxxxxxxxxxxxxxxxxxxxxxxxxxxxxxxxxxxxxxxxxxxxxxxxxxxxxxxxxxxxx
xxxxxxxxxxxxxxxxxxxxxxxxxxxxxxxxxxxxxxxxxxxxxxxxxxxxxxxxxxxxxxxxxxxxxxxxxxxxxxxxxx
xxxxxxxxxxxxxxxxxxxxxxxxxxxxxxxxxxxxxxxxxxxxxxxxxxxxxxxxxxxxxxxxxxxxxxxxxxxxxxxxxx
xxxxxxxxxxxxxxxxxxxxxxxxxxxxxxxxxxxxxxxxxxxxxxxxxxxxxxxxxxxxxxxxxxxxxxxxxxxxxxxxxx
xxxxxxxxxxxxxxxxxxxxxxxxxxxxxxxxxxxxxxxxxxxxxxxxxxxxxxxxxxxxxxxxxxxxxxxxxxxxxxxxxx
xxxxxxxxxxxxxxxxxxxxxxxxxxxxxxxxxxxxxxxxxxxxxxxxxxxxxxxxxxxxxxxxxxxxxxxxxxxxxxxxxx
xxxxxxxxxxxxxxxxxxxxxxxxxxxxxxxxxxxxxxxxxxxxxxxxxxxxxxxxxxxxxxxxxxxxxxxxxxxxxxxxxx
xxxxxxxxxxxxxxxxxxxxxxxxxxxxxxxxxxxxxxxxxxxxxxxxxxxxxxxxxxxxxxxxxxxxxxxxxxxxxxxxxx
xxxxxxxxxxxxxxxxxxxxxxxxxxxxxxxxxxxxxxxxxxxxxxxxxxxxxxxxxxxxxxxxxxxxxxxxxxxxxxxxxx
xxxxxxxxxxxxxxxxxxxxxxxxxxxxxxxxxxxxxxxxxxxxxxxxxxxxxxxxxxxxxxxxxxxxxxxxxxxxxxxxxx
xxxxxxxxxxxxxxxxxxxxxxxxxxxxxxxxxxxxxxxxxxxxxxxxxxxxxxxxxxxxxxxxxxxxxxxxxxxxxxxxxx
xxxxxxxxxxxxxxxxxxxxxxxxxxxxxxxxxxxxxxxxxxxxxxxxxxxxxxxxxxxxxxxxxxxxxxxxxxxxxxxxxx
xxxxxxxxxxxxxxxxxxxxxxxxxxxxxxxxxxxxxxxxxxxxxxxxxxxxxxxxxxxxxxxxxxxxxxxxxxxxxxxxxx
xxxxxxxxxxxxxxxxxxxxxxxxxxxxxxxxxxxxxxxxxxxxxxxxxxxxxxxxxxxxxxxxxxxxxxxxxxxxxxxxxx
xxxxxxxxxxxxxxxxxxxxxxxxxxxxxxxxxxxxxxxxxxxxxxxxxxxxxxxxxxxxxxxxxxxxxxxxxxxxxxxxxx
xxxxxxxxxxxxxxxxxxxxxxxxxxxxxxxxxxxxxxxxxxxxxxxxxxxxxxxxxxxxxxxxxxxxxxxxxxxxxxxxxx
xxxxxxxxxxxxxxxxxxxxxxxxxxxxxxxxxxxxxxxxxxxxxxxxxxxxxxxxxxxxxxxxxxxxxxxxxxxxxxxxxx
xxxxxxxxxxxxxxxxxxxxxxxxxxxxxxxxxxxxxxxxxxxxxxxxxxxxxxxxxxxxxxxxxxxxxxxxxxxxxxxxxx
xxxxxxxxxxxxxxxxxxxxxxxxxxxxxxxxxxxxxxxxxxxxxxxxxxxxxxxxxxxxxxxxxxxxxxxxxxxxxxxxxx
xxxxxxxxxxxxxxxxxxxxxxxxxxxxxxxxxxxxxxxxxxxxxxxxxxxxxxxxxxxxxxxxxxxxxxxxxxxxxxxxxx
xxxxxxxxxxxxxxxxxxxxxxxxxxxxxxxxxxxxxxxxxxxxxxxxxxxxxxxxxxxxxxxxxxxxxxxxxxxxxxxxxx
xxxxxxxxxxxxxxxxxxxxxxxxxxxxxxxxxxxxxxxxxxxxxxxxxxxxxxxxxxxxxxxxxxxxxxxxxxxxxxxxxx
xxxxxxxxxxxxxxxxxxxxxxxxxxxxxxxxxxxxxxxxxxxxxxxxxxxxxxxxxxxxxxxxxxxxxxxxxxxxxxxxxx
xxxxxxxxxxxxxxxxxxxxxxxxxxxxxxxxxxxxxxxxxxxxxxxxxxxxxxxxxxxxxxxxxxxxxxxxxxxxxxxxxx
xxxxxxxxxxxxxxxxxxxxxxxxxxxxxxxxxxxxxxxxxxxxxxxxxxxxxxxxxxxxxxxxxxxxxxxxxxxxxxxxxx
xxxxxxxxxxxxxxxxxxxxxxxxxxxxxxxxxxxxxxxxxxxxxxxxxxxxxxxxxxxxxxxxxxxxxxxxxxxxxxxxxx
xxxxxxxxxxxxxxxxxxxxxxxxxxxxxxxxxxxxxxxxxxxxxxxxxxxxxxxxxxxxxxxxxxxxxxxxxxxxxxxxxx
xxxxxxxxxxxxxxxxxxxxxxxxxxxxxxxxxxxxxxxxxxxxxxxxxxxxxxxxxxxxxxxxxxxxxxxxxxxxxxxxxx
xxxxxxxxxxxxxxxxxxxxxxxxxxxxxxxxxxxxxxxxxxxxxxxxxxxxxxxxxxxxxxxxxxxxxxxxxxxxxxxxxx
xxxxxxxxxxxxxxxxxxxxxxxxxxxxxxxxxxxxxxxxxxxxxxxxxxxxxxxxxxxxxxxxxxxxxxxxxxxxxxxxxx
xxxxxxxxxxxxxxxxxxxxxxxxxxxxxxxxxxxxxxxxxxxxxxxxxxxxxxxxxxxxxxxxxxxxxxxxxxxxxxxxxx
xxxxxxxxxxxxxxxxxxxxxxxxxxxxxxxxxxxxxxxxxxxxxxxxxxxxxxxxxxxxxxxxxxxxxxxxxxxxxxxxxx
xxxxxxxxxxxxxxxxxxxxxxxxxxxxxxxxxxxxxxxxxxxxxxxxxxxxxxxxxxxxxxxxxxxxxxxxxxxxxxxxxx
xxxxxxxxxxxxxxxxxxxxxxxxxxxxxxxxxxxxxxxxxxxxxxxxxxxxxxxxxxxxxxxxxxxxxxxxxxxxxxxxxx
xxxxxxxxxxxxxxxxxxxxxxxxxxxxxxxxxxxxxxxxxxxxxxxxxxxxxxxxxxxxxxxxxxxxxxxxxxxxxxxxxx
xxxxxxxxxxxxxxxxxxxxxxxxxxxxxxxxxxxxxxxxxxxxxxxxxxxxxxxxxxxxxxxxxxxxxxxxxxxxxxxxxx
xxxxxxxxxxxxxxxxxxxxxxxxxxxxxxxxxxxxxxxxxxxxxxxxxxxxxxxxxxxxxxxxxxxxxxxxxxxxxxxxxx
xxxxxxxxxxxxxxxxxxxxxxxxxxxxxxxxxxxxxxxxxxxxxxxxxxxxxxxxxxxxxxxxxxxxxxxxxxxxxxxxxx
xxxxxxxxxxxxxxxxxxxxxxxxxxxxxxxxxxxxxxxxxxxxxxxxxxxxxxxxxxxxxxxxxxxxxxxxxxxxxxxxxx
xxxxxxxxxxxxxxxxxxxxxxxxxxxxxxxxxxxxxxxxxxxxxxxxxxxxxxxxxxxxxxxxxxxxxxxxxxxxxxxxxx
xxxxxxxxxxxxxxxxxxxxxxxxxxxxxxxxxxxxxxxxxxxxxxxxxxxxxxxxxxxxxxxxxxxxxxxxxxxxxxxxxx
```

REBEL HELL

xxxxxxxxxxxxxxxxxxxxxxxxxxxxxxxxxxxxxxxxxxxxxxxxxxxxxxxxxxxxxxxxxxxxxxxxxxxxxxxxxxxxxxxxxxxxxx
xxxxxxxxxxxxxxxxxxxxxxxxxxxxxxxxxxxxxxxxxxxxxxxxxxxxxxxxxxxxxxxxxxxxxxxxxxxxxxxxxxxxxxxxxxxxxx
xxxxxxxxxxxxxxxxxxxxxxxxxxxxxxxxxxxxxxxxxxxxxxxxxxxxxxxxxxxxxxxxxxxxxxxxxxxxxxxxxxxxxxxxxxxxxx
xxxxxxxxxxxxxxxxxxxxxxxxxxxxxxxxxxxxxxxxxxxxxxxxxxxxxxxxxxxxxxxxxxxxxxxxxxxxxxxxxxxxxxxxxxxxxx
xxxxxxxxxxxxxxxxxxxxxxxxxxxxxxxxxxxxxxxxxxxxxxxxxxxxxxxxxxxxxxxxxxxxxxxxxxxxxxxxxxxxxxxxxxxxxx
xxxxxxxxxxxxxxxxxxxxxxxxxxxxxxxxxxxxxxxxxxxxxxxxxxxxxxxxxxxxxxxxxxxxxxxxxxxxxxxxxxxxxxxxxxxxxx
xxxxxxxxxxxxxxxxxxxxxxxxxxxxxxxxxxxxxxxxxxxxxxxxxxxxxxxxxxxxxxxxxxxxxxxxxxxxxxxxxxxxxxxxxxxxxx
xxxxxxxxxxxxxxxxxxxxxxxxxxxxxxxxxxxxxxxxxxxxxxxxxxxxxxxxxxxxxxxxxxxxxxxxxxxxxxxxxxxxxxxxxxxxxx
xxxxxxxxxxxxxxxxxxxxxxxxxxxxxxxxxxxxxxxxxxxxxxxxxxxxxxxxxxxxxxxxxxxxxxxxxxxxxxxxxxxxxxxxxxxxxx
xxxxxxxxxxxxxxxxxxxxxxxxxxxxxxxxxxxxxxxxxxxxxxxxxxxxxxxxxxxxxxxxxxxxxxxxxxxxxxxxxxxxxxxxxxxxxx
xxxxxxxxxxxxxxxxxxxxxxxxxxxxxxxxxxxxxxxxxxxxxxxxxxxxxxxxxxxxxxxxxxxxxxxxxxxxxxxxxxxxxxxxxxxxxx
xxxxxxxxxxxxxxxxxxxxxxxxxxxxxxxxxxxxxxxxxxxxxxxxxxxxxxxxxxxxxxxxxxxxxxxxxxxxxxxxxxxxxxxxxxxxxx
xxxxxxxxxxxxxxxxxxxxxxxxxxxxxxxxxxxxxxxxxxxxxxxxxxxxxxxxxxxxxxxxxxxxxxxxxxxxxxxxxxxxxxxxxxxxxx
xxxxxxxxxxxxxxxxxxxxxxxxxxxxxxxxxxxxxxxxxxxxxxxxxxxxxxxxxxxxxxxxxxxxxxxxxxxxxxxxxxxxxxxxxxxxxx
xxxxxxxxxxxxxxxxxxxxxxxxxxxxxxxxxxxxxxxxxxxxxxxxxxxxxxxxxxxxxxxxxxxxxxxxxxxxxxxxxxxxxxxxxxxxxx
xxxxxxxxxxxxxxxxxxxxxxxxxxxxxxxxxxxxxxxxxxxxxxxxxxxxxxxxxxxxxxxxxxxxxxxxxxxxxxxxxxxxxxxxxxxxxx
xxxxxxxxxxxxxxxxxxxxxxxxxxxxxxxxxxxxxxxxxxxxxxxxxxxxxxxxxxxxxxxxxxxxxxxxxxxxxxxxxxxxxxxxxxxxxx
xxxxxxxxxxxxxxxxxxxxxxxxxxxxxxxxxxxxxxxxxxxxxxxxxxxxxxxxxxxxxxxxxxxxxxxxxxxxxxxxxxxxxxxxxxxxxx
xxxxxxxxxxxxxxxxxxxxxxxxxxxxxxxxxxxxxxxxxxxxxxxxxxxxxxxxxxxxxxxxxxxxxxxxxxxxxxxxxxxxxxxxxxxxxx
xxxxxxxxxxxxxxxxxxxxxxxxxxxxxxxxxxxxxxxxxxxxxxxxxxxxxxxxxxxxxxxxxxxxxxxxxxxxxxxxxxxxxxxxxxxxxx
xxxxxxxxxxxxxxxxxxxxxxxxxxxxxxxxxxxxxxxxxxxxxxxxxxxxxxxxxxxxxxxxxxxxxxxxxxxxxxxxxxxxxxxxxxxxxx
xxxxxxxxxxxxxxxxxxxxxxxxxxxxxxxxxxxxxxxxxxxxxxxxxxxxxxxxxxxxxxxxxxxxxxxxxxxxxxxxxxxxxxxxxxxxxx
xxxxxxxxxxxxxxxxxxxxxxxxxxxxxxxxxxxxxxxxxxxxxxxxxxxxxxxxxxxxxxxxxxxxxxxxxxxxxxxxxxxxxxxxxxxxxx
xxxxxxxxxxxxxxxxxxxxxxxxxxxxxxxxxxxxxxxxxxxxxxxxxxxxxxxxxxxxxxxxxxxxxxxxxxxxxxxxxxxxxxxxxxxxxx
xxxxxxxxxxxxxxxxxxxxxxxxxxxxxxxxxxxxxxxxxxxxxxxxxxxxxxxxxxxxxxxxxxxxxxxxxxxxxxxxxxxxxxxxxxxxxx
xxxxxxxxxxxxxxxxxxxxxxxxxxxxxxxxxxxxxxxxxxxxxxxxxxxxxxxxxxxxxxxxxxxxxxxxxxxxxxxxxxxxxxxxxxxxxx
xxxxxxxxxxxxxxxxxxxxxxxxxxxxxxxxxxxxxxxxxxxxxxxxxxxxxxxxxxxxxxxxxxxxxxxxxxxxxxxxxxxxxxxxxxxxxx
xxxxxxxxxxxxxxxxxxxxxxxxxxxxxxxxxxxxxxxxxxxxxxxxxxxxxxxxxxxxxxxxxxxxxxxxxxxxxxxxxxxxxxxxxxxxxx
xxxxxxxxxxxxxxxxxxxxxxxxxxxxxxxxxxxxxxxxxxxxxxxxxxxxxxxxxxxxxxxxxxxxxxxxxxxxxxxxxxxxxxxxxxxxxx
xxxxxxxxxxxxxxxxxxxxxxxxxxxxxxxxxxxxxxxxxxxxxxxxxxxxxxxxxxxxxxxxxxxxxxxxxxxxxxxxxxxxxxxxxxxxxx
xxxxxxxxxxxxxxxxxxxxxxxxxxxxxxxxxxxxxxxxxxxxxxxxxxxxxxxxxxxxxxxxxxxxxxxxxxxxxxxxxxxxxxxxxxxxxx
xxxxxxxxxxxxxxxxxxxxxxxxxxxxxxxxxxxxxxxxxxxxxxxxxxxxxxxxxxxxxxxxxxxxxxxxxxxxxxxxxxxxxxxxxxxxxx
xxxxxxxxxxxxxxxxxxxxxxxxxxxxxxxxxxxxxxxxxxxxxxxxxxxxxxxxxxxxxxxxxxxxxxxxxxxxxxxxxxxxxxxxxxxxxx
xxxxxxxxxxxxxxxxxxxxxxxxxxxxxxxxxxxxxxxxxxxxxxxxxxxxxxxxxxxxxxxxxxxxxxxxxxxxxxxxxxxxxxxxxxxxxx
xxxxxxxxxxxxxxxxxxxxxxxxxxxxxxxxxxxxxxxxxxxxxxxxxxxxxxxxxxxxxxxxxxxxxxxxxxxxxxxxxxxxxxxxxxxxxx
xxxxxxxxxxxxxxxxxxxxxxxxxxxxxxxxxxxxxxxxxxxxxxxxxxxxxxxxxxxxxxxxxxxxxxxxxxxxxxxxxxxxxxxxxxxxxx
xxxxxxxxxxxxxxxxxxxxxxxxxxxxxxxxxxxxxxxxxxxxxxxxxxxxxxxxxxxxxxxxxxxxxxxxxxxxxxxxxxxxxxxxxxxxxx
xxxxxxxxxxxxxxxxxxxxxxxxxxxxxxxxxxxxxxxxxxxxxxxxxxxxxxxxxxxxxxxxxxxxxxxxxxxxxxxxxxxxxxxxxxxxxx
xxxxxxxxxxxxxxxxxxxxxxxxxxxxxxxxxxxxxxxxxxxxxxxxxxxxxxxxxxxxxxxxxxxxxxxxxxxxxxxxxxxxxxxxxxxxxx
xxxxxxxxxxxxxxxxxxxxxxxxxxxxxxxxxxxxxxxxxxxxxxxxxxxxxxxxxxxxxxxxxxxxxxxxxxxxxxxxxxxxxxxxxxxxxx
xxxxxxxxxxxxxxxxxxxxxxxxxxxxxxxxxxxxxxx

ooooooooooooooooooooooooooooooooooooooooooooooooooooooooooooooooooooooooooooooooooooooooooooo
ooooooooooooooooooooooooooooooooooooooooooooooooooooooooooooooooooooooooooooooooooooooooooooo
ooooooooooooooooooooooooooooooooooooooooooooooooooooooooooooooooooooooooooooooooooooooooooooo
ooooooooooooooooooooooooooooooooooooooooooooooooooooooooooooooooooooooooooooooooooooooooooooo
ooooooooooooooooooooooooooooooooooooooooooooooooooooooooooooooooooooooooooooooooooooooooooooo
ooooooooooooooooooooooooooooooooooooooooooooooooooooooooooooooooooooooooooooooooooooooooooooo
ooooooooooooooooooooooooooooooooooooooooooooooooooooooooooooooooooooooooooooooooooooooooooooo
ooooooooooooooooooooooooooooooooooooooooooooooooooooooooooooooooooooooooooooooooooooooooooooo
ooooooooooooooooooooooooooooooooooooooooooooooooooooooooooooooooooooooooooooooooooooooooooooo
ooooooooooooooooooooooooooooooooooooooooooooooooooooooooooooooooooooooooooooooooooooooooooooo
ooooooooooooooooooooooooooooooooooooooooooooooooooooooooooooooooooooooooooooooooooooooooooooo
ooooooooooooooooooooooooooooooooooooooooooooooooooooooooooooooooooooooooooooooooooooooooooooo
ooooooooooooooooooooooooooooooooooooooooooooooooooooooooooooooooooooooooooooooooooooooooooooo
ooooooooooooooooooooooooooooooooooooooooooooooooooooooooooooooooooooooooooooooooooooooooooooo
ooooooooooooooooooooooooooooooooooooooooooooooooooooooooooooooooooooooooooooooooooooooooooooo
ooooooooooooooooooooooooooooooooooooooooooooooooooooooooooooooooooooooooooooooooooooooooooooo
ooooooooooooooooooooooooooooooooooooooooooooooooooooooooooooooooooooooooooooooooooooooooooooo
ooooooooooooooooooooooooooooooooooooooooooooooooooooooooooooooooooooooooooooooooooooooooooooo
ooooooooooooooooooooooooooooooooooooooooooooooooooooooooooooooooooooooooooooooooooooooooooooo
ooooooooooooooooooooooooooooooooooooooooooooooooooooooooooooooooooooooooooooooooooooooooooooo
ooooooooooooooooooooooooooooooooooooooooooooooooooooooooooooooooooooooooooooooooooooooooooooo
ooooooooooooooooooooooooooooooooooooooooooooooooooooooooooooooooooooooooooooooooooooooooooooo
ooooooooooooooooooooooooooooooooooooooooooooooooooooooooooooooooooooooooooooooooooooooooooooo
ooooooooooooooooooooooooooooooooooooooooooooooooooooooooooooooooooooooooooooooooooooooooooooo
ooooooooooooooooooooooooooooooooooooooooooooooooooooooooooooooooooooooooooooooooooooooooooooo
ooooooooooooooooooooooooooooooooooooooooooooooooooooooooooooooooooooooooooooooooooooooooooooo
ooooooooooooooooooooooooooooooooooooooooooooooooooooooooooooooooooooooooooooooooooooooooooooo
ooooooooooooooooooooooooooooooooooooooooooooooooooooooooooooooooooooooooooooooooooooooooooooo
ooooooooooooooooooooooooooooooooooooooooooooooooooooooooooooooooooooooooooooooooooooooooooooo

REBEL HELL

REBEL HELL

REBEL HELL

ooooooooooooooooooooooooooooooooooooooooooooooooooooooooooooooooooooooooooooooooooooooooo
ooooooooooooooooooooooooooooooooooooooooooooooooooooooooooooooooooooooooooooooooooooooooo
ooooooooooooooooooooooooooooooooooooooooooooooooooooooooooooooooooooooooooooooooooooooooo
ooooooooooooooooooooooooooooooooooooooooooooooooooooooooooooooooooooooooooooooooooooooooo
ooooooooooooooooooooooooooooooooooooooooooooooooooooooooooooooooooooooooooooooooooooooooo
ooooooooooooooooooooooooooooooooooooooooooooooooooooooooooooooooooooooooooooooooooooooooo
ooooooooooooooooooooooooooooooooooooooooooooooooooooooooooooooooooooooooooooooooooooooooo
ooooooooooooooooooooooooooooooooooooooooooooooooooooooooooooooooooooooooooooooooooooooooo
ooooooooooooooooooooooooooooooooooooooooooooooooooooooooooooooooooooooooooooooooooooooooo
ooooooooooooooooooooooooooooooooooooooooooooooooooooooooooooooooooooooooooooooooooooooooo
ooooooooooooooooooooooooooooooooooooooooooooooooooooooooooooooooooooooooooooooooooooooooo
ooooooooooooooooooooooooooooooooooooooooooooooooooooooooooooooooooooooooooooooooooooooooo
ooooooooooooooooooooooooooooooooooooooooooooooooooooooooooooooooooooooooooooooooooooooooo
ooooooooooooooooooooooooooooooooooooooooooooooooooooooooooooooooooooooooooooooooooooooooo
ooooooooooooooooooooooooooooooooooooooooooooooooooooooooooooooooooooooooooooooooooooooooo
ooooooooooooooooooooooooooooooooooooooooooooooooooooooooooooooooooooooooooooooooooooooooo
ooooooooooooooooooooooooooooooooooooooooooooooooooooooooooooooooooooooooooooooooooooooooo
ooooooooooooooooooooooooooooooooooooooooooooooooooooooooooooooooooooooooooooooooooooooooo
ooooooooooooooooooooooooooooooooooooooooooooooooooooooooooooooooooooooooooooooooooooooooo
ooooooooooooooooooooooooooooooooooooooooooooooooooooooooooooooooooooooooooooooooooooooooo
ooooooooooooooooooooooooooooooooooooooooooooooooooooooooooooooooooooooooooooooooooooooooo
ooooooooooooooooooooooooooooooooooooooooooooooooooooooooooooooooooooooooooooooooooooooooo
ooooooooooooooooooooooooooooooooooooooooooooooooooooooooooooooooooooooooooooooooooooooooo
ooooooooooooooooooooooooooooooooooooooooooooooooooooooooooooooooooooooooooooooooooooooooo
ooooooooooooooooooooooooooooooooooooooooooooooooooooooooooooooooooooooooooooooooooooooooo
ooooooooooooooooooooooooooooooooooooooooooooooooooooooooooooooooooooooooooooooooooooooooo
ooooooooooooooooooooooooooooooooooooooooooooooooooooooooooooooooooooooooooooooooooooooooo
ooooooooooooooooooooooooooooooooooooooooooooooooooooooooooooooooooooooooooooooooooooooooo
ooooooooooooooooooooooooooooooooooooooooooooooooooooooooooooooooooooooooooooooooooooooooo
ooooooooooooooooooooooooooooooooooooooooooooooooooooooooooooooooooooooooooooooooooooooooo
ooooooooooooooooooooooooooooooooooooooooooooooooooooooooooooooooooooooooooooooooooooooooo
ooooooooooooooooooooooooooooooooooooooooooooooooooooooooooooooooooooooooooooooooooooooooo
ooooooooooooooooooooooooooooooooooooooooooooooooooooooooooooooooooooooooooooooooooooooooo
ooooooooooooooooooooooooooooooooooooooooooooooooooooooooooooooooooooooooooooooooooooooooo
ooooooooooooooooooooooooooooooooooooooooooooooooooooooooooooooooooooooooooooooooooooooooo
ooooooooooooooooooooooooooooooooooooooooooooooooooooooooooooooooooooooooooooooooooooooooo
ooooooooooooooooooooooooooooooooooooooooooooooooooooooooooooooooooooooooooooooooooooooooo
ooooooooooooooooooooooooooooooooooooooooooooooooooooooooooooooooooooooooooooooooooooooooo
ooooooooooooooooooooooooooooooooooooooooooooooooooooooooooooooooooooooooooooooooooooooooo
ooooooooooooooooooooooooooooooooooooooooooooooooooooooooooooooooooooooooooooooooooooooooo
ooooooooooooooooooooooooooooooooooooooooooooooooooooooooooooooooooooooooooooooooooooooooo
ooooooooooooooooooooooooooooooooooooooooooooooooooooooooooooooooooooooooooooooooooooooooo
ooooooooooooooooooooooooooooooooooooooooooooooooooooooooooooooooooooooooooooooooooooooooo
ooooooooooooooooooooooooooooooooooooooooooooooooooooooooooooooooooooooooooooooooooooooooo
ooooooooooooooooooooooooooooooooooooooooooooooooooooooooooooooooooooooooooooooooooooooooo
ooooooooooooooooooooooooooooooooooooooooooooooooooooooooooooooooooooooooooooooooooooooooo
ooooooooooooooooooooooooooooooooooooooooooooooooooooooooooooooooooooooooooooooooooooooooo
ooooooooooooooooooooooooooooooooooooooooooooooooooooooooooooooooooooooooooooooooooooooooo
ooooooooooooooooooooooooooooooooooooooooooooooooooooooooooooooooooooooooooooooooooooooooo
ooooooooooooooooooooooooooooooooooooooooooooooooooooooooooooooooooooooooooooooooooooooooo
ooooooooooooooooooooooooooooooooooooooooooooooooooooooooooooooooooooooooooooooooooooooooo
ooooooooooooooooooooooooooooooooooooooooooooooooooooooooooooooooooooooooooooooooooooooooo
ooooooooooooooooooooooooooooooooooooooooooooooooooooooooooooooooooooooooooooooooooooooooo
ooooooooooooooooooooooooooooooooooooooooooooooooooooooooooooooooooooooooooooooooooooooooo
ooooooooooooooooooooooooooooooooooooooooooooooooooooooooooooooooooooooooooooooooooooooooo

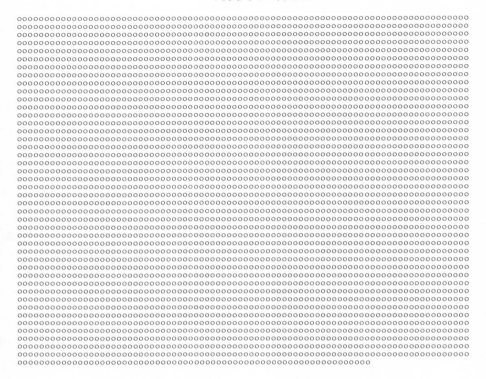

42,327 total marks = Illinois prison population of blacks & whites, via: www.icjia.org/cjreform2015/research/illinois-prison-overview.html [Illinois State Commission on Criminal Justice and Sentencing Reform, accessed 2/15/17]
28,190 O-marks [82/line] = total black population
14,137 x-marks [111/line] = white population

Is that shit not straight-up fuckin *asinine*? I mean, think of it this way: there are about 4.85 times as many whites living in Illinois as there are blacks—yet there are almost exactly twice as many blacks in prison as whites. In other words, a black person in the state of Illinois is nearly TEN TIMES MORE LIKELY to be imprisoned than their white counterparts.

Please read that last paragraph again. And again and again, until you're hopefully at least half as outraged and mind-blown as I am. I'll wait.

Since I mostly used **O**s, you—My Dear Beloved Reader/s—could perform a task I deliberately made very simple: you can help *rehumanize* them [if you'd like to [or if you *need* to because it'd help you!]] by adding simple stickfigure limbs, as in:

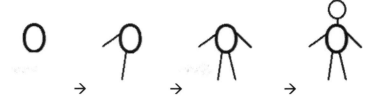

To humanize them even more [especially if you're somehow still, after we've gone through the everlovin goddamn philosophical fire together, after I've demonstrated all of it with clarity and abundant factual detail, you're *still* sitting on the fence like a . . . like a goofass fencesitting fool]— to further humanize them/us, if it would help you understand the precise #socioecopolitical dynamics at work, you could even color these guys in! This may facilitate a more thorough grasp of how astoundingly significant that *skin color* is in determining the presence or nonpresence of fair, true Justice in America—significant and also shocking, outrageous, infuriating, barbaric, archaic, et alia ad nauseum [NPI]. For the stickfigures of African descent, guess I would recommend a visual stroll through your crayon- or colored- pencil-carton's brownish hues; coloring in the cockasian fellows, though, might require a little more creativity, like using various iterations and possibly combinations of beige and/or pink and/or orange and/or red and/or etc. I said [well, *wrote*] the following not that long ago, but it most certainly bears repeating . . .

America is a *Prison Nation*. Plain & simple.

Exhibit A:

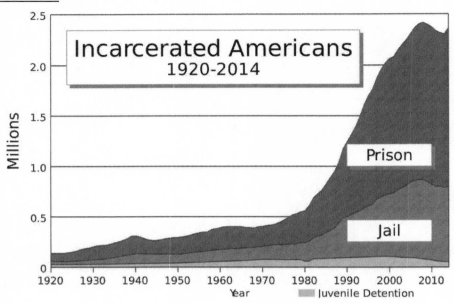

See the *massive* spike that's hinted at by the early 1970s and then skyrockets in the '80s? The spike that started at what seem like reasonable numbers—and they were, at least in the context of industrialized countries—and then nearly *quintupled* over the following 25ish years? Yah . . . that spike *IS* America's so-called War on Drugs. Both symbolically and literally. And blacks are disproportionately affected by this War. The disproportion's truly astonishing in scope. The following is an established fact: on average, blacks and whites use narcotics at very close to the same rate. Even more telling, whites are *more likely* to sell drugs! But blacks are prosecuted for drug offenses substantially more often. According to a 2009 report by the advocacy group Human Rights Watch, blacks are more than three times as likely to be arrested for simple drug possession than whites. And it's not just arrests, but convictions too. Per Bureau of Justice statistics, in 2011—right smackdab in the middle of my incarceration—about 225,000 Americans were serving time in state prisons on drug charges; whites comprised about 30 percent of that number, whereas blacks are all the way up at 45 *percent.* And that's total numbers; not taking into account how blacks only make up 12ish percent of the U.S. population! The discrepancies are more dramatic in some places than others [e.g. good ole Illinois is particularly stark], but it's definitely a nationwide issue. In fact, get this: There isn't

ONE.SINGLE.STATE in America where the percentage of blacks in prison isn't greater than the percentage of blacks residing "freely" in that state. *Every single one!*[45]

Finally, a couple telling little tidbits . . .

[1] America imprisons blacks at a higher rate than *apartheid South Africa* ever did.

[2] More blacks are locked up in the U.S. today than were in bondage at the *height* of *antebellum slavery.*

All in all . . . holy shit, right?! I mean jeezus, it's almost as if . . . as unbelievable as it may [though shouldn't] seem, it's almost as if the War on Drugs is used primarily as a *weapon* to *target and incarcerate* people of color! Shit—given all this indisputable info, it's almost like the War on Drugs could more accurately be referred to as the WAR ON BLACKS! I think the Derrick Jensen quote I cited above from *The Culture of Make Believe* has become even more undeniable, so here it is again; I think it's as

---

[45] Info gleaned from numerous sources, including:

[A] *The Huffington Post*, www.huffingtonpost.com/2013/09/17/racial-disparity-drug-use_n_3941346.html

[B] Human Rights Watch—the following links to a 2003 report called "Incarcerated America," which includes, among other things, detailed state-by-state breakdowns of the abovementioned racial discrepancies that'll simply knock your damn socks off if you have half a brain or one-fourth of a conscience: www.hrw.org/legacy/backgrounder/usa/incarceration/

[C] A 36-page PDF—which contains an astounding 145 footnoted references [& you thought this book had a shitload of them!]—from the journal *Stanford Law & Policy Review*, available here: https://journals.law.stanford.edu/stanford-law-policy-review/print/volume-20/issue-2-drug-laws-policy-and-reform/race-drugs-and-law-enforcement-united-states

[NOTE: Some discrepancies in precise numbers among the materials cited in this book are inevitable, given that they come from different sources reviewing materials at different times, with sometimes-alternate definitions of important variables; that's why I've attempted to provide a broad range of source material—in addition to distilling the massive amount of information in somewhat more general terms as best I can. Naysayers should keep in mind that, while some sources may cite slightly different statistics, broad trends remain the same.]

good a way as any to end this section. "Our judicial and penal systems form a massive interlocking set of racist and terrorist organizations, [the latter of which] is defined, remember [*oh, I remember!*], as one that deters through terror."

#MicDrop

PART 3

Doin' Time
[*How the Hell is This Still a Crime?!*]

I.

Today, Rachel's visiting for the first time.
It's August 10th now and I've been at Jacksonville for nearly two months; haven't seen my darling since May 19th, on that early morning drive to San Francisco International Airport.

The C.O. lets me into the main visiting room after the obligatory strip-search and I see my beautiful sweetheart sitting at a table on the room's opposite side. By the end of the vending machine row. My heart *FLIES* the moment I plant eyes on her. I can't believe this is happening! Can't believe it's been four months since I've seen her! I'm almost fully integrated into prison life now; certainly accustomed to the routine. Everything outside the Prison Vortex seems *surreal*, like a different realm, and quite possibly fake altogether. Right now I'm seeing Rachel in a way eerily similar to how I saw her when we first met, at the vegan store in San Diego where she worked—when she was just this hot tattooed chick with a badass non-chalance, and I thought she was out of my league.

Rachel stands when I enter, smiling widely in her gorgeous, toothy, singular way that's reminiscent—but not the same—as Julia Roberts's smile. One that seems to say, *I'm crazy about you*—and *lucky to have you*. I'm sporting a grin now too, except mine's much goofier. Because it's mine. Our bodies nearly *slam* together when we embrace. I run my hands up and down her back, along her rump, across the soft flesh of her sensual neck. Then I scoop her off the ground and she giggles. Set her down and we kiss as passionately as two people can kiss without using their tongues—No Tongue Allowed!—and then we pull back to gaze into each other's eyes, then kiss again. You know what they say about absence and the heart? There's that, of course. But also this:

Absence makes the *hard* go *fondle 'er*!

[That might be my favorite selfcoined phrase ever.]

"I love you *so much*, baby," she says as we head to our table, drawing out each word to affect yearning adoration. We sit down side-by-side.

"I love you too. Missed you so fucking much!" My voice cracks.

"I *knooowww*."

The words may be unneeded—our bodies maximally communicative. We clutch hands, my forearm wrapped around hers like snakes entwined in a mating dance. Several minutes pass with few words. I'm studying her face, recommitting each curve and freckle and hue to memory so I can summon every last detail once she leaves. Marveling anew at her beauty: those lovely light brown eyes flecked with hazel, her full sexy lips, her skin so soft. She grins, dipping her eyes and head several times [which motion causes an adorable pendulum-sway in strands of her redwood-colored hair], laughing repeatedly, bashfulled by my laserlike attention.

"You're laughing at me?" I say. "Haven't seen each other for almost four months, and first thing you do is *laugh* at me?!" I'm grinning.

"No!" she cries. Giggling again. "I'm just so happy to see you! I can't believe it. Like it's not even real."

"Ditto. Totally know what you mean." I press a smooch atop her hand. She's wearing the engagement ring my mom gave me to give Rachel [the ring Dad #2, Jim, bought when he and Mom got engaged in 1990]. I'm glad the prison staff let her wear it. It brings her great joy—not because she's materialistic, but because of what it represents. "Is it my haircut?" I ask, and rub my stubbly scalp. "That why you're laughing at me?"

"No," she insists. "I like it! You look badass."

"Oh! Sweet!" I say in this weird growly voice—one of our unique intra-relationship idiosyncrasies. All couples have inside jokes, but we also have inside *affects*. "What about the CHOPS?" I ask, turning my head to provide a good look. I'm growing out my sideburns for the hell of it. They're approaching Wolverinishness.

"Rad. Totally rad." She runs her fingertips through one side. All three of my inmate photos [County, Stateville, Jacksonville] are saved on her computer. Apparently she'll stare at them and daydream while in class.

We talk about what's been going on: music, including the six new cassette tapes I just ordered for my Walkman; prison life; my writing; her classes. And we brainstorm wedding ideas, a lot.

Sexual tension runs through the entire visit like a severed, crackling powerline, its mighty electrical surge exposed, cord whipping between us spastically, metaphysically singeing us: it's hard for her, and *unbearable* for me. I've got half a boner just from touching and kissing her hands! Then she starts describing all the hot sexual things she wants to do. I'm fully hard in about six seconds. I feel an enterprising bit of sliminess atop my penis. A gob of eager, go-getter jizzum. From an evolutionary standpoint, I'm thinking some aspect of our DNA must've evolved to produce the whole *pre-cum* phenomenon. As if predicting that "Come *on*, please lemme stick it in for a few seconds—just the tip, that's it!" would become a ubiquitous desire in men across countless languages and cultures. Though the gob serves no purpose for me. I'm vasectomized! Take that, you unpleasant pinhead of goo!

So then anyway, when the Guard isn't looking, Rachel and I sneak little pecks on the cheek or forehead or lips. We've turned partially toward each other; one of my legs is between hers. I push my knee forward. "Scoot up," I whisper, glancing at the Guard. She does, and her crotch presses against my knee. I push inward, and methodically describe a vertical-oval-shape with it. She moans softly.

"Feels so good," she breathes. Eyes closed. Per her request, I grab one of her breasts and squeeze, lightly pinching her nipple through the blouse. Now I'm horny as shit, aching for some rough sex. I glance back. The Guard's facing away, talking to an inmate's parents. I reach down under the table and rub her crotch with my thumb. She closes her eyes and bites her bottom lip—one of the single hottest things she does while fully dressed.

Sadly I have to stop, lest the Guard notice; at just the right angle, he can glimpse beneath the table. If we're caught doing this kinda stuff, her visit could be "terminated"—as the Officer told me when he saw my hand on her knee a while ago. I set my hands back atop the table.

Keep in mind I've been surrounded for three months by nothing but hominid-type creatures with—I can reasonably assume—swinging dicks. And my lady is super beautiful and sexy. Plus I'm a writer, a firm believer in aggressive, APPLIED *joie de vivre*. "Living" should always be an active verb. I'm not content with a timid, traditional, riskfree life of quiet desperation. MY desperation shall be loud, bombastic, and raucous fucking *fun!* I hate authority and get a huge rush out of pushing the boundaries of what I can get away with [and the boundaries of my own fear, trepidation, et al.].

Rachel and I find this hysterical: the visiting room contains *three* single-occupancy bathrooms; they're labeled MALE and FEMALE . . . and then INMATE. Ha! Our first visit lasts the maximum four hours. She'll come four total days in a row, then drive her rental car back to St. Louis and fly home to Northern California. We received a warning earlier. But things get serious on the second day, jeopardizing her remaining two visits.

The next morning, we discuss a novella idea that's banging around in my head. She helps me brainstorm, and flesh out some important plot points. We're clenching both our hands together on the table. She's so gorgeous. So much unbearable sexual frustration brewing mutually inside. "You're beautiful," I say.

Earlier, she flashed me the top of her sexy pink panties. I wrapped an arm around her hip and slid it under the waistband of her gray cotton skirt. Trailed my hand up and down her panties, tracing the delicious ladycurve of her rump. *Man,* I was thinking, *really seems like we can get away with a lot!* A visit between two adults—one of them incarcerated for a long stretch—*should* allow intimacy. Conjugal visits [meaning private ones with a bed] aren't permitted in Illinois; not even for married couples. In fact, only six states in the whole country have legalized conjugals![46]

---

[46] Although I've heard from multiple other inmates that, until about 10 years ago, you could bribe certain Guards to get sex; supposedly your wife or girlfriend would give the Officer 20 bucks, & then s/he'd sneak you & your lady into the small laundry room next to the bathrooms, locking you in there for 15 minutes of whatever you can manage [after 3 months' incarceration, I could probably squeeze in a DOUBLEFUCK-session! and pay triple the going rate if necessary!] It seems

I truly believe all the visiting restrictions are more about control and domination, beating people down psychologically/emotionally, than about safety or the putative aspect of prison. Some "Correctional" facilities in America don't even allow handholding! Hell, some don't allow *any* contact—the visitor/s and inmate sit on opposite sides of that Plexiglass—no goodbye-hugs, nothing. It's goddamn pummeling inhumanity! Even at Jacksonville, with their somewhat liberal policies, visits are an exquisitely painful form of low-level torture. Here's a simple, straightforward way to look at it: Prison administrators are SUPREME cockblockers [or *twat-blockers*, if it's a female prison].

Soon, the bad-thing happens—Rachel and I reap the consequences of our fervid rulebending. A very tall [6'5" or more] and buff and douchey Officer, who looks and likely is in dire need of a substantial bowel movement, stomps through the front entrance. This is Officer Batterson. An ex-Marine. A douche, and a giant beast—Officer DoucheBeast! He speaks to the visiting room's Officer for a moment, both standing at the check-in podium by the door. Then DoucheBeast barks, "SMITOWICZ!"

I look over and raise my eyebrows. Already know what he wants; I'm just trying to buy time. "Yeah?"

"Come'ere," he says, motioning with a finger.

"*Go*," Rachel tells me. She wants me toeing the line and even kissing ass if need be—whatever it takes to not jeopardize further visits.

"*Can't go!*" I hiss. "Not yet, I've got a boner!" It's like being in high school again. I lean close and gibber some meaningless thing to Rachel. Turn in my seat and stretch my legs. Time ain't for sale, but I'm buying it all the same. Now my hardon is down to that pleathery half-erect state. Officer DoucheBeast grows more pissed every second. So I stand up. But the crotch of my blue pants still bulges, noticeably! I jam my hands in the pockets and push outward, which obfuscates long enough for my happy-junk to settle down.

Officer DoucheBeast stares at me with pure acid loathing. "See that part there?" he nearly shouts in my face as I approach, pointing to the **Visiting Room Rules & Etiquette** sign tacked to the podium. "It says, 'Kissing and

---

that prisons in most European countries tend to be far more humane and non-dehumanizing than here. At one facility in Poland, they essentially provide *hotel rooms* for married folks, complete with a pack of condoms. The Warden says it's overly cruel to deny married couples intimate privacy.

Hugging Only Permitted Upon Entering and Exiting.' So you two needa stop that goddamn happy-grabass bullshit!"

I yearn so very much to proclaim, calmly and with my eyebrows drawn down in feigned but believable confusion, *What about the part where it says No Profanity?!* But I'm already treading in deep and stingray-filled waters. So I just nod in placation.

"Wan'cher visits terminated, smitowicz?"

"No-sir."

"Ahright. So follow the rules, and DON'T make me come back here."

"Okay. You got it." I step back to our table. Correctional [sic] Officer DoucheBeast says a few words to the other Guard, then heads back to the Bubble—the central control unit where I'm assuming he saw us on the visiting room's camera feed.

Rachel's scowling. "Fuckin asshole," she mutters.

"Yeah." I'm pretty unaffected by it. Grown used to the typical day's dickheaded behavior of most Officers and Lieutenants [whose stern smarminess and general cuntishness tend to be that much worse than the stern smarminess and general cuntishness of most Officers]. Seems like the Guards' jobs have a lovely built-in mechanism of catharsis for them, whereby they can exorcise their anger at having such pathetic and worthless jobs/lives on us, the inmates. Most of the time I let their stupid horseshit slide past me. "Total prick," I say.

"And what happened to 'No Profanity'? He was cussing so loud up there!"

"Yup." Even though I've vented to her on the phone about how the Guards act, it's still shocking to see firsthand. Guess it's hard to believe how petty and moronic and spiteful they can be unless you're surrounded by it every day.

"Whatever," I say. "We just won't do that stuff anymore. Important thing is we're here together, talking, staring into each other's faces—your beautiful one and my ugly one."

"Shut *up!*" she cries. Tears well in her eyes and they take on a liquid sheen.

"What's wrong, babylove?"

"Just fuckin pisses me off! That asshole prob'ly has *no* passion in his pathetic, cushy life." A tear slides down her left cheek. Seeing its wet trail hurts me infinitely more than anything Officer DoucheBeast could say. "No passion with his ugly-cunt redneck wife, so he has to feel better about himself by making young passionate lovers like us miserable, n keep them from expressing their love. Not to mention humiliating you."

I stare at her and hold her gaze, conveying seriousness. Cork a thumb back over my shoulder at the door. "You think *that* was humiliating? Oh honey, you're so sweet. Guards do that kinda shit every day! How else'd they get their rocks off? Kinda like you said—they have pitiful lives in this lame-ass Podunk area, so they get entertainment and feel better about their shitty lives by putting us down. Wanna know what Mom told me that's helped me a lot?"

"What? Your mom's smart." Rachel's calmed down a bit.

"She made me promise not to allow these 'goddamn Podunk losers' to change the wonderful person I am—her words, not mine. Because that'd be allowing them to win. And you know what? I've gotten pretty good at ignoring their shit. I mean, of course sometimes it gets overwhelming and I can't stop it from being hurtful. Most'a the time though, I just focus on how it makes *them* more pathetic—not me."

Rachel's nodding, fervent. "That's really good advice. And so true."

"Yeah. Anyway, I want you to keep in mind how beautiful it's gonna be when we reach the end of this. Hopefully that'll help you get through at least some of the loneliness."

"We do have so much to look forward to." She gives my hands a quick, tight squeeze.

Each of her remaining two visits, we spend part of the time playing Scrabble. It's lots of fun in reasonable doses—a game or two at a time—especially when you allow words like *bung* and *schlong* and *cock*.

And then her final visiting day comes. As spectacular and ecstasy-inducing as her arrival was—that's exactly how emotional her departure is, except everything's reversed. Like grayscaled photos. Her visits were inexpressibly wonderful; but they also have a strange effect. Once the euphoria passes, I begin to miss her even more than I had previously—I'd grown somewhat accustomed to the separation, and now I'm back to where I was the moment we said goodbye at San Francisco International.

In some ways during incarceration, an emotional flatline can be better than having extreme happiness—with its corresponding letdown and depressing after-effects.

2.

I figured I'd begin the *Doin' Time* portion of this narrative on a happy note. Hence the above. Sorry for the timehopping; hope it wasn't too jarring. I wanted to start on an upbeat because, soon after making it to Jacksonville— though it was unspeakably better than County and Stateville—I realized it very much presented its own unique challenges.

Well so now I'm jumping back to June 13th, a couple months prior to Rachel's afore-described trip out here. Back to the day I reached Jacksonville. Feeling like a war refugee—and in some ways looking it!

After the intake process, I head to 3-House. The eight-foot-wide gravel "Walk" forms a loop around the big grass field near the prison's geographic center. The Walk connects everything: Health Care, Gym, Chow Hall, Yard, etc., with tributaries branching off at each building. The five housing units are identical in design. Here's a satellite view of the grounds. Notice the lifeless, almost total lack of vegetation.

I stop on the entrance path leading from the Walk to my new home for a moment; it's a squat redbrick building. Grass yards surround each unit and flank the paths. Concrete tables dot either side. "KEEP IT MOVING," a voice booms. I look up at the nearest Guard tower. An Officer with a megaphone stands there watching me. I hurry inside.

It's air conditioned; highly pleasant, restorative even, after trudging through the summer humidity. I lucked out bigtime here. Turns out only a handful of the state's prisons have air conditioning. Gotta appreciate everything positive now—no matter how small! I approach the front desk, occupied by two Officers on every shift. This area's called the "Bubble." Each house has two units, A and B, left and right, respectively. Mirror images. On opposite sides of the Officers' desk, the doors stand beside large Plexiglas windows [so Guards can look into the units].

I enter B-wing. The showers are immediately to the right, a tiled area of about 50 square feet demarcated by a five-foot-high wooden partition and latching door. The dayroom is on my left. It's about 20 feet long and 60 wide. Against the left wall are two payphone-type telephone boxes, each mounted inside a cubby the color of scuffed old nickels. A television rests atop their shelves in both back corners. Five wooden benches are bolted to the dingy tile floor in front of the TVs. Finally, maybe a dozen orange tables [identical to those in the Chow Hall] are scattered throughout the room. It's surprisingly quiet right now. A handful of guys are watching TV; others occupy a few tables, playing chess or dominoes or cards [the dayroom's open from six a.m. to nine-thirty p.m. Neither TV is *ever* off during these hours. And, between breakfast and nighttime, guys are always playing at least one game of chess and/or cards.] I soon realize the unit's relatively empty and peaceful because most guys are out at afternoon Yard.

The bathroom is next to the showers. A big open room with abraded white tiles lining the floor, like the dayroom. A line of thirteen sinks runs along the left wall. The first one is several feet deep and made of beige plastic, like you'll see in garages and auto shops; it's often used for washing dishes. The rest are white porcelain, each with its own mirror. Opposite those are the couple urinals and five toilets. Partitions of white stone sit on either side of each toilet; they're not quite tall enough, so your head is visible above them. The partitions extend a few feet past your knees—with, significantly, no door or curtain or viewblocking apparatus of any kind in front. Thus:

When you're sitting down to shit [or masturbate]—unless you're very short or you hunch over spina bifida-like—bathroom goings-on occupy your peripheral vision, sabotaging any illusion of privacy the stone walls provide. And since they're totally open in front, if someone uses a nearby sink, it further chips away at said illusion. Sometimes you'll lock eyes for a second with a dude through his sink's mirror, and all you can do is hope desperately that it was an accidental glimpse [in the mien of my seeing craig's bloated saggy ballbag through his 4XL boxers]. Yes, you do grow accustomed to this daily low-level degradation. But there's a clearcut limit to the normalization—you're always at least somewhat uncomfortable, a feeling you must actively suppress.

There's something to be said about the withering psychological effects of having no privacy, no *real* privacy, EVER—to which I will speak in the relatively near future.[47] [Though this future will be not-so-near for me: could be weeks or months before I discuss it in the long process of *writing* this memoir, but probably nearer in the future for you, through the process of *reading* this memoir—unless you're a slow reader, or this is a terribly boring book, or even worse, both].

A hallway past the bathrooms leads to our living quarters. Five doorless "dorm" rooms with ten bunkbeds each. I'm in room six; inside, a bald heavyset white guy with a scraggly goatee named shawn offers me use of his shower sandals until I can procure my own from Commissary. I'm simultaneously grateful, suspicious, and worried that he's only being nice because I'm white—and that accepting his offer will somehow constitute an association with the Aryan Brotherhood or something. Really need to learn the ropes here, and fast, lest I get *strangled* with one. This place is a whole different beast than County and Stateville. Applying County Jail logic to prison would be like cutting off the head of a Hydra because it worked on the Cyclops!

At least I've finally reached my bunk. Second on the left, up top. The checkered-tile dorm rooms are about 25 feet wide. Extending some 40 feet back from the entrance. Five bunks running up each side, dark shitbrown steel bunks, with a six-foot walkway up the middle. Each bunk is separated from the neighboring one by about five feet. This is where we get dressed, the space our bodies occupy when we're moving to or from bed, and so on.

My thin-steelslab bunk already has a mattress, but no sheets or pillow yet. Just a faded blue- and beige-striped mattress splotched with pervasive multihued stains, probably from coffee and various things of a DK-DWK nature [for the second and final time, that's an abbreviation I coined meaning Don't Know, Don't *Wanna* Know]. There's a ladder soldered to each

---

[47] Unless "There's something to be said" itself constitutes *saying something*; if that's the case, then in the relatively near future I will say *more* things about the withering psychological effects of never having real privacy ever.

bunk. My knees are so painweak it feels like they won't support my weight for much longer. So I climb up my bunk's precarious ladder and collapse onto the gross old mattress. Stomachdown, with only my hands for a pillow—still *vastly* more comfortable than Stateville. I try to relax; my body's worn ragged and exhausted, though my mind races with nervous agitation. So many new people! and here, I actually have impetus to *not* be antisocial. Such a strange and unknown environment; at least in County and Stateville almost everyone was "On the New." But there are guys here who've been locked up for *years!*

Apparently we newbies will receive our bedding and toiletries and property boxes sometime later this afternoon. All we can do is wait. I've always been an impatient person. Chronic pain makes it that much more severe. But I'll quickly learn that a veritably titanic amount of time in prison is spent just . . . waiting. Waiting waiting waiting, with nothing but pain and tormenting thoughts for company. *Hurry up and WAIT!* is one of innumerable prison-sayings; some of which are cringeworthy-moronic, others magnificently clever. It really is its own little world. Galaxy, even. So much waiting—I hope the prison experience, if nothing else, will buff down the sharp edges of my terrible impatience.

Soon hordes of people are storming the unit. Back from Yard. They're deafening and rambunctious and sweaty, offgassing prodigious B.O. They run into the rooms to grab towels and soap and shampoo and then dash back out to queue up for the showers. Christ, I don't even wanna *imagine* showering with four to six other guys at once! I vow right then and there to take mine, whenever possible, at low-traffic times. My cellie comes in and greets me [obviously we're not in cells, but I guess "bunkie" sounds a bit too . . . "faggish" for prison]. A short Texican with deep brown skin and stubbly black hair, he goes by the moniker *biz*. "Wassup cellie?!" he cries, grinning.

I can't tell if he's one of those douchey pricks who act excited to meet white boys, but they're really just teasing you. Sharing some nonsensical inside joke with other proximate nonwhites. biz, though, does seem to be genuine. "Hey man. I'm jan."

He regards me sidelong. "Oh, hell no! Y'gotta have a prison name, bro. 'jan' ain't gonna work."

Grin and shrug. "Guess it'll haf'ta work! It's the name my mama gave me."

biz nods, pursing his lips. He glances at his neighbor, kazeem. "All right then," biz says with a chuckle. "If you say so. I'm yer cellie, so I gotcher back." He respects that I stood my ground—didn't show weakness just because I'm white and/or On the New.

Eventually we of the Big Bird costumes—mine with its chocolate poo-egg in the laying region—are summoned to Personal Property [an Officer leans his head in from the Bubble and shouts out our bed numbers]. The Property Building's across the grounds, next to the Chow Hall. We each receive two thick black plastic boxes. One is the size of a small cooler, called the "legal box," for storing anything made of paper. The other box is way bigger, about four feet wide and three feet long. It's for everything else—clothes, Commissary food, toiletries, etcetera. The smaller, legal box contains: a tiny towel like you'll see in Motel 6 bathrooms, so thin it's impossible to fully dry a grown man, and just barely big enough to wrap around your waist; a fingersized, flimsy orange razor; a tube of the same shitty clear toothpaste craig and I used as glue and minty airfreshener; and one of those silly little goddamn antishank toothbrushes, which require sticking half your hand into your mouth to reach the back teeth. Better than nothing though!

By the time I manage to schlep the bulky-ass boxes back to my room, I'm drenched in sweat [and I don't perspire easily]. I slide the boxes under my bunk and collapse on my mattress. Now I yearn to shower and shave. Still don't have any clean clothes though; we won't get our state-issued "Blues" until tomorrow morning. There's one word that perfectly encapsulates my physical state—and it's a synesthetic word, too, one that sounds and even *looks* like its meaning. That word is GRODY. I have a pretty high acceptance-level of grodiness. But here, *here* I'm living in a room packed with 20 men. Many of them with utterly disgusting habits. This causes a de facto shift downward in my ability to tolerate grodiness.

A thought occurs to me; it's one of the only things that'd cheer me up: *talking to Rachel!* We've been contact-severed for thirteen days now. The longest ever by a factor of thirteen! I gingerly climb down once more from my bunk and head to the dayroom, harboring the uncomfortable, imagined [?] paranoia that everybody's staring at me. Appraising me. Searching for weaknesses—which are not exactly hard to find. I'm a back-clutching, kneerubbing, grimacing, sometimes limping *advertisement* for weakness.

First I try the phone-cubby facing the showers; it flings painful static screeching into my ear. Broken. I walk around to the other side's phone;

its cubby-alcove opens toward one of the blaring TVs. I enter my ID and then Rachel's cellphone number. It begins to ring! I'm hopeful, despite the crushing heaps of learned despair heretofore experienced. But this time my hopes don't prove toxic and hurtful. Rachel picks up! I can tell by the first two phonemes of her "Hello?" before the operator cuts her off. An electric surge crackles inside me, and chills shiver throughout my whole body. "BABY!" she cries with unfettered joy after accepting the call.

I slump against the gray wood partition of the booth, tears rapidly filling my ocular cavities. I let them come—they'd be impossible to suppress anyway, and I know it. I'm overcome with relief and love and happiness [and yes, grief too]. "Hi baby."

"Oh honey, I'm so glad to finally hear your voice! I got your letter from Stateville. SO terrible, all those awful things you went through. My poor angel!"

I *whoosh* out a diaphragm-deep lungful of air, shaking my head. "The things I wrote in that letter were barely anything. I mean it—you can't imagine how fuckin miserable it was. But I didn't wanna make you even more bummed 'n worried."

"I could tell it was terrible, but you sounded so upbeat! Given the circumstances, I couldn't *believe* how positive you were. I'm so proud of you, my janny-darling. You're unbelievably strong and brave. And now the worst part is over!"

"Should be, yeah."

"It is, baby. It is. How's . . . um . . . Jacksonville?" She giggles. Smile audible. "I actually knew like several hours ago that you were being moved today. Prob'ly before you even got there! I randomly checked your IDOC page at school, and it said you were located at Jacksonville Correctional Center." So she researched the facility, found its geolocation, and learned some stuff about the place before I even arrived.

I grin, my flesh still tingling all over with that charged elation. "Such a clever girl!"

"Yep." Smiling again, I can tell.

"Well, things're okay so far here," I say. "Just barely got to my unit like an hour ago. It's been insanely exhausting." I mention the bus rides and intake process. We chat for about 20 minutes, then agree to speak again in the morning.

The call has lifted my spirits tremen . . . wait. No, it didn't *lift* my spirits—it *skyrocketed* them! Lifting implies a slower, measured pace, and not much height—after all, you can only lift something so high. And now it seems like there's far less gravity sucking me down. Tugging on my entire . . . ENTITY, on every little aspect comprising this thing called *jan*.

Point is, now I actually have some energy—time to shave!

The short, flimsy, cheddar-orange razor is absurdly shitty. I'm forced to *rake* its single cheap blade across every square inch of my face, six or seven times each![48] And still it leaves stubble and whiskerpatches. I finally decide it's good enough after some 30 grueling minutes. The process has left about a dozen scarlet dots on my face, and a couple wide, surface-layer scrapes that leak blood for several rounds of holding wadded toilet paper against my skin. After such a long time without shaving, my face feels decidedly *naked*.

I grab my dormmate's shower shoes, along with my dainty towel and weirdly fat slab of white state soap, and hit the showers. Thankfully they are now unoccupied. I'm able to surreptitiously wash my boxers, scrubbing out the shitstain until there's only a phantomy splotch remaining. The shower is glorious. Revitalizing. And the water temperature is actually adjustable [imagine that]! So it's not scalding, skinreddening-hot like the flooded-sewer Stateville showercage. I wring out the boxers as best I can, but they're still too damp to wear. So I climb back into my banana suit with nothing underneath. There's no way I'll continue wearing that filthy t-shirt after such an invigorating shower. It'd been exactly a week since I last showered, and two weeks since shaving—I truly feel like a new jan. There's something gratifying about watching dirty gray water slough from your body; it feels like you *deserve* the shower's resource-usage, as if you've earned it.

Back in the room, I hang my boxers to dry on a coathook next to the bunk. My "upstairs" neighbor on one side, whose bunk sits against the entrance-wall, introduces himself as *dutch*. A handsome black guy who looks like a perfect cross between NBA stars Carmelo Anthony and Kevin Durant. dutch gives me a brand new stick of roll-on deodorant; another unexpected gesture of kindness. Naturally—given my luck—3-House goes to Commissary [aka "Store"] tomorrow, but I have zero monies "on the

---

[48] I feel like Mac [played by actor Bill Duke] in the movie *Predator* [1987]—the guy with skin the color of 72% dark chocolate—who's shaving anxiously with a blue plastic razor while Schwarzenegger et al. wait for the Predator to enter their jungle boobytrap. Mac presses down on the razor so hard it snaps in half & his face is cut & oozing blood. This feels like a legitimate possibility here for me.

books," as it's called. Mom dug through her purse on the back stoop of Henry County Jail right before I turned myself in. She pulled bills of every denomination from her wallet and various purse pockets and crevasses, pushing the crumpled wad totaling $174 into my hand. I then immediately turned and handed it over to the female Officer who stood there waiting for us. The money went on my books; but it has to transfer electronically from County to Stateville to here, and hasn't yet "caught up with me." So I won't be able to shop for eight goddamn days. Which sucks tit.

At least now I have sheets on my bed. An Officer in the Bubble gave them to me—but they're out of pillows. I have to wait till someone leaves and snag theirs, and do it before somebody else gets the chance; this process often involves bribing a guy who has a nice pillow, *weeks* before his release date, to give it to you when he leaves. The prison economy's full of ruthless competition. Until I can procure an actual pillow, I'll just use my gray blanket folded into a thick rectangle. The room's full now. It's six p.m., so they'll be running Medline in about 90 minutes; it'll be nice to finally have at least *some* relief from my anxiety and increasing pain.[49] I manage to doze off despite the room's noisiness. Twenty convicts in each dorm, five dorm rooms to a unit; that's a *lot* of inmates in these cramped quarters. I foresee many problems arising from this alone.

At 7:35, they run 3-House to Medline. As is customary, an Officer from the Bubble dips his head into the unit and bellows, "Medline! Medliiine! runnin now, let's go!" Those of us taking meds gather at the gate; each building is surrounded by its own tall chainlink fence, with a gate just off the main Walk that's always kept open except during emergency prison-lockdown; whenever we leave the unit, including for Chow, we assemble at the gate and then wait until the Officer who's "running lines"—which basically just entails standing somewhere in the central grass field and controlling inmate movement—signals for us to hit the Walk.

About a dozen of us head out for Medline. Though it's dusk, with the horizon severing that dark-orange orb in half, it's still super muggy. Damn Midwest! I'm sweating before we've even walked the hundred yards to Health Care [sic]. Luckily it's a cloistered building; the A/C has it nice

---

[49] During our intake-visit to Health Care earlier, the Doctor begrudgingly prescribed some light opioid pain meds—50 mg of Tramadol in the morning & night—on a potentially temporary basis, and only if I agreed to get my outside medical records mailed in ASAP, and to come back within a couple weeks for a full evaluation.

and cool inside. We hand our ID cards—which must be clipped to our shirts whenever we're outside "the crib"—to the frontdesk C.O. Then we take a seat on the waiting room's clustered wooden benches. Several posters hang on the walls. An antismoking advertisement displays two lungs; the 40-year smoker's shriveled, gnarly organ looks like something you'd find smoldering on the barbecue of an unceremoniously abandoned party, from which someone pried off several blackened chunks. Disgusting! Horrifying! Gruesome! Repellent!

It makes me yearn to smoke. Because it *reminds* me about cigarettes, and how they're no longer available. I don't even think about them most of the time. Couldn't care less. But every cigarette on TV—every charcoaled-lung poster—brings the roaring jones.

Back in 3B, I meet jaime, an extremely muscular black dude who sleeps below dutch. jaime's pecs bulge no matter what he's wearing—MuscleTits, as me and some of my friends would call him. Both he and dutch are practicing Muslims, as is kazeem, my neighbor on the other side. To be more specific, they are—according to the back of their ID cards—"Al-Islam Muslims."

At 9:30 p.m., the dayroom closes and everybody heads to his bunk. Two Officers powerwalk through the unit for count. Some guys are absent, working the night shift in Dietary. If anyone's unaccounted for, they move through the rooms for a recount. If there's *still* a discrepancy, the whole prison clams up—no movement—until they figure out where the person is. It's typically a simple mistake, quickly corrected. But now and then it'll be difficult to find the missing inmate. Hilarious example: six months or so into my Jacksonville residency, movement shuts down when they can't find a guy who should be folding napkins in the Chow Hall. Almost an hour passes before they manage to locate him. Turns out he accidentally got locked inside a walk-in refrigerator; he wrapped himself in layers of plastic bubblewrap against the cold. This becomes a high-mileage incident that provides laughter for many months.

I lie on my stomach after count, still tired despite my siesta. I fall asleep quickly. I'm graced with a long, unbroken block of sleep. Probably seven hours straight, the most I've had since my second night in Stateville. I'm awoken at five a.m. by the shuffling movement and not-so-quiet talk as guys get ready for breakfast. I'm not a fan of breakfast and I'm definitely not a morning person, usually sleeping till 10 or 11. But right now I need to cram as many calories as possible into my body; it'll help me recover from my dramatic weight loss of 19 pounds in 27 days.

[One last time: I LOST *19 FUCKIN POUNDS* IN 27 DAYS!!]

I slip my canvas shoes on and head out with maybe a quarter of the unit. Most guys skip breakfast; it's just too damn *early*. Unless there's something "special" on the menu, like pancakes or donuts.

They serve a large splatter of grits [hot, unlike Stateville's congealed globs], scrambled eggs from reconstituted powder, and bran cereal. I let a guy next to me shovel the eggs from my tray, repulsed by the smell alone— this happens to tons of people once they've gone without meat/eggs/dairy for a while. I cram down a few bites of flavorless grits and dry bran cereal. We also receive the familiar four-ounce "juice" cartons. At least the label is truthful ["Orange Drink" and "CONTAINS 10% REAL JUICE"].[50]

Here's the complete ingredient list in order: *Water, Corn Syrup, Orange Juice Concentrate, Artificial Flavors, FD+C #1* [WTF?!], *yellow #5, Sodium Benzoate, Potassium Sorbate.*

Yum! Breakfast of Champions.

It's clear to me now—this dietary situation is untenable. Gotta figure out an adequate barter system. Or maybe they have a designated vegetarian tray? Doubtful, but possible. Better find out ASAP. I *cannot* continue eating anywhere close to what I did in County and Stateville. I'll get sick, dangerously underweight. Thank Earth I had the foresight to pack on some chub in the couple months before prison. I tell myself things will improve immediately once I get to Commissary.

My first week at J-ville is focused on acclimating rapidly to this strange and complex new environment. Everything you do [or don't do] is tangled up in *two* codes of conduct, and sometimes they're diametric opposites! There are prison rules [1], and then there's *inmate* etiquette [2]. The latter is far more nuanced and extensive, and of course no guidebook exists. You have to learn as you go; often through trial and error and frantic correction-slash-atonement. Violations of [2] may produce repercussions far worse than violations of [1]. A truism I'll learn the hard way.

---

[50] Reminds me of a hilarious standup bit by Dave Chappelle about the so-called grape juice he'd drink as a kid, which had "only three ingredients—water, sugar, and purple."

There is one thing that helps me feel like less of an outsider during this initial adjustment period. I'm fully aware that it's silly—screw it though, whatever helps! I'm talking about the NBA Finals between the Celtics and Lakers; the final, decisive Game 7 is happening just two days after I got here. Can't believe I escaped Stateville in time! Recall my telling craig how badly I wanted to see at least one game of the series; we agreed there was very little chance, yet here I am—just in time. I'm so restless for the entire gameday that I go to afternoon Yard. Something I didn't anticipate doing so soon after my arrival.

The Yard's surprisingly big. A rectangle maybe 100 meters by 300 meters.[51] Lots of thick, still-green grass. There are two volleyball nets— suspended over sand, no less! Two highschool-sized basketball courts. A big graveled area with free weights and benches and dumbbells. A horse-shoe pit. A side-by-side pair of handball courts with gray cement walls. An ovular gravel track, each lap an eighth of a mile. There's even a baseball diamond. With like the fences and clayey dirt and plastic bases and all that.

I stroll around the Yard's perimeter a couple times—right next to the dual fences. It'd be nice to pump some iron; the stereotype of returning from prison all muscleripped is a stereotype I wouldn't mind upholding. But not yet. I'm most certainly not ready for that scene, not comfortable or confident enough—because I'd be using the "girly" 15-lb. weights right next to swollen, tumescent-veined beasts with softball biceps hoisting 50-pounders like beer bottles.

So I just stroll. The heat-humidity combo is oppressive, especially since I'm wearing navy blue pants and a button-up shirt. These are my "blues"— the prison-issued uniform we have to don whenever we're outside the unit [except during recreation-time, when we're allowed to wear gym clothes; obviously I don't have that option yet]. Being outside is nonetheless glorious. The sky is an effervescent, cloudless blue, the grass so vivid; everything's, like, *technicolorish*. Another effect of my dim cell-bound month. Perspective can be such a powerful modifier! Even better, my knees feel okay right now. Maybe 3 out of 10 on the Pain Scale. This is connected to my feelings of relative freedom; my emotional/psychological state

---

[51] That's right, I used the metric system! Didn't want to use *yards* b/c I had, by necessity, just used the same word multiple times [i.e. *Yard*-as-proper-placename]. Look at this—you're getting a prison story *and* a periodic mini-primer on linguistics & wordsmithery! This memoir could rightly be idiomaticized as *Bang for your buck!*

cannot be separated from my pain. Same way race and socioeconomic class can't be detached. Nor can overpopulation and consumption levels.

After about an hour, a tower-Guard bullhorns that Yard's over. We head back to our units. [Yard and Gym schedules are staggered; for example, when half the prison—Houses 1, 2, and 3A—has afternoon Gym, the other half—Houses 5, 4, and 3B—gets Yard.] I'm tired. Leg muscles sore. But the endorphins are pumping and so I've got a headful of joyjuice. I'm feeling more upbeat, truly upbeat, than I have in at least a couple *months*. Now I just need to load up on Commissary food and toiletries, and get prescribed more appropriate medication. Then I'll be set to *cruise*. Establish a routine and let the months whisk away.

I'm stoked for tonight's championship game between the Lakers and Celtics! Haven't been this excited about basketball since 2003. I grew up watching the Lakers and was obsessed with them from ages 9 to 18. I still liked them in theory after that; but when I started college in late 2003, I had no TV in the dorms, and—in addition to class workload—I got really serious about writing and my then-girlfriend Veronica. Basketball wasn't very important to me anymore. And yet in prison, it seems like a helpful distraction. I already restarted the story based on my wild Stateville Lizzy-dream. I checked out a Stephen King book from the library called *Lisey's Story*, and I've been reading that like crazy. It's only my third day here; yet I've already undertaken productive, worthwhile activities. I deserve some mental distraction. *Need* it. Something that sends my mind into a largely worryfree zone of entertainment.

Thank Earth for my cellie biz. He's pencil-drawing with the game on, listening and every so often glancing up. [Commissary sells 13" personal TVs, which sit on the flat shelf extending out from the top of your bed—they're modified to work only with headphones, for obvious reasons.] He knows I'm from L.A. and excited about the game, and so invites me to sit on my legal box beside his bed to watch. Instead I plop down on the floor so I can stretch my legs out and lay them flat. biz even lets me use his headphones. He is indeed a nice, kindhearted guy. Really sweet, friendly, and thoughtful. He's locked up on a Manslaughter conviction. Or maybe it was Conspiracy to Commit, but close enough; he's been incarcerated for some four years already, during which he worked his way down from a maximum-security joint to a medium and then here via good behavior. This is the case for many guys at Jacksonville. dutch's cellie jaime has been down for almost *21 years*!

The game's second half is spectacular. The Lakers are losing for most of the game, sometimes by a lot, but they make a late run. Nearly everyone in the unit's watching. It's getting more loud and raucous by the minute. Guys yell at their TVs constantly . . .

GET THAT SHIT OUTTA HERE!

It creates a fun

POP THE FUCKIN 3!

sort of competitive

GUARD THAT BITCH!

atmosphere.

The final six minutes are epic, nailbiting fun. Every scored point brings cheers from that team's fans. In the end, the Lakers squeeze out a victory to win the championship.

That's awesome. But what happens afterwards here in the unit is even cooler. All the Laker fans are cheering, whooping, clapping and highfiving. I dash out to the hallway, joining guys from every room; we're elated, double-highfiving repeatedly, pumping our fists, even *hugging!* All of them total strangers to me and vice versa. It's a bitchin sequence of camaraderie and shared excitement, helping me feel dramatically more comfortable and welcome here. This is far from insignificant—silly though it might be. At last, a bit of happiness and connection to others in my new prison life!

A pleasant residual delight lingers for several days; but I'm worrying bigtime about pain relief, and terrified of being forced to work. Everyone needs to have a job assignment, whether it's porter [cleaning the unit], Dietary, cutting the grass, picking up trash around the prison grounds, tutoring in the classrooms, or myriad others. Porter's the only one that wouldn't leave me in ceaseless misery. Get this: even the higher-paying jobs make *25 cents an hour.* Which amounts to forced servitude, slavery.[52] I *need* the Doctor to place me on "Light Work Status." Not hopeful about my chances though, so my anxiety is nearly constant. My neighbors jamie and dutch keep insisting I'll be assigned to Dietary within a couple weeks.

---

[52] "Slavery is back—in fact, it was never abolished. In 1865, the 13th Amendment [to the constitution] . . . abolished slavery—*except in prison.* At the current rate of incarceration, by the year 2010 the majority of all African-American men between 18 and 40 will be in prison; the State as their captor, and their labor on the auction block" [emphasis added]. From historian Howard Zinn on aforementioned death row inmate Mumia Abu-Jamal's spokenword CD *All Things Censored, Volume 1.*

I tell them about my disability. But they just laugh. "Well," jamie says, "you *gon'* be workin, ain't no doubt about that. No, sir!"

Commissary rolls back around at last and now my money's available; whatever I end up getting, it's bound to feel like a windfall after a month-plus of scrounging. I'm so lucky to be a privileged white boy with a loving and well-to-do Mom of unparalleled generosity. She sent me an additional $400 before 3-House's Commissary day. I spreeshop, supplementing the paltry vegan food available at Chow. Bags of spicy dehydrated pinto beans, rice, Tapatio hot sauce, jars of pickled jalepeño slices, salsa, knockoff Ritz crackers, granola bars, peanut butter, knockoff Ramen Noodles, bars of cocoa butter soap [with CONTAINS NO ANIMAL INGREDIENTS right on the package!], dandruff shampoo, several pairs of socks and boxers and white shirts and gym shorts, a large towel, deodorant, and a couple washcloths. I also order a $220 digital TV [total gyp and borderline shake-down, though well worth it for the two years I'll be here], a "hotpot" to heat water for cooking, and a $40 Sony cassette player [also ludicrous, but music is so important to me—plus it greatly aids my writing, and writing is my life]. Finally, a pair of cheap, nonleather tennis shoes; mysteriously called "Bob Barkers." They do have nicer shoes—Adidas, Reebok, Nike— for $40 to $90. But I won't support huge multinational corporations that use sweatshop labor if I can avoid it; plus it's just the principle. Frugality is part of who I am. Mom would be proud. Hopefully she'll find a few admirable things in this memoir, mired though they are in the muck of my grossness and depravity and deviancy and foul language.

Guys schlep Commissary items back to the unit in their mesh laundry bags; mine's fit to bursting with my haul. As I walk back through the unit, people stare hungrily at my bag [*mesh* bag, not *ball*bag]. The vultures have pegged me as a mark, and I'm a focus of their hovering intrigue. Guys with few resources—nobody on the outside sending them money—seek out unsuspecting people who don't yet know the ropes. Acting like they're your buddy, watching out for you in the spirit of simple kindness. It's all part of their manipulative grift.

This one dude, casper, starts talking to me one afternoon on the way to Chow. Telling me about a "bitch" he dated from California; the vultures will latch onto any connection, no matter how oblique, and try using it to their advantage. Like you're suddenly their best pal. Later that same day— having in his mind established kinship—casper asks me for writeouts, noodles, other random things. Sorry but no, I tell him. "Can I jus' get some hot sauce then? You got any spicy cheese? Oh, yer vegan? Don't eat *no* cheese? Ahright then, that's cool bro! I respect that. Think you could spare a shot'a beans?" When biz got to 3B, casper helped him carry his boxes into the room—and then asked not for something specific, instead saying, "Ey, whatchoo got?" As in, tell me all the stuff you have and I'll pick what I want from there. Ha! Also, biz and a couple other dudes tell me that casper may well be into young men. Eek! I love gay people, but only platonically. The closest I've come to experiencing rape is watching the prison shower scene in *American History X* [1998] when Edward Norton gets assaulted. That's plenty close enough for me, thanks!

I'm learning prison culture fast now that my bit has begun in earnest. So much *gossip!* A shocking amount; so pervasive it's damn near impossible to know whom I can trust. Who's being sincere versus the massive number of humanoids "on bullshit," acting disingenuous to try gaining power or material goods. Then there's a particular strain of convict that enjoys the simple satisfaction of getting over on people.

Guys here run *some form* of hustle in droves. The inmate microeconomy provides endless fascination. Some dudes offer manual labor services for a fee—cleaning shoes, washing dishes, fixing broken electronics, etc.—while others draw portraits or create hallmarkesque cards for guys to send their loved ones. The craftsmanship and ingenuity is astonishing [I'm always witnessing crazy new ways to utilize everyday objects, which you'll see throughout this narrative].[53]

I sign up for "Sick Call" about five days after arriving. Oy!—Sick Call is for people who have acute injuries, or like the flu—as if my debilitating condition were a temporary malady that just popped up! But see, each bureaucratic barrier erected between you and the Doctor weeds out ever more people. It's oh-so-telling that there's precisely ONE medical Doctor for all nonpsychiatric issues. One Doctor for *one thousand* inmates. Think

---

[53] Uh-oh, another chink in the Fourth Wall ... Good! I'm tearing that bastard barrier *down* in this memoir. I wanna speak directly to you, my Dear Beloved Reader. I hope you'll get to know me—as both author *and* person—more & more. I want you to be thinking about this #Januscript as a painstakingly crafted narrative *and* as a completely true, unembellished personal story. B/c I have literary integrity, unlike some memoir-writers. I won't name James—I MEAN NAMES!! Shit. This footnote alone has shattered the Fourth Wall into "a million little pieces." HA! A joke *totally* worth risking a lawsuit! [*Ed. note: we strongly recommend the author remove this sequence about James Frey's* A Million Little Pieces *to avoid admittedly ludicrous but nonetheless existent potential legal issues.*]

we'll receive anything remotely approaching adequate medical attention with that ratio? The whole charade is eerily reminiscent of the vicious [and viciously effective] Social Security Disability process; they force you to jump through so many hoops, in such a difficult, drawnout process, that people who *truly* need help have extreme trouble completing the myriad requirements.

I'd like to please grind my ax against Social Security for a moment. I learned the heartbreaking way: their goal is *not* providing aid to people with disabilities; on an institutional level, they don't give a shit about determining whether or not you need help. Their goal is to *find a way* to deny your claim for benefits. Not only that, the whole process takes four to six months. Sometimes far longer. HOW THE FUCK DO THEY EXPECT YOU TO LIVE DURING ALL THAT TIME IF YOU'RE ACTUALLY DISABLED?? If you truly can't work—as I couldn't, which is why I had to leave my hardware-delivery job in San Francisco—how're you supposed to afford rent, food, and other basic necessities while you wait to be accepted or denied? Not only that, how's this one for yet another wicked, impressively pernicious catch-22: If, during the 4-6+ month process, you're making more than [in my case] about $900, you can't even *apply*. Think $900/month is enough to live on ANYWHERE in California—let alone San Francisco?! I literally would've been better off if I'd been *fired* from my job than had to leave for medical reasons. No joke. If you're fired, you can start getting unemployment in a couple weeks, and continue getting it for up to *two years* if you're "looking for a job." I know people who got fired and just rode that gravy Unemployment Train, putting in not a single job application the whole time. But I couldn't get Unemployment, because I wasn't fired—I left for medical reasons. Similarly, I know or have met a bunch of people, like easily upwards of a dozen, who aren't truly incapable of working [based on their lifestyle, or the fact that they actually *do* work in addition to getting Disability, getting paid under the table]. Yet they managed to get on it. What I said earlier about the U.S. "Justice" System— that the best minds of a generation couldn't *design* a more idiotic and unjust system—applies just as well to the Social Security Disability system.

Contemplating the similarities between prison health [sic[k]] care [sic] and Social Security [sic] is helpful in understanding the very basic purpose and function of the modern Bureaucrazy. Social Security . . . the health insurance industry . . . the "Justice" System . . . the Prison-Industrial Complex . . . governmental institutions and their politicians . . . all of them operate on the same basic principles, and the Bureaucrazy is the best way to facilitate and enact those principles. Not to help people who need help. Not to better the world or particular communities. Rather: to prop up the false veneer of fairness and democracy, and to best enable the control of tons and tons of people, and finally to ensure the smooth operation and further growth of the industrial economy. Everything in prison is a perfect microcosm of these ideas.

It's infuriating and nauseous, inspiring a cancerous hatred for society; for the System. The great hero Nelson Mandela—still alive when I was in prison [Mandela, not me]—knew it. At one point my mom suggested— and I heartily concurred—that there'd never be a more appropriate time in my life to tackle his autobiography *Long Walk to Freedom*. It proves to be spectacular, monumental, and terrifically inspiring to my prison-self. The entirety of his life represents a staggering achievement: to wit, the glorious triumph of the human will over unspeakable suffering and injustice. I pro-claimed earlier that his memoir should be required high school reading. Well, every prisoner in the world with sufficient means should also make it a priority to read *Long Walk*. Reading the memoir as a current or ex-felon provides a vastly more expansive understanding of Mandela's experiences. [NOT that I recommend committing a crime with the intention of getting imprisoned so that you can more fully appreciate Nelson Mandela's auto-biography—unless, that is, we're talking about effective, dramatic crimes of compassion that save animals' lives, whatever wildly variable form said crime/s may take—if that's the case, I'll admit that I *miiiiight* recommend it after all!] Yes, President Mandela learned a thing or two about prison in his life. "It stands to reason," he wrote, "that an immoral and unjust legal system would breed contempt for its laws and regulations." I agree! It *does* stand to reason! Though perhaps I'm biased: eventually, you may decide that the quote from Mandela perfectly expresses an *entire subtheme/leitmotif* this memoir's attempting to demonstrate!

In any case, this contempt being bred for America's legal system seems to be accelerating in growth. In my opinion. This contempt-breeding is birthing an evergrowing population [hey, just like human breeding! except the latter is destroying the planet.] It's not merely the people who are themselves incarcerated, or those who evade prison by copping guilty but still have that pesky felony remaining on their record like a turd in a punch bowl; that alone constitutes millions of Americans. No, it's their *friends and family* too! More and more, as the Drug War and other unchecked atrocities affect ever more individuals, it seems that more people than ever before now harbor mistrust or outright contempt for American "Justice." Doesn't help those in power that we've also ostensibly witnessed a large upswing in mainstream-consciousness-entering stories of nonblack and/or wealthy corporate twats receiving preposterously short prison terms [see Stanford rapist-douchemonster Brock Turner], or even no jail time at all [see banking-crisis executives' receiving bonuses]. More and more contempt. Growing all the time. Which may well prove to be a *very good* thing in the long run. The dying planet and all her endangered denizens, including humans, *need* more anger, more hatred for the Systems of Control that surround us. *Don't Just Get Mad*, I proclaim; rather, *Get **Even Madder** and then **Do Something About It**!*

   Sorry, one sec, gotta climb down off this scuffed ole soapbox . . . woop, careful, mind the knees . . . okay. So it took several days for me to foment the mental-emotional energy to seek better health care. I've been through such unfathomable, nearly con-stant medical-related bullshit since my initial knee injury way back in 2003. Innumerable condescending doctors have insultingly treated me—*before even examining my medical history*—like a fucking drug addict, simply because I was taking [prescribed] narcotic pain meds! Thereby revealing complete ignorance vis-à-vis treating severe chronic pain. When you take into account the veritable medical shitstorm I've been forced to deal with, the Stateville nightmare and its lack of health care was, believe it or not, the iceberg's tiniest tippytop. The iceberg to my life's Titanic.

   Hopefully this clues you in to my trepidation, my gutlevel dread, of visiting the Doctor here. In prison. The Prison Doctor. But I don't have a choice; I *cannot* survive for two years without an adequate medication regiment—I'll kill myself. No, seriously. And that's not something I say lightly; my wonderful older brother David killed himself in 2003 when he was 27 and I was 18—I found out about it literally two days after starting classes at UC Irvine. It had profound effects on me [both good and bad]. Certainly, I know the gravity of suicide and the devastating emotions it leaves in its violent wake. So I don't just go around saying I'll kill myself with impunity. It means something.

So believe me when I write that I'll kill myself if forced to endure two years in prison without at the very least a *livable* amount of pain relief.

The morning after I sign up for Sick Call, an Officer rouses me awake at 4:30; I clumsily throw on my blues and stagger off to Health Care. It's *already* warm outside, the air thick with mugginess; and dawn hasn't even lifted its blue gaze above the horizon! Midwestern weather is madness. Yet another thing to which I must acclimate. Why anybody would choose to live here is mystifying; the shitty ass weather being just one of numerous dealbreakers. Though I very much hope Midwest-residents adore living here—there's already far too many damn people occupying my beloved, native coastal California. Not to mention too many people occupying *non*coastal California. And every other state. There's really just too much human[un]kind on the planet. Period. Don't let doofus overpopulation-deniers fool you; they're *just* as deluded and ignorant about undeniable, straightforward ecological facts as evolution-deniers are about science.[54]

The Health Care Unit's fluorescent lights sting my groggy eyes—but at least it's cool inside. I assume the A/C runs all night, for the half-dozen guys so sick they're staying in beds here. The Nurse on duty takes my vitals, asking with total disinterest what's wrong. I'll soon learn this is the most abrasive and heartless of all the Nurses. And her appearance matches her personality: she's squat and fat and pointy-nosed; hair rustcolored and wispy like an ancient Chinese man's; plus she's balding, so much that you can see her scaly, brownsplotched scalp. She looks distinctly . . . *trollish*. I'm just one of the many guys who reach this same conclusion. Normally I'd feel sympathetic. But she's an unwavering cunt to me and everyone else I know during my entire Jacksonville residency, so from now on I'll refer to her as the *TrollNurse*.

---

[54] The easiest & quickest way to demonstrate the fallacy of overpopulation-as-myth—my antinatalism-advocacy-equivalent of *Study the damn fossil record!*—is this: even if ALL 7.42 billion humans alive today were to adopt the consumption habits of the average person in *Uganda* [hardly a bastion of conspicuous consumption], we'd *still* be extracting Earth's "resources" at an unsustainable rate! So unless you're <u>Sarah Palin-level bonkers</u> & think the average Ugandan lives w/ inappropriate luxury, you *must* admit we're overpopulated. Which we are. Hence my being vasectomized. And my staunch pro-adoption, pro-choice, antireligion advocacy. Source: www.worldometers.info/world-population [accessed 5/20/16].

I begin nutshelling my medical history for her. But she cuts me off after about 40 sec—

"So what is it you want?" Voice highly nasal.

I'm taken aback. "Uhm. Well, I hope to start getting better medication to control the terrible pain in both knees. And to make sure I don't get assigned a job that—"

"Okay." She scribbles briefly in my chart. "You'll be scheduled to see the Doctor."

"Uhhhm. All right then, thank you. Do I need to . . . uh . . ."

"Have a nice day, mr. smitowicz." She waddles off without another word. *Fugly McTrollNursington*, I think, shaking my head.

The next day is so miserable it's reminiscent of the endless day I left Stateville. In the morning, an Officer moves through the unit handing out "Call Passes," which're slips of paper with appointment information. I'm supposed to see the Doctor at 10.

Eight other inmates sit in the Health Care waiting room. I plop down on a bench. My knee pain's flaring badly within just 20 minutes; sitting for extended periods is one of my biggest pain-triggers and -aggravators. I didn't bring anything to read, assuming [foolishly, it turns out] I'd see the Doctor *sometime* in the remote vicinity of my 10 o'clock appointment. The ticking clock above the front desk has passed 10:45. I try to keep my mind occupied, brainstorming story ideas. But the ever-intensifying pain has begun to overwhelm my concentration. I'm unable to even *think* cogently for long enough to develop meaningful mental threads. THIS is why it's impossible to write without pain meds—and not for lack of trying!

I stare at the charred-lung poster. Thinking of Kurt Vonnegut, one of my very favorite writers. A lifelong smoker starting around age 15, he tried to sue Pall Mall cigarettes in the mid-'80s for false advertising—because they hadn't yet killed him! [The guy *lived* his art.] Really hope I don't pick up the Cancer Sticks again when I'm released. Mostly because I want *Rachel* to stop. I won't be able to resist if she's smoking when I get out, and vice versa. Pretty stupid to contemplate life-after-prison minutiae, but I can't help it.

Now it's been 90 minutes since my alleged appointment time. Still waiting for this elusive Dr. Williams. No magazines or reading material in the waiting room, of course. I'm going batshit from boredom and pain, fidgeting like a speedfreak as I try in vain to find a magical undiscovered position that'll ease the maddening stabbyburn-pain in my knees. It's getting *really* bad.

The Health Care Officer sends everyone off to lunch. That takes about 30 minutes. After returning, I wait another fucking HOUR. I've literally begun to sweat and breathe harder from the pain. By the time they finally call my name, it's past one p.m. More than *three hours* since I was forced to show up here! For the love of dog, where is the sense in bringing people here *three goddamn hours* before they see the Doctor?! We're already sick, uncomfortable—I could understand a half hour, even an hour early; you never know how long things will take, and of course it's better to waste our time than the Doctors'. But THREE HOURS? I'm absolutely not hyperbolizing—this is literal *torture* for me. Unconscionable! Pathological!

I start describing my condition to Dr. Williams in the examination room, and it takes a whopping 20 seconds for me to think, *Well, so much for getting decent care—this bitch doesn't give a* fuck! I'm perched on the butcher-papered exam table. She sits at a little desk just outside the room, looking at my chart. "Doctor," I call softly, "can I please move back so I can stretch my legs out? I've had five knee surgeries and I'm really hurting."

She leans over and her head appears in the doorway. Staring at me. The head looks hypercondescending and smarmy. Dr. Williams is a short and plump black woman, early 40s or so, not unattractive. Purple eye shadow. Black glasses resting low on her nose. The Doctor's head radiates a long, scrutinizing glare onto me. Somehow the head's face is guarded and self-righteous and bitchy all at the same time. She tilts the head at an angle, amplifying the effect. Her voice is even more smarmy and rude than the head/face. "You've had five knee surgeries and you're in *prison*?"

I'm flabbergasted. The hell's that even supposed to mean? My mouth must be gaping dumbly. Just what the Christ can I say to that? My first impulse is something like, *Are you* Doctor *Williams, or* Judge *Williams, you asshole? I -think- it's your job to treat patients, not make intellectual judgments on their mistakes!* If she utilized the spongy gray mass between her ears for half a second, she might realize disabled people have even more reason to commit crimes of financial desperation than other, able-bodied people.

Even Doctors discriminate against people with disabilities. I saw it well before prison, saw it in prison [especially], and yes, after prison too. I'd LOVE to see this uppity bitch try living for a mere couple months with the constant pain I've lived with for the last three years.[55] Bet she'd be *clamoring* for that OxyContin! But clearly she has no empathy—or even sympathy—whatsoever. She's become institutionally incapable of it. Or they hired her because she was already like this.

Finally I speak. "Uhm. I don't really see what that has to do with anything. I'm here."

She saunters into the room, staring at me with a smirk. It makes me feel subhuman. No matter how sure you are that you're not a bad person, that you don't deserve all this nasty resentful treatment, it still digs into your heart and your psyche, with sharp claws. And it hurts. It really does. Especially when your crime happened to be as victimless and nonviolent as they come. "Well, mr. smitowicz, you obviously did something to *get* here!"

I feel a powerful urge to suggest that, just maybe, the legal system isn't always fair. To bring up how the vast majority of the inmates here are black; and that, particularly since she's a woman of color, maybe she needs to question this. Question that cavernous racial disparity. Then again, she is a jaded, smarmy asshole, and I wonder if she's devoted even a moment's consideration to it.[56] I suppress—with no small effort [picture me, holding a fully conscious man's head underwater]—my profound desire to scream at her, to plunge my fist through the nearby glass cabinet, to smash the blood pressure machine against the wall. I wanna see blood. Even if it's just mine. And yes, I wanna break down crying, too.

I steel myself. Take a deep breath. Imagining a gentle wave that swells over me and washes off the black rage-muck in which I'm mired. "Yes," I tell her calmly. "I made mistakes that brought me here. *Huge* mistakes. But that doesn't change the fact that I'm here, and I have a serious illness, and I need medical care to function, and . . . yeah." I almost say, *and so I don't get suicidal*, but that's the last thing I need. They'd hustle me off to the "Naked Room" [suicide watch] before I could utter word one about how I was just hyperbolizing.

Dr. Williams smirks again. "So what's the problem, mr. smitowicz?" Her voice as flat as the surrounding cornfields.

---

[55] Now almost *TEN* years as I finalize this [early 2017].

[56] I actually think there's a decent chance it *has* occurred to her—and many others who work in prisons—but they've ACTIVELY, AGGRESSIVELY suppressed it. So they can do their jobs w/out succumbing to an insidious guilt. One that slowly eats away at their conscience like flesheating bacteria.

I sigh. Begin telling my extensive, complicated sob story; knee injuries long misdiagnosed and untreated, chronic debilitating pain, the countless different treatments I've tried over the years, etc. No surprise here: She cuts me off before I'm close to done. "Okay mr. smitowicz, but what is it you *want* from me?"

Once again I'm thrown off guard. Why's she being so abrasive, when I've been nothing but polite and deferential? "Well." My eyebrows draw downward as I decide how to best answer. "It seems like you're basing my medication regiment on what they gave me at Stateville, which kept me in debilitating pain. I couldn't do *anything*."

"I don't know what you expected before coming here," she says. "But this is a *prison*, mr. smitowicz."

I'm unpleasantly reminded—with an eery sort of echo—of that shithead emergency-call operator's words in Stateville when I pushed the button. "I understand that I'm in prison, ma'am. But it says right in the Orientation Manual that 'Health care is a *right*, not a privilege.' The medications I'm getting now are not adequately controlling my pain symptoms. Not even close."

"mr. smitowicz, we do not give out narcotic painkillers like OxyContin. We don't even have access to it."

"Okay." But I'm trying not to burst into tears; I've been prescribed just about every opiate/opioid painkiller in existence, and OxyContin helps by far the most, with the fewest side effects. Yet any legit pain med-dose is of course better than what I'm on now! "Surely there must be *something* more you can prescribe or do that'll help me get by, help me use my time here productively."

She gazes at me for a long moment. Considering. I practically hold my breath, trying not to even twitch a muscle. "We're not in the business of providing pain medication longterm," she says.

ohgawd-ohgawd-ohgawd kill me

"But how bout I increase your dose of Tramadol to two tablets in the morning and at night? We don't even normally do that."

I've been taking one 50 mg tablet of Tramadol twice a day. Dr. Williams has just doubled it. At this point it feels like a goddamn windfall! "That'd be much, much better. Thank you Doctor."

Writing the new prescription, she says, "I'd like you to get some x-rays. And please have your outside medical records sent in ASAP."

"Okay. No problem."

Back to the waiting room. Man, they sure do make good on the place's name! Another 20 minutes on that stiff wooden bench. Further stabbing-clenching pain. And my back's cramping now, too. Then the Nurse on duty, a goofy blonde I develop a pleasant rapport with over time, leads me into a different section of the unit to blast more needless radiation at me. I finally return to my unit and it's almost two o'clock; I spent close to four fucking hours in Health Care!

For many years now, writing—the expression and release of creative energy—has aided me in navigating countless difficult periods of life. The incomparable environmentalist and author Edward Abbey wrote my favorite novel, *The Monkey Wrench Gang*. It legitimately helped spawn the radical environmental movement, and generations of eco-activists. Abbey once said writers are the hardest people to live with, because we're either writing and obsessed, or not writing and miserable. That straightup *sings* to me. Ringing out with the perfect harmony of the deeply sagacious and true. For me in particular. My life feels worthless when I'm not regularly working on a project. This is the worst consequence of my pain [as I wrote before, it obliterates concentration and hence productivity]. Aside from the obvious palliative effect, narcotic medications are so worthwhile because they provide a vast increase in my ability to focus and accomplish complex mental tasks. [I'll say just one thing about addiction here: when you take opiates for a justifiable medical condition—not to get high—under a competent doctor's supervision, the rate of addiction plummets. We're talking a 30 percent rate for recreational opiate use that drops to under *two percent* with proper medical use!][57]

No matter what happens, I have to find a way to write. Have to have to have to. The mere thought of failing is unbearable; I *know* what will happen if I don't write a substantial amount—and not just in spurts—during this sabbatical. My depression and feelings of worthlessness will grow and grow, spreading like black mold to invade every last nook of my psyche. Then, since pain and depression and anxiety form that insidious, circular, self-feeding cycle, these symptoms will become ever more destructive. Devouring me like the Ouroboros snake in Greek mythology, whose body forms a circle as he consumes himself from the tail onward. Eventually—maybe I'd only last a couple months, maybe I could hold on

---

[57] *The Pain Chronicles*, Melanie Thernstrom.

for five or six, but it *would* happen—I'll feel so pitiful and miserable that I won't want to exist anymore . . .

The Living Purgatory.

My biggest consolation during this tough initial period of adjustment is that I have great music lifting my spirits, and a solid, fleshed-out story to write. Granted, at current medlevels, I can only write for a couple hours a day. Better than nothing though! And good music aides my writing process tremendously. *Even moreso* in here, with its obstreperous daytime noise. I begin working in earnest on my dreambased story, soon titled "Kissing Clouds." Writing by hand on yellow Commissary legal pads. I ordered a bunch of cassette tapes from a catalogue; stuff like Elton John, The Eagles, Supertramp, Bruce Springsteen, Creedence Clearwater Revival, and Neil Young. I'm really excited and motivated once those arrive. Unfortunately, we're only allowed 18 tapes at a time "on our books." So if I have 15 and order six more, I have to turn in three of them, which sucks. [Hey, even prisoners have First World Problems!]

The story and tapes help pass time wonderfully. No matter what's happening in my life, I can just push play and lose myself in writing and great music. Once the pain overwhelms my focus, I'll roll onto my stomach [the least uncomfortable position] with my headphones on and zone out for hours at a time. Contemplating plotlines, listening to my characters speak—for the current project and for others as well. The latter mainly being novels knocking around in my head. This all helps me avoid the prodigious ignorance and petty drama and dumb horseshit surrounding me. I'm awful at ignoring ambient conversations. If it weren't for cassettes and my TV's digital music stations, I do believe I'd bug up. Like mr. *it's mah birthday!* in Stateville.

I'm also reading a ton. When lost inside a book's world, I play classical music; it filters out most external noise without the distraction of lyrics. At this point I'm tearing through a shitload of Stephen King novels. This includes rereading his dark and wildly original seven-volume masterpiece of genre-mashup, the *Dark Tower* series. His books made me realize—very soon after I started reading him when I was twelve—that I wanted, more than anything else in life, to be a novelist. It's great that the library has dozens of King books. Also really helpful: I get loads of mail, especially my first couple months at J-ville. Rachel made a *Support Jan* Facebook page around the time we [unjustly, perjuriously] lost the Motion to Suppress hearing. It's paying off bigtime: Aside from the expected missives sent by close friends, I receive letters from people I haven't spoken to in years, and even a few from animal rights activist-allies I've *never met*! The outpouring of support is tremendous. Uplifting. I can't even keep up with all the letters! So Rachel sends a message to the group, saying how grateful I am for each and every one—that mailtime has become a daily highlight, whether I'm able to write back or not.

The first letter my Aunt Janet sends is memorably amusing; she pokes fun at the Guards, knowing they go through mail, and Illinois's rampant political corruption—

Dear Jan,

. . . .

So then I got to thinking that if someone has to read and censor your mail, he or she may be used to being referred to as a motherfucking cocksucker, but maybe one can't criticize the corrupt Illinois government. What state has more institutionalized corruption than Illinois? Maybe Louisiana on a bad day. What could be more pathetic than employment as a letter censor?
I got arrested once. The other arrestees were nice, but the guards were horrid. They were mean stupid and obtuse, but who else would chose that kind of career?

. . . .

Ah, that got me thinking, if someone is so pathetic as to be a letter censurer, paranoia and ignorance might lead them to believe that the above paragraph is coded somehow, so this next bit is for them.

6.21.3.11. 15.6.6. 13.15.20.8.3.18.6.21.3.11.9.14.7. 3.5.14.19.5.18.

With Love,

Janet

sent June 15th

P.S. Broadway Street is redundant don't those morons know anything?

3.

Every single morning at 7:15, I have to d r r r r a a a a a ag my ass outta bed for Medline. Weekends, holidays, terrible sickness; there are no exceptions, ever. If you're even five minutes late, you get a disciplinary ticket. I haven't been forced to overcome my natural sleeping patterns like this since I was a prisoner of that *other* soulcrushing shitheap of modern life— high school. Even then, at least I could sleep in on weekends and holidays! I believe with total certainty that humans should go to bed when they're tired, and wake up only once our bodies are ready. Within reason. That's how it *should* be—and I've had the wonderful fortune of being able to live that way, almost exclusively, since graduating from high school seven years ago. But no more!

One morning a few weeks into my Jacksonville residency, an older guy sidles up alongside me on the Walk. Probably in his mid-50s, with a salt-and-pepper beard, stubbled hair, and big redframed glasses. Far more people take medication in the morning than at night [there's a sensible reason, but it's irrelevant], and all five houses go to morning Medline at the same time [whereas at night it's one house at a time]. "Hey there," the older dude says to me. Voice kind and gentle. "Are you a born-again Christian?"

I look askance at him, chuckling a little. Seems like a weirdly specific question. "No, not at all. Why?" You rarely know what kinda jive prisoners are on; I've learned already to approach every new situation and person with caution. Hold my cards close to my chest in case they're trying to peep, and exploit the information to their advantage.

"Oh, no specific reason," the guy responds. "Just curious." We enter the Gym. The basketball court's polished wood panels creak underfoot. "If you ever have questions about that kinda stuff, please don't hesitate to ask— I'm always down to talk religion! I'm james, by the way."

I introduce myself and we shake hands. He begins walking briskly around the basketball court's perimeter, performing a kind of controlled-fling with his arms, way out forward and back with each step. Like a serious powerwalker, except he's eschewing the powerwalker's seemingly obligate psychotic pace. I join him, but sans armflinging. He lives in 3B as well. I've seen him around, and actually wondered about his last name; it holds ethnic intrigue for me. So I ask him, "Did your ancestors come from Czechoslovakia?"

"Yep!" We complete a lap. Passing the entrance and its obligate Guards' podium nearby. The Officer stationed there is a ginger with pale skin [even for a Midwestern ginger], and has a buzzcut despite his dramatically receded hairline. He fires a scathing glance at us for no discernible reason— other than your standard Correctional [sic] Officer◄─► inmate ire. "They did indeed," james says. "And hey, I'm impressed you knew it would've been Czechoslovakia back then, rather than the Czech Republic!"

I shrug with a halfsmile. "Knowing stuff is . . . good."

He gutlaughs, literally tossing back his head with a hand on his belly. As if he were a mad [though also goofball] prison-scientist. I didn't exactly think my sorta-joke about "knowing stuff" was *tummyclutching* funny! His endearing laugh and obvious intelligence have me immediately considering him for a potential friendship. I haven't made a single good friend yet; haven't even met someone I care to converse with on a regular basis! Even though I arrived almost a month ago.

Turns out james isn't here for Medline, but rather something called "Medical Gym." I've never heard of it. He explains how people with disabilities [that are Doctor-*approved*, anyway!] are provided with Gym access from 7:30 to 8:30 every morning. Normal Gymtime is packed like a factory farm, with lines for every machine, all of which tend to be set at weight levels varying from heavy to MuscleTits. But guys with Medical Gym—the Doctor has to "prescribe" it first—can exercise at their own pace; use whatever rehabilitative equipment is needed for their specific condition. And they won't be pressured and/or bullied into putting more weight on the equipment.

james got Medical Gym easily—he has a fuckedup, partially paralyzed clawhand. Don't worry, I'll describe the gruesome origins thereof soon. A dark little doozy. I'd *love* to get on the Medical Gym list with james. It'd be fantastic! Cautious, moderate exercise is crucial for me. Having at least some legmuscle strength helps support my knees, protecting them from yet more injuries. But I'm terrified; terribly worried about simply maintaining adequate meds from hefty, black, not-unattractive Dr. Williams. I feel like I MUST settle all that before thinking of anything else. Before exhibiting outrageous gall by asking her to sign a slip of paper so I can strengthen my legs under appropriate conditions.

My new friend james comes to Medical Gym every weekday morning to walk around the basketball court—22 laps = one mile, according to a posted sign on the wall. Right away, he impresses me with his unbelievable breadth of knowledge [except regarding the Christian thing—I do believe he's the first über-slash-outspokenly religious friend I've had as an adult!] He talks about the Czech Republic's different sociopolitical climates in the 20th century. When I mention that I'm technically a classically trained pianist, he shifts into a discussion about the great classical composers of

Eastern Europe—he's enamored with classical music. I relate [NPI] my Polish Gypsy and German ancestry, and that I'm related to the famous Bielski Brothers, Jews who led a forestdwelling underground resistance in Poland/Belarus during World War II. Bombing railroad tracks, raiding pro-Germany farms, killing Nazis, and other fabulous outdoor activities. I tell james how proud I am to be related to such incredible warriors. And how there's even a movie about them: *Defiance* [2008], with Daniel Craig and Liev Schreiber. james is a movie buff too.

I'm thrilled to've found someone intelligent, articulate, interesting, and socially conscious. As a lifelong knowledgeseeker I'm drawn inexorably to him, and vice versa. Like gravity. This despite his being a hardcore Christian; he's so great in such a multitude of other ways that I can find it in my heart to look past the religiosity.

We've both decided the vast majority of guys here are dimwitted, petty, ignorant, misogynistic, homophobic, and borderline [or not] sociopaths. Some combination of these—along with a hauntingly weird slew of other creepy ambiguous shit, plus some crack rock or crystal meth speckled on top just to further enrich the idea. I hear this guy in our unit tell the same unsettling story *three times* in the Chow Hall. And I mean identically the same—he probably tells it every day, and I just happened to be near him those three times. Supposedly, he got in a horrific car accident a few years ago, leaving him in a coma for several months. But he didn't break any bones, recovering quickly once awake. He attributes this to—wait for it— his mother's having breastfed him until the age of 12. Until the age . . . of 12. Breastfed. *Till twelve.* You can imagine the savage responses this elicits; yet he keeps right on telling it!

A guy in my room boasts that he facepunched his girlfriend for talking back to him. Real tough! we're all so impressed! Another time, a bunch of dudes in the room have a 45 minute argument that crescendos screamward and nearly escalates into a fistfight. The contention is whether or not Chicago's the murder capital of America. Forty-five goddamn minutes this shit goes on for! I wish all of them, instead of coming here to torment my life, had murdered each other. In Chicago. Since its dizzying homicide numbers are such an apparent mark of pride for some reason. This brings another thing to mind. Tons of guys here—often lifetime Illinois residents, mind you, plenty of them middle-aged—seem to think it's pronounced "ill-uh-NOISE." Wow! I really just can't even . . .

With this kinda stuff as a routine intellectual intrusion, at least I'm fortunate enough to see the tons of rabbits and ground squirrels gracing the campus with their lovely *nonhuman* presence every day. I'd never in my life seen a ground squirrel before; for the first couple weeks, I thought they were chipmunks—until lifelong-Illinois-resident james set me straight regarding their species classification. It's doubtless that most, maybe all, of the individual members we see from these two species live inside the grounds their entire lives. Generation after generation. james and I develop, and believe, a nuanced theory that the fences and other factors have serendipitously coalesced to facilitate the evolution of *everything* within, encompassing the entire natural community and its individual members, into a unique and selfcontained prison ecosystem. One completely independent of and different from the rural suburbia that encompasses us. This hypothesis provides hours of conversational fodder. And also engenders a whole new perspectival lens through which to view every minor action of these permanent nonhuman residents. Watching their patterns over the months, and *years*—james has already been down for some 26 months—is quite marvelous; figuring out whether new discoveries or information feed into our theory or not. I think this'd make a fascinating ecological study. Just putting it out there; now it's your turn to make it happen! smile emoticon

The rabbits and ground squirrels are both adorable species, but I'm enamored with the latter, having never seen them before. They're a "Great Plains Special," if you will. Like prairie dogs, they pop out of their ubiquitous burrows and stare around. Investigating local conditions with those big beautiful dark eyes. Sitting on their haunches, tiny hands suspended limply at chest level. They'll come running when you click your tongue, hoping to receive a treat. Guys smuggle bread from the Chow Hall in their pockets and toss pieces to the critters [risking a disciplinary ticket—for "stealing food" from Dietary, *and* for feeding animals], who've learned to wait for us on the big square grasspatch by the exit. They're smart—they know when the time's drawing near, and begin to watch; when the first unit's heading to Chow, dozens of squirrels from all over the grounds make a beeline for that grasspatch. You can see their pliable little bodies wiggling through the field. Then they're ready for us outside once we've eaten. Snatching up bits of food to sit back on their butts and nibble away. Jaws fluttering back and forth like ruminants with amphetamine-laced grass. Watching them always delivers me a smile, and some close approximation of momentary joy, no matter how miserable I am. What kind of person could hurt such sweet, helpless, beautiful creatures? Who?

inmates at Jacksonville, that's who.

Guys spit at the squirrels, yell and chase after them. Click their tongues, enticing the animals to get close, and then hurl breadballs at them as hard as possible. Or candy, hunks of sausage, vegetables, or worse. And get this: Certain workers in Dietary will apparently trap squirrels in plastic milk crates, then spit on them, terrorize them, piss on them, even pour fucking *bleach* on them. If that's not sociopathic, what is? When I hear about this, I'm despondent . . . and homicidally enraged. I must admit, Dear Reader— if I could get away with it, or if I already had a life-sentence, I WOULD · FIND THE GUYS DOING THIS AND KILL THEM. I'm not joking or hyperbolizing for dramatic effect. I'd fucking kill them. Maybe smash my TV screen, pick out a plastic shard, sneak up and plunge the sharpest end into their sidenecks. Or maybe fill a long sock with AA batteries and swing it like a medieval mace, crushing their skulls.

I've never heard the words *nigger* and *bitch* and *faggot* so much in my life. No female is a *woman* or *lady* or even *chick*; it's ALWAYS *bitch*. "You see that blonde bitch in the Visiting Room? That bitch was so fine!" Any gay, bisexual, or even remotely feminine person is without exception a *faggot*. Then there's *nigger*. My gawd! I've had two different best friends in my life who were black.[58] They both like/d to call *me* a nigger to mess with my lilywhite ass. I've watched tons of black standup comedy [much of which comprises, like, everything Richard Pryor's recorded]. Yet still . . . "Nigga, that nigga bogus as hell—tellin you nigga, that nigga crazy!" . . . So pervasive that I start getting offended by it, even when it comes from black guys.

That's enough for now. You'll see pllllenty more of my fellow inmates' ignorance and bigotry.

Back to james. He's 54 years old, a former hippie. Similar in many ways to my dear friend and 35-year vegan, Bob Linden—who hosts the nationally syndicated program and podcast *Go Vegan Radio*.[59] james goes completely

---

[58] Were & still are [black [as far as I know]].

[59] 10+ years' worth of shows are podcasted & archived on the show's website, www.GoVeganRadio.com! all of them hilarious & brilliant & informative. Now you can even search for specific guests by name—including me! I've been on the show a couple times over the years, & surely will be again [probably to promote this very book now in [I can reasonably assume] your hands].

vegetarian, and also stops eating eggs, not long after we meet and I describe the inherent barbarism of the meat/dairy industries and educate him about veganism's healthfulness [e.g. vegetarians and vegans live on average *six or seven years longer* than corpse-eaters, and your risk of heart disease and cancer and stroke and diabetes plummets—these are all well-documented]. james is a hardcore Christian who actually cares about the Earth—imagine that! He decries all the chemicals we're forced to breathe here. There's a tire factory across the street; we catch its terrible effluvium when the wind's blowing northeast. Smells like burnt clutch and charbroiled Band-Aids. Then there's prosaic old diesel exhaust, with freight trains chuffing past the prison repeatedly every day, just north of the Yard. We're even breathing awful stuff inside the Gym and unit. Few porters seem to have any concept of moderation or toxicity. ["Porter" is a euphemistic term for janitor. You'd think they'd have more pride in a job done right; after all, they're paid a handsome and near-prison-best of 50 cents an hour!] They literally twist open the spray bottles of bleach and industrial cleaner—toxic individually, fiercely toxic in concert—and fling-splash them into puddles on the bathroom floor. Soon, the whole dayroom reeks with such noxious pungency that it burns your nostrils and lungs. The Gym workers are especially bad; instead of Medical Gym, we start calling it *Chemical* Gym.

james and I talk about organic food, simple living, my wonderful monastic Mendocino cabin, environmental issues, writing. "Dude," I tell him as we're once more circling the basketball court—Medliners wait in the Gym until there's space in Health Care, so I've begun using this time to walk with james every morning. "You *have* to read Derrick Jensen! He's among my favorite writers; I'm getting a couple of his books sent in to me." Jensen is an anticivilization, environmental writer-activist whom I discovered near the beginning of my senior year at UC Irvine in 2006. I'd already been opposed to industrial civilization for some time . . . except I just didn't know that's what it was![60] Jensen helped validate my feelings. Demonstrating, with sparkling clarity, their veracity as legitimate and sensible ideas. He quantified precisely what it all *meant*. How it all came

---

[60] I'd been thinking & sometimes saying for a couple years that it'd be better if the human population were *far* lower, and if we all lived like American Indians were living for thousands of years before European conquest & genocide. But until reading Jensen, I didn't know there was actually an entire ideology & worldview that included these principles! [Nor did I understand how entwined, even inseparable, my first two aforementioned gutlevel feelings were.]

together in a neat package. Most importantly, reading Jensen gave me the boost in confidence I needed to actually start espousing these ideals! I no longer quivered at the thought of being branded a nutjob or extremist. The real extremist lunacy is that humans the world over are causing a **mass extinction** of flora and fauna, driving species into oblivion by the tens of thousands. Experts in numerous scientific fields have reached a resounding consensus: Humans [and our cultural systems, i.e. industrial civilization] have instigated the Sixth Mass Extinction; the first in planetary history *not* resulting from disastrous natural events, like a giant meteor-strike or an Ice Age. As I say in my overpopulation talk [see footnote 73 below], remember—

Extinction isn't just the end of life . . . it's the *death of birth*.

And we're literally causing species to go extinct at a rate faster than that of the *dinosaurs*! Estimates vary, but even the most conservative ones are devastating to consider; experts say the current rate is approximately 100 to 1,000 times greater than the normal, "background" frequency. Whatever the precise numbers may be, one thing is certain: many, many dozens of extinctions are occurring every single day—with estimates as high as *200* per diem! Destroying the planet's life-support systems. Making simple existence—eating, drinking, breathing—more and more hazardous by the moment . . . for us, and even more so for future generations of humans and nonhumans alike. The *real* extremist lunacy is letting this planetary holocaust to continue unopposed![61]

For a long time, james is my only real friend. On our third day of hanging out, we're walking to Chow and I finally ask what got him locked up. He's a peaceful older man, a true Christian, brimming with love and compassion and intelligence. It must be some kinda white-collar crime: corporate theft, money laundering, embezzlement—something white and middle class like that. So his answer floors me. "Attempted homicide," he says nonchalantly.

My jaw actually drops. "Are you *serious*?" He nods. "What happened?"

---

[61] For just a sampling of ideas, see *The Sixth Extinction: Biodiversity and its Survival* by Leakey & Lewin [1995], or *Under a Green Sky* by Peter Ward [2007], or really just anything by Derrick Jensen, especially the two-volume *Endgame* [2006] and *Strangely Like War: The Global Assault on Forests* [2003] and *What We Leave Behind* [2009]; on the web, the following is an absolute treasure trove of info regarding the current extinction crisis, with links to hundreds of articles & sites & studies: www.mysterium.com/extinction.html [accessed 5/16/16].

He doesn't tell me the whole story right away, but rather in pieces over time. He discovered she was having an affair with some British guy—we'll call him Rog [and not because that's the guy's actual name [necessarily]]. james and his wife were both alcoholics at the time, with long-untreated depression. He confronted her about Rog. Legitimately hoping they could work things out. But then she delivered the killer line [no pun intended]: "If it's not Roger, it'll be someone else."

james straight flipped the fuck out. Grabbed a butcher knife and hacked at her; as she tried to duck out of the way, it carved a long, deep wound into her back. He then tried to commit suicide. Slashing from his left wrist halfway up the forearm. Then sliced open his stomach so deeply his guts hung out. He staggered upstairs in a daze and kneeled at the foot of their bed. Jammed the knife to his throat to finish the job. Persistent bastard, wasn't he?! Last second, he passed out from bloodloss and shock. That's the only reason he's still breathing. Neighbors had heard the commotion and called 911. EMTs managed to save james's life; he woke up hours later handcuffed to a hospital bed.

I'm utterly blown away. *How could he do that?* I'm staring at him agape as we lean against the brick wall outside the Chow Hall. I know it's true, but he's such a peaceful, laidback, Christlike person that it's astounding. And goes to show how, under the right—or rather wrong—circumstances, almost anyone's capable of just about anything when they've long been simmering in the intense pressurecooker of modern society.

He was going to receive 12 years, but his victim, his by then ex-wife, wrote a letter to the Judge. Saying james is a good man and the conditions under which the crime occurred were wretched. She begged the Judge to be merciful. So james got "only" 8 years instead.

I'm *not* saying he should've received a harsher sentence. Violent crimes aren't much on my radar at the moment; let's end the vicious so-called Drug War [the number of people incarcerated for nonviolent drug crimes has increased *twelve times over* since 1980!] and immediately release all non-violent drug offenders.[62] This would allow the closure of literally over *two*

---

[62] From Human Rights Watch [accessed 6/21/16]:
www.hrw.org/legacy/backgrounder/usa/incarceration/
And remember that blacks are targeted FAR & AWAY more than anyone else for drug-related crimes; if needed, revisit *Inter-Mission 2: Seeing ≈ Believing* above, immediately prior to this current section we're on [Part 3], for detailed specifics and analysis.

thousand of America's 4,570 or so prison facilities. Can you even imagine what it'd do for national character, morale, and *morality* to forever clear out and shut down a couple fucking thousand prisons? That needs to happen first. Say what you will about violent crime, but I contend, and you should too, that it's absolutely fucking insane how—had I appealed Judge Hamer's decision in the Motion to Suppress Hearing and lost—I would've been hammered with a Class X Felony and 12-year mandatory minimum. For simple possession of cannabis with intent to distribute, I could've easily had a longer sentence than a wifestabber!

A couple weeks after seeing Dr. Williams, I have an appointment with the Psychiatrist. Everyone taking #headmeds is automatically scheduled to see the Psychiatrist every six weeks. Jacksonville doesn't have one on-site, so you sit inside a private room and talk to him on a Skypelike setup. This is called telemedicine. Guys refer to the Psychiatrist—a yarmulke-wearing South African dude with a long, scraggly gray #hobobeard—as the "Jew in the Box," because . . . well, because he's a Jew whom you speak to through a television set. He actually works back at Stateville—a physical location that ostensibly proves again and again to feature nothing but heartless halfwit staff, from Guards to emergency-call-button-answering-shitbags to Medical Doctors to Psychiatrists. Also, the technology is deplorable [no doubt a result of costcutting measures]. His image on the TV screen is blurry. Almost pixelated-looking. And there's a halfsecond lag, so his lip-movements precede their sound. I can only assume it's the same on his end. On a limb, I'm gonna go ahead and suggest this might not be the most reliable method of diagnosing and treating psychiatric maladies; body language matters. I try to explain my condition. He keeps changing the subject. I eventually just tell him straightout that I'm on a very low dose of pain meds, and that receiving even a little extra Klonopin would greatly help compensate. He flat-out refuses. Glancing down at my chart, he says, "You are incarcerated over the cannabis I see. You have clearly a drug problem, so I cannot increase your dose on the Klonopin."

My facial expression manifests the feeling of great bewilderment his ridiculous statement produces—but who knows if he can decipher even a rough approximation of this look given the techno-limitations, despite my expression's ostentatiousness. "*Drug problem?*" I say.

"Are you not here because of drugs, mr. smitowicz?"

Well yeah . . . no shit, Shylock! my paperwork's sitting right beneath your grody, tit-length hermit's beard. No way you're an actual vagabond;

but you're most definitely representing [unintentional?] hobo-solidarity with that wild #vaga*beard*! I could argue that transporting marijuana has no causal relation to drug addiction—especially since marijuana *isn't even addictive* in the traditional physiological sense, which any unbiased addiction researcher or modern drug textbook will unequivocally reveal. And demonstrate beyond reasonable doubt. But he's already made up his mind. I'm a drug dealer, and hence *must* have a drug problem! There are no gray areas in life, ever. Stop being so damn obtuse with all your stupid "logic" and "peer-reviewed research" and "well-established, unanimous scientific theorem"! I couldn't possibly mule pot without being a hopeless addict. The two are clearly inseperable, right? This sure seems to be every IDOC Doctor's outlook. Of *course* it is! it makes their asinine, Sisyphean task as sole Doctor for many hundreds of individuals substantially easier. To wit: If [1] the great majority of your patients have a tangible connection to illicit substances—which is a mathematical near-certainty [see the Drug War content above]; and [2] you're forced to figure out multitudinous ways to reduce workload and maximize efficiency, does there exist a better statistical fashion to accomplish this than immediately writing off every patient with a drug-related conviction? I don't think so. Sure, it's ludicrous and fucked up, even torturous in my personal case. But I cannot deny its surefire effectiveness!

This is the precise kind of abominable human rights violation that is both engendered by and rewarded in America's economics-first culture, and more broadly, our blind subservience to bureaucratic capitalist principles no matter what the [often invisible or willfully ignored] human cost. These things have become that much more blatant and brazen with the political ascension of Donald Trump, aka the Predator in Chief, and his vile so-called administration's climate change-denying, ecological-information-suppressing, civil rights-crushing attitude. [As I finalize this Januscript, he's been in office for only a week—and already he's lain down an executive order that the EPA and NPS aren't allowed to discuss climate change with social media or reporters. The *Environmental Protection* Agency has been prohibited from . . . *talking about the fucking environment.* George Orwell, eat your fuckin heart out while rolling over in your grave! I truly think this administration will be taking Orwellian doublespeak to stratospheric heights that not even Fox News would *dare* attempt for fear of losing their "credibility."]

You know what? Through the process of thinking and writing about everything, I've come to realize—and accept—that I actually *do* have a drug problem. A large one, as it turns out . . . HENRY COUNTY STOLE MY FUCKIN DRUGS AND UNCONSTITUTIONALLY STUFFED ME IN PRISON! *That's* my only "drug problem." Then again, I technically have another: my requiring pain meds every day to maintain something resembling a decent, tolerable life. This is indeed one more drug problem, which has been dumped onto my existence by awful luck, bad doctors, a wretched and barbaric health care system so bad that, in a functional sense, we're practically on par with third world countries, etc. [See *Rebel Hell: Disabled Vegan Goes to Prison* for extensive supporting details.]

I return to my unit after "visiting" the Psychiatrist; it's left me dazed, with the bizarre but distinct sense that my soul has just been #*gangfucked* in its asshole.[63] Not for the first time either; it's just that the #soulrape has grown more and more pronounced, and hence quantifiable, the more I go through. [*Haha! You've been through relatively* nothing *thus far, jannyboy. If you think yer getting existentially raped* now, *just you wait!*]

If I weren't in prison I'd be in tears. I am luckily able to stifle them— but it's close. The moment I return back to 3B, I shuffle straight for the phones and call Rachel to tell her everything. "What a fucking *cunt!*" she cries, referring to Dr. Vagabeard. Oh Rach, my lovable little firecracker.

"That's what I kept thinking—like, verbatim."

The sympathy and love she expresses is heartfelt, but only provides a modicum of comfort right now. I need to speak to a *real* doctor. I dial *mi mamá.* Explain everything that just happened. "Ass!" my mom interjects about the Doctor repeatedly as I'm speaking. "Turd! Jerk!" My voice cracks phlegmily several times. Can't help but smile though at her declarations, like: "Butthead! Ass! AssHOLE!" When I'm done, she says, "You know, honey, it's not at all surprising—"

"I know, but it's not fair! It's not right!"[64]

---

[63] Do souls have assholes? If they exist at all [souls, not assholes], we can certainly say the reverse is true: that assholes have souls. In any case, it sure feels like the Prison-Industrial Complex, and all its self-righteous idiot bureaucrats, have discovered that, at the very least, *my* soul has an asshole, and they're *joyous* over this discovery, and they're celebrating by relentlessly pounding my soul's asshole.

[64] Shut the hell up, whinyass punk—grow a pair! Don't just piss & moan when things aren't fair. Of course they're not fair! You have to *make* them fair.

"I know it isn't, jan, but you need to listen to me."

I fall silent, clutching the phone hard. Bottling the tears that yearn to flow.

Mom chooses her words with careful deliberation. "I know it's hard, sweetie. It's bullshit. But you need to understand that Doctors who work in prisons, the vast majority of them, are there because they couldn't get a job somewhere better! Either cuz they're not very good, or they screwed up somehow in their former practice. And working in prison is a pretty decent job for a person like that. Partly because they're not *expected* to be very good!"

Incredible—she's helped calm me down some. I tell her, "I'm sure *some* of em work in prison because they care and wanna make a difference. But not many. And definitely not this one!"

"Yes. You're right—not this one. So you're just gonna have to hang on and be strong. I promise it'll get better."

"Okay."

The dildo's been removed from my soul's asshole, and I'm hoping it'll stay out for a good long while. "All right. Thank you, Mom. I love you."

"I love you so much, my wonderful son. Be strong."

We hang up and my heart swells with gratitude. Affection. It is just amazing that my actions [well, the lawbreaking actions of the Illinois State Troopers and Judge Hamer, but those were ultimately predicated by my own choices] could cause her so much pain and anxiety, and cost her so much *money*, yet she has all but forgiven me. Her kindness and generosity and love is inspiring—even overwhelming at times.

Really, the two main things that help me survive the worst periods are Rachel and Mom's love and multifaceted support, and my writing. I'm only managing about two to three pages per day—like I said, it gets harder and harder to concentrate once the pain meds're wearing off. Nonetheless, I'm pleased with *Kissing Clouds*'s narrative development. Turns out this particular piece is building toward more of a novella than a short story.

I continue receiving many letters. Since Rachel and I talk on the phone several times a week, she only writes me about once a week by my second month at Jacksonville. But she covers each one in cute little stickers; they brim with loving content that makes my heart swell. Admission: I'm now getting nastier and more intense sexual fantasies than ever before, after a mere three months away from women! . . . but hey, I've only got 21 more months to wait.

x.

Oh shit, what? It's December 31, 2011, and I've served over 19 months of my sentence! Prison warps time like you wouldn't believe. I'm no longer at Jacksonville. They sent me here a few days ago on a Disciplinary Transfer, off to this *medium*-security prison called Logan. It's like a different world than the one I grew accustomed to at J-ville. I suppose that, if incarceration is its own parallel universe, then each prison is like a different planet or galaxy inside of it.

The so-called Doctors have taken *ALL* medications away from me except for my antidepressant. The world I occupy is, more than ever in my life, a world of *hurt*.

Midnight approaches. Many of us newbie-dorm occupants watch the New Year's Eve festivities in Times Square. Some baldheaded black singer called Cee-Lo Green is performing [term used loosely]. He's butchering "Imagine," and it's not even *kosher*—the butchering. John Lennon would be appalled. Yoko Ono would be rolling over in her grave if she were dead. Hell, it's such a grotesque version of such a glorious song that even the repugnant shitpile-loser who assassinated Lennon—Mark David Chapman—even HE might accuse Cee-Lo of *killing* the legendary ex-Beatle's music! It's bad, man. Green has donned a truly bizarre costume: flaring, red and black latex robes that spill over his gut and extend down to mingle against the stage. I'd say he resembles a colorblind wizard with Down's Syndrome who was allowed to select his own wardrobe; his handlers are likely smacking their foreheads for enabling such an abomination.

I cry almost every time I listen to "Imagine." And this time doesn't fail to produce some lachrymal moistness. It's because the song's lyrics are so powerful and beautiful, plus the whole thing makes me sad—the world is so fucked up, and Lennon's dreams of peace and no more religion or materialism have not come true. In fact, the things "Imagine" decries have gotten tangibly *worse*! This Idiot-Wizard isn't just brutalizing a gorgeous classic; that'd be unforgivable enough. But on top of that, this very man directly contributes to several of the societal issues Lennon critiqued! Cee-Lo's a materialistic tool who—despite already being fabulously rich—is a corporate whore, appearing in commercials to shill consumer garbage like Sprite.[65]

To me, the whole thing represents how we've fallen even farther downward as a society. When Lennon sang "Imagine," an electric current of kinetic energy and possibility crackled through the ether, the potential for dramatic transformation abounded, and people—masses of people—were actually *working* to effect positive change. Lennon wasn't just offering up ideas; his lyrics were also a *reflection* of contemporary forces for progress that folks were already working on. But look at us now. Apathy is today's chic. The masses are snatching up capitalist America's corporate Kool-Aid, and guzzling it like liquid Vicodin. John Lennon was an expression of his times. Cee-Lo, here committing an atrocity against that eternal piece of three-minute musical art, is a depressing reflection of *our* times.

THAT is why I cry.

And this memoir is my most barbarically yawping *rebel yell* in opposition to everything wrong today; all of it. All. Of. It. Imagine . . .

4.

Oops, sorry, slipped into a little wormhole there for a moment. Now I'm back in the present [which is actually less-recent than the above section, which is itself the more recent past than the distant past to which I'm now returning, but . . . ah, nevermind].

As my neighbors jamie and dutch predicted, I am indeed assigned a job in Dietary a few weeks after arriving. I'm incensed. Mortified. This should not be happening. For Christ's sake, I stopped going to concerts some 14 months before my imprisonment because they'd become overwhelmingly painful, just too much to tolerate—even though it was one of my favorite things to do! I gave that up due to pain. Yet now I'm being forced to *work*. Scheduled to begin the very next day, 11:30 a.m. to 3:30 p.m., five days a

---

[65] Makes me think of a bit by the late comedian Bill Hicks, who is fucking brilliant & would've been up there among history's truly great comics if he hadn't died at just 32. On his spectacular album *Rant in E-Minor* [1997], Hicks rips into Jay Leno for appearing in Doritos commercials: "Here's the deal, folks: You do a commercial, you're OFF the artistic roll call forever. End of story, okay? You're another corporate fuckin shill, you're another whore at the capitalist gangbang . . . you don't got enough money, you fuckin whore? You gotta sell *snacks* to fuckin bovine America?!" That's how I feel about this Cee-Lo Idiot-Wizard character, & yet he's singing [-ish] immortal antimaterialist lyrics like, "Imagine no possessions—it's easy if you try." Give me cancer now, gawd.

week. The next morning I head out for the Chow Hall. Slogging through the day's humid-ooze, which is already swamplike. I have zero intentions of working. At the entrance-podium, I tell its Officer, "Look, I'm disabled and can't be working."

"You got a Doctor's note? Did they put you on No-Work Status?"

Oh jeezus. Hear that? It's the sound

of

my

spirit

P
L
U
M
M
E
T
I
N
G

"Not yet," I tell the Officer. "But I just got here, and my medical records are being sent in, and then—"

"Well it's not up to me. For now you'll just hafta talk to the Dietary Supervisor. Miz Turner."

So I wander around back through the kitchen, with its giant stainless steel ovens and boiling vats and numerous walk-in fridges and freezers. Finally spotting her office at the very back. She's a fairly sweet middle-aged blonde lady, one of like two white women working amid Jacksonville's general population [excluding Nurses]. Ms. Turner tells me I can stick to light work—folding the plastic silverware into napkins. I sit down among half a dozen other guys in the first couple tablerows and give it my best shot. But even that grows miserable, sitting in place for several hours; recall the misery induced by my first Doctor visit's superlong wait. The Vise grips my knees and clamps tighter and tighter; only a matter of double digit minutes before the stabbing and burning invade my legs and begin to colonize. Problem is, it'll be really goddamn hard—I'm *sure* it will—to be excused from performing this "light work." But I think it's doable short-term; until my medical records arrive, I'll just lower my head and bulldoze through it, comforted [I hope] in knowing it's temporary [I hope]. Also, I'm able to sneak off and wander around every 20ish minutes. Be on my feet, moving, to alternate between uncomfortable positions. It also allows me to keep an eye on the loading bay out back. Patrol it, if you will. Because this is apparently where guys trap ground squirrels to torment them—and I plan to *do something* if I peep it happening. I don't know if this means stopping them with my words, or straightup fighting, but that shit is *not* happening on my watch!

I'm so glad Ms. Turner at least tries to be understanding. But [of *course!*] this advantage disappears once lunch starts and the place unmellows into a madhouse. A different Supervisor—the smarmy, paunched tub of shit named Watson—nabs me and forces me to join the floor crew. We're responsible for herding spilled food/liquid, once each row finishes eating, into plastic bag-lined milk crates. Broccoli florets, cake crumbles, rogue pasta noodles, meathunks, and every other repulsive thing. [Keep in mind I'm vegan *and* a germophobe!] Then we wipe down the tables with bleach-laden rags. Having to hustle manically to keep up; there are only 350 seats, but like 700 to 950 guys eat lunch in here. Depending on the menu. So each fourseat table gets used at least twice per afternoon. It's stupendously hard on my body. Bending over and back up, over and back up, over and over 'n overoveroverover etc. to wipe the tables; standing around while we wait for the next row to leave so we can rush forward and clean their spots. The aggregate pain on my knees and even my back is devastating. I plead with

Supervisor Watson to let me stop. But he brushes me off: I needa just *man the fuck up* and sit down t'rest while waiting for the next row to clear out.[66]

I start accumulating a reputation around this time; more and more humanoids, both inmate and Staff, are deducing that I'm a bigtime smartass who takes not a rabbit-pellet of shit from *anybody* without firing back. And if there's one thing I can do, it's talk smack—I'm quick on my feet, and have a hawk's eye for stupidity, irony, hypocrisy, and flawed logic. My sarcasm's visceral intensity can turn almost anyone into a blubbering fool. Especially these country-ass dumbfucks here in central Illinois cornland. To be sure, this reputation has its drawbacks: I think I'd've garnered like one-fifth the tickets I do end up getting if it weren't for that rep . . . Officers start to yell at and fuck with and threaten and target me; at one point, I'm a nanosecond from being *thwocked* on the skull with a wooden baton by a beefy C.O. in riot gear whose resemblance to Porky the Pig is unsettling. But my infamy can be advantageous as well.

Being disabled, particularly here in a world that neither understands nor cares, you do what it takes to protect yourself. No matter the rules. And as an anarchist, I have none of the blanket respect for authority this society tries to engender in us. You must *earn* my respect, especially if you have power over me. So I comply with Officer Forkface—but only when he's paying attention. Otherwise, I grab a seat at every opportunity.

Before I proceed: there's an interprison authority-hierarchy [yet another way that prison is just a self-contained microcosm of society]. The Pyramid of Prison Power looks something like this:

Warden
Assistant Wardens
Majors ≈ Internal Affairs
Lieutenants > Sergeants > Officers
Non-Correctional Staff [e.g. Teachers]
inmate/convicted felon ≈ cockroach ≈ smegma

---

[66] So during short lulls, I start taking a seat. Just the second time I do so, the C.O. directing lines douches up to me & says not to sit down on the job. I try to explain why it's necessary; he says, "I don't give a fuck, stand up." Turns out I'll have devastating run-ins w/ this cocksucking Officer. But that's a long, long way down the road. Right now he's just that small bitchy-looking Officer w/ the weird blurred cheekflesh—as a guy once observed, producing dormwide mirth, *It looks like Cook's face was on fire and someone* beat it out with a meatfork.

But I haven't yet been here long enough to understand the precise hierarchies; plus, there are particular C.O.s and Lieutenants you just *don't* mess with—Batterson, Forkface, Evans, et alia. Generally though, you can jivetalk many Guards with no repercussions except returned shit-talking. But you'd be wise to keep a wiiiide birth from the Lieutenants' bad sides. They're easy to spot in their white uniforms, as opposed to the Officers' and Sergeants' all-black ones. Most of us refer to Lieutenants primarily as "Whiteshirts." They're the ones with real power—and most dudes know not to mess with them. Not me though. Not yet. Also, don't forget my whole anarchist, rebel-yell-in-rebel-hell kick. So at one point, when Officer Forkface is turned away, I'm sitting backwards at a table; aching legs stretched out, shoesoles pressing against a seat in the adjacent row. The closest inmates happen to be from my unit, which unwittingly works out in my favor.

A stocky Lieutenant with his salt-and-pepper hair buzzcut approaches. Whiteshirts tend to be even more selfrighteous and smarmy than Officers. He's staring down at me, thumbs hooked underneath his belt. "You feelin comfortable?"

Every inmate within earshot has gone quiet now, watching and listening surreptitiously. Confrontations—whether inmate-inmate or inmate-Staff—are among the greatest forms of entertainment here. I answer the Whiteshirt honestly, a tack people have so often in my life mistaken for smartass sarcasm. Even when it's not! He wants to know if I'm *comfortable*, so I tell him. "No, not really."

I see a couple inmate jaws drop in my peripheral. The Whiteshirt stares at me like he wants to bash my face in . . . which he almost certainly does. I've just committed a bad unintentional prison-sin. "Putcher feet down," he says. "This ain't the fuckin Hilton." He starts to leave.

"Well aware'a *that*," I mutter to myself. Though still plenty loud. I hear some snickering, quickly suppressed; the wise inmate doesn't so much as court the *gaze* of a Whiteshirt.

He whips back around to face me. Like he's about to throw down. Several guys later tell me he looked very, very close to handcuffing and sticking me in Segregation [aka Seg, the Hole, the SHU [Segregated Housing

Unit]].[67] Lieutenant Whitey McShirtington stares at me caustically for a moment; perhaps considering whether he loathes me enough to deal with the headache of writing a trumped-up ticket that justifies cramming me in Seg. He decides against it. "Just keep your goddamn shoes off the seats and get t'work." He turns and lumbers off. Explaining my need to stretch out would've been a complete waste. He doesn't give a shit why I have my feet up; it sets a Bad Example for other inmates, and that's more than enough. Can't have workers looking *comfortable*!

After everybody's eaten and departed, we still have to stack tables and then mop the floors. I'm so fucking sore when I finally get back to the unit. Standing over a toilet, it feels like my knees could give out any moment and I'd collapse, cracking open my face and then floundering there with my head draped inside the bowl like I'm bobbing for apples. I lie in bed watching TV for a few zombiehours until Medline; at some point I call Rachel and bitch about being forced to work [the fact that Dietary workers are paid about 38 cents an hour is secondary or even tertiary heinousness— it wouldn't matter if I got 38 *dollars* an hour, I still wouldn't [be able to] handle it]. All I can do though is hang on, hang on and wait. A couple guys who witnessed my interaction with the Lieutenant accost me that evening. "Man," one dude tells me, "you crazy fam, talkin to a Whiteshirt like that!" Information spreads faster and more easily here than a winter cold. By the next morning, everybody in 3B knows about my run-in with the Whiteshirt; this is where my aforementioned reputation starts to build. On the inmate-interaction side of life, it's a definite positive. Even though everyone knows what I did was stupid, an inmate who doesn't take shit from the "*Po*-lice" gains automatic respect from many guys.

Now I must admit, there are *some* perks to working Dietary. We get the best food, and tons of it. Sometimes the cooks will prepare special meals just for us to enjoy. For example, one afternoon a teacher who oversees the agricultural class's greenhouse supplies our Dietary Manager with several MASSIVE zucchinis—picture an average-sized watermelon that's been strrrrretched out into a phallic shape. Huge! The kitchen staff dices em up, deep-frying them in bread batter. The resulting slices are crispy, flavorful,

---

[67] Another brilliant prison idiom: when someone's taken to Seg, it's called getting "Cuffed & Stuffed." [Prison vernacular is delightful for a punloving wordsmith like me.] If your offense is so egregious that you're transferred to a higher-security prison, you don a jumpsuit the morning of departure. So naturally, this is referred to as getting "Suited & Booted." Love it!

and mouthwatering, utterly extraordinary. I stack them up high on my tray, loading the entire platter with about 15 to 18 cutlets and nothing else. A veritable cornucopia, and for good reason—this is literally the *very first time* I've had the exorbitant luxury of eating fresh vegetables in prison! It's been some TWO MONTHS since I tasted fresh, noncanned produce; they simply don't provide any, ever! This must be yet another unconscionable, morally [and maybe even *legally*] unjustifiable way for Illinois's DOC to slash the financial burden of feeding all 45,000+ men living under its governance. So I make sure to take full advantage of the anomalous opportunity: When our shift ends, I roam the kitchen and dishroom area, tracking down a large serving-panful. Leftovers to be tossed. Instead, I summon several guys and we gorge, scarfing fully 10 pounds of breaded zucchini in like three minutes flat. Just think . . . not a single taste of fresh veggies for two months—in my case. Others had gone upwards of a friggin year! And but then we're windfallen with gutloads of zucchini that's not just fresh in the sense of being noncanned, but *fresh from the plant*; plucked off the vine that very morning! Not even I have the words to convey how special it is.

[It'd be remiss of me to not also further highlight the obvious: this occasion may be momentous, yet it's also tragically sad, right? The payoff was great—but the circumstances that created such awesome salience are hardly justified by that payoff. This nutritional destitution is yet another form of . . . I'll call it *weaponized inadequacy*. Similar to the medical-care and -consideration issue.]

Working in Dietary has one other *big* perk. The inmate restroom is *single-occupancy*. Which means . . . wait for it . . . **PRIVACY**!! Given Jacksonville's 20-man dorms, plus our open-layout bathrooms and showers, true privacy is as elusive here as a silver needle in a gray needlestack. Any chance for solitude must be seized to maximum possible extent. Thus, I retreat to that bathroom once every workday to jerk off in magnificent quietus. It is terribly hot and stuffy inside, so I always emerge sweating like—well, like someone who just spent ten minutes vigorously exercising in a small saunalike room. More than worth the discomfort, of course. And don't worry, I wash my hands afterwards. Although it does provide a sense of satisfaction—when fellow inmates have me feeling particularly hateful—to recall how I stroked my cock before preparing their utensils.

I spend a lot of prelunch, plasticware-and-napkin-folding time with a guy named baxter; he too enjoys dark humor, so it helps pass the time. One day we somehow bring up the private bathroom. baxter reveals that he gets *fully nude* in there to masturbate. For some reason. You routinely have to wait five or ten minutes for that restroom to become vacant. Now I understand why! Bet damn near every worker uses it to pound off in solitude.

After five straight days of bussing tables, I can't handle any more. The pain is intolerably overwhelming. I mean, it's bad enough that I'm miserable while actually working; but it also carries over into nonworking hours. This is untenable. And so I finally decide to do something about it. On my sixth Dietary workday, I check in and then beeline toward the back of the kitchen. The svelte blonde supervisor, Ms. Turner, is in there, as is Watson. As I mentioned, she's fairly nice. But Watson—he's a real dickwad. He's tall and ugly, with a wild thatch of dark gray hair; his gravitymelted face has that constant morose look of the unhappy, middle-aged man who suspects his life's a pitiful waste. I'm intentionally not even looking at him. Speaking only to Ms. Turner. Explaining why it's too difficult for me to bus tables.

"What *can* you do?" Watson interjects. His tone is like an oozing anus or something.

Finally I look at him. He's a heavy smoker, always emanating that funk of old sweatsocks and smoldering ash. Being around Watson—his unbearable smarminess and absent compassion—alternately makes me yearn to smoke a cigarette, and yearn to put out a lit cigarette on his eyeball. "Well, honestly, I'm in pain all the time," I say. "It's just that standing in place or sitting in place for long periods of time really aggravate it."

Watson holds up both hands. Palms out, as if being arrested on child pornography charges. His eyes are drawn open wider than usual. "Can't stand! Can't sit! Jesus, yer just a fuckin mess, ain't ya?"

"Yes, I really am, actually. Thanks for that."

I turn to Ms. Turner [NPI] again. Trying to maintain my focus on her alone, since she seems to possess a lingering touch of humanity. Human decency. "So yeah, it's really difficult for me to work the floor—"

She's nibbling her lower lip, staring at her desktop computer while she works the mouse. "So what can you do?" Watson says again.

I chuckle. Shrug a shoulder, shaking my head. Look back and forth between the two of them. "Honestly, the only thing that doesn't cause really bad pain is stuff I can do in bed. Reading, writing . . . what about like some kinda paperwork? I'm good with numbers. Is there something I could do back in the unit, filling out forms or dealing with inventory or somethin like that?"

Watson starts laughing with his head down, shaking it back and forth. "Gawd-*damn*."

I'm throttling toward full-on hatred of this heartless prick. Few things offend me; I'm well aware of my many limitations. But when someone makes light of my disability—especially because in this case it's someone with authority over me, during a personal crisis wherein I have *no* power, and he's taking it far beyond friendly teasing—I will only tolerate it for so long. No matter who's doing it.

Still chuckling, Watson looks over at Ms. Turner. "Guy in prison wants to work from his bed!"

"I really don't appreciate yer damn laughing," I say with heavy gravitas. Staring right into his faded bluegray eyes. "It's a serious medical condition, not a joke." I can feel my face turning red with heat, blood. I despise it. Why can't I just confront someone without becoming all physiologically embarrassed and worked up?

"Okay smitowicz," Ms. Turner says at last. "I'll figure out something easier for you to do, all right?"

*Twat*son [a far more appropriate name] scoffs and tries to fire off yet another snide comment, but Ms. Turner speaks over him. Seemingly also irritated by his relentless, crass imbecility. "Just take it easy and fold silverware today," she says, "and don't worry about bussing tables—I'll find someone else. Come talk to me tomorrow and I'll have easier work for you to do, okay?"

I nod and flash a smile. "That'd be great. Thank you Ms. Turner, I really appreciate it."

"Okay then," she says.

"*Lying down*," Twatson mutters, sneering. I lay a heavy stare on him for a couple seconds, then turn and walk off. He calls, "See ya later, *knees*!"

STOP. Dead in my tracks. My fists clench involuntarily. I want to rush back and show him both barrels, the fullness of my crushing and merciless sarcasm. But no. I can't. I'd be giving his pudgy pockmarked ass exactly what he wants—he *wants* to get under my skin. Best thing to do is simply ignore him. So I walk on, back toward the dining area and its endless piles of napkins and plastic utensils.

I make a pit stop at the bathroom to relieve some built-up stress.

The next day, I'm reassigned to the dishroom; Ms. Turner explains my situation to the inmate who manages the area. They task me with sorting plasticware after it's conveyer-belted through the dishmachine, an ancient, sprawling metal hunk. This job's not nearly as bad as bussing the tables. Though it does involve sitting in place for several hours straight. Still painful. Still accumulative, my pain intensifying more and more as time passes. I continue hanging with baxter, folding utensils with napkins, for the first hour before Chowlines start running. Sometimes Twatson will wander around to make sure we're keeping busy, his paunchgut leading the way. Every time he ambles close by, my heart beats faster and I grow uncomfortable, anxious he'll try to embarrass me in front of the dozenish other guys. Which he does indeed do [of course]. "Hey there," he says to me one day with his dumb shiteating grin. I look at baxter and shake my head. "How're them poor ole knees?"

"Bad. Always bad."

"I bet." He stares at me, mouth sagging open with mongoloidic idiocy.

"Lemme get a cigarette," I say to the pudgebellied turd.

"Yeah right."

"Fine. Soooo . . . piss off then, TWATson! Can'tcha see we got important work t'do here?" A few guys snicker. Plenty others also hate the prick.

"Watch yerself, knees."

"Whatever you say, Twatson."

It becomes a game for him—seeing how far he can push me. And he knows my sorest spots, literally and figuratively. Twatson will often stand behind the counter next to the servers while Chowlines run. Vigorous, it seems, in his apparent goal to waste as much time as possible; this is likely representative of his entire life. I'm filled with weighty dread every time he's back there. Just wanna grab my damn food and be left alone. But I cannot hold my tongue when he mocks and trivializes this fucking medical condition that has wrecked my life. "How're the knees?" he snidely asks me—always snidely—one afternoon.

"Almost as shitty as your entire *life*," I fire back in an instant, speaking with forceful surety.

The servers are cracking up. He doesn't even attempt a comeback. As I'm walking off with my tray, I hear one of them say, "Damn Watson, he just punked yo ass!"

And now I've given ample space to that mouthbreathing pail of liquid excrement; far more than he deserves. After hitting him with that first-degree burn, I just pretend he's invisible. Completely ignoring him.

I manage to continue for precisely two weeks in Dietary before deciding it's simply too much; I shouldn't be working here. Shouldn't be working *anywhere*. And that I need to at least try to extricate myself. This time I head straight to the top of Dietary's specific interprison hierarchy—to the Manager Mac's office. He oversees everything Chow-related. Turns out he's very nice and mellow. Once I explain my dilemma, he immediately removes my name from the Dietary-worker list! I return to the unit with an elated bounce in my step. Now at least I can relax to a degree commensurate with any given day's pain levels!

Or so I *thought*. Reasonably, in my estimation.[68] But nope—turns out I haven't reached this difficulty-mountain's summit after all, but rather a momentarily convincing facsimile; there in fact remain entire glaciers and jagged rock-cities and high, sheer cliffs to navigate. Should I be even a little surprised? I was stupidly quick to believe I succeeded in one of my biggest challenges here—convincing them for good that I'm *medically incapable* of performing any work that involves extensive time or physical exertion. As if my luck's track record thus far has demonstrated anything remotely resembling a chance that I could so easily vanquish said challenge on a permanent basis! As if the entirety of my work-problem could possibly be resolved by spending two meager minutes elucidating the issue for the Dietary Manager! This was a foolhardy and even *damaging* assumption. It's the whole blinded-by-hope-and-gratuitous-expectations deal. Again! Anyway, I'm graced with a whopping two days of mindease. And then, next day, it's afternoon count and mail-distribution time; the Officer hands me a slip of paper . . .

a *work* slip.

Whoever's in charge of job-delegations did indeed remove me officially from Dietary . . . *but then slotted me into a much, MUCH HARDER position!!*

"You gotta be fuckin kidding me!" I cry.

They've signed me up for an "Inside Grounds" job. This is bad. Oh gawd is this ever bad. Inside Grounds is, without question, *the* single most

---

[68] *You stupid fool. You poor, stupid fool. Still haven't learned much, have ya?*
Shut the hell up! It takes many brutal hits to force my spirit into submission.
And you haven't already had tons of them?
Just shut up. I'll learn soon enough, will I not?
Damn right you will. The madness is barely getting started.
Shhh! damn dude, can we at least get a spoiler alert?!
Just don't try'n say I didn't warn ya!

physically demanding job there is! Forget the dishroom; this is even worse, *far* worse, than bussing tables! Panic explodes in my chest constricts my lungs o shit can't breathe rises toward my throat trying to manifest as a scream or tears or fit of savage violence now able to breathe but it's *too much* it's too fast pulling in oxygen rapidfire o gawd huffpuffhuffpuff fuck plz this is calamitous dear earth letthisbeabadnightmare*please*........

I managed to escape working in Dietary because it was too hard on my disabled body—but so then they promptly assign me to a job exponentially more difficult. It's time; can I just go ahead and say it outright? I made the comparison at Stateville; it's become relevant again though, an unfortunate but inescapable truth, now in reference to Jacksonville [and I'm starting to think maybe prison overall, the American Justice System in toto]: this is fucking KAFKA-ESQUE.

Turns out those in power never *chose* to cease gangbanging my soul's asshole; they simply *misplaced* it for a brief period. Now it's returned to their demented, wicked purview. They managed to relocate it, and are now compensating for lost time by assblasting with a reinvigorated furor.

Inside Grounds workers perform a variety of tasks: trekking around the facility with garbage bags to nab trash using pointy-ended poles; rounding up the Dumpsters outside each unit in a tractor and towing them out to the big steel trash containers; mowing the many acres of grass—sometimes with a ride-on lawnmower, but then, for the fenced-in grass that surrounds each building, they'll use a heavy old exhaust-belching pushmower. A guy in my room [shawn, the dude who loaned me his shower shoes] was forced to handmow the lawns for five consecutive days. In the deadass middle of summer no less, when daytime temperatures routinely exceed 90 degrees, and the swampish humidity is *always* oppressive. He returned from work each afternoon sweat-drenched all the way through his clothes. This is how people get heatstroke. And now *I've* been forced into this assignment.

I'm supposed to start the next morning. One thing is certain: I will not *touch* a lawnmower. Doing that for just half an hour would leave my body in shreds. I don't give a damn what the consequences are; I'll sit down and get hauled off to Seg in handcuffs if that's what it takes to protect my body from agonizing pain and/or further injury.

After I return from Medline in the morning, I drag myself back outside. Utterly terrified—and boy do I ever mean it. Turns out one of the biggest redneck tools at Jacksonville is tasked with overseeing the I.G. workers: Sergeant Johnson, known for being a hardass. No sympathy whatsoever.

His selfrighteous shiteating grin is among the most selfrighteous and shit-eatingest of any douchebag here. His teeth gleam with the too-shiny glint of porcelain, like he chipped or cracked *all* of them and now they're capped with veneers. The teeth also look suspiciously neat and straight, which I find inexplicably unsettling. He has a bloated leathery face and a mustache [of course he has a mustache]. I try to impress upon him my total inability to perform the manual labor this job requires. "You got a note from the Doctor?" he asks. Hiking up a skeptical eyebrow. "Why aren'tcha on No-Work Status if it's so bad?"

Oy! this shit again! "My medical records're on the way—the Doctor won't do anything more until she sees em."

"Well, until then . . . y'see this?" He sticks out an arm and tugs on his black uniform's sleeve. Traces a finger over the insignia sewn there; I just mined MS Word's "Symbols" menu to find something that looks similar. The closest thing is the Greek capital letter Lamda, which is this: Λ . The insignia contains three blue Λs, stacked one atop the other. Johnson runs his finger along this raised pattern almost lovingly, sporting a creepy little grin—like he's stroking a woman's pert nipple [or a man's, no judgment from this goy], rather than a piece of fabric.

"I see it . . ." I say. He wants me to ask the question though; he's obviously waiting for it. Le *sigh* Fine, whatever. "What's it mean?"

Joyous, [unsettling] toothy grin. "It means *I'm* in charge unless the Doctor changes yer Work Status, 'n you hafta do what *I* say."

"Look Sarge, I don't know what to tell you—I'll straightup collapse if I have to push one of those lawnmowers around." We're standing right outside 3-House on the gravel walkway, flanked by grass on either side.

"Yew don't hafta mow the lawns if y'don't wanna," Johnson says. Which is strange, cuz shawn's been complaining all week that he fuckin *hates* mowin lawns, specially in this gawdamn heat, but he ain't got a choice. So Johnson's lying through those weird porcelainy teeth. Since Chowtime's approaching, he tells me to go back inside and he'll summon me later. After lunch, I swallow several cold pills from Commissary—which many other guys also use for sleeping—and pass out, hoping sleep will somehow ward off my being forced to mow lawns or poke-n-pickup trash. An Officer taps vigorously on my hip after 3:30 p.m. count. Hands me a couple letters and another slip. What *now?*—have I been reassigned to work as an electrician? Jumping-jack instructor? A mobile target [wild zig-zagging required] at the Officer's shooting range? For christ's sake?!

No—I have a Doctor's appointment! Tomorrow morning! Could this be the break I've yearned for, here at long last?

This time I embark for Health Care prepared to wait several hours, slipping my current reading material—*Cat's Cradle* by the inimitable Kurt Vonnegut—into a back pocket, since you're technically not allowed to leave the unit with such "contraband." As expected, the wait is once again a veritable smorgasbord of misery; nearly three hours of fidgety, borderline psychosis-inducing pain and discomfort. Doesn't help that I'm schlepping a horrible bloated dread in my gut, as if I guzzled two liters of carbonated sodafoam. That single brief, snide visit with Dr. Williams a few weeks ago was darkly suggestive. I'm already *so* fed up with traversing the excessive interprison maze of medical bullshit. And, squirming at a nearconstant clip on this merciless wooden bench, I'm trying to convince myself—via brute psychological force—that surely Dr. Williams wouldn't *reduce* my med levels [right?!]. But I'm having little success. As evidenced by my terror, and concomitant heart palpitations, nervous perspiration, and worse-than-usual joggling.

Then again, at least now I have some damn ammunition! in the form of my outside medical records, which arrived this week. At least now she can't dismiss me out of hand as a baseless drugseeker. My once-minimal chart has grown in one fell swooping fax to about four inches thick. Brimming with notes from dozens of doctor visits over the last seven years. It includes injury-exam reports, postsurgical writeups from all five separate procedures, and a slew of bilateral knee MRIs. This all combines like a thousand individual brushstrokes to form a crystalline portrait. One that provides inarguable verification of catastrophic fucked-upedness [for anyone who's seeking the unbiased truth]. This richly detailed portraiture illuminates, as with gaudy neon lights, a medical history that makes *going through the wringer* seem like a wildly inadequate phrase. My records also show how I've tried any/everything possible to gain the slightest succor. For example, my doctors wrongly thought I had an autoimmune disorder [wherein your immune system becomes "confused" and attacks the body's own tissues] for ten months. During which time I elected to receive the most aggressive applicable treatment. Taking immune-suppressing meds that catapult your risk of contracting the flu, infections, and tuberculosis to dizzying heights. Lastly, I have two letters directed expressly at prison medical staff—one from my rheumatologist and one from my chronic pain specialist—that delineate my condition's severity, and hence the great pertinence of daily pain meds.

These prodigious materials now here for Dr. Williams to peruse . . . countless bits of information about my painpuzzle, each lone piece both indivisible and inscrutable; yet they're cumulative. Patterns emerge. The puzzle's totality begins revealing itself in gentle fits and starts, eventually coalescing to form a single large, clearly discernible picture. One with perfect optical integrity. Beaming, for all to see, its simple but dramatic message: My condition is indeed very real and very serious, necessitating decent, legitimate care—irrespective of its being "against their policy" to prescribe pain meds on a longterm basis.

Given all this, I don't feel nearly as hopeless anymore. I now have *reams* of concrete, unequivocal evidence supporting my case. All of it pointing

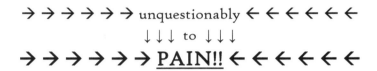

→ → → → → → unquestionably ← ← ← ← ← ←

↓ ↓ ↓ to ↓ ↓ ↓

→ → → → → → <u>PAIN!!</u> ← ← ← ← ← ←

"Well mr. smitowicz," Dr. Williams says, flipping through my pile of records and skimming the notes, "you certainly have been through a lot." This seems intended to be taken as an admission of tremendous good will from her.

"Yeah." I've decided, after extensive consideration, to try a different approach with her this time. "But it is what it is. I just try to cope the best I can. I'm writing and reading as much as possible, because it helps me feel better about having to be here. You know, staying productive? That's *really* important to me."

She looks into my eyes now, for the first time since I entered. "That's good, mr. smitowicz. Most inmates just float through their time without learning a thing."

"Oh, no way. Not me! I made a terrible mistake, and the only way I can atone is by using my time productively."

Is that a disbelieving hint of a *smile* on her lips?! "Good to hear." She continues skimming.

"Yeah." Now, the hard part. Heart's thrashing. If your serious medical condition is treated with dismissal by enough doctors, you start inter-nalizing the implications, no matter what you know and how you feel. "It's just . . . it's *so hard* for me to achieve anything substantial when I'm in the kind of pain I'm in."

"We don't even have OxyContin here, mr. smitowicz, and I wouldn't prescribe it if we did."

"Oh, that's fine! [sic] I feel like I can survive with a lot less here, if I manage my time and activities carefully. Believe me, I dislike taking *any* medication. But since that's not an option unless I want to just lie around watching TV in misery, I prefer taking the lowest amount needed to be semifunctional. Believe it or not, I do see the positives of not receiving OxyContin. It's forced me to adjust, and find more ways to cope." This actually does have a kernel of truth. Small though it may be.

Yep, she's definitely got a smiletype thing happening! "That's great, mr. smitowicz."

Now she's primed—I have to address the final, most crucial elements. "It's just that the . . . the amount of Tramadol I'm taking . . . it leaves almost no room to accommodate flareups. The pain's just too much to handle. When I saw you last time, you told me the meds were in all likelihood temporary. I'm not asking for a higher dose." I snatch a silent breath and hold it in; nervewracked, finding it extremely difficult to spit out my request. Already harboring in my gut a dreadful sense of fatalistic defeatism. At last I manage: "I'm just asking you to extend the prescription, um, indefinitely." Holding my breath again. Then I fire off a quick final thought. "Because I mean like it's not like my condition's gonna change anytime remotely soon!" Tension's intolerable; might just #spraypuke all over the place.

Dr. Williams flips to the back of my chart. "You're currently taking two 50-milligram tablets in the morning and two at night, correct?"

"Right."

She begins scribbling with her pen. "I'm gonna go ahead and put you down for three months at this dosage. We'll see if anything's changed then. How's that sound?"

How's it *sound*? Considering I thought there was a chance she'd take away the meds altogether, I almost start crying tears of relief! "That'd be great. I'll be able to continue being productive in my reading and writing, and this takes a whole lotta stress off my mind."

"Well, good. Just don't expect any more than this. It's the most I'll prescribe."

"That's fine! I really think I can get by." I almost keep talking, but force myself to stop. I tend to get overly talkative when I'm feeling grateful—don't want her misinterpreting it as a *YESSS, I'M GONNA GET HIGH!* sort of happiness.[69]

She finishes writing the prescription. I can tell she's about to excuse me, so I better get the rest out fast. "There's another problem," I say. "They've assigned me to work Inside Grounds, and there's absolutely no way I can do that. Mowing the lawns and stuff. I was working in Dietary for two weeks; I tried so hard to make it work—I really did—but it was just too difficult physically."

Williams frowns. "I really don't like to put healthy young men on No-Work Status."

OH MY GAWD! I almost scream. With a considerable effort to keep my jaw from flopping open. *THIS is what a* healthy young man *looks like?!* I yearn to say. *Does that look like the medical history of a* healthy young man?? But I have to be smart. So instead, I produce an expression of carefully measured shock. "Oh no, I'm not asking to be put on *No-Work* Status! I have no problem whatsoever with, say, being a janitor in the unit or something. It's the physically intense jobs that're super problematic for me. In the unit, I can go at my own pace and all that."

She's nodding. "Good to know. I'll put you on *Light*-Work Status."

"That'd be fantastic, Doctor."

"Okay, mr. smitowicz. Good luck with everything." She stands up. No no, wait! I rapidly explain why I'd benefit from Medical Gym. How it is, in fact, a borderline necessity.

She regards me with a skeptical smirk. "You're not gonna come back to me with an injury from tryin d' benchpress 200 pounds, are you? I can't even tell you how many guys I see for that kinda thing."

No, most definitely not, I tell her. Not interested in that. I just want to have the space to do my stretches, keep my leg muscles sturdy.

"Okay then. I'll put you in for Medical Gym; you should be on the list within a few days."

"Thank you, Doctor. I really appreciate all this."

---

[69] Pretty sad that I've sunk to this level—my paltry, barely workable medication regiment now garners extreme gratitude. But this *is* the level to which I have, by necessity, sunk.

She *should* assign me a Bottom Bunk Permit as well, so I don't have to drag myself up and down the stupid precarious ladder 30 times a day, but she's already ushering me out. Just grateful I somehow managed to secure all three things that I really needed from her!

Later that week, I receive my Medical Gym pass when the Officers hand out mail. james and I begin spending 45 minutes walking together every morning around the basketball court, instead of just the 10 minutes or so before the last Medline group. Sometimes we'll stand around and shoot free throws; he has to position the ball atop his good right palm with the deformed clawhand, then guide the shot almost onehanded. We're becoming closer all the time. He's a true friend. Always evolving into an even more compassionate dude [speaking of evolution, No, he's not a Denier]— bless his wifestabbing heart.

Around this time, my top-bunk neighbor dutch gets transferred to unit 4B, the Drug Unit. An entire 100-person wing with its own set of stringent rules; they have Counselors and daily meetings and classes/workshops. You earn time off your sentence in the Program. I'm on the waiting list, but last someone checked I was at like number 48. I harbor no expectations. Not even sure if I want to move there anyway, because it might involve a physically overwhelming amount of time sitting in place every day.

The guy who replaces dutch is an ambulatory nightmare [or maybe *wet dream* fits better]. A goddamn weirdo, compulsive masturbator, and total smutfiend pervert. Guys refer to him by the sole moniker "freaky ponytail." This is because he's a freak, and has a short, 1970s-style ponytail. Word on the street, or rather the gravel Walk, is he got booted from I-House when an Officer caught him sitting on a bench in the dayroom at 3 a.m., pants around his ankles, pounding off to *Girls Gone Wild*. Apparently he's infamous for getting bounced from one unit to another for various beatoff-related disciplinary violations.[70]

And now—what a shocker!—he occupies the bed right next to mine. A nice little treat, just for me! My prison experience is feeling more and more

---

[70] Masturbation is theoretically prohibited; if you're caught redhanded [or maybe red-*cocked*?], you can be written up for—oh man do I love this one—*Abusing State Property*. HA! See, since prisoners are "Wards of the State," we're also technically considered state property. Our bodies legally belong to the DOC! Hence, jerking off = *abuse of state property*. Parallel Universe Bizarro-World, amiright?!

Woody Allenesque, or Larry Davidian—except I'm not even Jewish, so it's totally uncalled for.

Nighttime is the worst; freaky ponytail really lets that freaky flag fly. Every night he lies on his bunk, staring at a single postcard-sized image for an *hour-plus*. No exaggeration. Depositing, I can't help but assume, every last pixel into his wankbank. Maybe it's just a naked woman's picture, but it could be *anything*. Several hermaphrodites fucking. Kiddie shit. A bucket of Stateville slop. His own cock, being yanked by his nondominant hand [titillating]. I frankly don't wanna know; every night for an hour or more, just lying there. Picture gripped in a clawlike hand eight inches from his face. Staring. Staring. Creeping. All of it screams SEX OFFENDER.

It's no big surprise when I awake late one night, opening my eyes to find they're trained right on freaky ponytail . . . who's hunched on his side, vigorously masturbating.

Aaaaaand so surely you can imagine how thrilled I am when, a few days later, I'm unexpectedly transferred to the Drug Unit.

5.

The reason most people enter the program is because you receive "good time." For every 90 days completed, they lop 45 days off your sentence. I'm nervous about adjusting to this odd new environment; you hear bad things galore about the Drug Unit—most of which are true, turns out, to varying degrees of shittiness. It also has its own large subset of unique rules. This all seems like a minor sacrifice though; I could shave *six months* off my sentence. Meaning I'd go home around November of next year, 2011, rather than May 2012! After unpacking at my new bunk, I call Rachel and tell her the spectacular news. She's probably more excited than I am! [she doesn't have to deal with any of its bullshit]. "Oh my gawd baby, that's so fuckin awesome!"

"I know—SIX MONTHS!"

"This is so incredible. I'm so happy, and so proud of you." Rare is the adjective she speaks without the word *so* beforehand. Bless her heart.

I'm feeling truly upbeat for the first time since arriving at Jacksonville [not counting that initial ecstasy induced merely by leaving Stateville, of course]. Since the Doctor put me on Light-Work Status, my dose of meds now seems survivable longterm; I have Medical Gym access; I'm far away from mr. freaky ponytail; and I'm poised to start accruing goodtime that'll shorten my sentence. There are also advantages to 4B that far outweigh the extra rules. It's *pristine* compared to 3B—and, indeed, every other unit—which is awesome, because in prison my mild germophobia's pitched way higher due to the cramped quarters. Residents clean the Drug Unit *four times a day*. And do it well. Everybody here must have an internal job, and so there's a designated Cleaning Crew that every newbie works on during their first two months. Two guys for the bathroom, two for the dayroom and dorm-hallway, and one for the showers. Plus someone else whose sole responsibility is checking to ensure the crew does everything right and does a good job! During each cleaning period, everybody else has to stay in their rooms. *Out of the way.* Being a porter in every other unit is a wildly scattershot affair: Some guys never once do any cleaning unless an Officer forces them to. And you normally have to work around people in the dayroom or bathroom; nothing shuts down to enable adequate cleanup. Not so 4B though! No shortcuts, no copouts, very little disorder. The program demands conscientiousness and accountability. Having to do so much cleaning sucks shit for me, but it's worth it. Especially since now I *know* how clean things are [and I have to admit, I love knowing *when they're cleanest*—preferring to call Rachel immediately after someone disinfects the phone booth].

Some other pleasant differences about 4B: chairs are posted up beneath each phone, so I no longer have to stand painfully in place, or contort my body to precariously sit on the quadrangular booth's shelf; posters adorn the dayroom walls, imbuing some color and life into the damn place; a couple bookshelves sit in there as well, and a magazine rack; it doesn't smell like musk, body odor, sweatsocks, dirt, and farts in here—mostly there's just a neutral smell due to the cleanliness; and perhaps best of all, it's often almost eerily quiet—again, compared to the other units anyway.

Three Counselors run the Drug Unit—officially called the "CiviGenics Program." Mrs. Meyer is its fearless head honcho, a short, plump, middle-aged woman with curly hair the color of a sequoia tree; she's super sweet, and, you can glean from any given five-minute timechunk, maintains a profound desire to help us enhance our lifelong wellbeing. Then there's Big John, a massive bearlike creature at least 6'3" tall, in addition to his graphic obesity [we're talkin 350 lbs., easily]. He's bald, scalp dotted with splotches of a grocery bag-brown. Finally, Jenny is the third Counselor. She's only 24 years old, and very beautiful—which presents a conundrum with calamitous potential for almost every inmate who passes through 4-House's entrance. A *woman*! An *attractive* woman, no less! And I don't just mean prison-attractive. After you've been locked up for maybe a few months, everyone measured by the Scale of Attractiveness seems to shift about two to four numbers upward.

men menmen

Doesn't help that we're utterly surrounded by men

men men menmen

men men   men

Jenny, though, is *real world*-attractive. If I saw her walking down the street, I'd surreptitiously admire her pretty face and light hazel eyes and taut little rump, which her taut jeans are always hugging. Some guys ogle her every day. They're seldom even discreet about it. People have been booted from the program [and unit 4A opposite our wing!] for committing "Reckless Eyeballing" on her.[71] Me, I'm subtle. I don't even raise my eyes toward her unless we're expected to, like when she's leading group. Then I eyeball her in what would otherwise be deemed a maniacally reckless manner—and she just thinks I'm being even more attentive than I already am!

My first day in 4B, a dude from my room leads me and another newb [dave] on a walkthrough. His name's jay; head shaved into a beige gleaming cueball. He's one of those guys who, because of premature hair loss and other factors, could easily be as young as 30 or damn near 45—and either way, your reaction would be *Yeah, that's about what I figured.* jay seems like a pretty cool guy. He gives a prosaic spiel on the unit's regulations.

Drug Unit-exclusive rules, some of which I'll list below, must be diligently observed at all times. *All* times. This is because they're enforced by—get this shit!—*we inmates ourselves!* If at any time you witness someone violating a rule, you're encouraged to, "write them up." Sitting on the sign-in/-out table by the unit's entrance, there's a neat pile of writeup slips. Once a week, one of the Counselors holds "court." S/he sits behind a dark-wooded desk at the dayroom's far end. One of the Drug Unit's four inmate "house elders," on a rotating basis, occupies a green plastic chair next to the desk. The Counselor pulls writeup slips one-by-one from a box. Then summons that ticket's alleged offender to hear the charges; if determined guilty, he's doled out a punishment. Ranging from electronic device rest-

---

[71] This is an *actual* disciplinary charge! Now it's become an inside joke between me and my good friend Romain, e.g., "Lookin forward to seeing you Saturday, dude— I'm gonna recklessly eyeball the *shit* outta you!"

rictions to special, detailed cleaning assignments to dayroom bans, et alia. The ticket box is kinda like a piggy bank filled not with hard currency, but rather with soft, petty bullshit. Many residents and even more outsiders at the prison consider this unit a glorified snitchfest, and thereby never for a *second* entertain the possibility of coming here. My position on this—which turns out so intensely prescient as to create a physically sickening reality— is, Give one inmate power over other inmates and that power will doubt- lessly, unfailingly be abused.

About 20 percent of the guys produce nearly every ticket. The other 80 percent includes a handful of residents who'll drop maybe a couple-few slips a month, and then several dozen who *never once* write a ticket. I fall primarily into the latter camp. Now I know this sounds impossible and absurd—you cannot "primarily never once" do something! but see, the aforementioned, inevitable abuse of inmate-power will at times *require* demonstrating to a certain cunty 4B-type that you're willing to write them up if pushed into a corner, to remain in the Program and hence continue accumulating goodtime. Look . . . it's complicated shit, okay? It'll make far more sense once, via my written explication, you've familiarized yourself with a particular example. In any case, here are some of the regularly enforced [see above] rules endemic to the Drug Unit:

•We're required to wash our hands—with soap!—after using the toilet. I personally love this rule to be honest

•You're prohibited from loitering in the hallway, and from standing there talking to guys in other rooms

•On weeknights, all lights and electronics must be turned off by 11 p.m. [In every other unit, you can watch TV all night if you want]

•Morning Meetings represent the beginning of every weekday, during which we stand and recite the CiviGenics pledge, house elders and Coun- selors make announcements, guys stand up and "give gratitude," and other dumb shit [Luckily Medical Gym is scheduled at the exact same time, and that takes precedence—so I'm one of just a few people allowed to miss any/all meetings! It also enables me to skip the Cleaning Crew's morning duties; I clean three times a day instead of the normal four—which may seem like no big deal, but is actually significantly better for my knees]

•We attend one classtype thing each weekday. inmates are separated into three different "phases" based on how long they've been in the Pro- gram. Each phase's meeting is led by one of the Counselors on a rotating basis. These classes last anywhere from 15 minutes to over 60, depending on subject matter and Counselor—Big John tends to ramble on, and on, and so on; it's so bad that he himself has fallen asleep while leading group![72]

• Etcetera

Now that the terrorizing threats of med-loss and a demanding job no longer occupy my head [and/or body] as a constant menace, I'm able to achieve much more. I already completed my dreambased novella *Kissing Clouds*. I've put in some work on this very prison memoir—already knowing my story needs to be told—but I shelve it after handwriting about 300 pages; it's just too damn depressing to live it *and* write about it. This leaves me in a major pickle. My goal is to produce at least one complete book while incarcerated, but I'm severely ambivalent about what I should write! Feeling total *unconfidence* that I'm actually ready to begin *any* of the three or four well-developed novels banging around in my head. I could of course work on short story ideas—and I do, for a couple weeks—but short stories don't interest or satisfy me the way novels do. Eventually, I decide to take what is for me a very "novel" approach; I'll come up with a *new* idea, come up with it on the spot and then begin immediately. I'm in prison. I have nothing if not time—might as well try something new and see how it goes!

The first ideas I latch onto are [1] drugs and [2] a San Francisco setting. Rachel and I lived there for 13 months in 2007 and '08. We adored it. And I love writing about [and taking] certain nonhard drugs. Note: I don't feel psychedelics are *hard* drugs. So I'm lying on my bunk late that morning, grooving to some tunes on my Walkman, letting those two idea-seeds sprout and grow in my skull. Then, in a flash of inspiration, it hits me. The story's thrust. It'll follow three people—a male-female Native American couple and their best friend Syd—on a drugfueled "Last Hurrah" in San Francisco, because the first two are about to move away. They have no agenda, no plan except wild fun; a trio of feathers in the swift breeze of S.F.'s mid-Autumn. This unscripted adventurousness should make a fun and entertaining story. Just as important, the characters' initial lack of interest in planning will allow *me* to advance all plot points on the fly. Eliminating my usual obsessive need to know exactly where everything's going in a story at all times. That very moment, feeling both thrilled to the max and trepidatious, I begin! After grabbing my yellow legal pad and a couple pens, I carefully select three cassettes that'll best aid the stream of

---

[72] Reminiscent of my birthfather, who'd read to me before bed when I was a kid. On at least one occasion, he fell asleep before I did.

creative juices—U2's *Joshua Tree*, *Diary of a Madman* by Ozzy, and *After the Gold Rush* from Neil Young [whom Rachel calls "the beautiful poet-rockstar"]. And then out of nowhere . . . just as I hold the writing pad up to my face . . . the book's title materializes in my head!

The Eternal City. A chapter title from one of my alltime favorite literary works, Joseph Heller's absurd comedic masterpiece *Catch-22*. It's utterly perfect. I weave my pen atop the page; rendering the title, freshly plucked from my mind's garden, in ink. Titular words flanked by crude drawings of San Francisco's famed 48-floor Transamerica Pyramid skyscraper. And then I start writing.

As the days and weeks pass, I grow more and more enamored with the book. I settle into an almost invariable routine that further enhances my discipline. Further enshrining my sizable work ethic into daily practice. Every morning I'm awake and out the building at 7:30—first Medline, then 45 minutes at Medical Gym. Conversing with james as we walk in brisk loops around the basketball court, lifting some light weights, and periodically shooting casual hoops. Then I hurry back to the unit. Fix a plastic mug of steaming Taster's Choice instant coffee and fire up a cassette and begin to write, ceasing after a couple hours for lunch. Then I attend that day's group session. By 3:30 p.m. or so, I take a nap. This is new to me; for the longest time, I've been straightup unable to siesta. To fall asleep during midday. Not in prison though! In time, not only do I manage a daily nap, I come to *depend* on them. Since I'm prescribed paltry meds that only last a few hours, napping allows me to bypass the very worst of each day's pain. Which unbearable scorching pain tends to last from late afternoon until I take nighttime meds. Some days the siesta lasts a couple hours, other times three-plus. Upon returning from evening Medline, I write for another solid stretch.

This nuanced and careful, highly evolved routine works to a remarkable degree. Before long I'm writing and reading as much or more than ever! *The Eternal City* rapidly assumes a life of its own; the story streams forth with little conscious effort, save for the simple physical act of moving pen across pad, of dictating that which flows from my mind. It's a beautiful and wondrous phenomenon.

The Drug Unit's fresh, stone-set schedule also helps facilitate my tremendous newfound discipline and dedication to writing. Other things here can help [or hurt] too. Like the degree of prisonlife difficulty or ease outside the world of my legal pads. I'm often paired for Cleaning Crew duties with dave, who got here the same day I did. He's a fellow Stephen King fanatic; we discuss his books at length. dave knows about my knee problems. One night I'm mopping the dayroom and he sees my torpid progress, so he offers to help me from then on. A munificent and touching gesture that I'm unable to turn down.

dave's got quite the backstory. He was a masterful burglar. Breaking into rich people's homes to load his van with flat screen TVs, fancy dishware, appliances, myriad electronics, furniture, and even *guns.* The cops never pinned him with any residential burglaries. Instead, he's locked up for driving a stolen truck from Florida to Illinois. On the very *day* he got arrested, dave learned his girlfriend was pregnant—he'd likely become a new father while in jail or prison. "If that doesn't sound like somethin right out of a country song," he'll say, "I dunno what does." I agree 100 percent; country music is dreadful, as is the thought of bringing a new child into this humanplagued world. Especially under the circumstances—and I'm not talking about incarceration, but rather the realities of climate change, pervasive and increasing pollution, mass extinction, water shortages, and so on. All stemming from overpopulation. I got my vasectomy in 2010; haven't regretted it for one single moment. Instead, I see/hear things each and every day that make me ever more grateful and relieved for having done it! With 415,000 [nearly half a *million!*] children in the U.S. foster care system alone, how bout we start acting like ALL KIDS matter by taking care of the ones already here![73] Imagine that. A ludicrous proposition, I know, since it requires the masses to set aside their selfish personal desires and work toward the greater good via sensible longterm planning. Not exactly typical behavior for industrialized humans.

Anyway, dave and I inspire a shortlived sort of revolution in our room that creates a ubiquitous upheaval, with great divisiveness between opposing sides. What happens is that we start playing the Fart Game. Perhaps you're not familiar with it; luckily the Game's simple. You eschew holding in your gas, or trying to silence it with maneuvers like the onecheek-sneak. Instead, you unleash those farts with maximum force. Louder the better. More bombastic the better. There are no real winners or losers—except for

---

[73] For further info, and my own detailed analysis, see "The Pathology of Human Reproduction," my 2016 presentation at Oakland University's *Evolution of Psychopathology* conference [organized to a large degree by Professor Todd Shackelford, author of this book's foreword], available on YouTube: www.bit.ly/2l5FbD7

the ways *everyone* is a winner!—or loser, if you wanna be a dick about it. dave, though, is the Game's unquestionable MVP. It's not just his particular biochemistry and physiology. Even *fate* seems planted in his corner. Best evidentiary support: One evening, a house elder ambles into our room to speak with dave's bottom-bunkmate; people with certain job assignments are allowed to move freely between rooms if it involves legit unit-business. This specific house elder's known as "kool-aid," a muscular and stocky Mexican. dave's lying on his side [i.e. dave's resting on *dave's* side; the "his" pronoun is not intended to suggest that dave's somehow perched on the side of *kool-aid's* body—just wanted to clarify in case there was any confusion [okay, ya got me, nobody was confused and I know it, I just wanted to turn what was technically an ambiguous pronoun into my little plaything for a bracket or two]]. Anyway, kool-aid enters the region next to dave's bunk, unaware of the toxic weapon that looms dangerously close. Even more ominous is the fact that dave is *also* unaware. He has no idea anyone's close—let alone a house elder in the direct line of fire! At the *exact* moment that kool-aid's head enters the vector comprising dave's butthole-blastzone, dave rips ass. And I mean *rips*; literally sounding as if someone snagged ahold of the fabric of spacetime and ferociously ripped it apart, like cleaving a long gash into a thin cotton sheet. The blast flares out for a solid 1.6 seconds. kool-aid's face and upper body jerk backwards in a flash, an instantaneous and violent thrusting jolt in automatic response to the explosive discharge—or perhaps, just maybe, the catastrophic brute force actually *does* tear a hole in spacetime, and kool-aid is physically displaced by it . . .

This event, aside from being hysterical to all but a handful of tight-sphinctered curmudgeons in the room, raises dave's status to unit legend. Sadly, the fabulous timewaster and smile-creator that is the Fart Game is soon relegated to the realm of memory: those guys start complaining to the "room strengths" about all the farting. The room strengths are two guys in each room who have been here for some time; they're supposed to try settling any interroom disputes and make sure everybody's being respectful and following the rules. What's funny is that our room strengths—jay and capone—are two of the biggest shit-stirrers around. Especially capone; an insufferable gossipmonger. Anytime someone has an issue with another resident, capone makes sure to spread this info. Always feigning nonchalance, of course. "So dave, they were sayin you ain't too happy with grif. What's up with all that?!" Furthering any existing rift. Dumb shitheads

[256]

with no imagination will often do this. I mean, Jerry Springer and Maury Povich only air for a couple hours a day! So these people create real-life drama in the unit. It's pitiful. As is a prisoner, especially in a cushy joint like Jacksonville, who calls himself *capone*—then goes around acting like a goddamn teenybopper bitch. You were a nobody on the streets, dude; just another run-of-the-mill Hispanic gangbanger. And you're *really* a nobody in here. "capone." Such absurd delusions of grandiosity!

The other room strength, jay, is remiss to stop the Fart Game—because he's among its greatest and most joyful participants! But he has to. Pretty pathetic that whoever had a problem with the farting didn't just approach us individually like the "grownass men" everyone proclaims to be. But that's something the Drug Unit setup provides: an easy excuse to relegate uncomfortable responsibilities onto someone else. Then at least *you* don't have to deal with it! This [the intentional abdication of responsibility] is one way the Drug Unit is a microcosm of the Prison Bureaucrazy; which, again, is itself just a microcosm of worldwide bureaucrazies in general.

Months begin slipping by as I entrench myself inside the smooth, deep groove of my routine. I complete *The Eternal City* on the morning of New Year's Eve; 520 pages handwritten. And by this point, I'm so disciplined and obsessed with my writing that I don't even take a break! After evening Medline, I get right back to work on a short story. Later, I put together a small vegan "cake" to celebrate my tremendous achievement. Sharing the decadent treat with a few supportive roommates. I create this cake using Oreos and peanut butter and knockoff Nutty Bars [which are interspersed layers of peanut butter and wafers, covered in chocolate]—these sorts of mass-produced, common junk foods that happen to not contain animal products are often called "accidentally vegan," though I prefer the self-coined phrase "*incidentally* vegan." I always celebrate upon completing a book; incarceration shouldn't stop me. My celebrations usually involve lots of whooping and hollering and joytears and loud music and strange bodily gyrations [in the vein of "dancing"]. Sadly, I have to stifle these urges— gyrations would be tolerated but mocked indefinitely, while crying'd be Just Plain Bad.

6.

Plenty of other shit happened in the three-ish months between my moving to the Drug Unit and my completion of *The Eternal City*. They replaced Dr. Williams with a heavyset white female, and she wanted to take away my pain meds. She cut the dosage in half for a couple weeks and it was wretched, but I miraculously convinced her to put the dosage back where it belonged. Also, a tentative sorta semi-friendship developed with Jenny, the pretty mid-20s Counselor assigned to me—well, it's precarious, but we do become the closest thing to "friends" a female Staff Member and an inmate can become—which is an odd dynamic that, looking back, simply *must* have contributed to the eventual personal-social disasters of unthinkable proportions that run utterly roughshod over my life. But not yet . . . at the time, my thoughts were focused on *Let the sentence reduction begin!*— 45 days of goodtime for every 90 days spent in the program, as I mentioned. Unfortunately, there are no partial completions; if you're 89 days into a three-month "contract" period and get booted from the unit, you accrue *no* goodtime. Those 45 days are lopped off your outdate only after you complete each 90-day contract. Anyway, I'm grateful Jenny is my Counselor. She's cool and mellow and sweet; and obviously cares about us a great deal. Not just as inmates, but as individuals. She maintains a strong, constant urge to help us alter our bad habits so we can *remain* free after escaping the Prison Vortex. Whatta gal!

Toward the end of 2010, I learn that Jacksonville does actually have a designated "Vegan Diet Tray" you can sign up for . . . but only for religious purposes. You can't receive it based on health or ethical reasons. Only religious ones. Isn't that great? Ethics and health—both of them tangible and factbased—are illegitimate. But if you want to eat a certain way because a religious text promotes it? well now *that's* legitimate! Yessir. Fine then, fuck it; whatever it takes! I claim to be Seventh-Day Adventist, which is one of the approved Vegan Tray religions I know at least something about [along with African Hebrew Israelite, Hindu, and Buddhist].

Some troubling developments really start to gain momentum a few weeks into the New Year, which *should* be my only full calendar year of incarceration. Which is the year that is 2,011 years after the birth [sic?] of Our [sic] Lord and Savior [sic] Jesus Christ. The problems start small, but then snowball into avalanches of life- and soul-crushing assfuckeries. They begin with a very simple [yet very dangerous] development.

To wit—I grow comfortable.

See, up to this point in prison, I've largely hidden *who I am*. Kept quiet about my radical politics. Made no hullabaloo about being vegan. I didn't really proselytize about anything, save for the occasional comment about guys' usage of words like "bitch" and "faggot" as universalisms [james has been the exception to my non-proselytistic ways, because he's likeminded and trustworthy]. The Person I Am, in prison and more or less today, is something I can trace back almost completely to one single event. All my radicalism, my ideologies, my rebelness—the entirety of *me*—can all be linked back to *Hurricane Katrina*. For a week during Winter Break of my junior year in college [2005], I did volunteer relief work in New Orleans with a group called Common Ground, which sprouted in the storm's wake. That trip BLASTED my eyes open. My entire universe, even. A sort of *life*-supernova; instant radicalization that changed everything, spreading to even the most remote corners of my life. Being in New Orleans and doing volunteer relief work was the nexus of my ideological evolution. No doubt about that.

Then again, strange as it may seem, I also know *I wouldn't've traveled there in the first place* to have those supernovic experiences if I hadn't gone vegetarian earlier that year! What's the connection? Well, I was raised on the so-called Standard American Diet [aka SAD; which it is, it's very sad indeed]. Steak 'n potatoes. Toxic fleshbased "food" at every meal. I loved McDonald's and KFC and Carl's Jr. and In-N-Out . . . all that shit. *Loved* it. I was also in love with this supercool black/Mexican vegetarian chick— we'll call her D.—in late highschool. One of my best friends also loved her, though, and it seemed like I had no chance with D. But her *twin sister* dug me, so I settled for dating her. That ended badly, and fast. I became really close good friends with D. our senior year, and she had a profound effect on me. Her *jois de vivre* was infectious. But any time I considered vege-tarianism, the idea was preposterous and my outlook remained steadfast: I could never give up "meat." Just loved it too much. Didn't help that I knew literally nothing about the universal, barbaric cruelty of animal products' creation, either.

Nonetheless, D. planted seeds inside me [that sounds extremely sexual, sorry]. Not on purpose—she was never the type back when I knew her to actively promote vegetarianism—but as a simple function of the example she set, and of my deep affection for her. Fastforward a couple years. Near the end of my sophomore year at UCI, my fisherman roommate brought home a two-foot catch. Then he showed our other roommate how to gut and clean the poor creature. I watched with a trepidation that rapidly trans-formed into aghast disbelief. He carved the animal open from head to fin— *while s/he was still very much alive and conscious and gasping for oxygen!* In an instant, for really the first time in my life, I made that oh-so-important and powerful connection between a hunk of meat and a sentient individuals' awful killing. Nor did I simply make the connection; I also *felt* it, on a visceral gut-level. An equation soon wiggled into my consciousness: [1] A few moments of gustatory pleasure vs. [2] an innocent, feeling creature's violent death. The scales tipped dramatically against [1] over the next 24 hours as I relived the scene, and contemplated that unavoidable equation, over and over. Things seemed increasingly unfair and inappropriate and just plain *wrong* the more I considered them. Giving up *meat* though?! How could I ever possibly manage? But then the next afternoon, something else very very significant happened. My Babcia ["grandmother" in Polish] and · I were together for our monthly luncheon; she lived just 20 minutes from UCI. I told her about the previous day's eye-opening and frankly traumatic experience. How I was considering an attempt at vegetarianism. Again, I knew zip-zilch about it. So I was taken aback when she explained how it's not only exceedingly easy to get ample nutrition sans meat, but that it is in fact *healthier*! Like by far. In multitudinous ways. [Christ, I was so damn ignorant!] Armed with this potent new information, I soon decided that I should at least *try* to get off the horrible meat-habit. Seeing what I'd seen, and feeling what I'd felt as a result, this seemed like the least I could do. Just give it a shot. See what it was like.

That was almost 12 years ago. My trial period seems to be going quite well! The meal with Babcia [at Olive Garden; ughh, so gross] was the very last time I intentionally consumed the flesh of a sentient being. So then—returning, at last, to my original point about Katrina et al.—the fact that I was vegetarian left me in total disbelief for many months, every time I considered my outlook up to and including the very *day* I made the change! It began to feel like I could do anything I set my mind to. *Anything* was possible! *I* went vegetarian [and vegan ≈ 11 months later] . . . **me**! Even now, well over a decade later, it'll sometimes *still* strike me as outlandish, hard to believe. That should tell you something. And me. It should tell all of us something! If I had the inner strength and resolve to 180 on such a fundamental, ingrained part of whom I'd always been . . . well, that showed me I had [and have] greater willpower and courage than I knew. Than I ever would've *guessed*. So, after deciding for certain that I wanted to help downtrodden New Orleans residents in Katrina's wake—selfconscious and uncomfortable and frightened though I was to embark on a solo trip into a torn, probably dangerous area—I knew it was doable if I just set my mind to it. That post-Katrina trip proved to be the nexus of my adult identity. But it would've never happened if I hadn't first initiated my boundless resolve by going vegetarian. Hopefully this all helps you understand one reason veganism is so important to me.

So then. *The me you see is the only me I can be, Mon chéri!* But for a long time in prison, I felt the need to suppress my true self with all its passion and unique experiences. Toned it down hoping to navigate my sentence in relative peace. Hoping to avoid confrontation as much as possible. But then I started growing comfortable there in the Drug Unit, and hence far too lackadaisical. Especially given just how fiercely my personality and beliefs clashed with average J-ville inmates—and indeed, the average American.

As I alluded to, part of the problem is Jenny, in some odd way. Every Drug Unit resident must meet privately with their Counselor at least once a month. But the Counselors also make themselves available to talk for the majority of business hours, willing to discuss just about anything on our minds. To me, this is a fabulous chance for some much-needed personal sanity-maintenance. I'll often have a chat with Jenny when something particular is upsetting me. She's a real-world person, not an inmate; they ain't the same, folks! #SorryNotSorry. For one, she goes *home* at night. She's not entrenched in prison culture like all of us—dug in like unwitting ticks. Engulfed in manic rushing bodies and all their drama as it and they swirl around cyclonically. The Counselors, though, occupy a space *outside* the Prison Vortex. They step inside four days a week—but not *all the way* inside, and not far enough to get sucked into its black hole-maw. It makes a substantial difference in personalities. Myself included! Talking to Jenny is like fleeing a smog-choked city for the mountains. Total, invigorating refreshment.

In addition to her job here, she works part-time at a women's shelter. I tell her numerous times how awesome she is, how noble these occupations are. She's flattered to a reddened-cheek degree—no inmate has ever even vaguely hinted something like that to her before. The value of having this connection to a noninmate-person is immeasurable. Problem is, it's also the *very thing* that helps me feel more comfortable being who I am. I'll be speaking to Jenny in her shared office, in the Bubble right by the building's entrance, and we'll discuss the rampant misogyny and racism and homophobia I encounter on a daily basis; how much it bothers me and pisses me off. She validates my feelings. Inadvertently, at the same time, validating my *anger* too. And so little by little I *stop* holding my tongue. I confront people on their disgusting attitudes and statements.

One afternoon in early 2011, Mrs. Meyer gathers everyone in the day-room to watch the movie *Philadelphia* in lieu of classes. Surprisingly, I've never seen it. I'm always interested in learning about the struggles gay [and other oppressed] peoples endure.

I think the movie's fantastic; terrific performances by Tom Hanks and Denzel, and so touching. I might've cried if I weren't in prison. Back in the room afterwards, guys bitch and whine about being forced to watch such an apparently gross and discomforting movie—it had *men kissing*, for gawd's sake! "Well that was totally fuckin pointless," my neighbor buft says. He's an ex-tweaker popped for cooking meth. Got locked up—this time—over two years ago. He once showed me a picture of himself from immediately prior; he was skeletal, ravaged, cheeks sunken #methward. buft damn sure turned it around in prison though [physically, that is—I harbor strong suspicions of lingering pathology]. Now he's a musclehead, able to benchpress twice his weight, beefy and t h i c k . Cueballed head and icy blue eyes. The kinda eyes that evoke the terror-trio of rape, pillage, and plunder: quintessential Viking eyes, if you will. Even more unsettling, a fierce rage smolders visibly within them—crouching beneath the super-ficial façade, ready to barge forth in a nanosecond if provoked.

One of buft's selfpurported schemes is that he'd seduce women in bars, get them to bring him home, and then, after they banged and the woman fell asleep, he'd steal her valuables and leave. So in essence, he was exactly like those cheap hookers you always hear about. Real standup dude, huh? Class act. It shouldn't surprise you that buft will contribute multiplicative bullshit, drama, and anxiety to my life.

jay's upstairs bunkmate pete also complains about the movie. He offers a more nuanced critique: "That was the gayest fuckin movie I've ever seen," he says, and guffaws in a peculiar buffoonish staccato unique to him.[74]

"Well," I tell pete, "it *was* a movie about gay people's lives and strug-gles, so it seems to . . . kinda make sense, just a little?"

Several guys stare at me now. buft says, "Did you like the movie, jan?"

---

[74] pete's another humanoid for whom I could make a strong argument for reclassi-fication as a distinct subspecies of homo sapiens sapiens—cuz he's such a vile fuckwit.

I hesitate

for

a moment. Then decide it doesn't matter a whit what they think. "Yeah actually, I did like it. Pretty damn good story."

. . . awkward silence . . .

pete gets his rocks off talking shit all day long, just like jay and capone. He's not the Gossip *Queen*—capone is planted atop that throne—but pete's the loudest, most obnoxious shit-talker. He has unkempt black hair, a thick goatee, and a big toothy grin evoking beavers and similar such woodland creatures. I think he's locked up for selling guns; at the very least, he claims longtime involvement in black market handgun-dealing. He has a pistol tattooed on his left pectoral muscle. More classy stuff. Not white-trashy at all! In this homophobic wasteland, pete's among the most outspoken gayhaters I ever encounter. He calls Spongebob Squarepants . . . wait for it . . . a "gay conspiracy to turn kids into fags." No, really—I wish this were a Freylike fabrication, but sadly it's not. That right there is a verbatim quote.[75] Seems farcically over-the-top, I hear you! But he's dead serious. Truly believes asinine shit like that.

The plot thickens—like a blood-engorged dong. Are you familiar with teabagging? It's when a guy squats over a sleeping or otherwise helpless person's face and dips his balls in and out of the prostrated mouth. Once again, we're talkin highsociety stuff here. pete celebrates having teabagged someone's mother, in addition to mouthballing numerous friends. Friends both female *and* male. The plot further thickens—like a fingered anus [not that there's anything wrong with that!] He frequently claims people on TV are "fuckin faggots." And mocks me on the regular for loving Elton John's music. I finally get sick of it one day. Time to fire back.

"You know," I tell him, purposefully loud enough for our dormmates to hear. "There was a huge study about people who dislike gays." The eight or ten guys in the room watch us closely. Eyes tennis-matching back and forth. "Two groups—the openly antigay ones, and those who claimed the opposite," I continue, "were shown gay porn. And do y'know what? The guys who identified as homophobes were far more likely to get aroused!"

---

[75] Amusingly enough, big tough musclehead buft *loves* Spongebob Squarepants [along with many other cartoons]. Of course, pete NEVER mentions his theory when buft's around. Shocking, right? LOL!

pete backtracks faster than an NBA point guard on defense for a fast-break. "Hey, I don't hate gay people! I just think th're *funny*."

"Oh yeah?" To be honest, I'm more than a little concerned he'll realize what I'm suggesting and kick my ass. Heart's clomping like wild Mustang hooves; I'm struggling to keep my voice casual, steady and free of the weakling-trembles. That's right, I'm scared—and willing to admit it [to you, my Dear Reader].[76] But I'm so tired of his brash goddamn bigotry. Just can't hold my tongue anymore . . . I feel obligated to confront him. "You think they're funny, that's really what it is?"

"Yeah! I think it's funny they like sucking cocks, HUH-HUH-HUH-HUH!" That's his laugh—like MTV's Butthead in warp-speed.

"Gotcha."

Riiight. He doesn't hate gay people at all! Even though one day, during a news segment about Clay Aiken, pete makes an offhand comment that "Fags like that should be hunted down and shot."

Man, this dude's a real scumbag bastard. All the more toxic because he has an *audience* for his idiotic verbal #shartblasts. His outgoing personality and ceaseless jocularity provide a sizable friendgroup, on top of general unit-wide affinity for him. But I see through the grandiose window dressing. He's a shitstain, plain and simple. Would've significantly enriched the world by perishing as a sperm in his father's crusted sweatsock.

pete's brand of unfettered, brazen hatefulness blows me the fuck away. I cannot fathom how people could actually feel like this. Let alone announce it to the world! It literally makes me ill, figuratively crushes my heart. It's the exact same sentiment that resulted in Matthew Shepherd's savage beating and slow, agonizing death in Wyoming. Same attitude that led to the rape and murder of transgendered man Brandon Teena. Same one, too, that held sway as countless black people were lynched-tortured-mutilated-murdered in post-Civil War America. Pared down to its fundamental core, it's the pathological fear/hatred of *the Other*. Of people who are simply different from the so-called norm. It's revolting; dangerous, even—see the wild popularity of Donald Trump and his insane, explosive political ascension.

Is it any surprise that pete's nasty attitudes extend beyond gays? He expresses a similar sociopathic lack of empathy for women.

---

[76] Love you! ☺

If we allow this kind of baseless and aggressive hostility to exist unchallenged, it will fester and rot like an untreated gangrenous limb, spreading outward to infect and kill our entire society. The overwhelming majority of these diseased individuals will *never* be enlightened and change their minds. Not through love, not through prayer, not through magical thinking, or psychic beams of positive thoughts and loving energy, not through brilliant rationale, or countless studies demonstrating that, for example, sexuality isn't a choice but rather the way you're *born*. Some people are too far gone for rehabilitation. Too sick. Sociopaths must be held accountable for their behavior—forcefully, if that's what it takes. They need to be removed from society to protect the innocent [especially nonhumans]. Would that entail some form of prison? Ones with only a passing resemblance to the monstrous for-profit institutions America has now? Or would it mean dealing with unremitting sociopaths some other way? I'm sure the complete solution is multifaceted; but here's what the main character of my second novel *Redwood Falls* proclaims about individuals who intentionally kill or maim living creatures or devastate ecosystems:

"Nothing changes a mind quicker than a bullet to the head."

Yessir. That is indeed one way to affect someone's belief-system and actions dramatically; and fast, too! [I know it may seem masturbatory to quote oneself—but hey, masturbation feels good, so screw it!]

George Jackson was a revolutionary black militant and Panther member; his collection of prison letters, *Soledad Brother*, is required reading for anyone interested in black liberation or prison reform [as if it's actually possible to untangle them into separate issues!]. He captures prison life, the human condition, and radical leftist politics like no one else. Jackson was gunned down in a San Quentin Prison exercise yard during an alleged escape attempt in 1971—though many people, including historians, believe he was simply assassinated. In part because he was an irrepressible and exceptionally influential far-left activist and a voice, a mouthpiece, for millions of disenfranchised people of color. One line from *Soledad Brother* that really resonated with me: "Capture, imprisonment, is the closest to being dead that one is likely to experience in this life." I feel it, man, feel that statement's truth in my bones. The soulkilling reality of incarceration is a principle reason I'm compelled to write on a daily basis. The process offers mental escape. It's the same reason I read close to zero nonfiction in prison; most worthwhile fiction engenders a liberating sense of bodily relocation that is seldom comparably induced by nonfiction. Plus, those books

I read from the latter category tend to contain miserable shit detailing the myriad ways we're all totally boned. My beleaguered psyche can't handle that noise right now. Once more quoting Jackson's letters: "Why can't I rid myself of the sorrow and emotion that awareness has brought me? I get rid of the self-destructive force of error and ignorance only to be torn and miserable by what I discover." This feeling of a double-edged existence, which often coincides with knowledge about the world's human-caused suffering, is a prevalent phenomenon among vegan animal rights activists. And I'm all but positive the same feeling will arise when any empathetic person harbors a concern for justice. Many of my several hundred vegan friends have said things like, *Life would be so much happier if I didn't know about animal suffering.* This whole concept is really just a nuanced, social injustice-specific way of saying "Ignorance is bliss." Or, more accurately, it's an explanation of what becoming *nonignorant* feels like—a reflective assessment of that cliché's unfortunate inverse. "Knowledge is misery," perhaps?

Around this time, early spring 2011, the prison chaplain finally adds my name to the Vegan Tray list. He's regrettably the sole individual charged with managing it; which means I had to meet with him first and feign religiosity. I expected this to produce squeamish discomfort and even embarrassment. I'm confident my anti-theist brethren can understand why. In reality, though, it was so simple and quick that I hardly felt anything. And the result is such a drastic improvement that I'd meet with the chaplain a hundred times if that's what it took! The Vegan Tray here is startlingly impressive—even moreso when you consider I'm in a Midwestern prison, and even more-moreso when compared to the regular meals! They bestow us with weighty mounds of food, including fresh, whole fruit for every. single.meal. Earlier I talked about the lack of fresh produce; this includes fruit as well. I haven't tasted real fruit in over six months! I cradle that gorgeous first Red Delicious apple in my palm. Staring in awe; it's become a friggin novelty! Like a semi-familiar object I barely recall, made strange and even alien via the extensive time passed. That first crisp, juicy bite tastes sweeter and more mouthwatering than any dessert I can remember. And I don't even really like Red Delicious apples!

We can only hypothesize about the reasons they don't serve real fruit. Too expensive? Taken for granted as a human right? Also though, a not-insignificant amount of blame lies with my fellow inmates. A substantial percentage would trash their fruit untouched. I'm truly stunned by how many guys don't eat the meager, mushy canned vegetables we do get; I think it's gotta be 25 to 30 percent. Some dudes even go so far as to *remove* the vegetables from their main dish! E.g. sifting through a corpse-centered ["beef"] casserole to pluck out the broccoli. It's a basic nutritional violation to exclude fresh fruit in toto from a thousand individuals' diet for years, even decades. Contrarians might argue we'd brew hooch if fresh fruit were available in bulk, but I can obliterate that claim with two short points: [1] it'd be impossible to brew alcohol in the dorms without an Officer noticing and/or a roommate snitching; [2] even if it were possible, that potentiality is far surpassed by our fundamental need for nutritious, unprocessed fruit! It really is that simple.

Hell, get this: For the regular trays, they only serve *canned* fruit three or four times a week at best! Usually it's a tiny scoop of peaches or pineapple or plums or mixed fruit, drowning in high fructose corn syrup with a little dribble of actual juice. Of course, the monthly menus are vetted by a professional dietician working in Springfield's IDOC headquarters; someone who -claims- the food is nutritionally adequate. But this is just like with the Doctors and Health [sic] Care [sic] Providers [sic[and sic**k**]]: they're *Company Men/Women*. Hired for the sole purpose of rubberstamping whatever the Bureaucrats want them to. What other explanation could there be? They *must* know the food's abysmally deficient. [The existence—and power—of such bootlicking #*Yessirs*, as I've dubbed them, working within "Corrections" should surprise no one; there may be an intentional produce shortage, but there damn sure ain't a shortage of selfish assholes with a degree and no job!] You don't need a vast arsenal of dietary wisdom to know that eating two miniscule mushcanned-vegetable servings a day and four syrupy, canned servings of fruit a *week* ensures that any grown man will be lacking an array of essential vitamins and nutrients. Madness, all of it! Nutritional Cruelty! **G**ruel and Unusual Punishment!!

FOOD/NUTRITION: yet another *hidden monster* lurking within the Prison-Industrial Complex.

Aside from all the great stuff discussed above, there's one more fantastical benefit to getting on the Vegan List: They automatically switch you to "Early Chow." Meaning that, along with the diabetics, we're summoned to Chow a good 20 minutes before they even *start* running regular lines. This is nothing short of spectacular—hell, I'd even say it's SPEC-friggin-TAC-U-freakin-LAR! Because what it means, you see, is that it means that for Chow I'll *never again* have to endure one of prison-life's most odious aspects. No longer will I be required to trudge—gloriously, oh goddamnit oh-so-gloriously goddamn glorious!—my ass to the Chow Hall every day along with my entire unit, with its lunchgoing masses of like 70 to 99 guys.

[Before getting on the Vegan Tray List, I'd sometimes stay back and eat lunch in the room [remember, I already *never* went to Chow for dinner because it came during obligate nappytime] from my Commissary supplies. Simply because the whole ordeal was so stressful and nerve-wracking. To wit: Almost without fail, during a typical Chowtrip, the Officer controlling movement would force everyone, the entire 50-yard-long scattered cluster[fuck] of ≈ 70 to 100 guys, to halt over and over while the laggards caught up; this densely populated journey often also featured a complex, multitudinous sequence of disparate microlines—viz., a line at the unit's gate, a line to enter the Chow Hall, another line for food, yet another lining up afterwards at the building's gate, and so on and so awwwn. Me engulfed the whole time by many dozen sadsack schlubs. So many, all at once, and with so much *energy*! excited to load up on that gourmet prison cuisine. Assaulting my fragile nervous system with constant,

intensely loud   FAM, GET TH' FUCK UP HIR, ON E'RYTHANG

and obnoxious   dude, preeeety sure that newbie's a fag--biller told me capone said he was checkin im out in th' shower! HUH-HUH-HUH-HUH

and *relentless*   Ey jan, could I getcher cake if you ain' eatin it?

noise pollution   **FUCK that dumbass bitchass nigga!**

Now then, I think you can imagine my bliss at discovering Early Chow is mellower by nine-tenths or more; instead of ↑that↑ gawdawful ordeal, it's actually *relaxing*! [I know, I couldn't believe it either!] Everyone at Early Chow combined occupies no more than three table-rows—as opposed to normal mealtimes' three *dozen* rows. As you can see, simply getting myself onto the Vegan List produces several very tangible upgrades to my life.

Soooo, with all this good stuff . . . the Vegan Tray, Early Chow, Medical Gym, tolerable meds, a blitzkrieg of writing . . . by now, why haven't I begun *anticipating* a barrage of terrible shit to splatter over my life, enough to more than compensate for these positive things? The cosmic scales have always seemed improbably tilted against me. Prison and every screwjob involved is merely their latest iteration.

At some point back/up there I was discussing this memoir's writing— or rather how I *wasn't* writing it. How I've now [well, not *now* now; I mean the story arc's now, meaning early 2011] set aside this memoir for the time being.[77] The purpose of bringing that up again? Well, I *need* something to write! You know, the whole staving-off-suicidal-urges-via-always-having-a-project-in-the-works thing? And this hardly seems uncommon among writers. In the terrific collection *The Eleventh Draft: Craft and the Writing Life from the Iowa Writer's Workshop*, author Chris Offutt says that completing a project means "snatching [that book's] life away. A part of me goes with it. Nothing will fill the absence but another project, another imaginary world. Nothing will save me but the act of writing." Indeed, *señor* Offutt—and now I once more require saving. More than ever, given my circumstances.

So I wrack my brain. At least four unwritten book ideas are knocking around in my head. A couple have been in there, developing, for several *years*. But I don't feel ready to write any of them. I struck a mental wall on the first two after trying to develop the narrative arc. The other two are problematic because they're ultra-ambitious, complex stories, and I think I'm not yet capable of rendering them just right—of juggling the huge cast of characters and their dense, nuanced plots. Matching on paper the complete visions in my mind.

. . . .

Then again, I have nothing if not time to experiment here; it may in fact be the perfect time, given my newfound discipline, the necessity of escape, and the mental space granted by my environment. Plus, mentally considering the possibility of writing one of the badass epics has gotten me

---

[77] By the way, do you find it at all strange that memoirs almost never seem to mention the physical reality of said memoir's writing? In other words, you rarely read about the memoir *being written* within said memoir. Does most every memoir's writing process begin only *after* everything in the memoir has already happened? Surely something must be written down or recorded amid the course of events! Maybe it's conventional to not bring it up unless absolutely necessary, like movie characters' using the bathroom.

Just for the record, this whole talking-about-writing-the-memoir-within-the-memoir-itself thing is NOT [just] an attempted parlor trick by me, some clever über-metafictional technique [or maybe metanonfictional would be more fitting—or meta-*metafictional*, or *meta*-metanonfictional—are any of those even a thing? well, they are now!]; this memoir's writing is itself both a significant part of the story and helps demonstrate a point [viz., that the "story" was so witheringly depressing that I couldn't write it while having to live it as well.] And I'm also genuinely curious: Why have I never read a memoir that discusses the writing of that memoir—outside of, like, the introduction? Maybe it's just me. Is it you, too? Or just me? It's just me, isn't it? Damn.

amped at the prospect. Screw it. Might as well try! I might discover I *am* able to wrench forth a novel sufficiently commensurate with my vision thereof.

It's the next morning, 21 January 2011 [I maintain a daily log—see image below—to keep track of pages written, encourage myself [note the repeated use of #autobackpatia via smiley faces and exclamation points], try to maintain goals, and know my per diem averages].

4/25 — 9 pgs.
4/26 — 9 pgs.
4/27 — 10 pgs.
4/28 — 7 pgs.
4/29 — 7 pgs.
4/30 — 10 pgs. [216 total]

(April avg = 7.2 pgs/day!!)

5/1 — 6 pgs.
5/2 — 6 pgs.
5/3 — 11 pgs.
5/4 — —
5/5 — 10 pgs.
5/6 — 10 pgs.

5/7 — 9 pgs.
5/8 — —
5/9 — 8 pgs.
5/10 — 6 pgs.
5/11 — 4 pgs.
5/12 — —
5/13 — 7 pgs.
5/14 — 6 pgs.
5/15 — 4 pgs.
5/16 — 9 pgs.
5/17 — 8 pgs.
5/18 — 9 pgs.
5/19 — 7 pgs.
5/20 — 7 pgs.
5/21 — 9 pgs.

5/22 — 10 pgs.
5/23 — 7 pgs.
5/24 — 9 pgs.
5/25 — 7 pgs.
5/26 — 10 pgs.
5/27 — —
5/28 — 12 pgs!
5/29 — 13 pgs!!
5/30 — 8 pgs.
5/31 — —

(May avg = ≈ 8.2/day!!)

6/1 — 5 pgs.
6/2 —
6/3 —
6/4 —
6/5 —
6/6 —
6/7 —
6/8 — 4 pgs.
6/9 — 9 pgs!
6/10 — 7 pgs.
6/11 — 9 pgs.
6/12 — —
6/13 — —

6/15 — 8 pgs.
6/16 — 9 pgs.
6/17 — 7 pgs.
6/18 — —
6/19 — —
6/20 — —
6/21 — —
6/22 — 8 pgs.
6/23 — —
6/24 — 4 pgs.
6/25 — 6 pgs.
6/26 — 7 pgs.
6/27 — 6 pgs.

6/29 — 5 pgs.
6/30 — 8 pgs.

TOTAL = 120

(7 pgs/day!!)

7/1 — 13 pgs!!!
7/2 — 6 pgs.
7/3 — —
7/4 — 7 pgs.
7/5 — —
7/6 — 8 pgs.
7/7 — 4 pgs.
7/8 — —

Immediately after Medline that morning, I get my stuff together and stick my headphones in and then compose the first sentence of what'll become my most radical, sociopolitically meaningful, complex, badass, and twice-over longest book I've ever written.[78] That first, guiding line: *Four figures, clad in black, move through the darkness.*

The story focuses on an uncompromising group of underground animal liberators: their political activism—which includes releasing caged mink at fur farms, breaking into laboratories and stealing files on animal research to expose experiments that are even more ghastly than usual, torching slaughterhouses and meat trucks, and staging cyberattacks on corporations that inflict savage cruelty and mass death on nonhumans; it focuses on the FBI's attempts to infiltrate the group and various related political dealings; on the group's strategies and intricate ideologies and their multitudinous tricks used to evade capture; on the ways they maintain their necessarily indefatigable, impassioned spirits despite being faced with barbaric mass cruelty and David-versus-Goliath odds; and it focuses on the group's interpersonal relationships, how they watch out for and take care of one another. Like I wrote—one complex bastard of a novel!

Almost right away, a spectacular truth unveils itself: I was wrong about being unprepared to take on this project! I very quickly drop into a deep groove, cranking out *70 pages* in the first two weeks alone. I'm thrilled; and, amazingly, the story's coming out even better than I'd imagined. All the absurd prisondrama bullshit—which is clamoring, always, for my attention—only further enhances the book's escapist value, and also aides my discipline-motivation-commitment to the project. The shittier things get, the more heavily, even desperately I fling myself into the story. It reaches a point where *The Liberators* [its early title] occupies my mind the great majority of waking life. No exaggeration: I'm thinking of the book like 95 percent of the day. james and I discuss it during our Medical Gym laps. I ponder it during Chow and while drifting off to sleep for my siesta. Upon waking, I mentally review the scene/s I hope to compose after evening Medline. I fall asleep at night planning the next day's chunk of compo-

---

[78] And that's no easy task—my novels tend to be *l o o n n n g*. Especially first drafts, since I often "type my way" to the juicy morsels, & explore things in tremendous detail. Only upon completion can I begin to glimpse things w/ true objectivity, & then parse it all down until the best stuff remains. I try to cut out 15-20% during second draft revisions. Hell, this book's first draft was 230,000 words, which would be well over 700 pages in book form!

sition, orchestrating its architectural design at every level—sometimes even seeing it take shape in my head with no apparent willful thought or effort on my part, as if viewing a geometrically rendered computer model of a building that comes together piece by piece. It's a beautiful, exhilarating, wondrous process.

What's not beautiful, though, is . . . basically everything else. buft—ex-tweaker, current musclehead cumball—has grown to loathe me. I think it stems from how different we are. He goes out to Gym and Yard every day and lifts heavy things from a variety of positions many many times. I stay in bed and write/read all day. He's tough and sinewy. I'm weak and flabby. I enjoyed *Philadelphia*; he thought it was a massive queerfest-timewaster. I was a pioneer of the Fart Game; he whined to our room strengths about it. More than anything though, I think buft hates me because of my personal lamp. Other people have them, but I use mine a *lot* more. I have to! This lamp-as-symbol-of-everything-wrong-with-possible-fag-jan will turn out to be a recurring theme. It's fuckin astounding how so many of these big tough hardened criminals and gangbangers are unraveled by a puny desk lamp! Pathetic, really. At least now you know—if you're ever attacked by a psychotic ex-con, apparently you just gotta shine a 30-watt bulb in his general direction and he'll morph into a bitchy nutless child. This advice may just save your life one day.[79]

Several other guys in the room hate me because I use my lamp a lot—even though I cover and dim it with a washcloth. buft by far more than anyone though. He's my neighbor, and seems the most vulnerable to its strange poison. He asks me to stick a folded cylinder of paper over the bulb so the beam's more focused. I grant the request; but within a few days a hardass Officer [same one who nearly thwocked me in the head with his baton during a unit-shakedown, and whose pasty, bloated face resembles Porky the Pig to a startling degree] removes it and says he'll confiscate the lamp if I cover it again.

That's all bad enough. But then it gets worse. Doesn't it always?

buft's curled on his side one night watching *Kung-Fu Panda*, dozing; he faces away from me. It's quiet in the room and I'm reading. A short burble

---

[79] No thanks necessary if it does indeed help you—although any gratitude would certainly be welcomed! I think the best way to thank me would be by purchasing, say . . . 60 or 70 copies of this memoir, and then distributing them to your friends/colleagues/children/fellow church members. Muchos gracias!

of gas flutters out of buft's ass. After a moment, without turning back to look our way, jay drones out, "Ey buft, 'z'at you?"

"Uh?" buft grunts, undozing. "Nah."

"It was youuuu, buft," pete cries. "Don't deny it, you supplied it!" He guffaws in that singularly obnoxious, knuckledragging way.

"Man, shut the hell up." buft says. Fully conscious now. "Musta been jan. Came from behind me."

"Nah dude," I say. "That was you, trust me. Y'all know I *claim* my farts!"

"Man's got a point," dave mutters.

"Wasn't me!" buft says. "It came from behind me."

"That's where your ass is," I cry. "Of course it came from *behind* you!" Half a dozen guys start cracking up.

buft scoffs. "Whatever." He's pissed now; and this is one guy who tends to haul grudges around like they're affixed to his fucking body, like hemorrhoids or something. And recall his preexisting ire, with its foundation in my demonic lamp. I just want this to be over so he calms down. Dude is straightup dangerous.

It does end—for the night. As so often happens though, the minor incident gets rehashed with roomwide cracks for at least a couple days. So buft's embarrassment and anger at me grows, fermenting. A few mornings later, almost everyone's in group or out at Yard. I'm writing. buft and pete are the only other guys in the room. A laundry porter strolls in, handing me my whitemesh bag of clean clothes. I want to keep writing ASAP. So I'm folding and stuffing the clothes sloppily into my box. buft sits on his bunk sideways, legs dangling off the edge. Just staring at me. pete's lying on his bunk diagonal to us, watching a typical "Who's the Baby's Daddy?" segment on the cultural cesspool known as *The Maury Povich Show*.

buft chuckles at me. "Yer mom teach you'da fold like that?"

I fire back without pause. "Your mom teach you to cook meth?"

A pall drops over his face so fast it's like a spell—black magic. *Expecto Douchebaggum Psychosis!* His facial muscles go slack, and a murderous fury burns in those Viking eyes.

But there's also a sense of deadness in his expression
an emotionally numb quality
as if deaf to remorse
or the pointless bleating of a malformed conscience.

Sociopathic, in a word. And now he's staring at me with that violent pathology carving his features. "I will beatcher fuckin ass." Voice dead, too, flat as a casketed corpse.

I puff out air in a sort of chuckle, smirking. Yet a fierce heat flushes my cheeks, and it's suddenly hard to breathe, chest constricted like there's a fat dumbbell perched on it. The Terror is palpable and physiological in me. Yet I cannot allow it to show; can't display weakness, or I'll be even worse off. "Dude, you brought up my mom first. I was just returning the favor."

"I. Don't. *Give a fuck.*"

Now pete's noticed and he clambers down from his bunk and hurries over to buft. Looking up at that withering deathgaze. "Hey man, it's cool."

buft hasn't removed his eyes from mine for a millisecond. "I swear to fuckin gawd jan, I'll come down off this bed and choke you out right now."

"buft, buft," pete says with both hands held up. "You don't wanna do that, bro, take it easy."

"I was just messin around." I can barely breathe—yet I must stand my ground. [But he could *kill* you—RUN, ya idiot!!] "You made a crack about my mom, I shot back. Simple."

"Do you *want* me t'choke you out? I don't give a fuck what happens, I'll fuckin do it."

"*buft!*" pete seems positive buft's about to attack me. "It's not worth it, bro, you know what'll happen. Think about the goodtime. You wanna get home to your family as soon as possible. *Think about all your people!* It ain't worth it, he don't know what he's sayin."

I knew/know precisely what I was saying, but I'll let it slide—in the interest of continuing my important life's work filtering oxygen.

"Don't fuckin talk about my mom, *jan.*" Snideness on the name's perceived femininity.

Still I don't back down. "I don't wanna talk about your mom," I say. "It's simple—don't say anything about my mom, I won't say anything about yours."

You may not understand—you, Dear Reader, may think my crippled ass should just choke down my pride and apologize, withdraw, acquiesce, suck his cock, do whatever the hell it takes to assuage him. He's got like 80 pounds on me, rippled muscles sprouting everywhere. And yes, my Dear Reader, you may be absolutely right!

The whole thing's near-impossible to understand unless you've been imprisoned, though. I *cannot* back down, especially as a young white man.

Maintaining this attitude and behavior could get the shit beat out of me[80]—but withstanding one pulverization, and thereby demonstrating you won't back down, is better in the long run than having everyone think you're weak—because then your entire prison life will be hellacious; guys'll know they can walk all over you. And so, though I'm terrified, I must suppress my natural instincts and stand up for myself. No matter the odds.

Luckily the worst of buft's rage has passed. "Better watch what you say, jan, or someday somebody's gonna seriously fuck you up."

"It's cool buft," pete says. "Let's just move on."

The threat's over. I lie down and jam my headphones in and continue writing.

. . . .

Ah, who am I fooling? It's more like I *pretend* to write. I'm shaken up. My nerves are jagged, spitting white-hot sparks like a severed powerline. I'm sweating, can't think straight. The scene plays over and over in my head, lodged on repeat like a gawdawful song you can't stop hearing. I'm hugely relieved when they call Early Chow and I get to evacuate the unit and decompress.

Now you know the necessary dynamics and players; so I suppose it's time to relate the sequence of events that result in a catastrophic debacle, and contribute as much as anything to the wreckage that follows.

jay and I have grown into casual buddies. He's the baldheaded "room strength" and gossiper occupying the bottom bed in the room's far right corner. And when I write *occupying*, I mean it in the sense that American troops occupy foreign countries once they've established a presence: He almost *never* leaves bed. Goes to Chow once or twice a week—which is also how often he takes a shit. jay's extreme constipation is a big running joke in our room; he seems impervious to Metamucil or milk of magnesia. His face has the flat affect of someone who is—well, devastatingly constipated—but also stuck in a constant depressive state. His features seldom deviate from total stolidity. Even while laughing, only his lips move.

Hence my surprise when we develop a competitive chess rapport. Don't forget my own highly sedentary lifestyle either, and how I abhor the dayroom. Aside from a half hour on the phone with Rachel every other day, I

---

[80] Or the life choked out of me, or the [*noun*] [*verb*]ed out of me . . . choose your idiom.

avoid the place like it's full of squawking children [which in many ways it is]. Given that sitting aggravates the knees, it really is a shocker when jay and I start playing chess several days a week.

He's way better than me—winning about four of every five games. I used to love playing; even got second place in a middle school tournament. Now though, I'm just bored after more than a couple-few straight games. One day I violate Prison Etiquette bigtime. This is right after I fork his queen and a rook with one of my knights. I'm jacked with excitement; it's so damn satisfying to execute a solid fork like that.[81] "BOOM!" I cry, and shoot to my feet. "How you like that shit, bitch?!"

His eyes dart up from the board to me.

I start to realize my faux pas even as it's still exiting my mouth. I'm lucky he's the only one who heard me [call him *bitch*]—a forbidden insult with violent potential in prison. "Shit dude, I'm sorry."

"You shouldn't—"

"No I know, it's my bad. I was amped up, it just came out."

"Just fuckin be careful, bro. I don't fuckin care if you say it, personally, but you gotta fuckin be careful." jay utilizes the word *fuck* so often it's borderline-Tourette's. It functions as his *Umm* or *Uhh*, his thoughtpauses. "You can't . . . fuckin . . . just don't fuckin . . . don't do that."

"You're right, that was my bad." I'm being genuine; this is not to be taken lightly. Many guys would swing on you, without hesitation, for calling them a bitch.

My hands are clasped motionless on the table; I'm staring at the board, but no moves or plays are running through my head. Like the game just finished. "Hey." I'm looking into his eyes to show how serious I am. "My bad, all right? Cool?"

"It's done, don't fuckin worry bout it. Fuckin just, you know, fuckin watch yourself."

"I will."

"Your move." He flicks a finger. "Go."

And with that it's over. We continue our unending tournament.

---

[81] A *fork* is when you move to a spot that threatens two of your opponent's pieces. Forking two valuable pieces can be spectacularly demoralizing for your opponent, b/c then they have to decide which one they'd rather lose. Pulling off a good fork blasts an almost godlike power into me, and I have the tendency to then slam my palms on the table and shout something like, "I JUST FORKED THE *SHIT* OUTTA YER ASS!" This often creates confused stares and/or raised eyebrows.

From then on, though, a subtle undercurrent of animosity and edginess runs through our interactions. Don't even know why [although I'm certain that capone, jay's neighbor, goads him into furthering the drama]. And it is building, too, as days pass. jay singles me out for mockery more than usual. I naturally return the trashtalk in kind.

One night, we're all in the room after count and pete asks jay who won our chess matches that day. "Smoked his ass," jay says. "Got two outta three, but I fuckin should'a won em all."

"Smoked me?" I cry. "Dude, every game was close!"

"Only cuz I let you get close."

"Ohhh!" pete hollers, and then unleashes his Butthead-laugh.

I make a *pshaw* sound. "All right, whatever you say—chump!"

Several guys draw out long-O sounds. jay rises onto an elbow and turns toward me, glaring.

"He's just hatin on me," I announce to the room, "cuz he's jealous I can take a shit more'n once a week."

A bunch of our roommates are cracking up. mikey, lying on his bunk near the door and watching his neighbor's TV, says, "That right there's what you call a burn, jay. He just torched yo ass. On e'rythang." mikey's scruffbearded and so scrawny he's nearly massless. Also funny as hell. Able to deliver witty and incisive observations all the time. The slang is one of his humorous shticks; though lilywhite, he'll use idioms and phrases derived from Chicago black-vernacular—except he renders them with perfect enunciation. Creating even funnier and more absurd statements.

With the escalating acrimony between jay and I, things seem to be nearing their conclusion. Something's gotta give. Lest it all intensifies to spark an explosion that cannot be contained to our room; cannot be handled internally. I feel it coming. No idea what form it'll take, though.

Amid this drama and psychological dread, other bad shit's happening. No surprise. Rachel's a mess—her father just died after an extended, courageous fight against a litany of illnesses. He'd lived in San Francisco for decades; when Rachel and I lived there in 2007 and '08, they reconnected. Spent lots of time together and grew very close for the first time in her adult life. I also got to know him. He was always very sweet and kind hearted to me. His early death devastates Rachel. He wasn't much older than 60. Naturally, the whole thing is even harder for her because I'm INCARCERATED 2,000 miles away! His passing saddened me, but the worst part is I'm all but powerless to help Rachel cope, to offer comfort and mitigate her lonesome suffering. The emotional support-capabilities offered by the damn stupid telephone are meager at best. It really highlights the unquantifiable value of *physical* comfort.

So I'm lugging that omnipresent weight of dual sorrow, amplified by my near-complete inability to provide the emotional support she so needs and deserves. On top of that, I'm still [always] navigating the shadowy, narrow path of daily despair. The baseline sorrow of living not only in a world being destroyed by human greed, but at the same time living in this toxic, grotesque place, surrounded 60/60/24/7/365/2 by humanoid-type shitheads and their blaring bullshit, their insufferable noise and ignorance and bigotry. This mad, diseased Vortex. Which is—I'm understanding more and more—a perfect microcosm of the mad, diseased world outside the razorwired fences. It's all the same, the "Free World" and this Prison Vortex, except here the scales are densely compressed; so many identical problems, except here pitched to glass-shattering heights, and epitomized, and also right out in the open. Whereas truth in the outside world is buried under layer after layer of obfuscating enculturation and brainwashing. The uglier aspects of life are present in both places; outside the fences, though, we're able to turn away. Convince ourselves human activities aren't as hideous as they really are. My dear friend Jo expressed this idea with great elegance in a letter she wrote me: "Your observation that every other word you hear is 'either racist or misogynist or otherwise ignorant' underscores what a lot of people say: that prison is a microcosm of society. I think *most* americans are ignorant, misinformed, xenophobic, and narrow-minded. If this were not true, the country wouldn't be in such sorry shape; the public would not be able to be so easily manipulated by selfish greedy politicians and corporate executives whose blatant lies and mindless soundbites are so instantly believed by the zombie masses." [This has proven even more sagacious than it already was with the recent election of Donald Trump!]

Prisoners—whether you want to believe it or not—are truly One of Us, just as we are One of Them. Maybe that's why we try so aggressively to *not* think about them! because we're unconsciously aware of the terrifying, awful truth that the neighboring realities are far more alike than they are different . . .

7.

I'm back home in coastal California; the only place I belong. No—not *back home*—I never left in the first place! The whole arrest-incarceration thing was just a horrible, and horribly vivid, nightmare. One that continued for an absurd length of time. But now it's over. I've returned to my real life.

Rachel, Rikki, and I are running down a tunnellike path created by huge ferns in the woods, through the towering oldgrowth redwoods of Humboldt County. We're laughing at my ridiculous nightmare about being in prison. Even so, the laughter is tinged with immense relief. Rikki darts around joyously; she slips under the ferns' arcing arms, hopping onto a log and jetting down its tremendous length, and then weaves her way back to us. Being Forest Rikki, as we refer to it. Bolting in and out of the thick vegetation, flashing for a second onto the path and then disappearing again in the dense growth. A fog bank furls lazily into the forest, carrying with it a scent of the nearby Pacific. Air so clean, fresh, moist, invigorating, lifegiving. I close my eyes and extend my arms as the fog swirls around me and I breathe deeply, inhaling for so long there's a spike of pressure in my chest—but it's good, oh so good, everything's good, even *perfect*. I'm with my two favorite people in the world, in my favorite place. I'm smiling so much it aches, cramping my lips. But I can't stop.

To stop would infringe on the magic surrounding us.

Rachel comes to me. Spreads her arms around my back and presses her body to mine. Faces close enough now to share oxygen. She's smiling too, her perfect toothy grin of pure happiness that lights her up with an almost-tangible aura, as if her inner glow shines through her face. Like the bright wash of a fresh Polaroid beginning to reveal its subject.

Rikki bounds up to us for a moment, checking in. She looks up at me with beaming adoration. Those glacial blue eyes melting my heart. Then she dashes off.

Rachel kisses me. Pulls back. Leans in and pecks my lips again. The fog envelopes the three of us, as if creating a sanctuary for us alone—for *these fleeting moments* alone. The moist woods harmonize briskly in our nostrils. This is my home. It's where I belong; the only place I should ever be. Then Rachel's saying something, but too faintly. I can't hear her. Can't hear anything anymore. My darlings, and the forest's natural beauty, perfect down to every last twig and mushroom spore and dewdrop, is fading as well. Back to a mere silhouette of memory.

Because I'm coming out of the dream.

I realize it, too; I'm still there with her arms around me and her smile and the fog and the redwoods and the wild *joie de vivre* of Forest Rikki and the fecund earthy woods, but I understand now that I'm just dreaming. Everything's fading, dropping away, the crystalline Polaroid in reverse. I try to cusp in my mind the images, the smells, the soft damp soil under my feet, the press of Rachel's body against mine, but I can't make them stay [oh goddamnit no, please let it linger, let *me* linger, just a few more seconds even—PLEASE!]. No matter how hard I try. I'm shackled, powerless—bitter reality's helpless slave.

Then I'm conscious, the dream's over, sensations gone, all the incredible vividness gone except in difficultly conjured flashes; my eyes are still closed, but the images appear only in flitting pops, like the silver-white dots that can pulse in your eyesight after a powerful camera's flashbulbing effects.

And now I'm fully aware it was just a dream

[*vision?*]

and that I am indeed in prison, and won't see Rachel/Rikki for another year, minimum. At least 52 weeks, and with them 360-plus opportunities to once more be duped while sleeping. Right now, though, I'm refusing to accept this information. Not after a dream like that. I still, intentionally, haven't opened my eyes. They're clamped shut and they're staying that way. This is damn foolish and I damn well know it—but I'm trying, with all my mighty mental might, to *will* reality into changing. Why the hell not? What can it hurt? [Don't answer that, jan.] After all, there's no justifiable SENSE behind any of this. Starting with Trooper Beau Marlow and Interstate 80; ending just last night when I fell asleep. And seemingly updating its senselessness every bastard day.[82] If the crazy, unthinkable sequence of soul-assfucking-bullshittery that has proceeded this moment can happen, who knows what's possible! Perhaps I've woken up inside

---

[82] Might actually be more accurate to posit that it started NOT with Marlow-life, but rather when the Social Security Administration denied me—twice—for disability. You're aware, Dear Reader, that I now take huge responsibility for the pain I've caused. All I'm saying though is that I'm saying that if their disability screening process was even remotely on target, I'd've received the aid I needed—and that I fucking *paid into*—many months before I ever received the job offer in the first place. And a *Yes* to my application for disability would = a *No*-response to the trafficking proposition. I *know this* to be true. With the financial stability I would've had from those more than adequate [for my monastic lifestyle] monthly S.S. Disability Insurance checks, the immense risk *would not* have felt justified.

some parallel universe—an actual physical one, not in the metaphorical sense I've written about wherein prison exists as its own separate universe, as a fractured mirror of the Free World—but rather an alternate reality in which I'd still been arrested, but where *sensible* legal priorities and *legitimate* justice were the overwhelming norm rather than aberrations; where Judge Hamer actually *didn't* pretend to believe Marlow's blatant, despicable falsehoods; where Hamer decided the Fourth Amendment—and my young life, present and future—and my loved ones—and the everlovin goddamn *truth!*—was more important than scoring another prosecution, imprisoning another young man over flower buds—more important than political gain and by extension money and power; a parallel but just-rightly-askew world where I dodged the prison-bullet and I'm free. And so now I'll open my eyes and I *will see* Rachel's peaceful sleeping face, which like in the dream is close enough to share oxygen, and I'll also see Rikki tucked into her tight trademark curl at our feet—paws twitching from *her* dreams. That's what will happen! If I just yearn for it badly enough, and will it hard enough, reality will undergo a R^{E}ALIGNMENT into something . . . Sensible. Right. Humane. Just. _____ [fill in your own appropriate[ly sympathetic] adjective/s].

Still—*still*—my eyes are closed. How many minutes have passed?

Almost time. Just have to allow a few more seconds for the shift to finalize. I can wait; I've made it this far, what's a few more lil seconds? I think the nightmare improved my patience somehow! I'm exhilarated though, a tiny bit longer and then I can open my eyes and everything will be right again. I'll be free, and we can collect the shattered fragments of our lives and piece them back together, together, and begin to move on. No wait—what am I talking about? *There are no shattered fragments! Nothing to move on* from! It was all just a nightmare, jan. Remember?

I've been awake for five minutes, probably, and—yehhp—eyes're still closed. But now it's time. I've waited long enough; allowed ample time for the realignment, for me to become unstuck from that absurd, insanely illogical, nightmarish dream-universe. I slowly peel my eyelids apart.

Ah, seriously?! What.the.*Fuck!* Welllllp . . . this sure is strange. A bit disappointing, if I'm being honest [which I am [being honest]]. No bright, early morning California sun shining through the windows next to our bed. Casting a warm little yellow triangle across the inside bottom corner. Rachel's not here. Nor is Rikki curled at my feet. No Humboldt County redwoods, either. No ocean smell or fog. No freedom. No hope.

The dormroom *is* brushed with light—but it's a dingy gray; clouds obscure the morning light through our single narrow window in back of the room. The dark-shitbrown bunk frames are oh-so-apt. I stare at one of them for several moments. Thinking how apt that shitbrown color is given what led up to this moment. Given everything in, you know, the last few pages above—or back, from your reading perspective.

In the drab light, I can discern the 19 slumbering figures of the men I share this small dorm with. My spirit dips yet lower. You see . . . *sigh* . . . my Dear Reader, I feel we've developed a rapport. That we trust each other. So I want to make a confession—intended for you alone! Here it is: I *hate them*, Dear Reader. Hate their motherfucking goddamn bastard fucking guts, not just in this room but in the whole prison. With the exception of literally fewer than 10 individuals, everyone here is the collective bane of my existence, and I'd without question rather spend my entire bit completely alone in a single cell; solitary confinement can be torture, but it depends on the person. Solitary would be delightful for me! [so long as I had my books and writing tools and electronics]. Almost every last person here is a gross pile of excrement, with variations only in severity; some excrements are solid and don't reek *all that* bad, while others are liquidjet diarrhea with a cloying, sour stench; as if your poor Rottweiler—who has a terrible gastrointestinal sickness from eating implausible quantities of broccoli and asparagus and raw liverwurst and spicy blackbean chili—has filled a cloistered room with numerous massive loads.

Some people will guilt trip me for not "showing solidarity" with my imprisoned brothers. But I say *Fuck that! let em hate.* How many of these armchair warriors have done <u>hard</u> <u>time</u> in prison, and therefore possess sufficient personal knowledge? Probably almost none. Before anybody lobs such accusatory grenades, I'd like to head them off. Wanna talk solidarity? How bout my boots-on-the-ground volunteer work [on two different occasions] after Hurricane Katrina, staying in and working to help rebuild one of New Orleans's most impoverished neighborhoods, which also happens to be like 96 percent black?

Ugh. I feel so embarrassed and stupid about my thoughts. And I'm not talking about my merciless hatred for the average prisoner here, or that excrement-laden diatribe. No shame in admitting those feelings. Rather, I'm talking about my eyeclamped first several minutes after waking up. When I truly hoped to WILL myself home. That's some dumbass hippie-woo shit, and I want no association with such things. I'm not interested in magical thoughts or claims. Just goes to show the profound challenges and psychological torment induced by prison. Especially for gawdless heathens like myself, who don't have a spiritual crutch to lean on.

When I cracked my eyes to this miserable scene, after that phenomenal and vivid dream, I felt more thoroughly hopeless than ever before at Jacksonville; my lowest point since being trapped and dangerously ill amid Stateville's hellaciousness. That emotional post-wakeup sequence paralyzed me. I thought I'd break down, simply unable to continue. And here's something else: it may have been the first time I seriously contemplated suicide. A soulwithering-type sorrow like I've never felt in such a hyper-condensed moment.

Would you believe me if I told you that that particular sorrow seems *tame* now? Compared to what the future has for me, waiting to pounce with sharp claws and fangs bared?

And today, it turns out, all the tension that's been building will coalesce into a veritable firestorm. Nothing will be the same after tomorrow.

I'm feeling especially depressed. I need to talk to someone—and not an inmate. Somebody outside this horrific collective reality.

Jenny. It's gotta be Jenny. She's an outsider, but still close enough to understand my feelings. The Counselors' offices are occupied, and I want to speak in private. So we spend a solid 45 minutes sitting at a plastic table in the superheated laundry room, voices raised above the dryers' loud mechanical buzz.

We have a simple and pleasant discussion. I vent about the usual stuff, like how the surrounding bigotry makes my heart ache. She provides what I most need: a sympathetic, understanding ear—that's it. She *gets* why these things bother me so much; her validation is uplifting. We also chit-chat about random inconsequentials. I do mention my friction with jay, and the irritating hypocrisy of having capone as our room strength.[83]

After we're done I head back into the unit; still depressed, but a helluva lot less than this morning! I spot jay at a table in the dayroom and head

---

[83] "For such a big tough guy who's been to prison numerous times," I tell Jenny at one point, "that guy's a serious drama- and gossip-monger. Latin King?" I say, referring to his gang affiliation, "more like Latin *Queen*!" Jenny cracks up. One of my fondest memories with her is when I read an excerpt from this very memoir to her, w/ all my righteous anger. She thinks it's hilariously fantastic, and isn't the least bit fazed by my crass language and unadulterated rage.

over. He's staring at me, arms and hands extended questioningly. "The fuck took you so long?"

I sit down, the chessboard between us and already prepared. "We were havin our one-on-one."

He slides a pawn two spaces forward. "Been wait'n here like fuckin forever." He swipes at his lips. "What were you up to, fuckin . . . *doin 'er* on top of the dryer?"

I stare at him. Unmoving. "*What?*"

"Nothin. Yer move."

"Seriously, wha'd you just say?" I know what he said. But I can't believe it. He's supposed to set a good example in the unit. Not only that, he pulled me aside the day I arrived, suggesting I avoid joking about Jenny in any regard. I took his words to heart. But now he's making a directly sexual and personal comment about her!

"Nothin," jay tries to insist.

"Prolly shouldn't be sayin shit like that," I tell him with a sidelong stare.

"I didn't fuckin say anything." He knows he messed up; a small worm of worry has nibbled into his apple. "*Your turn.*"

I move my knight to an idiotic spot, where he snatches it up without risking a thing. We play a few games. I don't mention his comment again.

It prods at my conscience all day though. Lying in bed for my normal afternoon siesta, I can't stop thinking about what he said. Tossing back and forth with my thin sheet while it twists—as like my mind—into more and more of a tangled tornadic mess. Which I almost always use by itself, i.e. the sheet, even now in like the winter time [yeah, that is where we're at in a chronological-seasonal timeline sense]. Even though I do have that thick gray cotton blanket—the one I used as a pillow upon first arriving here, before I could secure my own pillow?—I just hardly ever use it. The sheet alone is actually kinda nice. Being of a thin cotton, it takes on my smell; not an odor, just the unique scent every human has—anyone in an extended current relationship knows precisely what their partner's, say, sweater smells like, and could sniff it out of pile of identical sweaters—and I like having the sheet imbued with my own smell. It reminds me that I'm still a living animal, that I can have a [benign] effect on my environment. Not dead yet!

Anyway, the Two-J Incident [Jenny and jay] continues to bother me. A lot. I hold that young woman in very high esteem; for her obvious compassion and concern about all of us, and for her bravery just in *coming* to this fucking place five days every week. Forced to deal with endless ogling from inmates and Guards alike.[84]

I awake from my nap and jay's misogynistic comment is planted right where I left it, in full occupation of my mind. That shit was so disrespectful. Especially given Jenny's unquestionable admirability and sweetness. I find it highly revealing that it still bothers me—that I seem unable to move on. What the hell can I do though? There's really only one thing within my power, but the thought of it makes me nauseated. I.e. the universal prison no-no of snitching; telling Jenny and Mrs. Meyer what he said. It *would* send a profound message to everyone here . . . I consider myself a feminist, a staunch enemy of patriarchy and legit sexism [not the pseudo-sexism some feminists accuse me of for using words like *bitch* and *cunt*]—so isn't this in fact a great opportunity? I could take this #fucky situation and turn it into something hugely advantageous; making it clear as a cut diamond that every man here had better treat her like the stellar person she is, rather than thinking of her mostly in sexual terms and hence trivializing her terrific kindhearted presence. As I parse this all out in my mind, it's proving far more complex than a simple dichotomy of snitching versus not-snitching. I'm no squealer—I demonstrated my mettle in that regard pretty damn strongly the night of my arrest! You say yer a feminist, jan? That you find the dominant culture's oppression and hypersexualization of women repugnant? Well then, here's your chance to prove it!

That's it then. Mind's made up. I'll talk to Mrs. Meyer and Jenny about this tomorrow morning. Delicately though; very delicately. I do *not* want serious repercussions for jay. I just want these attitudes dragged into the great wide open. It's the least I can do.

---

[84] She once told me the Guards are often worse than inmates [makes sense—they don't have to worry about getting booted on Reckless Eyeballing charges like we do]; how they're constantly coming onto her, whether they're married or not, and how it's pathetic & gross. Hell, I've seen it myself! During one of our counseling sessions, Sergeant Johnson—that infinitely slimy dickwad—saunters into the office & openly hits on Jenny, which is like so vulgar it's uncomfortable for *me*; can't even imagine what it's like for *her*. Dude's gotta be over twice her age! and she's so young, only 24. Sergeant Johnson is practically a parody of the central Illinois redneck-tool, replete with a beergut & obligate smarmy mustache. Plus a demeanor flashing out from him that's almost like a *quasar-pulse* of false entitlement & grandeur; the kinda guy with an internal vision of himself that you just *know* is warped & distorted to funhouse-mirror levels.

And so. The next morning [Friday], a roommate and fellow Medliner joggles my foot until I awake, which he does every morning—a difficult task that often requires numerous attempts of escalating force. Once a month, I bestow upon him a bag of Taster's Choice instant coffee [the *crème de la crème*—sans actual *crème*, naturally—of our local options] for this invaluable service. Dude's name is scott k. Everyone calls him "sling blade" though, because he sounds just like Billy Bob Thornton's character in the eponymous movie. Like, uncannily so. A mushmouthed and gravelly voice with that backcountry twang.

We all hit the walk for Medline and I converge with james as usual, our hilarious interactions commencing right away. We bring one another so much joy. Bitching about prison and joshing and talkin shit as we lap the basketball court. These days, I often spend the first 15 or 20 minutes inside the actual weightroom, slowly working the leg machines with low weight. Which'd be impossible during regular Gym's packed madness. This is such a wonderful resource for me. Sadly, most of the guys at Medical Gym— referred to as "Retard Gym" by everyone else—are bullshitters who don't need it, or don't use it, for legitimate medical purposes. Big surprise, right? They just manipulated the Doctor in order to access the Gym when it's almost empty; their activities are obviously in no way limited. It's a solid grift. No denying that. Normally I wouldn't give a damn, either—but soon it'll have a tragic effect on people like me and james, who really do *need* it. That's when their swindle becomes problematic in my eyes. There's a nice anarchism-rooted slogan that works perfectly here: *Your right to swing your fists through the air ends where my face begins.* Meaning, do whatever the hell you want—so long as it doesn't infringe on someone *else's* rights or bodily integrity. This Retard Gym-situation seems analogous to those who abuse pain meds, and the effect it has on people like me who seriously need them.

To wit: there's a guy in my room. We'll call him m. hunt. Actually no, let's go with mike h. [teehee x 2]. This mike h. has a Bottom Bunk Permit, and Medical Gym. Supposedly he has a bad back. I think it's reasonable to infer that, if your back is so messed up that it's dangerous to climb a short ladder, your physical abilities would be limited *somehow*. Yet he plays in the prison's competitive and very intense Intramural Basketball Tournament! So . . . yer telling me he can play aggressive fullcourt basketball, but can't climb a fourstep ladder onto a top bunk?! I call bullshit, man. Makes me fuckin sick. His grift is blatant, and yet he never encounters a hint of trouble. Meanwhile, I get busted for almost every last little rule I break. A number of cassettes in my possession over the permitted 18—ticket. Late to Medline—ticket. Toss a pack of noodles on a friend's bed that sits right adjacent to the entrance—ticket. All the time! Shit has my knickers in such a twist they're like the wires behind a stack of video game consoles.

As james and I stride around the Gymnasium, I explain my Two-J dilemma. He fully supports my discussing it with the Counselors. "You're a rogue, buddy," I tell him. "A dying breed. You don't follow the prisoners' code—you have your own moral compass."

"I have a compass all right." Grinning, he thrusts his non-clawhand-arm's elbow against his crotch and executes a sort of rigid arm-stiffening-upward gesture. "And it likes to point due north no matter what!" He throws back his head and his Adam's apple bobs up and down from his gleeful high-pitched cackle. I've already joined him, starting with a very alto, or maybe falsetto, screechyawp-thing. This guy's seriously my life-line in here. I don't know what I'd do without him.

After Medical Gym, I return to the unit and immediately step into Mrs. Meyer's office. She's working at the computer; Jenny sits in a chair against the back wall, a stack of folders in her lap. "Morning," I say.

"Hey jan," Mrs. Meyer says. "How are you? Feeling better than yester-day?"

I smile a little. "Yeah, actually, thanks for asking. Talking to Jenny really helped." Mrs. Meyer is head of the program, and has decades of experience in drug rehabilitation. Jenny's only 24 though, without much experience. So whenever possible, I like to tell Mrs. Meyer how wonderful Jenny is. How adept she is at leading workshops.

"Good to hear," Mrs. Meyer says. "So what's up?"

I heave a deep sigh and lean back against the door. "Something . . . inappropriate happened, and I really think y'all should know about it."

Mrs. Meyer's face becomes colored with a brush of concern. "What is it?"

"Here," Jenny says, getting up, "have a seat."

We trade places. I sit down next to the combination desk-shelf that's bloated and barfing out files, pamphlets, books, pens, and various knick-knacks. "So what's up?" she says, crossing her arms.

I try to steel myself. Had no idea it would be this difficult. I usually have no trouble saying uncomfortable things, but this is different some-how. Partly, of course, because the "object" of hypersexualization is sitting right in front of me. I finally manage to speak. "Okay. So you know how yesterday, we were talking for quite a while in the laundry room?"

"Uh-huh," Jenny says.

"Well . . ." I glance at Mrs. Meyer. Then I talk, slowly, choosing each word with care. "Um. Well afterwards, jay and I were playing chess, and he said something I found extremely uncalled for. And I just thought . . . listen, I do *not* want him getting in trouble—I just think it was so inappropriate that someone should speak to him about it."

"What did he say?" Meyer asks.

"It was just basically asking if . . . if Jenny and I . . . gawd this is embarrassing, I'm sorry."

"jan, you don't have to feel uncomfortable," Jenny says. "This is not the first time something like this has happened. I can handle it, okay?"

This really helps ease my squirmy discomfort. I nod. Can't look Jenny in the eyes, though. "He said, 'What took so long, were you *doin her* on the dryer or somethin'?"

After a quiet moment, Mrs. Meyer says, "Yeah, pretty inappropriate."

"Look," I blurt, "I don't want him in trouble. I just don't feel like I should be made to feel uncomfortable to seek counseling from my *counselor*. If that makes sense."

"Definitely does," Meyer says. She pauses, lips pursed in contemplation. "How about this," she finally says. "It's Friday. Let's see how you and jay do this weekend, and we'll go from there. These things usually have a way of petering out on their own. That sound okay?"

"Yeah. Yeah, that sounds good. I kinda suspect it'll blow over, too. The animosity does seem to be cooling off."

"Good," Mrs. Meyer says. "Well then, just, you know, try to relax and not worry about it too much. We'll talk on Monday."

"Okay. Thank you." I stand up and step to the door.

"Thanks for letting us know, jan," Jenny says as I walk out.

I really did think the enmity with jay was dying down. Mrs. Meyer's suggestions seem like good ones . . .

Little do I know the beginning of the end will come that very afternoon.

It's about four p.m. and I'm lying in bed reading *The Girl with the Dragon Tattoo* by Stieg Larsson. Rachel and my spermdad both gave it high praise, and I eventually checked it out from the library. It's fantastic! I normally can't stand genre fiction, but this one's different. Special. In part because of its great characterization. The timing's also perfect, as it turns out: One of my main characters in *The Liberators*, Carrie Marie Nelson, is a hardcore hacker and techwhiz. So Larsson's brilliant protagonist Lisbeth Salander—among the more badass and memorable female characters I've ever read—provides a jumping-off point for me to brainstorm Carrie's activities.

Almost everyone in the room is preparing for Chow. Even jay! They're serving tacos, one of the few things decent enough to get him off that lazy ass. He's sitting on his bed sideways, feet on the floor, tying his shoes. I'm about to climb down to refill my plastic water jug and, after Chow's called and the unit's almost empty, give Rachel a call.

jay glances up at me. "So what's goin on, jan? You gonna go get some *vegan* tacos?" In a snide tone, blatantly mocking me. Loud.

I turn and look at him, stepping down to the floor, and fire back without hesitation. Almost shouting so the whole room can hear, I gesture to my groin: "Why don't you suck my vegan *dick*?" I grin widely to the chorus of *Ohhhhhhh*s and laughter—I roasted his ass. As I'm slipping my orange shower shoes on, suddenly jay starts coming at me fast.

He stops right before me. The bustling noise has dropped to near silence; everyone's watching now. As are several guys straight across the hall in Room 10. jay's face and shiny bald head are flushed with anger. "Wha'd I fuckin tell you about sayin shit like that?" He's so close I can feel his hot breath on my skin.

I chuckle in his face. "Ey, you mock me, I'm'a fire back! Pretty simple."

"I wasn't fuckin *mocking* you, the fuck're you talkin about?"

Head tilted, I give him a smirk that says *Come on dude, don't bullshit me.* "Come on dude, don't bullshit me," I say. "You were raggin on me cuz you think I'm missing out on that *delicious, high-quality* meat." There are some chuckles, but the room's tension is palpable, like high humidity. I'm sure my face is bright pink too; I can feel it burning. Hate confrontations.

jay turns his face away and sighs, scratching his bald pate and forehead. "jan, how many fuckin times we gotta talk about this?"

"Ain't shit t' talk about! You put me on blast in fron'a the room." I smack the bottom of a fist into my palm repeatedly for emphasis. "I'm just toastin your ass right back, that's how it works!"

Now he takes another step forward and our faces are less than a foot apart. He jabs a finger at my chest as he speaks. "You needa stop sayin shit like that to me. Fuckin tired of it, jan."

With a glance, I see just about everyone in Room 10 watching now; it's gone quiet in there, too.

"I've let it slide cuz, fuckin, whatever," jay says, "but this is like the fourth fuckin time I've had'a tell you—" Now his finger's actually stabbing against my chest. "—and you aren't fuckin getting it."

There's gonna be a fight. His radishcolored face, his piercing eyes and jabbing finger . . . this is it. Shit!—I'm gonna have to fight him. He's made physical contact, crossed the line, and I can't have people thinking I'll tolerate such a thing and so I'm gonna have to throw down. These thoughts aren't formed solid in my head like clay fresh from a kiln it's not like that in the moment in the burning heat of the moment it's just a rush of emotions and physical reactions preparation for what's coming and a kind of blasé resigned certainty.

"I get it just fine, jay. Don't *fucking* touch me." I smack his hand away. "I think *you're* the one who doesn't get it. You stop talking shit, I'll stop talkin shit, straight up. Simple!"

He starts poking me again. "I wasn't fuckin talkin shit, you're outta fuckin line and you needa stop that shit or yer gonna fuckin be sorry."

I smack his hand away, harder this time. Producing an audible *tuhk!* sound. "Keep. Your. *Fucking hands* off *me*, jay."

That's when a house elder, the diminutive but beefy kool-aid [he of ass-blasted-in-the-face-by-dave fame], rushes in and separates us, insisting we cool down, cool down and stop right now right now fam. "You guys realize whatcher doing? D'you see who's *watching*?" We look across the hall into Room 10 and see chohan—a Sikh Indian and convicted kiddie-diddler who tickets people like it's his life's calling—staring at us. kool-aid says, "And over some petty shit, no doubt. Just *chill*, guys."

"Awh shit dude," pete mutters. "Goddamn chohan, already write'n the ticket in his head!" He chuckles mutedly.

"Ain't a fuckin joke, man," I say. The heart-in-my-throat anxiety about fighting jay has transitioned smoothly into a morbid fear of our confrontation's repercussions. jay was jabbing me and I smacked his hand away. Twice. Putting your hands on another guy in 4B is grounds for immediate ejection from the unit, which means no more accruing good time. "*Shit*." I run a hand through my short-buzzed hair.

jay has backed off several feet, hands on hips, a similar psychological crisis-process flashing across his face. kool-aid speaks calmly, hand on my shoulder. "It's gonna be cool, aight?" He looks from jay to me and then says quietly, so people outside the room can't hear, "I gotch y'all's backs, dig? Saw the whole thing—nobody touched anybody, it was just a lil argument. No more'a this shit tho, aight? Chill. You cool?" he asks me.

"Yeah." I'm parched; the corners of my lips have accumulated that thick [#smegmatic?] white stuff. I swipe at my mouth with the back of a hand. "Yeah, everything's cool."

"jay?" kool-aid says. "Good?"

"Yeah man," he says. "Just . . . yeah, whatever, it's fine." He stares at me. "Just don't . . ."

I hold up my hands. "It's all good. I'm chill, bro. Let's move past it."

"Shit ain't worth goin t' Seg for," pete says.

"Straight up." kool-aid looks back and forth at us. "Go take a nap, hit the back stall and get some money . . . whatever you gotta do t'cool down, aight?"[85]

"Yeah," jay says. "Fine."

"Aight then. Straight."

Then they make the call for Chow, and nearly everyone leaves. My fight-or-flight chemical mechanism seems defective; it takes an inordinate length of time to dissipate. I'm trying to read, sprawled out in bed. Place is dead silent. But I can't focus—often having to read the same paragraph several times before it finally sticks. For a good 15 minutes, my heart still thumps, nerves jagged, breathing shallower than normal. The scene plays over and over in my head uncontrollably, like a DVD segment stuck on A-B Repeat. kool-aid's support definitely helps—*I gotch y'all's backs*—but I do *not* feel good about how this will play out with the Counselors, and beyond into the long run future.

My anxiety will prove wellfounded.

8.

The weekend passes without incident. jay and I don't say a word to one another. Then, Monday morning, the shit officially hits the fan. As soon as I return from Medical Gym, I'm summoned to the Counselor's office. Mrs. Meyer and Jenny and kool-aid are all crammed inside.

I'm slammed with a wavewall of anxiety, instantly so very nervous and ⸾J⸾I⸾⸾T⸾T⸾E⸾R⸾⸾Y⸾ ⸾J⸾I⸾⸾T⸾T⸾E⸾R⸾⸾Y⸾ ⸾J⸾I⸾⸾T⸾T⸾E⸾R⸾⸾Y⸾

---

[85] "Get'n money" and "Hit'n a lick" are two of our euphemisms for masturbation.

The reality is that jay put his hands on me with aggression, and I returned the favor. The reality is that we will probably both be kicked out, and I'll lose six months' potential good time for it. The reality is that I refuse to acknowledge this reality as such.

"So jan," Mrs. Meyer says. I'm standing back against the closed door. "Guess the problems with jay didn't fizzle out after all."

I'm staring down at the muck-scrimmed beige tiles and it's hard to look up and I breathe out with a sigh. "Yeah," I murmur. "Guess not. Unfortunately."

"Well listen," Meyer says, "this'll all be sorted out, all right? Just relax; no one's getting kicked out—"

FWOP! The moment she speaks these words, that familiar old leaden ball seems to've vanished from my guts and I actually hear it happen, as if the lead ball, with a corklike pop, winks out of this universe's fabric: *fwop!*

". . . just want to make sure this stops for *good*. Okay?"

"Okay." Struggling to keep the eagerness unexclaimed from my voice. "Good, okay, thank you!" The woman knows how to set a mind at ease damn quick. Bless her heart.

Mrs. Meyer has to rush off for an important meeting in Springfield. As Program Director, this is part of her regular duties. She bids us goodbye, pulls on her warm winter jacket and hurries out.

Now it's just me and kool-aid and Jenny. This is good. Jenny hates seeing decent guys in serious trouble even more than does her boss—to the point where she'll even bend the rules and coax your answers in a better direction. Bless *her* heart!

Just because they're not kicking me out, though, doesn't mean there can't be severe consequences. They've meted out some pretty brutal punishments just in the few months I've been here: loss of all electronics for days, six-hour cleaning marathons, etc.

"So," Jenny says, "tell us what happened." Bubblegum smacks around in her mouth; she's taken to chewing the pink fruity crap this winter. Somewhat similar to the way I've "taken to" just dealing with having chapped lips this winter. [Well, similar but like on requisite opposite ends of the reaction-spectrum [given her non-Prison-Vortexed ability to purchase fancy lip gloss [and quality drinks of unlimited choice [and gum [to help ward off the central Illinois wintertime's dry, windy, mouthparching effects [whereas I, being inside [and hence having extremely limited options [forced to live within the means available to me here [i.e. there's no lip balm [available from Commissary [so you see how the general state of our mouths/lips are total products of our specific abilities [and so hence similar in their very oppositeness! [Right?!]]]]]]]]]]]] A pen and small writing pad wait on the desk before her. kool-aid's sitting in the back wall's chair. I remain against the door, on my feet but leaning way back with my butt pressed to the wood, eliminating some of the kneepressure.

I summarize the events for them both. Leaving nothing out.[86] Jenny's demeanor—and Meyer's parting words, of course—facilitate my decision to lay out the plain, honest truth.

As I speak, Jenny scribbles notes. "Mmkay, go on."

"So then I told him I was only responding to his mockery. He kept jabbing his finger at me, so I kinda . . . smacked it away."

She pauses. Flicks her pen against the desk several times, nibbling on her lower lip. Then she looks up at me. "But there was no like *real* contact, right? He was kinda wagging a finger, and you just brushed it aside?"

Now it dawns on me in full what she's doing, and the clarity is like being bathed in warm delightful morning sun—she wants to portray the incident in the most benign light possible! I glance at kool-aid. "Right . . ."

"I was in their doorway by that time," the house elder says. "I saw what was goin on. Wasn't no aggressive contact at all."

Yes, hell yes!—kool-aid's using his seniority and status as house elder to downplay the confrontation. Intimating that he not only witnessed the whole sequence, but also saw it *more clearly* than chohan across the hall did. "Riiight," I say, now fully on board. "Yeah, I mean, there was anger, but I never thought we were gonna *fight* or anything! We were just talkin shit, which is part'a the culture of our room, y'know?"

"Gotcha." Jenny scribbles a quick note.

"And I was under the impression that jay was kinda putting on a show, like acting madder than he really was."

"So it was more like you were *playfully* pushing his hand away?"

"Yep, uh-huh."

"T' me," kool-aid adds, "looked more like horseplay than aggressive confrontation." Wow!—he told us *I gotch y'all's backs*, and he's made good on that pledge bigtime. Above and beyond and over and past all expectations by far. Whatta guy!

---

[86] When I tell her that I suggested jay "suck my vegan *dick!*" she can't help but emit a cute little snort of laughter. Shine On, Jenny!

"All right, good," Jenny says. She jots on the notepad for ten seconds and then looks up at me. Those stunning hazel eyes; her ceaseless support and concern; the indefatigable strength of her character; and most of all, she loved the memoir scene I read to her, laughing at all the right places and more; gawd I love this woman! *All right, good* in-fuckin-deed! "Think you and jay can put this behind you and get along?" she says. "No more talking shit, even if it's playful?"

"Oh yeah, definitely! I'll be fine, long as he can move past it as well."

"He will," kool-aid says. "E'rything's cool."

"Okay then," Jenny says. "Thanks, jan."

"Thank *you*!" Walking out, I'm unable to suppress a big dumb grin.

I truly believe that's the end of it. kool-aid and Jenny graciously helped downplay the situation, and hence nullified any devastating repercussions . . .

Or so I thought, at least. But just like in the so-called Free World, a significant interpersonal event in here can have a host of far-reaching consequences that cannot be predicted or assumed, and which may take a long, long time to entirely manifest. Or sometimes, a slice of those consequences gets cut and served immediately. That's the apparent case here, because one of *the* worst possibilities comes to fruition the very next morning. As in, literally the second worst plausible outcome. Something I never ever wanted—even if it weren't destined to foist militant scorn upon me!

In the morning, Tuesday morning, I sign back in after Medical Gym and then the front desk Officer tells me I've been reassigned to bed 6-9 Uhhm! . . . . WHATHEFUCK?!

Now wait just a sec! [heart leaping as if jolted over and over ZAP!ZAP! ZAP!ZAP! with a defibrillator.] Wait wait *wait*! [breath snags on something in my throat no not something but nothing, snags on *nothingness* in my throat.] This does not make sense. Bed 9 is a bottom bunk. "Hold on," I tell the Officer "Are you sure?" I stare at him, bafflement cranking deep ripples into the skin above my septum. This should be great news—no, spectacular news. Scoring a bottom bunk this early in my Drug Unit residency would be phenomenal, but something's wrong. It's not my turn yet, so there can be no GOOD reason for this. Only bad reasons. Potentially calamitous reasons. At least two—maybe as many as four—top bunk guys are ahead of me in "seniority." Meaning they've been here longer, and should therefore get a lower bunk before me. Rumors have been rippling throughout the unit that a black dude in my room called doc has long been flirting with ejection. It's seemed only a matter of time for a while now. But that's only one bottom bunk that'd open up; what about the other one or two or *three*? [doc has a bottom bunk permit, and also happens to be one of the guys in Medical Gym who clearly has no limitations physically, so good fucking riddance.] I tell the Officer, "I don't think it's my turn to move down yet, so just wanna make sure."

He glances down at his notes and then back up, wearing a glaze-eyed look. "Yyyuhp. It's right awl right—bed 6-9. Move yer shit."

I shuffle off to my room, baffled. doc's area is already empty, mattress stripped of its sheets. Then there's another guy with a gleaming bald head like jay, a middle-aged black dude who goes by "west" and basically adores me—I allowed him to lock in a perpetual trade for my tray's fried chicken-corpsemeat [before I was getting the Vegan Tray, obviously], in exchange for all his vegetables. That repulsive, veiny, low-grade, carcinogenic product of barbaric cruelty against the single most abused animal species on the planet is also far and away the most popular "food" item Dietary serves—guaranteed to empty every unit like nothing else. People with no outside monetary support will sell their serving of chicken carcass for two or three dollars, which is also the going rate for a haircut! Our longtime trade had west thinking I'm [1] out of my mind and [2] impossibly generous beyond his capacity to fathom].[87]

---

[87] From a numeric standpoint, chickens are inarguably the most abused/exploited individual species on the planet, with over 50 billion [50,000,000,000!] slaughtered every year worldwide [source: United Poultry Concerns, a wonderful nonprofit that advocates for "the respectful treatment of domestic fowl." See www.upc-online.org/chickens/chickensbro.html]. Marine animals in general, though, are far worse off. What humans are doing to the oceans—cradle of *all* life—and its denizens is an atrocity that may well be unparalleled in human history; unthinkable in the fullest sense of the word, i.e. it's basically impossible to even comprehend the level of annihilation & mass death. I'd even argue, with utmost sincerity and also a crippling array of supporting evidence, that it's a textbook example of GENOCIDE. Not a word I use lightly. Trying to conceptualize the dizzying magnitude of our oceanic destruction is akin to the most mindboggling thought experiments in astronomy, like attempting to grasp the size of our universe. I mean for fuck's sake, it's literally *not possible* to determine the actual numbers of aquatic animals killed—the best anyone can do is estimate, with wild variability; human & corporate greed are so monumental, and fishing methods so wanton, so indiscriminately fucking gluttonous, that worldwide "production" isn't measured in numbers of individual sentient beings; they're not even measured by, say, gross tonnage. Rather, fish "harvesting" is measured in *millions of metric tons per year* [see www.adaptt.org/killcounter.html]. We are straightup killing the planet, my Dear

Hot damn that was a long footnote! I think that maybe, while describing my bafflement at being inexplicably moved to another bunk, I latched onto a couple topics I'm quite knowledgeable about. Well-trodden mental territory—yet also, much like the current bewildering circumstances, hard to fully comprehend.

west is right now beginning to transfer stuff from his previous bottom bunk to doc's old spot. I start unplugging cables and moving my belongings. If my brow remains this furrowed for much longer, it might get stuck that way; this actually seems feasible in my baffled and mangled thoughts. Suddenly jay rushes in and starts packing his shit—and I *still* don't understand. "What's goin on, jay?"

He's wrapping several electrical cables into a compact loop. Doesn't look up. "Whatchu think man?" he spits, dripping with bitter spite.

Then it hits me like a stiff, sudden gutpunch. Ohhhh NO! *Not* this! I open my mouth to say I-don't-know-what, but I'm crestfallen, speechless.

He's been kicked out.

Dear gawd. I'd never, ever wanted such a thing to happen; never even considered the possibility, except in the context of us *both* being ejected. "Fuck, dude. I . . ." But what can I say? An apology would seem insincere, and might even be taken as a sick, smirking joke! Trying to explain would

---

Reader. Overpopulation & consumption by humans—who're not the pinnacle of evolution [or creation if you're a fact-denying idiot], but rather just one species of 10 million—WILL make the majority of Earth unlivable by the end of *this century* unless we take radical, effective, *immediate* measures to drastically reduce worldwide population as well as First World consumption, and also begin the wholesale dismantling of industrial civilization [for proof of the latter's absolute necessity, see *Endgame, Volume 1: The Problem of Civilization* and *Endgame, Volume 2: Resistance* by Derrick Jensen, who [I mentioned this before, but it's obviously a mark of huge pride, so I wanna say it again] provided this memoir's front cover-quote; for ideas on a praxis that could accomplish said task, I recommend *Deep Green Resistance: Strategy to Save the Planet* by Aric McBay & Lierre Keith [the latter is quite the scumbag—she's a bigot against transgendered folks, and über-zealously promotes unfounded antivegetarian pseudoscience—but the book is so important that I can't help mentioning it; McBay publicly denounced Keith's anti-transgendered stance and severed his professional and personal association with her, so that's pretty redemptive]. *DGR* was published during my incarceration; Rachel sent me a copy and I handwrote a glowing review, which was actually published by the *Earth First! Journal.* You can check out *DGR*'s entire step-by-step strategic proposal—which they call Decisive Ecological Warfare—by downloading a PDF file here: www.deepgreenresistance.com/en/deep-green-resistance-strategy/decisive-ecological-warfare [all sites in this footnote accessed 8/1/16].

only make things worse [and what would I even explain?]. Anything at all coming from me right now'd be a slap in the face. Man did I screw up bad! I'm in serious jeopardy now. Sure seems likely, anyway—not a single good thing can come from this, no matter the specifics, i.e. *Why the hell wasn't I booted as well?* I vacate the room in what feels like a drunken stagger, dazed, supremely uncomfortable to be anywhere near him. He must despise me. The kind of savage murder-fantasies that'll soon be running through my head all the fucking time are no doubt running through his head this very moment. And I'm frankly unable to assert, in good conscience, that such #ragethoughts are inappropriate! I stand in the dayroom. Hands planted against my hips. Inside my skull, it feels like a continuous cinematic over-head shot of a newspaper press running at hyperspeed. Is everyone staring at me, or is it my imagination? Could it be both? *Neither?* Christ, my head hurts!

I need to visit with the Counselors. Have to. Can't take much more I'll implode I *need* to know what the hell's going on. I beeline for the office, where Jenny and Mrs. Meyer are working. Big John recently had a big heart attack. Not his first. Nor his last. I collapse into the green plastic chair and stick my elbows on my thighs, dragging a hand through my hair. "I don't understand—jay got kicked out?! I just . . . I just wanted to do the right thing! Wanted people to know they shouldn't be saying awful sexist things, especially in regards to . . . I had no idea . . . I would *not* have—"

"You did the right thing, okay jan?" Jenny holds my gaze, heavy on gravitas. "People shouldn't be saying things like that."

"He's been treading water for months now," Meyer says. "What he said about you and Jenny, and the way he confronted you . . . those were just the final straws. I've been telling him to straighten his act for a long time. jan, we know what goes on in the rooms—you'd be surprised. We're aware how much trouble he stirs up. This is not your fault; you need to under-stand that, jan. We explained the same thing to him. If he tells anybody it was your fault, we'll know. And we'll take care of it. So you don't need to worry about being targeted or anything."

"I think I do."

Jenny speaks. "Try to move past that worry. It'll be okay, jan. Things'll cool down."

I wipe my lips with the back of a hand. The Leaden Weight's posted up in my gut again. Becoming all-too-familiar.[88]

". . . to relax, okay?" Mrs. Meyer's saying. I didn't catch the first part.

I try to ease my jangling nerves. Force a smile. "Well, not like I was popular anyway . . . guess it doesn't much matter, eh?"

9.

Not surprisingly, turns out it very much *does* matter. Not only am I quietly but unambiguously scorned by most guys in the room, but I have indeed acquired a big fat target on my back. Things soon go from shitbad to worse.

Amid the clusterfuckery of internal 4B issues, leaving the unit brings paltry reprieve. It's the dead of winter; here at J-ville we're only about 150 miles from Lake Michigan, and its icy wind lashes out across these flat plains like a coldhearted dominatrix. That biting wind cracks its whip right over the Walk—and our exposed necks, lips, noses and eyes. We're not allowed to wear Commissary headbands around our necks because they're a "choking hazard." A ludicrous goddamn proposition—they're made of cheap cotton, and stretch almost as easily as Trooper Marlow's version of the truth. Know what else is a choking hazard? Freakin *hands*! If one of the many candidates for strangling me wants to strangle me, keeping my headband on the forehead ain't gonna stop em. This rule just seems like another specious tool for Officers to harass us with and make us uncomfortable.

It's early February now. The ground wears a snowblanket several feet thick everywhere but the Walk—which gets cleared daily with shovels and icepick-poles by shivering Inside Grounds workers [which would've involved me, if Sergeant Porcelain-Toothed Podunk Shitheel Johnson had his way]—and yet even so, guys slip constantly. Happens to me several times a week. Feeling every last time like my knees could be ripped apart. When

---

[88] **Jan:** *You just wait, bub. You have NO idea.*
inmate: What're you talking about?!
Jan: *How could I, with the knowledge I have, possibly tell YOU anything? It's a chronological impossibility, at least given the spacetime paradigm to which we hairless apes are bound.*
inmate: But you just fucking told me that I 'have no idea'! That strongly implies we *can* communicate.
Jan: *You're confused. The* Just you wait *warning came not from me, but from YOUR heart, YOUR own worried mind.*
inmate: This makes no sense.
Jan: *Hush. Pay attention—someone's talking to you.*

someone *falls* on the Walk, those present—including Officers, of course—
enjoy a good laugh. Everyone else hears about it within the hour, a source
of great fraternal mirth. We're not much better off even when managing
to stay upright. That wind sweeps by, flinging shards of snow against our
exposed flesh. Shit *stings*, man.

Morning Medline; 7:30 a.m. Temps in the high teens if you're lucky—
and that's not accounting for wind chill! The Officers love making you all
stand at the gate. Waiting several minutes for no good reason, layered in
thermal shirts and thick sweaters and your navyblue jackets, teeth *still*
chattering. You try to warm up; bouncing on your heels and scurrying in
tight circles like monkeys rendered insane by torturous "research" laboratories. Hands jammed into pockets and going numb anyway, same as
your poor frigid lips. Then the Officer'll halt the line halfway there; again,
no reason except probable sadism [is he *smiling* under that nice long neck-
band?]. And you'll huddle all together like a cluster of navyblue penguins.
Waiting . . . waiting . . . waiting.

This shit is the norm, for two or three months straight. Letups are a rare
exception. Seems like it'll be gloomy and cold and windy, with hardly a
glimpse of the sun, for weeks on end. Accumulating snow mounts ever
higher alongside the Walk. For a week or more at a time, it'll feel like we're
trekking through slot-canyonesque cracks within glaciers, the walls radiating cold like dry ice splashed with water. And the unrelenting wind that
pushes everything over the edge to complete intolerability. Whipping and
lashing mercilessly—ranging only between *terrible* and *even worse*.

And yet . . .

I have to admit: This winter of miserable discontent still releases the
occasional flash of astonishing beauty. Like when we're trudging to morning Medline a couple days after a blizzard, one that dumped several feet of
fresh powder; but now the air's cloudless, an unsurpassably clear blue, and
sunlight flares off the snow in an almost blinding whiteness. Winds have
shoved huge snowdrifts up against the brick buildings. These deposits rise
five feet high in places. Resembling hyperwhite sand dunes, windswept
sand dunes with trails woven across the surface—trails that become patt-
erned, a visual record of the winds' paths—kinda like its *fingerprints* are
pressed into the fluffy powder. As we stand in place, stopped yet again on
the Walk, I'll examine a patch of snow. Stare at it and phase out the noise
around me. Then my brain starts helping me glimpse the configurations;
soon, like those optical illusions whose subject takes a moment to reveal

itself, I can see a sort of *physical map* of recent wind currents. Infinitely variable patterns brushed into the snow hour after hour. Like a lifesize topographical map of wind—unfurled on the ground for studious inspection. Though it's constantly changing, just like sand dunes. Or, on a macro scale, like an entire region's tectonic ridges and peaks and craggy edges—except here it's enacted on a visible timescale, easy to witness, to grasp and examine.

Or it'll be snowing as I walk to Chow, and I'll extend a hand. Within seconds my palm is strewn with flakes. I stare down at them. Glancing up only often enough to avoid ice patches on the gravel. The most wondrous complexity of form, a Natural Geometry of the Earth, with infinite possibilities. My gaze flits from one snowflake to the next, trying to memorize their intricate patterns. But they melt so quickly. That shape . . . that one shape, like no other before . . . gone forever. In one moment they're examples of magnificent proliferating complexity, and then they crumble and cave in and liquefy until they're nothing more than tiny spots of water, clinging to my flesh like dewdrops. The latter rendered prosaic solely because I'm accustomed to rain.

These oh-so-rare and fleeting moments of startling beauty in prison: I must cusp them in memory's careful hand and survey immediately, ascribing words and meaning, because, sadly, these assignations often persist long after the images have faded. Beauty—especially natural beauty, unmarred by the relentless destruction of humans—is the rarest commodity here. Not sold on Commissary. Almost never found on TV. Nor even via sterling descriptions in books. Because the levels of majesty and wonder required to, as Kafka wrote, "break the frozen sea within us," have been driven so high by the ceaseless grinding realities of prison life that they're devastatingly elusive now. Uncommon even in the few [tainted] glimpses of the natural and real world we do have.

This natural beauty only provides momentary reprieve though. Rumors are intensifying that guys with Medical Gym will soon be prohibited from using the weightroom. This was catalyzed, we discover, by dickhead Gym workers' complaints that we've been abusing our privileges.[89] This *is* true for some guys, as I already addressed, like doc and mike h. But the totally unexamined [natch!] swindle and hypocrisy here is that these same whiny workers aren't supposed to lift weights during Medical Gym in the first place—they're supposed to be working! So *all* of them are abusing said privileges. Whereas not everybody with Medical is acting inappropriately. The difference? Their boss Louie isn't just Recreation Director; he's also their buddy! Louie is grayhaired and bespectacled with a fat paunch. Every day he wears a white golf hat emblazoned with the word **TITLEIST**; shouldn't surprise you by now that james and I hence rechristen him. "Look," one of us will cry, "it's the *TIT-lee-ist* man in all of Jacksonville!" And then we both cackle in delight. Our lives may be plunked in the shitter . . . but if we're steeped in excrement, by gawd we're gonna laugh about it![90]

So it turns out the Gym workers—those "tough" and massive muscleheads, so burly you can't help but wonder how they manage to reach and wipe their own assholes—are a pack of selfish squealing cunts. Brawny and beefy and powerful; aaaand punkass goddamn snitches! Just like buft. [If you're thinking *Well just hold on now, señor smitto—smitowih—sipowit—**jan**, didn't you like just finish an extensive confession of how you snitched?!* then my response would have to be *Yes, that is true, but context matters and the circumstances are not comparable; the workers' squealing was an act of pure selfinterest—*

---

[89] I am unquestionably privileged as a Straight White Male; but I wouldn't quite consider guys like me and james *privileged* to have Medical Gym. Something that helps maintain whatever physical health still present in a disabled person is not exactly a privilege. In these cases, we deserve such a thing. It's one of the facets of appropriate medical care—and like I mentioned before, according to Jacksonville's own alleged policies, "Health care is a right, not a privilege." But if you've read this far, Dear Reader, surely you can predict whether or not prison Administrators will make the appropriate, fair, sensible decision regarding Medical Gym . . .

[90] james is so hilarious, & largely fearless. He abides his own ethics first over the "Inmate Code" of behavior. Back when he hadn't been here very long, if Gym workers were shooting hoops and the ball rolled toward him while walking laps, he'd punt or throw it back. But they never once thanked him. So he simply stopped returning it. Now, when we're walking together & an errant basketball approaches, he'll just kick or bat it away with his non-clawhand. Making zero effort to send it in their direction, & not even bothering to see which way it goes. I love it! Brings me the giggles every time. "You've got some serious chutzpah, dude!" I once told him after he sent two workers' basketball sailing toward the opposite basket. "Yer not worried they're gonna get pissed?" He spat a dismissive guttural sound & flicked his claw at me, smiling. "Eh, I'm a peaceful old cripple, what're these retards gonna do?" Then we shared a hearty laugh.

they simply wanted the weightroom all to themselves; whereas I was trying to combat widespread sexism against Jenny and in general. World of difference 'n all that.] Isn't it strange how some of the biggest, strongest men are sometimes the greatest wimps? Cowardly, thin-skinned losers who only bully people much weaker than them. Like the sources of domestic violence; like child/animal abusers. Does the Gym workers' obsession with appearing tough and ultramasculine-slash-supermuscular [or is it the other way around?] stem from something as simple as LDS—Little Dick Syndrome? Or is it more complicated than that?

Quick story about the worst, most obnoxious worker of them all; he's also the most ridiculously muscular guy in the entire joint. I witnessed him benchpress 475 pounds. He goes by the moniker—wait for it—*poo-poo*. No joke! And this troglodyte actually refers to *himself* this way. Sorry, but how can a grown man calling himself poo-poo be taken seriously by anyone? A mountainous hardened con named after dookie, feces, poopy. Ah, prison: you provide such endless amusement, such absurd fodder! If you didn't engulf me with murderous rage and make me wanna die, I might just love you.

I'm imagining a scenario; one that may well've actually happened, and I'm just picking up the psychic afterglow—

What up Counselor Davis, I wanna sign up fo that Foundry class.
Q.
Sho, ain't no thang. poo-poo jones.
Q.
Say what?
Q.
poo . . . poo . . . jones.
Q.
J-O-N . . . uhhhm . . .
Q.
Oh! Yeeah, no doubt. Iz poo-poo. Like, y'know . . . wit two Os 'n e'rythang.
Q!?
Right. Diznookie, sheeyit, caca—you got th' idea!

True story? Anyway. This silverback-sized tool acts like the toughest lad around. King turd of shit mountain [or rather poo-poo mountain]. He seems to possess just one volume setting; doesn't matter if he's talking to a benchpress-spotter right above him—he's SHOUTING. And to be honest, it's scary. *He's* scary. Pro wrestling-level massive, muscles bulging him into shirts at least a couple sizes up, with a deep, booming voice that shudders your bones like heavy metal drums mic'd through an arena's PA. He's been down some 15 years. So I'd expect heavy adherence to the Inmate Code. Nope! Turns out he's one of the more adamant voices trying to get Medical Gym guys banned from the weight room. Instead of sharing it for 45 whole minutes with eight or ten of us, they'd rather sabotage our interests so the dozenish of them can have exclusive access—again, despite the fact they're supposed to be working.

We check in for Medical Gym one morning around early March of 2011, and the Officer informs us we're no longer allowed to utilize the weight-room. Shocker. It's become more and more apparent that, when a rule is enacted that benefits one group at the expense of another, you can be damn sure the less fortunate group will get screwed! Seems to be the natural order of prison—just like the broader societal order. Think tax breaks for big cor-porations and the megarich with coinciding social program cuts; think of how relatively easy it is to receive unemployment vis-à-vis the absurd, unconscionably commonplace difficulty of getting on disability; think of the [genocidal] Drug War's effects on blacks compared to whites, and on poor people compared to the wealthy; just *think*, plain and simple.

Bravo, tattling Gym worker punks! Now all we can do at Medical is walk around the basketball court, shoot hoops, use yoga mats [if it happens to be a weekday and the equipment room is hence accessible], medicine balls [same], and the single stationary bike [same again]. No more weight machines for my legs—which were so very helpful in *safely* strengthening the muscles, enhancing knee support and stability. Fuck those wannabe-macho gymrat guys and their bitchy childlike squealing. They wound up being diametric opposites of what they try to portray with their muscles and attitudes.

This storyline does have a lovely postscript though, albeit morbid. After spending a decade and a half in prison, poo-poo's release date finally arrives and he's gone. Couple months later, we learn of his fate. I assume via the Gangbanger-Grapevine. Sounds like getting ripshit-buff—and spending his last few years at a minimum joint—gave him a grossly inflated sense of indestructability. He grew accustomed to having great social power due to his size and comparatively nonviolent prison-residence. But then, he obviously made a halfwit's error by continuing to act untouchable in the

"Free" World. Word is that poo-poo visited a woman with whom he'd maintained correspondence over the years. He learned she had a boyfriend, who soon showed up at her place as well. poo-poo tried his macho posturing routine; puffing out his giant chest, talking tough with the boyfriend. But this wasn't prison anymore . . .

The guy pulled a pistol and shot poo-poo dead.

After 15 years' incarceration, he was free [well, free and *living*] for all of 46 days.

"Oh my gawd!" I bellow when james tells me. Voice bouncing around the Gym like a rogue basketball punted off by his clawhand. He overheard the story in his room—he's in the same unit as several workers. I burst out cackling from the gut, tossing back my head. Hysterical laugher. The laughter of someone beaten down by life, by the demoralizing System—but who has now received an informational tidbit showing that, sometimes, justice *does* get doled out appropriately.

james is tee-hee-heeing. "Guess the tough guy act didn't work so well out there, huh?"

Still laughing giddily, I say, "So poo-poo's dead . . . guess gawd finally decided to *flush that turd!*" Now james throws back his head and guffaws, clawhand pressed to his stomach.

10.

Alas—despite the Counselors' continued assurances, the target on my back seems only to be gaining clarity and size. I can feel its presence no matter what else is happening.

I've always been seen as untrustworthy here, treated with suspicion, merely because I'm different. In the face of widespread and vicious bigotry—homophobia, racism, misogyny, and most pervasive of all [here and In the World], speciesism—I've become brazenly outspoken in defense of gays, people of color, women, animals . . . any and all oppressed classes. That's weird enough to most people. And oftentimes infuriating. On top of all that I'm an atheist vegan environmentalist, I spend the bulk of my time reading and writing, I'm educated, and so on. Hell—these things make me iconoclastic *outside* the razorwire fences! So try imagining what it's like in the Prison Vortex. Then pile on the fact that most guys in the unit believe I'm the reason jay got kicked out, no matter what Jenny and Mrs. Meyer say. A result that should've been easily predictable. Especially for them! In essence, all bets are off now. I'm fair game. Certain guys no longer hesitate to write me up; in particular those who already disliked me. buft most of all. He hates me because I'm so different, and because I didn't back down when he threatened me; but more than anything, it's my light. My egregious 30-watt reading lamp. buft, with his rippling muscles and Viking-blue eyes. He embarks on what can only be described as a ticket writing spree. Not against everyone though. Just puny crippled young me.

Being an atheist in prison is not pleasant, and the Drug Unit's worst of all. Sometimes, now that the weightroom is closed, or if I'm feeling down or hurting more than usual, I don't bother with Medical Gym. In which case I do attend the Morning Meeting. Almost all 100 guys crammed in the dayroom together in green plastic chairs, and two or three Counselors standing in back. The penultimate portion is *Giving Gratitude*, where guys stand up and list some things they're grateful for that day. Gratitude— which I prefer thinking of as Ten Daily Minutes of Gawdcock-Slurping— since so, so many people mention gawd or religion in their pronounce- ments. I doubt there was a single meeting where gawd wasn't praised at least once . . . nauseating! And not just because I hate religion. In a letter to his mother published in *Soledad Brother*, George Jackson nicely sums up my thoughts on the ever-so-popular Jailhouse Jesus:

> *Ordinary people, the mediocre, need to feel or believe in something greater than themselves. It gives them false security and makes them feel that help may be forthcoming. This is self-delusion in the extreme. I cannot partake in any foolishness . . . When I need strength, Mama, I reach down within myself. I draw out the reserves I've built . . . I call on* myself, *I have faith in* myself. *This is where it must always come from in the end—*yourself [emphasis added].

Brilliant. But in the case of prison and, yes of course, the outside world too, it's not just the baseless illogical fantasies, the herdlike mentality, the general absurdity of all religion—which is often transparent to those who weren't indoctrinated at a young and impressionable age; no, what's most irritating of all is the blatant goddamn hypocrisy! The vast majority of individuals merely pay lipservice to "god." They don't actually *practice* the teachings of Christ—they aren't peaceful, or truly compassionate toward all "creation," or humble, or interested in a simple lifestyle [though james *is* all these things, which is why I do respect him]. It's like Gandhi supposedly said: "I like your Christ, but so many of you Christians are so unlike Christ." Few such statements have been uttered that're more bitingly, tragically accurate. There are exceptions like james, but they only serve to prove the rule. Right after thanking gawd for this or that routine occurrence, these guys'll return to their rooms and slip without a hitch right back into their usual hateful, petty, homophobic, misogynist, compassionless, human-supremacist behaviors. It's the case with almost all religious people across all faiths. Most here identify as Christians though, so that's the hypocrisy I see most.[91] buft is one of the inmates who expresses gawd-gratitude on the regular. This is the guy, remember, with ultraviolent predilections, who threatened to choke me out, who cooked and sold meth, who slept with women just to rob them, et alia. The most common sentiment people express is something like, "I want to thank gawd for wakin us all up this morning." [What about all the people who died in their sleep, or were bombed by the U.S. military, in the last eight hours? Did they just draw a bad hand? Where was gawd for them? If you're thanking gawd for waking all of us up, isn't it equally appropriate to denounce gawd for *not* waking up the tens of thousands who DIED?]

One day the room is three-quarters empty and someone makes an offhanded dig at the prevalence of "Jailhouse Jesus." I agree aloud. scott k. grumbles about "hating that bullshit," and we have a brief moment of atheist solidarity. Then *surprise!* he obliterates this anti-theist brotherhood immediately; after calling me over, he pulls down the collar on his skyblue State shirt to reveal a burning cross tattooed on his upper pectoral. It takes me a moment to realize it's not an awesome symbol attacking Christianity—but rather a goddamn fucking piece of Ku Klux Klan imagery! "Ah," I mutter flatly, lips gnarled in disgust, and shoot him a look that says *You fuckin kidding me dude, REALLY?!* and shuffle off without another

---

[91] I've seen it a lot recently from Catholics as a result of Pope Francis's comparative progressivism. He came to America in 2015 and announced that taking action to combat climate change is a religious and moral imperative [!]—prompting feeble-minded political figures like then-presidential candidate Rick Santorum to say things like, "[The Catholic church is] better off leaving science to the scientists." The great & terrible hypocrisy is that people like Santorum are constantly doing the very *antithesis* of his suggestion, e.g. rejecting global warming as a hoax, denying the reality of evolution, etc. So it's almost as if . . . as if so-called religious people . . . *it's almost like they* pick and choose *what they* want *to believe!* I know, this revelation must be a <u>serious</u> shock! Heh. [Source: www.huffingtonpost.com/2015/06/02/rick-santorum-pope-climat_n_7498768.html]

word. [Rather than shoot him a look, I'd rather just *shoot him*.] Fabulous! Just when I think I've found an ally . . . ! Why am I even surprised at ridiculous shit like this anymore? I shouldn't, that's the answer; shouldn't even be surprised. At ridiculous shit like this. Not anymore.

Naturally, the ludicrous irony is disheartening and repugnant, but I'm *me*—so I can't help but find amusement here as well. Let me be clear, as President Obama's said a time or two. The racism itself isn't funny. It's the whole concept of racism from white people *like him*. Their quiet, cautiously muttered proclamations—often when black guy/s are being loud and obnoxious—of "Dumbass fuckin niggers" are always accompanied by a disheartened headshake. And these things're almost always spoken by a very specific type; these such white dudes tend to be . . . not exactly sterling representatives of their own race. Take scott k. He didn't finish high school, reads at about an 8th grade level, tops, lives in a trailer in one of Illinois's shittier Podunk counties [he once told me about cruising the local country roads with a pint of Jim Beam between his legs, and if he got pulled over, the cop would let him off so long as he "had an extra bottle d' give the cawp"]; and in general is just a perfect example of poor white trash. It is of course sadly tragic, but also laughable for its fundamental irony. Its transparent lunatic idiocy. I'd guess it stems from an unconscious fear that, delusions of white supremacy aside, *they're* the inferior ones.

In any case, just like with Jenny and proving my feminist solidarity, I feel obligated to do the same with people of color. After all, I'm privy to the things white guys say when blacks aren't around! So I call out scott k. as a racist. Informing people in the room about his tattoo. Also publicly rechristening him "scott *kkk*," since his last name was [and presumably still is] *kay*. He's none too pleased with that. But my black friends in the room appreciate it, and that makes exposing him totally worthwhile.

After being in the Drug Unit for several months, and especially after attending some half-dozen a.m. Meetings in a few weeks, the incessant religious statements make me want to puke all over the person's shoes. Jam a pen into my earballs just so I don't have to listen anymore. Or bite my own fingers, hard, to distract myself. As I surmised before, getting comfortable here contributes to my downfall. The subtle mockery I start pulling when I do attend the Meetings certainly falls under that umbrella. Back before I discovered scott kkk was a horrible racist and outed him, he'd wake me up every morning for Medline. At the Meetings, I often stood up to

Give Gratitude. First just mentioning a couple innocuous things to set the stage—like how grateful I was for my fiancée, and my mom's tremendous support; then I'd insert my sarcastic little flourish at the end: "Finally, I'd like to thank *scott k.* for waking me up this morning, and I'd like to thank *sunlight* for waking up the rest of us."

I wonder how many guy actually realized I was jabbing at their gawd-bullshit. Sadly, it seems the percentage was small.

II.

I decide the best thing to do is double down on my writing commitment, flinging myself back into *The Liberators*. I continue to make great progress. In February, I wrote over 130 pages. Averaging over five per day. A spectacular pace to sustain, especially given the tumultuous environment. Now it's mid-March, and I'm still moving at a strong, steady clip.

I have writing and books; Rachel leans on our darling Rikki for strength. She tells me how much fun they're having; even more now that the weather's improving. They visit the nearby dog park almost every day. She recently also discovered a wonderful new spot: a small, isolated beach on the San Francisco Bay with stunning views of a treelined jetty and the expansive, breeze-rippled baywater. Dogs are allowed offleash. It also happens to be literally 100 yards from infamous San Quentin State Prison's razorwired fences.

"That's crazy," I say. "How weird!"

Rachel's doing a lot better. Moving past the grief of her father's death, and growing at least somewhat accustomed to life without me. Her improving mood is sweet melody to my ears. "Just think," I say, "if everything goes right, I'll be home in just eight months, hon! Already *well over* halfway done!"

"Oh baby. That's so amazing. And hard to believe—can't fucking wait!"

"More than halfway done," I repeat. Assuming there's no reason to suspect otherwise.

Then tragedy strikes like a bolt of lightning on a cloudless day. Senselessly, in a word.

The electricity starts gathering when they rotate the Officers' assigned stations [which happens every 90 days], and our main nightshift Guard becomes Officer Cook. You might remember Cook as "Officer Forkface"; he of the bizarre, gruesome rivulets and blurred flesh-splotches covering his cheeks. As per dave's astute, previously quoted observation, it looks as

if Cook's "face was on fire and somebody beat it out with a meatfork."
Hah! Cook is a short, scrawny little spitfuck. No more than 5'5" and maybe
140 pounds—if he carried a semen-crusted rubber vagina in one pocket and
a fat stinky dildo crammed up his bung. Dude definitely has a raging Napo-
leon Complex. Trying to compensate for his puniness with a constant
bearing of haughty superiority and faux-toughness. Yep, he is one smarmy
bastard [sorry, just had to sneak in the S-word—it fits him even better than
the other Officers]. A genuine highgrade hardass, too.

This scumwad starts shitting all over us right away. Invariably copping
a bitchy, prissy attitude. For no reason! He's truly a cumstain on the tighty-
whities of humanity—and that's saying a helluva lot, since humanity itself
is nothing but "a virus with shoes," as the hysterical late comedian Bill
Hicks observed. One morning soon after he starts working the Bubble in
4-House, several of us return from the newly restrictive Medical Gym and
stand at the front desk, waiting to check in. Cook's reclined way back in
his chair, the *Jacksonville Journal-Courier* held open before his gross fucked-
up face. Five of us stand there. Just loitering like a bunch of ass-thumbing
buffoons. After waiting at least ten seconds, the guy in front—my buddy
jerome—says, "walker, 10-17."

Forkface doesn't move for a long, stretched-out moment. Then he sets
down the newspaper with an irritated expression, lips flat. He blinks—
once, s l l l O O O w w l y. "Did I *ask* fer yer infermation? Couldn' choo
see I 'as readin?"

jerome, mellow black dude with a gleaming shaved dome and slight lisp,
doesn't speak for a second. Then, "S^th orry, Offic^th er."

Sighing with a hard frown that says *Christ, WHAT did I do to deserve
this?*, Cook leans forward at the speed of sloth and grabs his pen. "Sorry,"
he intones with a sneer.

"Yep, that's^th what I s^th aid." Ah jeez, jerome, be careful! "S^th orry."

Cook shoots him a withering glare. Then shakes his head and scribbles
down our numbers. This uppity-bitch-type shit happens *all* the time with
Forkface. Given my almost pathological inability to tolerate such heaping
horseshit without eventually grabbing a shovel, I should've known it was
only a matter of time before we clashed.

One evening, I'm preparing dinner right in the midst of 9:30 count, and
he tells me I can't be cooking this late. You know me by now, though—it's
writing *über Alles!* So I choose not to alter my fundamental routine; I'm
simply more cautious about it. If I'm having fried rice for dinner, I make

sure it's finished and hidden in my box by 9:15, then wait till after count to eat. Watching all the while to see if Fuckface-Forkface is on the prowl.

As it turns out, my ultimate undoing [aside from Forkface] is caused by—wait for it—*brown rice*. The healthful food item. The high-fiber grain, grown in paddies, retaining throughout production its innate brownness, unlike its more common, nonfibrous white sibling.

No, really. My world—torn apart by brown . . . friggin . . . rice!

See, a couple months prior, they began selling the more healthful rice at Commissary. An exciting development for me; I almost never ate white rice until prison, when it became the only option. A few nights after Fork-face warned me about cooking late, I decide to try preparing a stir-fry with brown rice for the first time. Basically, I cook the rice in my hotpot, then add an offbrand Cup O' Noodles, minced garlic and onion, and some dyna-mite powdered seasoning mix. I begin cooking at 8:30 this particular night, knowing it will take longer than its de-pigmented [whitey] relative.

But it ends up taking way, *way* longer. At 9:20, the rice maintains crun-chiness all the way throughout each little grain. By 9:50ish, it's no longer crunchy—but *still* too tough for consumption. Same thing at 10:10 . . . and 10:30, and 10:45. This is getting goddamn ridiculous!

The Officers will come around for another count at eleven o'clock, so at 10:50 I say *Screw it!* and dump the pot's contents into my Tupperware "bowl" atop some now-cold refried beans. Then I begin shoveling into my gourd the meal, with its too-firm brown rice, in a desperate rush to finish before count. But I don't make it; too much food, too little time, too much undercooked-rice-mastication required. So I stick the bowl in my box and feign sleep. After the Officers make their rounds, I continue eating. Now savoring the meal—as much as one can be said to "savor" a meal featuring severely undercooked brown rice that is quasi-edible at best.

After count, you're typically safe for at least 20 minutes; the Officers have just walked through the whole unit. They have seminal responsibil-ities in the Bubble, e.g. reading the news or paperback genre-pulp trash like Dean Koontz, or passing out with upturned faces parallel to the ceiling, or pounding off in the bathroom while fantasizing about deviant violence, or discussing pussy or baseball in bored monotones—you know, crucial C.O. stuff. Of all nights though, this is the night Officer Forkface returns to the unit a mere *five* minutes after count. Catching me totally off guard as I cud morosely through my terrible meal.

He steps into the room and toward my bunk with purposeful intent. "You." Pointing a finger Napoleonically. "Bring your bowl 'n hotpot in'da the Bubble, right now." He marches straight back to the front desk. Did someone tip him off?! Sure seems like it [*coughBUFT!cough*].

I'm frowning while I gather up my shit. "There goes my hotpot, gawddamnit," I mutter.

If only!

I enter the Bubble and Forkface stands over the desk, filling out a ticket. Fine, whatever. No biggie. Without looking up, he kickslides a small gray trashcan toward me. "Dump outcher food and set down the bowl 'n pot." Still jotting. He shakes his head like I'm a puppy who won't stop urinating on the carpet. "Fuckin warned you bout this just th'other night."

The second Officer isn't around; maybe he's in 4A, or the bathroom. "Sorry about that," I say. "It's just . . ."

Forget it. No sense trying to convey the intricacies of my medication-and-food routine to this country-ass douchenozzle. "I'm a lil confused," I say. "Can you please tell me what the exact rule is?"

Now he stops writing. But it's weird . . . that's *all* he does, for a long awkward stretch. Remaining in the exact same position, corked over the desk [Spud Webb-short, he doesn't have to bend very far], pen hovering over the ticket-in-progress. He finally turns his head to look at me. Voice unsettling—totally affectless. Enunciating with care and repeated pauses. "Dump out yer food . . . and then place yer pot an' bowl . . . on the desk."

"Yeah, definitely! I just wanna clarify for future reference. Is the rule no *cooking* after count, no *eating*, or what?"

Now he straightens himself up, extending to his full and intimidating height of . . . well, of like my shoulders. "You needa stop arguin with me right now," he growls. "You been here long enough, you know the fuckin rules."

"Sir, I'm not arguing! Just that I've seen people cooking and eating after count all the time, but I've never seen another Officer say anything; just wanna know what the exact rule is, so I can—"

"Fuck it, ya hadger chance." Forkface grabs the walkie-talkie from his belt. "Setcher shit down an' get back in the fuckin unit." He holds the radio up to his gross, forked-up face and he's **kshh** requestin assistance from th' lead Lieutenan on duty **ksh**.

Oh *shitsickle!* He's just summoned reinforcements to come whisk me off to Segregation oh shit shitfire-bastard SHIT! If they throw you into

Seg [the Hole, jail, whatever, it all means the same thing—fucked], you're *automatically* ejected from the Drug Unit. Oh gawd. Oh please no. I drop my mouth open to protest, but this vile sonofabitch, this pile of uniformed excrement who should've crusted up and died inside a condom with his "siblings" after being plucked from a rural hooker's wart-ridden twat, he's already made up his small malformed mind, and speaking any more will only do further damage. I just hope the lead Lieutenant gives me a chance to defend myself. I set my Tupperware bowl and hotpot on the desk and move toward the unit's entrance.

"Don't go far," Forkface says.

Back inside, I stand near the Bubble's glass window, trying to steel my nerves and keep from freakin out. From crying outright. Need to remain calm and cool so I can explain what really happened—without appearing like I've been pissed off and arguing.

After a minute, Guards start filtering into the Bubble, and "cavalry" is almost an understatement. Three non-Whiteshirts arrive first; Sergeant Johnson with his discomfiting fake teeth is among them, and naturally he's wearing that big ole shitkickin redneck grin [does he *sleep* in that thing?]. Then two Lieutenants arrive. Finally another Lieutenant with a Sergeant and two more Officers. Bloody hell! you'd think I knocked the stupid cunt unconscious! Over the top response, much? The nightshift's lead Lieutenant opens the door to the unit, holding it half-open [or half-closed, if yer a pessimist] with his forearm, and stares at me. "So what's going on?"

I step up close. "Look, sir, I don't know why Officer For—er, *Cook* is making such a huge deal out of this." Calmly and politely, I explain what actually just transpired. How I wasn't arguing, I was simply asking for clarification on the rule. When I'm done, the Whiteshirt says, "Okay, well, you're not getting that bowl or hotpot back . . ."

"Oh hey, that's fine! I broke *that* rule, and accept the consequences. But I don't deserve to go to Seg over this. Please."

"You're fine. Go head and return to your room. No more eating after count, eh?"

. . . .

Back in the room, I'm shaking a little. But also awash in relief. Tragedy averted! Gooseflesh easing back down into normal human-flesh. Guys in the room are asking what happened, if everything's okay.

Fine, I tell them. It's all good.

. . . Buuut it's *not* fine. *Not* good, at all. A few days later I receive my yellow copy of Officer Cook's Disciplinary Report, and **The Dread** returns. With poison-dripping fangs bared. The modus operandi for *all* these powerdrunk cunts—which has proven itself over and over to be blatantly predictable—is remarkably similar, from Trooper Marlow all the way through to Officer Forkface and beyond. His writeup of the "Incident" is overflowing with the same precise brand of absurd lies and half-truths and hyperbole as Marlow's Police Report. Check out just this one section and you'll see.[92]

I/m Smitowicz SAiD thAT He wAsn't Going To Dump ouT [his rice]. I/m Smitowicz sTArTED ARGueing [sic] with this C/O ABouT why he had To Dump his Food. I Told I/m Smitowicz there wAs No EATing AFTer 9:30 pm [sic; **recall how I all but begged him to tell me the exact time!**]. I/m Smitowicz wAs Told AGAin To Dump IT ouT. I/m Smitowicz keep [sic] Telling Me He wAsn't Going TO DumP IT ouT. [**Excerpt and entire ticket sic passim.**]

Now, I rendered the scene precisely how it happened, so just consult the few pages above if you wanna compare our distinct versions. I submit to you the following, though: if Cook overreacted in the angered heat of the moment [and he did, he did], wouldn't it very much behoove him to make it appear like I did something terribly insolent—i.e. much worse than it really was? Because then his summoning the cavalry would actually seem justifiable to his superiors!

---

[92] Also notice Cook's bizarre mix of capitals & lowercase letters; I've painstakingly [and *painfully*] recreated it here.

And thus, for this one so-called incident, they charge me with three separate offenses: Disobeying a Direct Order, Insolence, and Violation of Rules [which is the <u>sole</u> offense I committed, in reality, by eating after 9:30 count]. As I wrote about the felony charges that got me locked up in the first place—also consisting of three different charges for one crime—it's like they heave "prodigious gobs of shit at a wall, knowing at least some will stick" [*Rebel Hell: Disabled Vegan Goes to Prison*, <u>Part 1</u>]. The worst part about the ticket by far is that Cook marked it as a Major Infraction, rather than a Minor. This means your charges are reviewed, your punishment doled out, by a committee—a hardass *troika* of Staff you might articulate as Officer + Sergeant + Lieutenant = unjust shitshow. This triumvirate-council brings even more frightening gravitas to the whole situation. Two of my confidants in the unit inform me that receiving a Major Infraction commonly results in a monthlong-or-more sentence of "C-Grade." While on C-Grade, you're barred from using the telephone and allowed only one trip to Commissary a month. That's bad enough.

But the final putative aspect is far far *far* worse. Incomparably worse.

If they stick you on C-Grade, it results in automatic, immediate, and incontestable <u>ejection</u> from the Drug Unit. Returning to now-unthinkable regular housing.

No more [relatively] pristine living conditions.

No more special rules that help corral the most odious behavior.

And of course, by far the most soul-crushing and -obliterative of them all, *no more <u>goodtime</u> accrual!* . . . Meaning my anticipated release—the date, toward the end of this year, that I and all my loved ones have expected for over *six* months that I'd be going home—would be pushed back. WAY the fuck back: As of now, I've only secured a pitiable 45 days of goodtime credit. And if they do indeed slam me with C-Grade, there's *nothing* the Drug Unit Counselors can do to help me. It's a Prison Rule, so their authority is superseded. Their influence utterly nil.

12.

Next a.m., they call me to Seg. Time to "hear" Cook's Major Infraction ticket. To receive my sentence. Oh christ is this unbearable! This is

B A A A A A D

The stuff of nightmares—
except worse, because there is
no waking up from this. No
reprieve
or justice
or hope.
This is [I just know it] where
the *true* **hard time** begins. It's the place where
life-ennui and vague anhedonia
smash together and gel into legitimate
SUICIDAL <u>IDEATION</u>.
Surely, it's the
"Think this is bad? You just wait . . . !"
that that guy in the footnotes keeps harping on,
finally come to awful, awful fruition.

. . . .

The *first* **stages** of it, anyway.

. . . .

Let's get this over with
before even *Jan-now* starts crying

SERGEANT EVANS opens the door and ushers **jan** inside. Two people—**LIEUTENANT CHEEK** and **OFFICER PATTON**—sit side-by-side at a wooden desk in the small room. There's a large rectangular window in the wall beside the desk; an electronic switchboard sits beneath the glass. Through the window **jan** can see a hall, with doors running up its side: the Segregation cells.

EVANS
Take a seat.

jan sits down on the other side of the desk from **PATTON** and **LT. CHEEK**; **EVANS** stands, arms crossed, against the door. **jan**'s nerves are stretched tighter than banjo strings, and just as jangly. The desk is built with a perpendicular wood panel running down from the edge and almost to the floor, so **jan** cannot stretch his legs out beneath the desk.[93] **LT. CHEEK** and **PATTON** stare down, skimming what appear to be triplicate copies of **jan**'s Disciplinary Report.

jan [*voiceover*]

Dear gawd, it's this bitch——Patton. Same one who popped me for having extra cassette tapes. And the same woman [term used loosely, since being a *woman* requires you first be a *human*, about which I'm not entirely convinced] who was a total asshole to Rachel in the Visiting Room. I think Rachel's exact words describing her were "fucking cunt." Patton's fugly appearance perfectly matches her inner nature——the spitefulness, witheringly smarmy powerdrunk attitude, and just the meanness in general. She's one of Jacksonville's worst Officers in terms of the all-too-common unfounded elitism and utter lack of even the faintest compassion. This is why I feel no hesitation and/or remorse whatsoever in describing her ugliness. If she weren't such a scumbag, I'd be far less ruthless w/RE/to how she looks. Nutshell: Officer Patton is a hideous beast of a humanoid-type-creature. Short and pudgy. Half-black, half-white, whole-ugly. She missed out on the good fortune of many mixed-race people, wherein they inherit some of the best characteristics from each parent, resulting in an

---

[93] I realize the above sentence could be interpreted to mean the desk is *intentionally* designed so **jan** can't stretch out his legs, but that's not what he's implying—it's fairly unlikely the desk was designed this way for him and him alone, so that he specifically, here today, would be unable to straighten out his legs and get less-uncomfortable; having said [or rather *written*] that, **jan** cannot completely rule out the possibility. *Stranger things* & all that.

intriguing sort of exotic beauty. But there's nothing beautiful about Patton, and the only thing *exotic* is how much of a meanspirited cunt she is.

She's about 45, balding heavily. The curly lightbrown hair she does have is wispy, with a fine, almost *translucent* quality. You can see four-fifths of her scalp, most of which matches her skin's mocha color, but the scalp is also grossly mottled with darker, auburnish splotches. Scalp surface like the torn segment of a discarded Jackson Pollack experiment, too unseemly even for him to work with. Her face also has a definite *piggish* quality; not as much as the male Officer who looks almost identical to Porky the Pig, but it's certainly there—in her marshmallow-shaped face, her sizable upturned snout with large prominent nostrils, and the soft, gradual meld of her chin into neckflesh. Even her voice grates on the nerves. It's discordant with her chunky frame; highpitched and whiny, and nasally, too. A gross ugly beast, inside and out. Just gross. Her presence does not bode well for me.

EVANS
Putcher fuckin chair forward and sit up! Have some damn respect!

jan had angled his chair and slid it back a couple feet, so he could stretch his legs to the side.

jan
Sorry, I've had five knee surgeries, it really hurts to—

EVANS
I don't give any kinda fuck! Slide your chair back in fron'a the desk. Not like this'll take very long.

jan does as instructed, and the Visegrip tightens immediately. **EVANS** runs a hand through his silver beard.

                    jan [*voiceover*]
Officer Cook, Forkface, I hope you choke to death at lunch today you fuckin miserable cunt. Are they serving the infamous cock-in-the-sock? Gawd I hope so. I hope you choke to death while eating a cock-in-the-sock! Hope that weird condomy plastic that's wrapping the repulsive graymeat gets lodged in your vile turkeyneck gullet, and you suffer bugeyed terror for the several minutes it takes to finally DIE. And I hope there's precisely one person in your vicinity when it happens, and it's another male Officer, and he tries to give you the Heimlich maneuver, but years ago on the morning he trained for it, he was painfully hungover, with a slicing headache, and so he can't quite perform it well enough to save you, although as he's trying, the rubbing friction of his crotch against your ass gives him a throbbing hardon, and as your vision fades and your already-feeble brain shuts down from lack of oxygen, you're disgusted that the other Officer's hard penis is jabbing into your buttocks; and but the last thing you experience is confusion and a sort of mid-*death*, *end*-life crisis when you realize that *you also* have an erection, and instead of having the joyous bits of your pitiful life flash before your eyes as you descend into the dark eternal nonconsciousness of death, rather than experiencing a vision of your loved ones waving goodbye, you die in a tornadic whirl of bafflement,

terror, misery and selfloathing.[94]

LT. CHEEK looks up at **jan**. His face has a hardened, leathery quality, and he's got a neat, darkbrown mustache. He, too, is an uptight bastard.[95]

> ### LT. CHEEK
> Well, mr. smitowicz, let's see . . .

CHEEK speedreads Officer Forkface's writeup of the event aloud.

> ### LT. CHEEK
> Okay, so. First, would you like to make a statement in response to these charges?

> ### jan
> Yes, please.

> ### PATTON [*nasally*]
> Sit up straight. Keep your hands on the table.

> ### jan
> So, yes: I *was* cooking after 9:30 count. I admit to being guilty of that Violation of Rules, and take full responsibility for it—and the consequences attached—but that is *all* I'm guilty of. I absolutely *did not* refuse to throw away my food, as Officer Cook wrote in his report. I never once told

---

[94] This is NOT to imply that there's anything wrong or bad about two males' getting an erection while either receiving or giving the Heimlich maneuver while one of them is asphyxiating on the condomesque plastic casing of a gray sausage of unknown Animalia-origin; this sequence is merely a commentary on the rampant homophobia among inmates & Officers alike, and a suggestion as to the possible *basis* for their frequent expression of homosexual-abhorrence.

[95] In fact, this triumvirate—EVANS, PATTON, & CHEEK—*epitomizes* what George Jackson was talking about in *Soledad Brother* when he wrote, ". . . prisons attract sadists . . . a group of individuals demonstrably inferior to the rest of the society in regard to education, culture, and sensitivity."

him *No*. The only thing I did was ask for clarification as to the rule—

PATTON
Come on, mr. smitowicz, you're well aware of the rules. I know you've been here for long enough. How long have you been here for?

jan
Uhhm . . . about eight or nine months.

PATTON
Right. You should *know* the rules by now.

jan
I honestly didn't. I see people cooking and eating after 9:30 all the time, so I was confused. I was only asking him to explain exactly what the rule was, so I could avoid it in the future. And besides, I already admitted that I'm guilty of violating the rule! I'm just saying that Officer Cook misrepresented what really happened. I never refused him, not once. I wasn't even arguing with him. In the ticket he says that I was argumentative, and refusing over and over to throw the food away. That just did not happen.

EVANS [*cuntishly*]
Seem pretty fuckin argumentative to me.

LT. CHEEK
All right, I think we've heard enough here. Please step outside for a minute while we discuss your punishment.

jan opens his mouth, but then shuts it, frowning. He rises and **EVANS** opens the door and **jan** stands outside, on the verge of tears.

> **jan** [*voiceover*]
> Oh gawd. I'm so screwed. What's the point of even having a goddamn hearing if they're not gonna *hear* you out? It's a farce. Yet another masturbatory bureaucratic maneuver whose only purpose is to *appear* like there's a chance for justice. Fuckin *exact same* as the System on the outside! Theater—a way to *make believable* the Justice System's "fairness," and that you're Innocent Until Proven Guilty. Babyshit! Guilty Until *Proven* Guilty would be more accurate. Now, hideous gross balding blackhearted Miss Piggy-looking cunt Patton and redneck smarmy douchebag peabrained cunt Cheek are gonna believe Fuckface-Forkface's lies unquestioned [or pretend to]. No justice. No decency. Just a farcical little piece of theater to make it *look like* there's a legitimate accountability process.

EVANS opens the door and ushers **jan** back inside.

> **jan** [*voiceover*]
> Oh Christ. I can't breathe. They're about to wreck my life even worse than it's already wrecked, without a goddamn nanosecond of hesitation.

jan stands in front of the door. They don't even sit him down this time.

> **LT. CHEEK**
> Okay, mr. smitowicz. Based on Officer Cook's report, this Committee finds you guilty of all charges. We're giving you one month of C-Grade.

jan utters a low groaning sound.

jan

Could you please, *please* reconsider? I'm in the
Drug Unit, and C-Grade means I'll be automatically
kicked out. I'm really working the program and
trying to better myself—you can ask the
Counselors. I made a mistake, I know I screwed up,
just please don't put me on C-Grade. *Please*. Two
months of B-grade, three months, six. Three months
without Commissary. *Anything*. Please, *anything but
C-Grade*. Please.

PATTON

Maybe you should've thought about all that before
you disobeyed the direct order from Officer Cook.

LT. CHEEK

Our decision stands. One month of C-Grade. It's not
our concern what happens as a result, our job is to
simply decide the appropriate punishment. You can
always get your name back on the list and return to
the Drug Unit after you're off C-Grade.

jan

The waiting list is *huge*, it'll take me months and
months to get back there. Please, just—

EVANS

Didn't you hear them? This hearing is over, inmate.
Return to yer fucking unit.

13.

inmate smitowicz shuffled out of Segregation in a daze. Although of course he didn't know it at the time, he'd eventually return to that building—and remain inside for two entire weeks. His shoes susurrated lightly over the Walk's gravel as he stepped along. Eyes down. An inmate in 5-House watched smitowicz through the window in his room, wondering why the kid was staring at the ground the whole time. Now there's a guy wit a lot on 'is mind, the 5-House inmate thought.

When smitowicz reached 4-House, he looked into the office on the right, where Mrs. Meyer sat. She saw the look on his face and ushered him in. The Officer at the front desk yelled at smitowicz to CHECK BACK IN! first. smitowicz gave his bed number [soon to be someone else's bed] and entered the office.

He tried to hold it together, but within just 60 seconds he was weeping. Slumped at the waist in the chair, head dropped into one hand, the other holding a wad of Kleenex. Weeping. Mrs. Meyer was very sympathetic. She did her best to comfort him. The best thing she did, though, involved no softly spoken words or shoulder pats. The best thing she did was make him feel it was okay to cry, that there was no judgment or annoyance. smitowicz was extremely grateful for this.

smitowicz was already flush with anxiety over how hard this'd be on his fiancée. Guilt plied at him like a tick, digging into his flesh. He knew he had little fault in the whole debacle. But he couldn't stop the guilty feelings. How easy it is, through careful retrospective analysis, to see the ways things could've turned out differently! How this tragedy, too, could've been averted. The trick—the Hard Part—is performing this analysis in the moment, avoiding serious trouble in the first place. But within an environment as volatile and unpredictable as the Prison Vortex, it's indescribably difficult to behave with perfect rationality. To unerringly do what's best. smitowicz was unable to even fathom that he'd lost FOUR AND A HALF MONTHS of potential good time credit. It was abstract; too much even for consideration yet. If his psyche snagged on the idea, it'd leave him a cracked and functionless shell before long, all but dead inside. The idea of going home not this November, but rather next April . . . Unthinkable! He had to focus first on getting through the month without access to Commissary or vocal communication with Rachel. That hurdle alone seemed insurmountable enough.

smitowicz thought the whole situation and its fallout was so utterly fucking senseless, so sickening and wrong in its fundamental injustice, that dwelling on it would open the door for Suicidal Ideations and/or Desires. This didn't surprise him in the slightest, because he felt it In the World, too. Quite often. Depression resulting from humans' barbaric cruelty and wanton destruction, feeling impotent in the face of power beyond comprehension, and the emotional trainwreck of living with a strong conscience and awareness in the horrorshow that is industrial civilization: he experienced all these things in the Prison Vortex, same as in the socalled Free World. The two places like mirror images, except as viewed through distorting funhouse glass. Everything fucked up about society lived, thrived in the Vortex; the primary substantive difference was simply that, in prison, all those things were intensified to a dangerous feverpitch, and right out in the open—no disguises, with very little of the enculturating propaganda [surrounding us since birth for countless generations] that insists everything destructive and murderous and wrong about the dominant culture is Just the Way Things Are and Must Be. But living in the Mad Carnival of Industrial Society is no more natural or necessary than living in the Sociopathic Circus of Prison.

smitowicz felt all of this running through his very blood, down to the deepest core of his being. But he also knew succumbing to despair was not an option. He had to survive, had a moral obligation to continue his literary endeavors; if nothing else, then at least for his ability to help others both see and navigate [and maybe escape, even DESTROY] Industrial Civilization. And so—he decided during the week he remained in the Drug Unit, in limbo, merely waiting for the paperwork to go through before he was ejected—in order to traverse this labyrinth of sorrows, to occupy the industrial megamachine's black-greased belly and emerge with his spirit more or less intact, smitowicz would paradoxically best survive by adopting the ideology of a machine! The Ideology of the Bulldozer, to be exact.

In other words: No thinking. No vacillation. No stopping. He'd simply put down his head and GO GO **GO**! Bulldozing his way through the labyrinth's concrete walls. Not because it would bring joy. Not because it would make him stronger. Not for anything at all in the whole wide world, except the only thing, the one single thing, that mattered . . .

Because he had to. Because he had no choice.

14.

A couple days later, the Guard handing out mail tells me to pack my shit— they've assigned me to Unit 2A and it's time to move on. As I stuff my clothes and TV and shower shoes and sheets and everything else into my property boxes, working hard to stifle the tears, I vaguely anticipate some kind of sad farewell. Aside from a few Good lucks and See ya rounds though, there's no pomp to my leaving, despite being here for over seven months. But that's just the way it is. Guys come in, they depart . . . they get kicked out, they go home, they hate the place and request a transfer; constant shuffling. Don't get too attached to anyone, because they—or you!—could disappear in an instant.

With so much dread and misery floating around my entire person, it's actually amazing that I have any to spare . . . but I do, and it's because I haven't yet told Rachel about all this. Any of it. [Well I mean she knows about my going to prison and all that, and about the Stateville Horrors and medical assrapery etc.—she just doesn't yet know I even received a major ticket.]

I use a wooden pallet with wheels to schlep my boxes a hundred yards down the Walk to 2-House. The wheels clunkroar over the gravel, sounding like the apocalypse if the apocalypse's roads were graveled. Soon after unpacking at my new bunk, I see that my old pal austin's here. He's the 6'4" tall, reedthin guy with whom I worked in the Chow Hall dishroom. We'd talk a lot; he was always very kind and helpful. I'm glad to know at least one person here. My new cellie is a devoted Muslim, a black dude called naseer. The guys in my room seem pretty cool overall. Ethnic make-up: about 75 percent black, with a couple Mexicans and a few white guys. The Drug Unit's weird in respect to ethnicity; way fewer black guys reside there than in the regular units. Easily 20 or 30 percent less. This might correlate to the Chicago gang culture so many black men here were steeped in: their fervid snitch-avoidance. Most J-ville residents consider 4B the "snitch unit."

I can't put it off much longer: Rachel deserves to know the tragedy that has befallen us. Yet the idea of explaining my [our] fate is threatening to induce a paralytic state. I just need to bulldoze my way through the phone call, *force* myself to just get it over with. I wait until dinnertime before calling—when the unit's almost empty—due to the very real possibility of my breaking down into tears. I may be the one incarcerated, but she too is locked up in many ways. We're *both* enduring the hell of imprisonment. Injustice's tentacles flare out to snatch others in its grotesque suctioning clamp.

Knowing just how volcanically this info will scorch her heart . . . my outdate getting pushed back in her mind by **four and a half months** in a literal instant . . . this is genuinely among the most difficult moments, amid one of the two or three most genuinely difficult periods, of my entire incarceration. My heart still cracks anew—with a feeling like the sound of a thick porcelain plate dropped on cement—even now, a full 5+ years after it happened.

"Hi baybeee!" she answers.

Hearing her voice, and her excitement for my call, sends yet more jagged shards of hurt plunging into my spirit. "Honey, I have bad news. Really, *really* bad news."

What can I write? She's decimated, shattered. Nothing I'm able to come up with could ever truly represent the depth of our collective sorrow. I could try to describe it—but sometimes, I think maybe sometimes the best way to convey emotional devastation in words is to not even *try* describing it. To just let the events speak for themselves. Any attempt at fancy linguistic wordsmithery will fall flat. So no. Not this time. This time, here, now, I will merely offer . . .

Silence.

Though I do need to describe the precise character of this silence, clarify it at least, render in plain detail the important dynamics of this particular sort of silence: it is like the overwhelming, earpiercing silence that would come roaring at a deathmetal concert, an *arena* deathmetal concert, if you had your forehead pressed against a tower of speakers, the noise so blisteringly loud it's little more than distorted cacophony . . . then suddenly there's a power outage, the arena's delved into a pitchblack, and it's like the music was breakneck-rushing through the desert and plummeted off a vertical cliff. Gone, dead. And all the crazed ferocity blitzing around inside your ears and your head at that moment . . .

That kind of silence.

After I tell her what happened, she maintains a glimmer of hope—one of the many things I'd long ago looked inside myself and found, like the machine-creature implanted in Neo in *The Matrix*, and I'd ferreted and clawed it out of me and destroyed it, killed it mercilessly. Out of sheer necessity. Survival. But perhaps I was wrong. Somehow it survived; like the shimmering mirage of *hope* inside Rachel. Desperation in her voice. "Couldn't you, I dunno, try talking to Jenny or the other counselor lady? Maybe they could do something! Like maybe write a letter or make a call or . . . or . . . *fuck*, baby, there's gotta be *something*!"

"Already talked to Mrs. Meyer. This goes above them. I'm sorry, sweetheart. So, *so* sorry. There's nuh-nothing . . ." and now the tears come, the walls crumble to dust and I begin weeping openly. "There's n-nothing . . . anyone c-cuh-can do. I'm fucked, baby I'm so sorry if I'd known he was gonna run me through like that I would've just thrown the shit out without saying a *word* I'm so s-s-sorry Rachel please don't be mad at me *I love you so fucking m-much.*"

She's crying now too.

Goddamn Forkface. Goddamn Trooper Marlow and Judge Hamer and my lawyer Bruce. Goddamn this prison, this state, this country, this sick, demented, sociopathic culture that gobbles up lives and shits out mere fragments. Goddamn this miserable existence, which would be Heaven on Earth if it weren't for human civilization. We're destroying the remaining pieces of heaven . . . for the luxury of a few, for inertia, for fear and cowardice. Goddamn *us*.

And goddamn *gawd*. I'm sure it doesn't exist—but when life is this fucked up and hideously cruel, might as well put it out there just in case. Goddamn *gawd*.

I manage a quick adjustment to the new environs; my frequent relocation has rendered the process largely mundane. Lots of extra free time here in 2A—I no longer have to turn off my lamp at eleven p.m., with no more classes or meetings—so I vow to entrench myself even deeper into *The Liberators* [which has now been reimagined as two long novels instead of one massive tome—*The Liberators, Volumes 1* and *2: Strong Hearts* and *Strong Hearts Forward*]. Within a mere day or two, my writing pace accelerates. A lot! Returning to general population, particularly after living in such a restrictive and micromanaged unit for seven months, is strikingly mellower in its relative freedom.

There are of course downsides: It's far messier. Most guys don't bother to wash or even rinse their hands after peeing, and many don't even do it after taking a *shit*. There's no sense of unit camaraderie. Not even a façade, nothing. And it's *way* way louder. This last is by far the hardest part for me. Overhearing conversations so idiotic it's positively stupefying; trying to relax with a book while steeped in noise like the background chatter in a movie party-scene cranked to 11 [if said party were filled with boorish, misogynistic, antigay bigotry and hypocrisy—so, in other words, like a Republican fundraiser].

Thank Earth I have earplugs! an even bigger necessity now. They're not available on Commissary—which seems like gratuitous cruelty—but earplugs do exist within the prison. Maintenance workers have access to them, as the job involves using loud machinery. And this is a certainty: if there's a demand for something, and inmates can smuggle it from their job [which means pretty much anything small that has little chance of being weaponized], there *will* be acquisition-opportunities. james goes to church service with a maintenance employee. Every few months, when my plugs have become so grimy and inelastic that they're useless, I give james three bucks' worth of writeouts to trade for a new pair. That's right—I pay *three dollars* for two little foam earplugs! And I'm perfectly content with it. I'd pay **$20** if that's what it took!

The singular thing that staves off suicidal depression during this period is my writing. I force myself to think about the current novel's plot, about every little nuance of its characters' lives, in large part so I can *avoid fixating on my own life*. Because the crushing deepsea-like despair has fantastical, wildly original new problems heaped upon it all the everlovin time. Hell, only a couple weeks after I get ejected from 4B and lose all that good time, yet another terrible thing happens! At the now-sorry excuse for Medical Gym, I'm exercising with a couple guys from the Drug Unit. We're using 10 lb. medicine balls. Sitting on vinyl mats that reek of sour, accumulated sweat and stale #cheesefeet, and radiate toxic, sinus-burning vapors—as if, after each use, the workers submerged the mats in barrels containing a 50-50 mix of industrial cleaner and bleach [wouldn't be at all surprised if they really were doing so—james and I don't call it *Chemical* Gym for nothing!]. Somehow, though, the mats' heavy miasma fails to overcome all those grody organic odors [#groders?]. Instead, the smells all just effluviate outward in asphyxiating unison.

My knees're bent up near my chest. Heels almost touching my butt. I twist left and right at the hips, swinging the ball over my knees to tap the hardwood floor on either side. As I'm rotating and lowering the dense ball, a sudden breathless pain erupts on the right side of my lower back. I drop the ball and holler out. Terrible pain like rapid pulses of lightning zaps up and down my spine. Feels like poo-poo jammed a bayonet into my oblique abdominals, slicing through the flesh, and the needlesharp tip then plunged straight into my spinal cord's dorsal root ganglion nerve-clusters. It's truly up there with the most intense flashing *blitzkriegs* of pain in my life—and I've torn knee cartilage and ligaments, cracked bones both large and small, gotten barbed by a stingray right into the fine, tender flesh atop my foot, fallen off a bike at 20 mph to go skidding across the concrete . . . so I'm no stranger to sudden painflares. This one is *bad*.

I'm fetal on the mat, groaning, the misery utterly consumptive. "You all right?" my buddy mick asks.

"Hur-m'-back," I manage to blurt between sucks of air hissing through my teeth.

That turns out to be a vast understatement. I'm favoring my lower back for the remainder of the day, but not until the next morning do I realize the injury's full debilitating extent. A fellow Medliner throttles me awake; I start to climb down the ladder and can't help but unleash an embarrassing bleat of agony. Jagged, slicing adamantium pain snatches my breath away. It's comparable in severity to how it felt right after tweaking the muscle—except now, a similar level of anguish bursts forth *every time I move*. Like a machete that's been crudely rock-sharpened tearing through my back's lower right quadrant again and again, a region comprising one-fourth of its entire surface area.

I'm literally hobbling on the Walk as my shoes scuffle across its gravel. Clutching at the injury. Facial features knotted in a perpetual grimace that only changes while uttering a hiss or groan or long drawn-out mewl. Each and every footstep shoots that fierce stabbing pain all along my spine. I've only ever limped this heavily in the immediate aftermath of my most traumatic knee injuries and subsequent surgeries! The oldtimers with their four-pronged canes easily limp past on the Walk. An Officer yells at me ta hurry up 'n stay with'a gawdamn line. "Does it *look* like I can hurry?" I shout. "Back's killin me, man." Step-blade-stab-dig-grunt, step-stab-twist-hiss, over over overover SHITFIRE HELL! Luckily I'm way far back from anyone else now; I release a low sort of keening sound, tears leaking, and a pitiable little whimper floats from my mouth.

As if the emotional trauma of getting booted from 4B and losing four and a half fucking months of goodtime and being further severed from Rachel and Rikki weren't bad enough, on *top* of my normal everyday pain, now I have to contend with *this*? Will the nightmare ever end—this puke-worthy joke that stopped being funny long ago [if it ever truly was except in retrospect]? I really don't know how much more misery I can withstand. Does each person have their own built-in limit to the amount of suffering they can endure before finally just breaking down? Feels like that indeed may be the case . . .

piling piling
piling piling piling

Because alllll the bad shit just keeps piling and piling.

When I finally limp back into 2A after Medline, I head straight for the phone and call Dad #2—Jim. It's barely 7 a.m. back home on the west coast, but this can't wait. He answers on the third ring and sounds tired, but he was already awake. "How's it goin, buddy?"

I explain what happened, and the awful fallout. "What do you think it could be?"

"Most likely you strained or pulled a muscle. That's what it sounds like."

"Makes sense . . . gawd this is bad." We talk for a few more minutes, and then he has to take my little brother Jimmy to school. Jimmy—14 years old when my incarceration started, he'll be 16 by the time I'm released. A monumental stretch in a teenager's life, filled with unprecedentedly rapid changes. I'll see his dramatic transformation only once I get out; he'll have stretched a foot taller, voice dropped half an octave or more, grown during my forced sabbatical from a nice early-teen boy into a fine, brilliant young man. And I miss it all. Talking on the phone once a month doesn't capture the transition. I'm absent during the crucial, profound, once-in-a-lifetime pubescent changes in my little brother's life. Unable both to witness it and to be there for him. To be the rad big brother mine never was. I hate myself for it. Even more, I hate The System for it. Just one more thing stolen from me and my loved ones by the skewed reality of American so-called Justice. "All right then," I tell Jim before hanging up. "Love you Dad, thanks!"

"Love you too, janno."

My eyes fill with tears for the second time this morning—I quickly duck through the wave of emotion. Which gets easier and easier all the time. Jim's been a father to me since he and my mom started cohabiting when I was a toddler. They married when I was five. My spermdad was around—I still visited him every other weekend—but Jim raised me for the most part. When I was six, I tumbled from atop a wooden playground structure at Wilderness Park down the street from my childhood home, bashing head and face against bulky wooden beams four or five times; Jim held watch at my bedside all night. When I had severe asthma attacks at ages four and twelve, he took me to the hospital in the middle of the night for breathing treatments. All the way through college—his was the first face I saw upon waking from most of my knee surgeries.

I never called him Dad, though. Always Jim. It just felt weird. Like a subtle betrayal of my birthfather. But Jim helped raise me so much; he's been supportive in every way all through this horrific ordeal. Not only that, he and Mom'd been separated for several years when I caught my case—yet still he treated me like his son. I'm more than a little inspired to grant him this small titular gesture. I had to get incarcerated for me to internalize and actualize this simple truth: Calling him Dad is the absolute least I can do![96]

After mulling it over during lunch, I decide *To hell with my injury!*—I cannot allow it to stop me from writing. Thankfully the back pain isn't sharp and invasive when I'm supine. So I can still do my thing. This injury occurs toward the end of March 2011. In April, I set a new personal record for total number of pages written [216], averaging over seven a day! That helps mitigate the period's emotional difficulty. By the end of April, I'm on a role. DEEP in the zone.

It's almost *dizzying* to consider how much I could've accomplished with a better medication regiment. The reasons I'm capable of writing so much despite this impediment, to lay them all out in one place, are [1] I've cultivated a blistering level of discipline; [2] I'd be bored out of my skull otherwise, with life-threatening "creativity blueballs," to coin a phrase; [3] my environment makes mental escape a non-negotiable requirement—no matter how mindbustingly difficult the writing is, any alternative is unspeakably worse; [4] simply put, I'm having a blast with the novel. Its complexity, populous cast of characters, giddily fun plot to imagine and render, and personal/social significance all coalesce to make writing *The Liberators, Volumes 1 & 2* a wondrous, phenomenal, stupendously obsessive task [in the best possible way]. And I think every single last one of these weapons-grade elements are indispensable to my overcoming the endless obstacles.

I'm hobbling with every footstep for *two full weeks* after the initial back injury. Then it finally diminishes a shade; I continue to experience regular

---

[96] He was by no means perfect—I vividly recall the spankings & fingershaped bruises on my little arms, as well as the psychological/emotional trauma of feeling like nothing I did was ever good enough, and being made to feel like a gross piece of shit when I was chunky as an adolescent—but he *was* and *is* a father to me, & deserves the title. I think our society places WAY too much emphasis on genetic family vs. what I might call, for lack of a less hippie-dippy phrase, your "soul family," composed of kindred spirits with whom you are bonded in ways that can be far more powerful than any familial ties.

spikes of intense pain, especially climbing up and down my ladder, but overall it's far less intolerable.

Not only am I zipping through *The Liberators*, I'm reading a ton as well. Averaging at least a book a week, although sometimes up to six or seven a month. I'm currently on a big John Irving trip, working through the yank-author's entire oeuvre. My reading habits mirror the way I consume music. After discovering a writer whose style and stories capture me, I devour most or all of their books. This is why I've read 15 Vonnegut novels [most of them twice], 40+ by Stephen King, everything published by Tom Robbins, Donna Tartt, Derrick Jensen, Jennifer Egan, and so on.

I read and adored Irving's *The World According to Garp* when I was 18— my high school drama teacher gave it to me as a graduation present—but never delved any deeper until prison. I finished *A Prayer for Owen Meany* a few weeks after leaving the Drug Unit. Thought it was fantastic. Then I flew through *The Hotel New Hampshire* and loved it even more than *Garp*! I'd found a new literary obsession. Over the next eight months, I read most of his stuff: *The Cider House Rules*, *Garp* a second time, *The 158-Pound Marriage*, *A Son of the Circus*, *A Widow for One Year*, *Setting Free the Bears*, and 2005's *Until I Find You*. Discovering a fantastic new author with a large body of work is truly among the most exciting things in life. Particularly when they've written numerous spectacular books.

In May, I once again crank out more than 200 pages on *The Liberators*. Damn thing is becoming a serious beast; I've surpassed 700 pages. It's already substantially longer than *The Eternal City*, and when I examine the plot arc in my head, it seems like I'm only about halfway done! Looks like the project, my sixth novel, will be far and away my fattest tome.

Around this time—late spring—a Psychologist begins working at Jacksonville. Till now, people have been seeing a "Mental Health Professional." She was really sweet and kind. So they replaced her, of course! supplanted with someone who is . . . well, *not* sweet or kind. Takes me all of five minutes during my first session with this new Dr. Camerer to realize she's just like all the other #*Yessirs*, towing the Company Line—or rather *prison*, not *company*, though is there really much substantive difference?—and upholding the cruel, unconscionable status quo.

There's something decidedly . . . *off* about Dr. Camerer. Very strange attitude and affectations. She's white, early 30s, with chestnut hair drawn back in a lazy bun; when rogue strands fall across her cheeks, she quickly swipes them back behind an ear with her finger, as if studiously avoiding anything in her appearance that could be interpreted as easygoing. She has high-set cheekbones, the hint of dimples. Grayish-blue eyes behind black-framed glasses, which create a touch of that smart-girl-next-door air.

What she doesn't have a touch of is *affect*. Not so much as the teeniest little touch. Her face's muscles never appear to shift; even while talking, only her lips move. When most humanoids speak, it influences like their zygomatic muscles, for example. Or the eyes do something. Their voices' inflection rises and falls depending on context and meaning. But not hers!

I've surmised—following extensive cogitation—that she spent several hours a day sitting before a mirror for at least a month prior to her first day here. Practicing. Honing her craft. Mastering the delicate art of non-nonverbal communication. Picture it:

Hi, I'm Dr. Cam—NO! Don't even consider allowing your lips to spread even a millimeter smile-ward—Daddy always said *Loose lips, stink shits*, and nobody wants that! Those filthy perverted criminals could interpret such wanton bilabial reck-lessness as weak or even a come-on! Pretty sure that's how most sexual assault cases start. **Try again**. Okay . . . Hi, I'm Dr. Camer—NO! Your cheeks moved that time! Definitely don't want cheeks moving. And get that damn glint of friendliness-slash-professional-courtesy out of your eyes! You need to remain totally deadpan. As deadpan as an actual dead pan. At LEAST! Maybe even more. Especially the eyes. Eyes are the window to your soul—do you really want those lowlifes to look into your dual face-windows and catch a glimpse of your very soul?! No, that's what I thought. **TRY AGAIN**.

All that preparatory mirror time paid off fully. She's a physiognomonic tabula rasa, the proverbial blank slate. There's *nothing* gleanable from her expressions—because she has none! She offers only words; and I'm frankly a little surprised she didn't train herself how to produce phonemes without lip movement. Like a ventriloquist. She very likely tried, though. I'm ima-gining her husband [she has a gold band on the correct finger] walking into their neat bedroom; he hears her flat, lowpitched voice, but her face appears motionless. He steps closer. Then he sees it: minute lip-twitches on the Ms and Fs. *Honeyshmoogenboogenlips*, he coos, *you've GOTTA* let the ventrilo-*quism go! It'll be way too weird. Freak people out, y'know?*

I don't give a FUCK! she shrieks, hurling his Einstein-faced buttplug at him. Do you want me to get beaten or raped? I can't show them a thing. What about . . .

hey! Maybe I could, like, put up a cardboard barrier or something in the middle of the desk! Her husband—a data-reconfiguration and statistical analysis expert, most likely—sighs. *Pumpkinbunnykittenmittens, please. Let's discuss this.* Eventually he somehow convinces her to ditch the ventriloquistic aspirations, but she refuses to budge [LITERALLY!] on the cheeks, eyes, or vocal monotone.

That's another thing: her *voice*! It may be even more affectless than her face, which I would've considered impossible. Like trying to snatch a pencil from the hand of someone holding zero pencils. Her vocal intonation is flatter than a ten-year-old bulimic girl's chest [not that there's anything wrong with having a flat chest]. A Medline-acquaintance of mine one day mentions that Dr. Camerer resembles the cartoon woman from the Abilify medication advertisements on TV. It's a genuine Holy Shit! Moment for me. Because she really, really does.

The animated commercials feature a woman whose regular antidepressant isn't working. She's slump-shouldered and lethargic and flatfaced, utterly devoid of spunk; Abilify is a brand new antidepressant purported to supplement and enhance the efficacy of more common such meds. The manufacturers' ad campaign is vigorous and well-funded—with commercials airing all the time across numerous channels. Dr. Camerer looks like the woman in her pre-Abilify state—like, eerily so. I find it entirely plausible that some bastard working for the Bristol-Meyers-Squibb professional drug-pushers spotted her on the street during a selfguided walking tour of outdoor sculptures in Chicago [I imagine she'd enjoy this; admiring the sturdy lifelessness, the stolid immutability of the statues and sculptures]; a campaign director watched her staring up—face and craned neck held unmoving for several minutes as she marveled, seemingly fascinated yet stupendously emotionless, at the "Eye" sculpture on Van Buren Street in downtown Chicago—saw her and knew immediately and with increasing confidence that she was the one; she would be his perfect muse for the pre-Abilify cartoon star.

My first time seeing her is not as dramatic [though no less stoic!]. I step into her little office in the building next to Seg. "Hi," I say cordially.

mr. smitowicz?

"That's me."

i'm the new psychologist—dr. camerer. because you're on psychiatric meds, i'll be seeing you on a regular basis.

"Okay, sounds good."

so how are you doing?

"Oh, you know." I scoot my chair sideways to extend my legs. "Sorry, I just need to stretch out, my knees are really messed up."

okay.

"I've had five surgeries on them."

wow. that's a lot.

"Yeah . . . anyway, I'm okay I guess. Actually I'm struggling, a lot, but I try to stay upbeat and productive. I'm a writer. Working on a nice long novel right now."

i see. well that's good. staying productive is a good goal in here.

The hell's wrong with your *face*? I urge to ask. "It's really really hard, though. I'm in pain—no exaggeration—24/7, and it severely impedes my concentration. Especially because, you know, I'm not receiving anything close to adequate pain management."

. . . .

Her corpselike brown eyes just stare at me. It's pretty discomfiting. "Uhhm. Yeah. Also, I recently pulled a muscle or something in my back, and that's made things even worse."

did you see the doctor for that?

"Yeah, but she didn't really do anything. Gave me some Ibuprofen. I don't know if you know, but the medical care's kinda terrible here. Not-talkin-about-you-of-course," I quickly add, "since you just got here 'n all."

mm hm. why don't we just focus on things you can control. your own mood.

"Well but see my mood is very much influenced by the pain. I wish that wasn't the case, but it is." I shrug. Raise my hands off the table to flip them palms-up. "That's just my reality, y'know?"

. . . .

"Uhm." We stare at each other. The small office's deadweight air makes me squirmy. Such physical anxiety always seems to tug at my pain-awareness, drawing it to the forefront of my mind. Feels like she's waiting for *me* to speak; but I've seen myriad talk-therapists, and never ever had to personally slog the conversational load. Isn't that their job? I try to grasp something to say. She just stares.

. . . .

See what I mean? It's fucking *weird*. Creepy, even. Heading "home" from our first appointment, my head's clouded with a surreal disconnect. What reality is this? Not one I much understand, that's for sure. It's that damn funhouse mirror-distortion again, rendering everything unrecognizable, bizarrely contorted. I already feel angsty about our next meeting in two weeks.

Since I'm on C-Grade my first month in 2A, my dishroom-friend austin offers to buy me anything I want from Commissary, for which I can just reimburse him when my shopping-prohibition ends. Sometimes in prison you have to exercise extreme judiciousness about becoming indebted to people. austin is legit, though. A genuine brother; he's not "on bullshit." So I accept his fabulously generous offer, and he helps keep me stocked with the basic gastronomic necessities for my nightly suppers—spicy refried beans, rice, pickled jalepeños, noodles, and chili corn chips. He even offers to let me call Rachel using *his phone minutes!* I decide not to take him up on this one because it's a little risky for us both, but still . . . such phenomenal kindness; such unbelievable magnanimity!

Truly, it's guys like austin who keep my compassion for prisoners alive; my belief in humane treatment for all. I indeed find most guys here to be scumbags—petty, spiteful, willfully ignorant, homophobic, sexist, and/or racist [usually a combination of many]—but even if there's only one austin for every *ten* buft-types, that's enough for me. It's impossible to pick and choose; no prison could or would implement the complex oversight necessary for such a thing. It's a zero-sum game. An all-or-none sorta deal. And I know in my heart that it's worse to treat one Austin and ten bufts like garbage than to treat them all humanely. Not just from an ethical standpoint, either. If all American prisons are inhumane in some way or another [which they are], and every inmate gets treated like shit in some way or another [which they do], you're only further decreasing the already abysmal chance for rehabilitation. But if you treat every prisoner humanely—grant them a semblance of basic human dignity—a greater percentage will spend time reflecting on their lives, their behavior, and how they can ditch criminal activity and avoid recidivism.

Even though I despise about 94.6 percent of the people here, I know my conclusion is sound. Don't get me wrong: I'd love to witness, say, sexual assaulters' prison time made into a Living Hell. But it's *not* best for society. When those in power dehumanize prisoners and piss on their dignity—*especially* shitbag filth like child molesters and rapists—they'll leave prison as even bigger scum. As George Jackson observed about the too-common sadism of prison guards, "How can the sick administer to the sick? . . . It's socially self-destructive to create a monster and loose him upon the world." And that creation is a precise result of American prisons' inhumanity.

One final thought on the mess that is the American Prison-Industrial Complex—in the form of a statement from Jeff "Free" Luers, an environmentalist who set fire to several gas-guzzling trucks in Oregon under the banner of the Earth Liberation Front [an underground nonorganization that, along with the Animal Liberation Front, the FBI ludicrously considers "America's Number-One Domestic Terrorism Threat," even though they've never even *injured* a single human being!]. They hammered Luers with a staggering sentence of nearly 23 years [!!] for an arson that only caused about $30,000 in property damage. Luers ultimately served "only" ten years after winning his appeal for a reduced sentence in 2009. He wrote the following about his prison bit, which nicely sums up the last couple pages:

I can watch a man get stabbed in the neck and keep eating. I can pretend to not see a man lying helpless in his own blood [along with everyone else on the Yard]. And I can watch a man die and be completely unmoved. Would someone please tell me **how this is supposed to make me a better person?** *[emphasis added].*[97]

---

[97] Quoted in *Green is the New Red: An Insider's Account of a Social Movement Under Siege* by Will Potter. I highly recommend this phenomenal book; it's absolute required reading if you want to learn about the U.S. government's overzealous pushback against modern animal rights and radical environmentalism, and the Orwellian nightmare augured therein [e.g. In this mindboggling age of creeping techno-fascism, trespassing for the sole purpose of opening cages to free tortured nonhumans is considered TERRORISM—apparently on par, somehow, with suicide bombings and mass shootings. Transparent governmental prioritization of corporate interests over life is transparent!]

15.

Springtime is just wonderful here. The snow melts, little by little unveiling the long-hidden grass; trees a couple hundred yards outside the fences burst awake, blooming with gorgeous and vivid greens; and those big clustered flowers right outside Health Care, the bright orange flowers on long stalks that rocket from almost nothing to full-bloom, an impressive three feet high, in just a couple weeks.

But the descent into summer is rapid and horrendous in the Midwest. Especially for someone like me; again, I've never lived more than 25 miles from the Pacific Ocean in my *life* before this! In central Illinois, spring and fall are quick, ephemeral, but wintertime is long and brutal—and summers are just as bad [in the opposite direction]. I moved from 4B to 2A amid the early awakening of spring. Yet I've barely grown accustomed to my new digs when summer first exhales with its moist, hot canine mouth. My back *still* isn't quite right. Despite the initial injury's having whipcracked almost three months ago! I can walk fine, no longer limping; sudden or torque-heavy movements, though, continue to fling that acute slicing pain into the muscle. Thankfully, most of the time it's just a knotted pinching sensation. Worst during the mornings' first hour or two. Since it still remains incompletely healed after all this time, Jim and I conclude that I might've *torn* rather than just pulled the muscle. I've experienced the latter before; it was nothing like this one. In both pain-intensity and duration.

I've managed to make a few buddies in the new unit. Guys I talk to way more than austin—he's a terrific buddy, but we really don't have much in common. This dude in austin's room becomes one of my only legit *friend*-friends at Jacksonville. Name's mike. A short, lanky guy in his early 40s with a russet-hued mustache. His head's bald dome gleams. Except he—like so many other balding men—maintains that weird wraparound hair on the sides and back, à la Jason Alexander from *Seinfeld*. I don't understand that whole business. It's strange. Why not just shave off all your hair? At least then it'd seem like a choice.

mike's breath reeks of stale coffee; he drinks so much, with so many scoops sludged into each mug of hot water that it resembles the blackest, densest motor oil-muck. He attracts near-universal scorn, which is sad and pathetic. As if his sole utility in others' feeble minds is to serve as a piñata for verbal battering. The vicious backlash against him occurs partly because he's a hardcore, outspoken anti-theist. He was already like that when we met—but, as so often happens, being around me has a decided radical-izing effect on him. My knowledgeable-ish presence and routine validation seem to instill a brazen confidence in him. A feeling of supreme certainty in his beliefs. He becomes so unafraid that he tells his whole room how religion is nonsensical bullshit, necessary only for the weakminded who can't handle reality on their own. I don't even pull that kinda shit in here; defending women and animals and gays and being vegan is "bad" enough! There's something else about mike that causes huge problems . . . some-thing even worse than his outspoken hatred for religion. People in his room [and then the whole unit before long, because chatty-kathies] suspect he's gay, or at least bisexual. "Are you?" I ask him one evening. We're lounged on a bench in the dayroom, waiting for Medline.

"Yeah," he says without hesitation, taking me by surprise. "I am." He's staring vacantly at the TV. "I mean, I love women. But I like guys, too."

"Wow—I had no idea!" Hadn't picked up even a hint of homosexuality from him. Maybe my vision's skewed, given where I'm from, and given that I have tons of jubilantly gay friends and acquaintances.

"Yep."

"Well listen," I tell him, voice muted, "I'm prolly the most gay-friendly straight guy in this entire prison. So you don't needa feel uncomfortable or shy or whatever around me. You can talk about anything, okay? No judgments here!"

He nods, lips pursed. "Hey, I really appreciate that. Thanks jan."

mike turns out impressively blasé about people knowing he's bi. Within a few weeks he'll end up admitting it—when somebody in his room accuses him of "Being a fag," he responds with, "Hey, I like girls, but I like guys too. Fuck off if you got a problem with it." An action for which I have tremendous admiration, and tell him in no uncertain terms how proud I am.

One morning mike and I are strolling along the Walk. Morning Med-line is a very strange phenomenon. I've mentioned how all the houses leave at once in a big scattershot line, and only the first 12 or 15 guys are allowed to head straight into Health Care, while everyone else waits in the Gym a little farther down the Walk. A handful of dudes are *obsessed* with being part of that first bunch. They habitualize a veritable monsoon of sheer humanoid lunacy. Pushing at the boundaries between powerwalking and jogging, they'll step onto the grass to rush around others, surreptitiously sneak forward to cut in line when we're stopped, and even slam against guys in the way as they rush by. Absolute madness. These are "Grownass men," as they say all the time; so why are they acting like unsupervised gradeschoolers on a field trip? Why do they harbor an apparently terminal aversion to waiting five extra minutes? This asinine nonsense happens EVERY SINGLE MORNING. It makes everyone else want to stab the halfwit fucks.

There is one particularly eventful morning around this time. mike and I laze at the line's back end. Discussing how religion provides a feelgood pass for even the worst scumbags: *It's okay, Jesus will forgive me for what I've done!* To me, this is among the more toxic aspects of religion. Making the dimwitted think their actions don't *really* matter; they can simply repent and be forgiven later, and everything'll be peachy. Certain sex offenders here epitomize this idea. One of them is alan goodson. And yes—if you were wondering—this is indeed his real name. I believe in revealing humanoid sewage like goodson, people who are and always will be a threat to the innocent. His coffeebean-colored hair's braided in a long ponytail; he has a black goatee and a perpetual, intensely creepy look occupies his dark eyes.

People talk shit to goodson every day, calling him *chomo* and *pervert* and the like. Sex offenders despair at being exposed. It's one of their biggest fears, for good reason. They're stuck on the very lowest rung of prison's pecking order. At hardcore joints, chomos and rapists get their asses kicked [and/or *fucked*] on a routine basis. Which is why they're often placed in P.C., or Protective Custody. Severed from the general population in a special unit. Man! I wish children and women were protected In the World as diligently as their *assaulters* are in prison. It'd make so much sense— that's probably why it doesn't happen!

Rachel finds goodson's rapsheet for me on the Illinois Department of Corrections [sic] site. He was convicted of "Criminal Sexual Assault— Victim Can't Consent [Handicapped]." From people who've talked to him, the prevailing word is that he worked in a nursing home . . . and utilized this grand opportunity to molest disabled women. So, while not a chomo in the strict sense, his crimes remain deliriously repulsive. Aaaaand he's a regular churchgoer. His victims are no doubt scarred for life, but at least he can still be forgiven! Fuck *that* shit. Some acts are so loathsome they should never, ever be absolved. But that's [a tiny thinmint-slice of] dumbass religious illogic for ya.

goodson receives morning meds. No surprise there—hopefully some kind of mood stabilizer—nor is it the least bit surprising that he's utterly fanatical about getting to Health Care first. He might be the worst of all these inexplicable dipshits. Even starting at the very back of the line, every morning he somehow manages to blaze zig stampede zag veer around zig slam into zag sneak forward and make it past 30ish guys to the front, zipping inside with the first group.

This morning, goodson and another idiot from 3-House are barreling down the Walk and bump, hard, into my severely disabled friend terry, nearly toppling him to the ground. terry grew up in Huntington Beach—which is half an hour from Downey, and my high school friend-group's favorite hangout. He lacks muscle coordination in his hands and can't grip anything well. Trouble walking, too. He uses a prison-issued aluminum cane; his left foot frequently lands partway on its side; he's wobbly. Talks as if his lips are permanently Novocained. I often help him at lunch, carrying his tray from the serving area to his table. Poor guy—I wonder how he *masturbates*!

"Wadge where yer goin yew fuggin idiots!" he yells after them. "I'm fuggin handicapped an' yew almoz knogged me over!" Other guys actually laugh then at terry. The two dickwads never even look back. mike and I exchange a dismayed glance, shaking our heads.

Things soon turn a little crazed. It started when goodson rammed poor ole terry; then goodson mutters *Faggot* at mike as the former exits Health Care. It pushes mike over the edge—he's PISSED. We get our meds and hit the Walk. Goodson is about 40 yards farther ahead. "I hate that piece'a shit," mike fumes. His face has bloomed a pinkish hue. "Pervert chump even *looks* like a creep." Then he handcups his mouth and hollers to make sure goodson will hear: "I CAN'T *STAND* THAT HANDICAP MOLESTIN PIECE'A *SHIT*!"

goodson whips around to face us; his braided ponytail, running halfway down his back, swoops in an arc. Like a horse's tail swishing against flies. "Th' fuck you say?" he calls. His voice is hoarse and strained and muted, almost like a yelled whisper. Reminiscent of Marlon Brando's voice in *The Godfather*, sans accent. No; no, not quite like that . . . but familiar *somehow*.

"I SAID YER A FUCKIN HANDICAP MOLESTIN PIECE OF SHIT. *FREAK!*"

alan goodson—the Wheelchair Bandit, Cripple-Creeper, Handicapped-Handler, Fiddler of the Functionless [now I can't help but wonder: would he try forcing my disabled ass [NPI] to be a prison surrogate for his apparent predilections toward the defenseless if we were in a max joint?]— darts his oh-so-dark-and-creepy eyes around the prison's open interior . . . circumscribed by the buildings and housing units . . .

No Guard[s] in sight. The Officers pulling line-management sometimes duck into Property or Chow or the Bubble or Visiting Room to shoot the shit so time will bleed out. Hence the occasional de rigueur standing at the gates for several interminable #thumbassed minutes. Just waiting. Beset with mounting impatience for a Guard to summon us onto the Walk. The current absence of visible authority—right when sociopathic goodson is growing hot enough to singe anything he touches—strongly supports my theory [which, admittedly, I just now thought of]: Murphy's Law could be physicists' fabled Theory of Everything—but it only applies to the *Prison Vortex*! This'd explain towering mountains of otherwise baffling, incomprehensible evidence.

After his visual sweep, goodson bursts toward us in a speedflash, eyes burning with psychopath fury. My blood goes cold. "Oh, shitballs!" I cry. "You kidding me?"

"Don't worry," mike says in a monotone, "guy ain't gonna do jack."

"*Why don'tchu say it to my* face?" goodson shouts hoarsely. He's pumped the muscle-brakes, now just ten yards before us. Heavy leather boots stomping across the gravel. mike and I just stand there on the Walk, motionless. Exposed to onlookers. And to goodson's volatile, capricious wrath. Then suddenly, I'm walloped by an unwelcome revelatory eruption. There is a perplexing, somehow unsettling quasi-familiarity to his voice. But I understand it now! And—when examined from a satellited, macrocosmic view— its strangeness actually makes a certain contextual sense there in the Vortex. Here it is: the creep's voice sounds exactly as I imagined, in my mind's ear, the *wrecked voice* of John Irving's diminutive, unforgettable title character from *A Prayer for Owen Meany*. While reading the book—*before* I ever met or heard alan goodson—Owen's always-capitalized dialogue sounded to me precisely like goodson's hoarse whisper-yell . . .

The Prison Vortex, where the surreal feels as, or more, real than actual reality—not *surreal*, but *suprareal*. I completed my imprisonment almost five years ago now. And yet the sum experiences continue walloping my psyche in new and complex ways, seeming to amplify-grow-morph and even *come alive* within my memory. The Vortex and its crushing gravity does not just warp time, it does not just warp time and memory, it warps *itself*, too, and the people within it. Warps us so much we'll never regain original form. Fiction and real life, incarcerated and free, reason and nonsense, memoir and novel . . . the Prison Vortex even warps fundamental realities of the world, until, from the outside looking in, from the present looking back, from the me-now examining the me-then, something strange begins to happen, something discomfiting and even uncanny . . .

THE LINES BEGIN TO FADE.

goodson stops. Just a few paces in front of us. "Say it to my face," he breathes.

"I don't give any kinda *fuck*," mike says, flushing even more [face now an unripe heirloom tomato]. "I'll say it t'yer creepass face: You're a piece'a shit and I can't stand yer ass, you sicko pervert. Gropin old ladies in wheelchairs! I heard you talkin shit t'me in the waiting room, callin me *faggot* 'n all that. You better fuckin STOP that shit, or I'm'a beatcher sorry pervert ass into the fuckin dirt!"

"Pervert? I ain't no pervert, you fuckin faggot—I'll beat *your* ass."

"FUCK you, pervert. FUCK YOU. I'm sick'a yer bullshit, you better watch yer ass!" mike's seething, literally spitting-mad. Face turnip-colored now. "*Goddamn creep, somebody oughtta slit yer fuckin throat, an' I hope somebody does, I'd fuckin laugh watchin yer sicko pervert ass bleeding on the ground!*" He's taken the shade of a beet. Dude's cycling through produce faster than an immigrant farmhand paid by the pound.

"Just try somethin," goodson says. "See what happens. I ain't no fuckin chomo, don't believe everything you hear!"

Now I can't help but laugh. Get involved. "How bout Criminal Sexual Assault on handicapped people? I had you looked up, alan goodson. It ain't what we heard, it's what we *know*. Fuckin creep."

He turns to me for the first time. "Fuck you, yer a faggot too! Bitchass punk."

Poor mike's gonna burst a damn blood vessel. Pop an artery or something. He moves to get right up in goodson's face, and that's it—this can't go any further. They'll toss all of us into Seg if they peep this confrontation. I grab mike's arm hard and start dragging him past goodson. "COME ON," I demand. "Chester the Molester here ain't worth it, buddy." I'm still gripping his arm, but now mike walks along with me and we're several yards past the creep. mike fires a burning stare back at him. "Keep movin bro," I say. "He ain't worth get'n in trouble for. Everybody knows he's a fuckin perv. You could stomp the dogshit outta him—but he'd prob'ly run squealing to I.A. like the little bitch he is." Now we're shuffling homeward at a good clip.

I've managed to calm mike down some, drawn him back to the produce section's tomato bin. He and goodson are still shouting back and forth, but we pass 4-House on the Walk and we're now a good 50 yards away. Bullet dodged; tragedy averted. Another 30 yards and at last mike faces forward and stops lobbing threats. Settling into a pleasant carnation-hue. "Can't *stand* that fuckin guy."

"I know, mike. I know. And you stood up to him, didn't back down. It was good. Don't think he'll be messin with you anymore. But it needed to stop before it got physical and the police came runnin."

"Yeah, you're right. Thanks man." He unleashes a sigh, rubbing at his temples. "I just get worked up sometimes . . . gawd, that dude is a serious scumbag."

"Yep. Total creep. But not worth goin t' Seg for, and you know it. He'll get what he deserves soon enough. Talk shit to the wrong motherfucker and get tuned up good."

We step inside 2-House and check back in. "Well that was fun," I tell mike in the dayroom. "Now it's time for me to do some work before lunch. Talk to you later, buddy."

"Thanks jan. I'll see ya later."

"Yep." Back where I belong—sprawled in bed—I'm preparing to write. Then I can't help but burst out laughing. I don't stop until tears are running down my cheeks. This place, man. This bloody nuthouse!

Apparently mike retained some lingering aggression, which he exorcises on a stray bible in the dayroom. He hands it to me with a proud grin after lunch. I flip through it and start chuckling. He defaced it with joyful, vociferous blasphemy. Some pages are scratched or **X**'d out in pen, with more than a dozen others ruined by giant words obscuring the text. mike made sure each phrase or few words occupied a whole page for maximum surface area-wreckage. Graffiti [all errors sic; I simply *must* preserve its singular flavor] such as:

BULLSHIT!!
FICTION
RELIGION IS FOR THE WEEK-MINDED
BULLSHIT LIES!
STOP BELIEVING THIS SHIT, IT'S ALL LIES,
THINK FOR **YOURSELFS**!
QUESTION EVERYTHING.
CHECK OUT <u>GOD DILUSION</u> BY RICHARD DAWKINS.
DON'T BELIEVE WHAT THEY WANT YOU TO BELIEVE.
THIS SHIT IS STUPID, RACIST, SEXISST **CRAP**!!

I look up at him, smiling. "Nice work—much improved!"
He beams. Satisfied at a job well done.

Another guy I befriend in 2A is xavier, an Albanian dude. He also goes to Medline. Recognized him the moment I saw him here in 2A. He's one of the most visually memorable guys at J-ville. Suffers from near-complete paralysis in his left arm, which is always propped in a blue sling unless he's showering or in bed. His Origin Story for Prison is among the saddest and most interesting I ever hear.

He was motorcycling home in suburban Chicago late one night. Girlfriend perched behind him. They were both above the legal blood-alcohol level; xavier was zipping along the highway at 80 or 85 mph. Then he lost control and spun out into a cataclysmic accident. Their flailing bodies were both struck by at least one other vehicle. Nobody stopped after hitting the bodies. Just kept right on driving.

xavier awoke in the hospital. On top of prodigious lacerations and road-torn flesh and bruises, there lay his left arm, pretty much destroyed. A Cop was posted in the room. xavier discovered he was handcuffed to the bed's railing. His girlfriend was killed in the crash—and he'd been charged with her death. Reckless Homicide. He didn't even remember the accident until much later.

What an awful tragedy. For xavier and his family, but especially for the girl and *her* family. A miserable situation all around. I can't help but have compassion for him. He made a monumental error, but, unlike most people who make socially irresponsible decisions, he paid a *heavy* price. Can you even imagine? Waking up to find you'd been in a savage vehicular accident, your left arm now paralyzed for life, girlfriend dead, and you're being charged with Reckless Homicide . . . frightening to even think about!

Luckily for him, it seems the Judge felt sympathetic. Sentencing xavier with two years on a Class 2 felony. Reminder: I copped out to Possession with Intent to Distribute and got the same sentence. In addition, we had to pay that $25,000 "fine" [bribe?] to get my plea deal down from 42 months to 24, and from a Class X to a Class 1. xavier's crime directly resulted in a death. Mine was one of the most nonviolent felonies you could commit— irrespective of the DEA's outlandish *How the Hell Is This Possible?!* drug classification, the first two parts of which are reproduced below.[98]

Schedule I

Schedule I drugs, substances, or chemicals are defined as drugs with no currently accepted medical use and a high potential for abuse. Schedule I drugs are the most dangerous drugs of all the drug schedules with potentially severe psychological or physical dependence. Some examples of Schedule 1 drugs are:

heroin, lysergic acid diethylamide [LSD], marijuana, 3,4-methylenedioxy-methamphetamine [ecstasy], methaqualone, and peyote

Schedule II

Schedule II drugs, substances, or chemicals are defined as drugs with a high potential for abuse, less abuse potential than Schedule I drugs, with use potentially leading to severe psychological or physical dependence. These drugs are also considered dangerous. Some examples of Schedule II drugs are:

cocaine, methamphetamine, methadone, hydromorphone [Dilaudid], meperidine [Demerol], oxycodone, fentanyl, Dexedrine, Adderall, and Ritalin

---

[98] www.dea.gov/druginfo/ds.shtml [accessed 10/12/16]

So marijuana is officially jammed into Schedule 1: same category as heroin and ecstasy. Making it even worse than *cocaine and meth* from a legal standpoint—but when you subtract legalese from the equation, everyone with at least one-fourth of a brain knows this classification is positively scandalous; and yet, despite my crime's inarguable, pristine nonviolence, we had to shell out $25,000 just for me to receive the same sentence as xavier! Dead Body versus Munchies. Someone please explain to me how in the fuck that makes sense.[99]

I want to ensure crystalline clarity here. Just like with my earlier discussion of james's backstory. It's not per se that I want harsher sentencing for xavier and other people whose crimes, unlike mine, resulted in direct injury or death. I accept xavier's two-year sentence. Given that his left arm is paralyzed; that his girlfriend died; that he has severe chronic nerve pain in one arm; and given that he must endure two years in the Prison Vortex, I'm confident he will never drink and drive again. No—what I'm saying is that "crimes" like mine should receive *shorter* sentencing, if any! How do you think it makes me and other folks feel about Cops and Judges and the American political system when people serve the same amount of time for transporting flower buds as people whose negligence *killed* someone? How do you think it makes, say, my friend deandre feel—he was unwittingly present when a couple friends committed Armed Robbery, and got eight years—when his sentence is the exact same as men who've raped children? How should this pervasive madness be interpreted; what message should we take away?

There's only one thing with the potential to redeem all this madness. Considering how blatantly unjust and racist and classist the "Justice" System is, I maintain hope that more and more people will realize these innate truths. That people will start saying *Enough is enough!* and stop allowing these inequities to continue—by any means necessary. And that they'll finally begin fighting back against the state-sanctioned kidnapping of their children, fathers, mothers, brothers, sisters. That we'll reach a critical mass and people will rise up to *smash* the fucking System. Then build something

---

[99] Think you could produce a legit and sensible explication to account for this absurdity? One that'd rattle my saber, or force me to reconsider, or hell, even blow my mind out of my asshole? Then I very much wanna hear it! You can email me at ████████@gmail.com [*Ed. note: author's email address has been obscured for a litany of what seem like obvious reasons. Yet again.*]

new and just atop its ashes. I truly hope defense attorney Tim Lohraff was correct when he said "We're not producing justice here. We're manufacturing revolutionaries."

A Jan can dream, right?

So paralyzed-arm xavier and I start walking to and from Medline together every morning and evening. He's a funny bastard; we crack each other up. We love unleashing random lines—in character, of course—from the *Borat* movie/show, and from Arnold. Several times a day, xavier will stroll past my room and shout, "GET DOWN!" [*Total Recall*—1990; *Terminator 2: Judgment Day*—1991; *Eraser*—1996; et alia]. Or, in a decent Schwarzenegger facsimile, the timeless classic, "GET TO THE CHOPPA!" [*Predator*— 1987]. We tell jokes, roast Officers and inmates alike, and bitch about the health care. He's also experienced heaping mounds of bullshit there. They haven't tried to screw with his pain meds [we take the same dose of Tramadol]. Possessing *visual* evidence of chronic pain makes all the difference. He gets the benefit of the doubt—the Sympathy Card, if you will. So unlike me, he's not besieged by constant attempts to cut off his pain meds. Buuuut . . . they did literally almost *kill* him this past winter! so I guess he has ample reasons to complain. Basically, he was suffering from internal hemorrhaging, with obvious symptoms, but by the time they finally sent him to the outside hospital, he'd almost died of blood loss. Upon cursory examination, the outside doctor immediately shouted at the Guard standing nearby, "WHY *did you people wait so long to send him in?!*" For this, xavier and his family are suing Doctor Williams, plus the prison, state, and the outsourced medical company providing so-called health care to the Illinois DOC.

xavier thinks religion is a load of shit as well. In fact, aside from james, all my legit friends at J-ville—all, like, four of them—aren't religious at all, and also grow mega-annoyed with the pious nonsense we're subjected to. I mean . . . It's bad enough to hear the drivel spewed forth by Slammer #Sermocinators [*Noun*: one who delivers sermons; it's mine, but you can use it]. By inmates. They alone provide a surfeit of forehead-smacking stupidity. Yet the Officers will proselytize, too. What happened to separation of church and state?

[OH WAIT! I forgot: This division, though constitutionally mandated, is largely a fantasy in America, seeing as how so many politicians— from city officials all the way up to national so-called leaders—are [or at least pretend to be] biblewhores too. Want an example? I need just *one* single word to demolish any arguments contrary to mine, anyone trying to say America DOES have strict separation of church and state: **abortion.**]

Here's just one illustration of certain Officers' habitual theistic impropriety. Back in the Drug Unit, I returned from Medline one morning to find a piece of paper taped to the Officers' desk in the Bubble. You couldn't miss it. It read:

ARE YOU READY ?

I stared with brow furrowed. Then looked up at the Officer. "Ready for what?"

He dipped his head sideways for a second. "Are you ready."

Thanks, Officer Turdsoup-for-Brains, but I can read. "Ready for *what?*" Maybe he wanted to warn us of an impending unit shakedown or something. I should have known better. He leaned back, chair squeaking, and clasped both hands over his head's bald spot, arms akimbo. He blinked. Slowly and dramatically. Staring at me in quietus for several awkward moments. Finally, in the sotto voce of some great revelatory dispensation, he said, "*The rapture.*"

". . . Uhhhm. Oh. I see." Anticlimactic irritation palpable in my voice. Gah, gimme a break with this shit! How many billions of dead people have believed with certainty that Jesus would return in their lifetimes? Right though, it's coming. Aaaaany day now! Been over 2000 supposed years, but it'll definitely happen, like, *this year*. Probably next month . . . December at the latest. Yeah, December—he'll come back for his birthday party! It'll be a totally righteous celebration. Better get ready, cause it's coming . . . hurry 'n pack your bags . . . don't forget that svelte gray coat you love . . .

[*crickets chirp*]

Right.

Rapture? More like *Rupture*: a <u>rectal</u> rupture, as I rageclench my sphincter to unload an atheist dump on your dumbass inappropriate sign.

16.

Yea verily, life is already pretty bad, but in June it swerves toward the much much worse. It's been some three months since injuring my back; quick movements still unleash that breathtaking dagger of pain. But my suffering doesn't linger anymore. The muscle feels about 90 percent better.

I began *The Liberators* on January 20th. From then until late May, four months, I was wildly obsessed with it. Not just obsessed, but also mentally *capable* of working at such a breakhand pace. How's this for devotion: Even with the pressurized daily sadness of incarceration, all the crushing sorrow and indignation of getting railroaded from the Drug Unit, and the awful reality of losing phonetime with Rachel for a month . . . through all that, in those four months—120 days—I worked on the novel all but *eleven* of them; many days writing 8, 10, even 12 pages. That's serious dedication! A four-month flurry that turned out to be the most efficient, prolific writing period in my entire life.

But then June's events wallop me like a battery-stuffed sock, and my output plummets off a vertical cliff. See, my pain meds' prescription is about to expire; the Doctors only write scripts lasting three months at a time. It's moronic—as if my chronic disorder could ever just magically disappear! Due to this idiocy, I have to see the Doctor every 90 goddamn days. Which of course by now you know means parking myself on the assbone-slaying wooden benches in Health Care—ones I've spent countless hours on, waiting for many many utterly pointless Doctor's appointments—for two to four hours [knee pain heightening ever more every minute until it's literal torture and I can't even *think* zombified mind mangled unrecognizable by the senseless alien invasion nerves like severed powerlines flailing and spark-spurting with overactive electroshock antitherapy and I have to just sit there squirming sweating trying not to hyperventilate and desperately hoping my skincrawling anxiety doesn't choose to swerve into a full blown panic attack]—ALL THAT to spend maybe five minutes with the Doctor. For a malady that traps-confines-torments me more than prison ever could. A disorder that in all likelihood drags a lifetime guarantee along with it; omnipresent and changeless, with the exception of changes for the *worse*. Their protocol—forcing me to return every 90 days in perpetuity despite the condition's bedrock-solid and dully predictable nature—is total cockeyed insanity. Treating nonviolent offenders [or anybody!] with such wanton disregard for their suffering is nothing short of MONSTROUS. The sadists in power are as bad as the scummiest inmates. Some are worse!

And yet . . . sometimes . . . in my fiercest, most laser-focused thralls of tilling at the deepest roots within this socio- and psycho-logical dirt . . . a suspicion will creep inside my head, wiggling in like a worm to nibble at the core of my laborious analyzing. And I can't help but wonder further: Are the sadists who're running things *here* the ones responsible for all this senseless cruelty?—Is it merely a matter of bad, unacceptable individuals exhibiting bad, unacceptable behavior?—Or is the reality more pernicious even than that? I've now become convinced it's actually the latter. As I dig deeper, probing ever closer to the root-tips, my inkling that it's *not* a simple issue of rotten individuals grows stronger and stronger. Now I'm thinking The System itself [the Bureaucratic Model] is what produces the worst, most mindless and asinine regulations—as with Health Care above—that gnaw down our spirits. The System fosters a lunatic dissociation. A disconnect from human decency via rules drawn up and laid down in ink by faceless bureaucrats who know little, understand less, and care not at all. Then, when you toss atop this shitheap a blind adherence to said regulations by lesser bureaucrats who're closer to us in proximity, the towering pile and its diverse contents sharpen into brilliant focus . . .

Aaand then it becomes crystal-clear what's really going on. At last! After all, I've been probing these ideas for a long time. Hell, I was trying to unpack all the variables and makes sense of them like 250 pages ago! Now though, I think it has been percolating in my skull long enough that I've finally pinned down the overarching truths—figured em out, and related a quantity of "narrative" sufficiently stocked with corroborating evidence, and, perhaps equally important as the rest, determined what I feel is the most compelling-convincing and clearest way to express these truths in no uncertain terms. So then!

Bad people can be dug up and tossed in the compost heap with relative ease. But to *uproot an entire broken system*—THE BUREAUCRAZY—is a far, far more daunting task. Although, given what's at stake [the very soul of society?], failure to instigate this *revolution*, as we might as well call it, has become not just untenable, but unthinkable. In the end . . .

It's not so much about rotten apples;
it's about a rotten SYSTEM.

Never in my life have I experienced the degree of longterm pain that I do in prison. Nor have I felt the level and frequency of homicidal *rage*—and I write that without the faintest whiff of hyperbole—that I do in prison.[100]

---

[100] *Just wait, buddy. You* <u>*still*</u> *ain't seen nothin yet.*

"You" keep saying that. Makes no sense! You're writing/editing this *years* after being released! How could you possibly warn me that I'm in for worse [as if it would even help—suffering is suffering, & the knowledge that further on up the road you'll be suffering even more does nothing to diminish the suffering you're experiencing at that moment]? You're *future-me*! We CAN'T communicate!

You dumb shit. I'm not warning you; of course I know it's impossible. I also know, of course, that this argument in & of itself is impossible, given the irritating constraints of the spacetime continuum. It's not about warning you—it's called foreshadowing, *dork. For my Dear Beloved Readers [well, I suppose you'd have to say* our *Dear Beloved Readers]. I'm almost 6 years older than you. My writing is far superior to yours.*

I fucking know what FORESHADOWING is.

Good. Glad to hear. You're quite the angry fellow, aren't you?

Oh, shut up! And by the way—I find your metafictional techniques [or metanonfictional, et al.] to be problematic in a bunch of ways. Don't even know where to begin! You already mentioned this debate between jan-in-2011 & Jan-in-2017 is functionally impossible—

Think I don't know some of this stuff is problematic?! If you know, it's very very basic, fundamental chrono-logic that I'd know.

Would you let me finish? Cute little pun there, btw [that's sarcasm, case you couldn't tell].

You know you liked it. "Chrono-logic"—you & I both know you'd be proud if you'd come up with it. But you didn't, so you're jealous.

This makes me feel like a legit insane person.

Don't blame me. Blame Trooper Beau [teehee] Marlow, blame Judge Hamer, blame your lawyer, blame that racist stain of excrement on history's pages, Harry Anslinger, for lying and manipulating data and almost single-handedly railroading antimarijuana laws through Congress, blame the American "Justice" System as a whole—but not me! We're products of our environment, don't you think? And for two years the Prison Vortex was my environment. I doubt I'll ever be completely healed.

That's . . . damn, man, that's pretty depressing to hear. Or at least it would be, if it were even possible logistically.

I understand there will no doubt be problems and possibly confusion regarding this whole meta-debating technique. But what you, and our Dear Reader/s—

I see what you did there, with that *potential*-plural. Cute.

Anyway, I'm waiting in Health Care yet again to hopefully get my meds extended. xavier doesn't have to go through this shit; his identical-to-mine prescription is automatically renewed. But he's *visibly* disabled, and I'm not. Trust me: this makes a galactic difference in how a person is treated. Not just by Doctors, but by society at large. It's quite phenomenal.

After 2+ hours, I'm finally summoned—limping from the #scorchurous pain—into the examination room. The new Doctor is a white, overweight middle-aged woman with short auburn hair. Can't remember her name; so we'll just call her Dr. Fatbody. She glances through the last few pages in my file—only looking at what the *prison* Doctors have said about me, in other words. Since [naturally!] that's the only stuff that matters. It's the Vortex, folks, and it swallows *anyone* who spends real time inside. Even those who return home after eight hours. She glances up at me for the first time. "So what's the problem?"

"Nothing new, just the same daily pain I've had for several years now. I'm just here to renew my Tramadol."

"Hm." She eyes my chart. "You know, I really don't like prescribing longterm pain medications. They're very dangerous, in terms of addictiveness and things like that."

She almost couldn't be more wrong. I just recently finished a spectacular book called *The Pain Chronicles*. Written by Melanie Thernstrom, a

---

What you & especially they [bless their hearts] need to understand is that all of these are imagined *conversations.*

Yeah, no shit. I get it dude. Pretty sure *everyone* gets it. But I damn sure do.

I know you do. Ha!

I'm hypothetically smacking my hypothetical forehead here. Hard enough to hurt—hypothetically. Tell me: just how much are you willing to deliberately annoy the *shit* out of our reader/s?! Because if this kinda ridiculousness makes it into the final draft, it'll produce *lots* of irritation.

Well, I'd like to think, & I also strongly suspect, that people who read my stuff—my Dear Readers, especially ones who've come this far *down into the Vortex with me—will be sharp enough to 'get' what I'm doing, and appreciate it as well. But even if they don't appreciate it, and are, as you worry, severely annoyed by this stuff, my hope is that they'll at least have developed—after all the time we've spent together—some level of [perhaps reserved] affinity for me, compassion & concern for me, interest in my welfare & the development of my story, & will therefore be willing to put up with some irritation. But yeah—hopefully some readers will actually* appreciate *what I'm doing here.*

Okay. Hope you're on the money. You've at least got *me* partially convinced—I think you may indeed be right!

I know that's what you think.

Oh, goddamnit!!

fellow chronic pain-sufferer, it's wonderful, poignant, and even *useful*. It helped me *understand* the physiological basis for my particular chronic pain. Which may not seem like a big deal, but it is. A MASSIVE deal. Coping with a debilitating medical condition is terrible. Not knowing what it is or how/why it developed makes it all that much worse. The book was . . . empowering. I now feel like less of a physical-medical freak. Maybe I'm *not* defective on a fundamental level. Reading that great book improved my life forever—no doubt. Here are two of its most amazing, monumental factoids: [1] Any and every surgery that involves slicing through tissue has an estimated *10 percent chance* of producing chronic pain. That statistic brought a certain lucid sensibility to my condition's development; [2] It cites a ground-breaking review of several dozen major pain-medication-related studies. They confirmed the expected: that addiction rates for narcotic pain meds are indeed up there with alcohol and cocaine and other such hard drugs. Here's the salient, though: this rate only proved accurate for people ingesting the medications *recreationally*. Getting high? You have an addiction frequency around 25 percent. If you're taking them for a severe pain condition though, under a qualified doctor's supervision, watch the probability nosedive to about *1.2 percent*. My gawd, what a revelatory stunner! Something I already believed in the back of my mind based on experience. Yet this tangible confirmation—by such respectable and trust-worthy empirical analysis—is so damn validating. Of course it's wretched for the unfortunate 1.2%, but a quick cost-benefit analysis may provide fencesitters some crucial clarity. Imagine: A pain specialist has 1,000 patients to whom they prescribe opiates. Statistically, twelve will form a habit. But up to *988* will experience relief from a life turned miserable. Consider those numbers and what they mean for a moment. Please. Hundreds will be capable of going back to work. Hundreds will feel [like I do when prescribed adequate meds] they've been graced with a semblance of their lives back. Almost every single one of those 988 will have an improved quality of life. Many seeing *dramatic* improvements. So a doctor can choose to never prescribe these narcotic meds, which many do, to avoid culpability in providing recreational drugs to twelve addicts [though true addicts absolutely WILL find another way to score]. But at what cost? Sure, you don't personally bestow twelve or so addicts with their drug of choice. Yet you simultaneously [torment, hurt, terrorize] deny succor to 988 suffering people. Which situation is worse? Help 988 and hurt 12, or [maybe!] help 12 at the expense of 988?

Not quite a Final Jeopardy!-worthy question. These numbers NEED to be known. By *everyone*.

Problem is, most doctors—especially when they are untrained in pain management, and even more especially when they're the pitiful, over-worked, heartless, bureaucrazy-and-cost-shackled ones working in corrections—don't have an everloving clue about these crucial truisms.

I try to collect myself before responding to Dr. Fatbody's proclaimed distaste for doling out pain meds. "Well . . . uhhm . . . You know, I recently read this amazing book called *The Pain Chronicles*." I describe the massive study-analysis cited above and its findings.

"Oh wow," she says with, by the sound of it, little interest, "that's interesting." Yet I can't help but wonder if she even considered the information. Because then she says, "Either way, 100 milligrams of Tramadol twice a day seems like an excessive dose."

"Doctor, I've been taking that amount since I got to Jacksonville almost a year ago! it's the exact same dose I know for a fact is prescribed to other guys here; I'm personally acquainted with two of them."

She grunts a vague noncommittal noise. "I'd like to try you on a lower dose and see how you do."

A freefall sensation in my guts, replaced after a moment with thick, curled ropes of nausea; face heating up. Deep breath, mah dude. "Doctor, I know precisely how it'd go—because I've already *tried* a lower dosage. You can look in my chart. Dr. Williams first tried me on half my current dose, but it was miserable. Overwhelmingly painful. So she doubled it; still hard, but I developed ways to make it work. I've been monumentally productive, Doctor. I'm a novelist; I handwrote well over a *thousand* pages in the last year." Christ though, lookit this woman! already inking a new scrip! Seems to have made up her mind. But I *gotta* keep trying. Because writing is life, and the inverse thereof is just as true, and just as truly frightening. "Ma'am [sic?], without an adequate dose, that phenomenal accomplishment would not've been possible. Absolutely not possible! Please don't take this ability away from me."

Another ambiguous throatnoise. "Yes, well." She finishes writing and then raises her multichinned face—labial rolls at its base seeming to prop up her head, like a fat blobby ass perched atop an airport "donut cushion"—to look at me. "That was a year ago, mr. smitowicz. Things may well've changed."

I groooaaaan. Head drops as if unhinged from neck. IDIOT! Evil heartless bitch! Try'n stay with me here, Doc: I'm still in pain every single day. If my condition had improved, I would've bloody well noticed! Gah!

"So let's go ahead and try 100 milligrams a day instead of 200 [fuck you], see how that goes [already told you]. Don't worry though [lol]—I'll see you again in six weeks [suck a poisonous dick]."

x.

jan
It's really, really hard. Dealing with my pain is a constant struggle. I'm forced to structure my entire life around it, so I can still at least be *somewhat* productive. I can't even express how important that is to me—using my time in here constructively, making the most of this awful situation. But it's a constant struggle nonetheless.

DR. CAMERER
You seem obsessed with your pain. It's almost the only thing you ever talk about.

jan regards **DR. CAMERER** with a perplexed stare.

jan
Well . . . uhhhm . . . of course? It dominates my life!

DR. CAMERER
Seems like you're *allowing* it to dominate your life.

jan
Look, I've been dealing with this ceaseless condition for like over four years now; and that's just the omnipresent nerve pain. The inciting injuries go back even longer—wayyy longer—than that! I've tried practically everything there is,

including a ten-week course on strategies for coping. But there's a very distinct limit to what I'm capable of controlling!

> DR. CAMERER
> I just don't think it helps to focus on it so much.

jan lays another baffled look on **DR. CAMERER**.

> **jan**
> Sure. Course. I can only ignore so much, though— the pain is my reality; it affects every hour of every day.

> DR. CAMERER
> But you obsess about it. You relate everything you talk about to your pain.

jan hesitates, unsure how to respond. Could this be a bad acid trip? He may've heard about those.

> **jan**
> Well . . . it seems kinda . . . *normal* to focus my talk-therapy on the biggest, worst, most dominant uncontrollable issue in my life, no?! It's like... it's pretty much equivalent to asking a diabetic person not to focus their doctor's visits on their diabetes!

jan stares down at the desk, brow furrowed.

> DR. CAMERER
> I don't know if I believe that.

jan's eyes seem to glaze over. He's staring up at the steel filing cabinet behind **DR. CAMERER**—a small plugin fountain sits atop it, its small pool of water gently burbling. He's unsurprised that it feels depressing somehow. The fountain may or may not act as a symbol for the Psychologist's flailing attempts to convince herself she's still an individual, rather than a mere minor cog in this grand, tragi-comi-tragic, nightmarish bureaucrazy [though she most definitely *is* JUST A COG], in the megamachinery of the monolithic American so-called Justice System—thereby representing [**DR. CAMERER** does] the indi-vidual-trying-to-both-establish-and-retain-individuality-in-a-dehumanizing-and-deindividualizing-System. **jan** finally speaks [sic].

jan

This is starting to come off as surreal. What's going on? I thought I was seeing a psychologist. I'm really fucking confused, to be honest. And I feel an intense disconnect from you, and the things we're saying. Which disconnect and weird surreality are the reasons I've chosen to render this particular memoir scene in script format. Attempting to reflect my experiences in *form*, too—thereby hopefully giving you, Dear Reader[s], a stronger sense of what this experience actually *feels* like.

DR. CAMERER

To me, it's just another attempt to do something unique and memorable—stand-outable, you might say. Playing transparent parlor tricks with the narrative. I think it's one more unnecessarily ambitious literary device, piled on all the others. I highly doubt you can utilize it successfully. Are you even *aware* that ALL OF THIS may simply come across as a *Hey-look-at-me-and-my-cleverness!* type of statement, and nothing more? I'm talking about the whole über-selfaware metafictional thing.

jan
You don't even sound like *you* anymore!

DR. CAMERER
That's exactly what I mean. It's yet another
exhausting literary contrivance. Pretentious too,
if you ask me. And yes—I, the real human Doctor
Camerer, may not, in reality, even know what
"metafiction" and "literary contrivances" are, but
that doesn't change the potential truth of what
you've had "me" say . . .

jan
I'm aware. Believe me. You're not telling me
anything I haven't already considered [and worried
about] to a great degree. After all, this whole
imaginary sequence is a pretty stark concession
that I'm very much conscious of the criticism "you"
are offering—am I right?! Also, I HAVE to tell you
this: you look so much like the cartoon Abilify
chick it's scary.

DR. CAMERER
jan?

He looks back down at her affectless face, which,
yes, makes him think even more strongly of the depressed cartoon woman.

jan
Oh! Sorry, got lost in my thoughts there for a
second.

DR. CAMERER
Let me ask a question. Do you think you *allow* your
pain to, as you claim, control your life?

jan
No. No, I don't *allow* it to do anything. It's my
unfortunate reality. It seriously feels like you're
suggesting that a paraplegic's inability to walk,
his need of a wheelchair to get around, is nothing

more than his *allowing* the paralysis to control his
behavior!

DR. CAMERER
Know what I think might be the case here? I think
maybe you're intentionally amplifying the true
severity of your pain and suffering to get your
pain medication increased.

jan
What?!

DR. CAMERER
It's pretty common among prisoners.

jan
Okay . . . ! But have these prisoners you're
talking about had a bunch of surgeries on the same
body part? Are you aware that, with *any* surgery
that involves cutting through tissue, there's a ten
percent chance of developing chronic pain? That is
a demonstrable, recorded fact, not conjecture.

jan is growing more and more agitated [**DR. CAMERER**
remains as unagitated as ever].

DR. CAMERER
Okay.

jan
That statistic in and of itself suggests a massive
chance for my having legit chronic pain. So there's
that! And these other drug-seeking inmates you're
talking about—do they have *stacks* of medical
records, years' worth, outlining their journey
through the medical ringer? Have they gone through
countless attempts to get better—like numerous
rounds of physical therapy, a multipronged Chronic

Pain Management course, and visiting specialist after specialist—including *pain specialists*?

DR. CAMERER
You know, a patient's use of the phrase "drug-seeking" is itself an indicator of drug-seeking behavior.

jan
Oh wow. Are you . . . I only used it because *YOU suggested that's what I'm doing*!

DR. CAMERER
And regarding your medical records—it's all based on what you've *reported*. You told doctors you were in terrible pain and they believed you . . .

jan
That's only partly true. These people are specialists, they've had professional training to help tell the difference between someone with a legitimate pain condition and someone who's just trying to score drugs. Plus it's *not* just what I've reported—my MRIs show severe damage! So there's *plenty* of evidence backing up my "claims."

DR. CAMERER
I think you're just really good at manipulating people into getting what you want.

Color has risen in **jan**'s cheeks. He's burning with anger, indignation, even shame. It's unspeakably demoralizing and repulsive to have one's debilitating medical condition trivialized—by a Doctor, no less!

jan
Look, my stepdad is strict and hypercritical. And he's been with me every step of the way, from the

very *day* I first injured my knee EIGHT years ago. Knows my history inside-out. And he believes unequivocally that my pain is precisely as severe as I say it is. Plus he's brilliant, pretty much immune to manipulation. Always has been.

DR. CAMERER
You say he's so strict and can't be fooled—and yet you managed to manipulate him into believing you.

jan stares at her, mouth agog.

jan
That is *seriously* uncalled for.

DR. CAMERER [*with finality*]
Well, you'll be free again soon enough, and then you can get your stepdad to prescribe your drugs.

jan
. . . Do you really think that's an appropriate thing for a *Doctor* to say to her patient?!

DR. CAMERER
This appointment is over. Have a nice day.

jan rises from his seat slowly . . . almost paralyzed by the accusatory repugnance of their discussion... by its surreal, Kafka-esque turn. He feels numb... almost like he's gone into shock. He's been through multiple inappropriate, fuckedup doctor visits, in which they treated him like nothing more than a drug addict trying to get high . . . but NEVER anything as insulting and dismissive and ethically disgusting as this one. **jan** turns to leave the claustrophobic office and it's like he's an automaton, completely sans agency or personhood-rights or hope.

jan [*shaking head*]
Jeezus Christ, that's CRAZY! *Wowww* . . .

17.

Immediately after Dr. Fatbody halves my Tramadol dose, I call Jim upon returning to the unit. Ask him to *please* call the Health Care Administrator and explain how this new dose is woefully inadequate, and how there's no way it'll keep the worst of my pain in check. "I'll try," he says after a moment's consideration. "But I doubt it'll make a difference. You might just have to tough it out this time, janno. Be strong, okay?"

"Thanks, Dad. Love you. I'd feel *completely* helpless without you advocating for me out there."

Then I call Rachel and can't help but cry a little. Venting. Expressing my despondency, my hopelessness, my *fierce* rage. She's furious, too. We brainstorm things I might do to stop this medical neglect and under-medicating. A hunger strike? Contact the media? Or maybe she could post on the *Support Jan* webpage, explain my awful situation, and ask supporters to call the prison and complain, insisting on better treatment. But Rachel's hesitant—would it change anything? What if it backfires, and things get even worse?

"I just don't want you getting in trouble, baby. Seems like a lotta Officers are *already* gunning for you . . ."

"Sooo . . . what then, I'm just spoz t'lie around watching TV 'n *suffering* for the next *ten* months?"

"You'll get through this, honey. Be strong. This won't last forever—things'll change! You were on that low dose when you first got there, remember?"

"Yeah, but I *did* something about it! Went to Sick Call. Had Jim call Administrator Sudbrink. Got Dr. Williams to actually look through my records. Know what . . . I can't talk to you right now. You're not helping, and I *need* your help! You can do things out there that I can't. You have resources and I have jack shit. Whatever, I'm gonna go lie down."

"Love you sweetie!" she cries.

"Love you too." I jam the phone into its cradle. Teeth clenching. I want to demolish something. Run my fist through a goddamn window. Make someone bleed—if not an Officer, then *myself.*

I'm at a loss. Plain and simple. Don't know if I've felt this frustrated and impotent since the distant nightmare of <u>Stateville</u>!

I call Mom to lament the situation to yet another loved one. Soon, she and Jim and Rachel will all have called to complain. Maybe *something* will come from it . . .

. . . Yeah, well, *something* does indeed come—just not anything I would've suspected even in my worstcase-anxiety. Next morning, I'm writing with the headphones on when a dormmate taps on my shin. I press pause and raise my eyebrows at him. "They callin you t' I.A.," he says.

"The hell? Seriously?!"

I climb down from bed and quickly throw on my Blues. Getting called to Internal Affairs is never good; it produces suspicion and gossip without fail. Someone *always* uses it as an excuse to label you a snitch. I hurry to the I.A. Office with a sick feeling in my gut. These people are frighteningly good at intimidating and tricking people. It's their stock and trade. I enter a hallway of offices and an Officer tells me to sit down and wait—that Major Robinson wants to speak to me. "Am I in trouble?" I say, half-joking, half-nervous. Can't think of a single thing I've done wrong.

My skin ripples with the tinglies when the Officer says, "Pretty much." And he said a *Major* wants to see me. They're a level above Lieutenants! Christ-bananas, what're they after me for now? The shitstorm never ends. If I'm lucky it calms down for a while before raging once more.

I step into Major Robinson's office. He's very fat, with the high-blood-pressure-reddened face that suggests a likely eventual coronary infarction. He wears wire rim glasses and a bristly mustache. "Sit down," he tells me. "Do you know why you're here?"

I answer with the plain truth. "Not at all. No idea."

He holds up an extralong sheet of paper covered in writing; it's a disciplinary ticket. I furrow my brow and cock my head at him. "I've already got this all written up," he says. "I'm prepared to tack nine months onto your sentence for Extortion."

My jaw seems to unhinge. Heart flutters for several beats. I have no *clue* what he's talking about. Extortion?! "*Extortion?*" I say. This has to be a mistake. He's summoned the wrong person. What the actual fuck is this?

"That's right. You really don't know what this is about?"

"Sir, I honestly have no idea whatsoever." I'm starting to sweat though. And get a sick pulsing terror in my gut.

"Havin all these people call in for you, tryin to get your medication changed."

I stare at him. This is incomprehensible. Seriously, did someone slip me LSD? This can't be real.

"I listened to your phone conversations with your girlfriend. Rachel, right? She's a smart girl, you should listen to her."

I try for several seconds to speak. Finally I manage to croak, "*Extortion?*"

"You wanna play with us? Go on a hunger strike? Keep havin your friends 'n family call in? Go to the newspapers? Let's do it! You have a <u>drug case</u>, mr. smitowicz. Think you'll get an ounce of sympathy in the newspapers? Go head and try! We'll make you look like a drug-addicted criminal. No one'll give a shit about you."

"I don't . . ." I shake my head. Heart pounding like wild mustang hooves.

"I get that you're in pain. I have knee pain as well. But you know what? You could pound my fingers with a hammer right now and I'd just keep right on goin.[101] It's mind over matter, kid. You need to learn how to ignore your pain."

I just *love* when people try to tell me what *my* pain is like, and what I should do based on what they do. Because, you know, every person experiences pain in the exact same way—there is only one type of pain, with no gradations of intensity. Pain is exceedingly simple and elegant like that!

"I also have recordings of you on the phone, calling the Doctor and Ms. Sudbrink . . ." He glances down at his notes. "'Bitches' and 'cunts' and 'assholes.' That right there is *Harassment*, and I could add even more time to that nine months! That what you want?"

"No. I don't." This continues to feel nightmarish. The surrealism has walloped me, and I'm dazed and reeling still.

"Then you need to stop having people call in for you. That's extortion. And you need to stop harassing the Health Care Staff into giving you the medication you want. It's not up to you to decide. That's their job."[102]

I fail to see—and feel the same to this day—how getting outside people to call and complain about my abysmal treatment constitutes extortion;

---

[101] I wish he would've let me test that absurd claim. It would've been *awesome*.

[102] Do I even need to comment on that? Or can you just surmise the kinds of things I'd say based on what I've already said—how they wouldn't give two fucks about me even if *acres* of wild fucks grew right outside the Health Care building? Just go ahead and surmise something like that.

denying and/or constantly trying to deny appropriate care for someone with a severe medical condition is tantamount, in a case like mine, to a sort of low-level medical torture. If you think I'm being hyperbolic, imagine the equivalent for an able-bodied person: What if a prison forced people to sit in a box, knees against their chest, for six hours a day? Because that's what it feels like when I wake up, every day, and it's even *worse* now with less medication.

Major Robinson stares at me. "So are you gonna stop?"

I'm utterly helpless. Maybe if I were stronger, or not suffering so much already, or if I had several years left on my sentence, I'd risk going on a hunger strike or contacting some kind of medical advocacy group for prisoners. But simply *getting by* is difficult enough. I don't have enough left to aggressively challenge the status quo here.

"Yes," I finally say to the Major. Defeated, heartbroken: "It'll stop."

"Sounds good, jan. Listen to Rachel. She's a smart girl."

"Yeah." [Rachel also happened to refer to the Doctor as a *Fucking cunt*—but I guess we'll just ignore that part.]

"Okay. Good luck—you're free to go."

Fuck you, fat disgusting sheepcock-sucker. You should be killed, and I should be the one to do it. I stand up. He actually expects me to express gratitude for not submitting the ticket, I can tell. Stupid savage bastard. Heartless, powerdrunk, repulsive, smarmy, bullshitting bullfucker.

The impotent rage I feel carries over into my interactions with inmates and Guards alike. One day in the room several guys are having a basketball argument. People like to try and rub it in any time the Lakers lose, knowing I'm from L.A. There's this huge, very strong black dude with massive buckteeth named joe. He's an obnoxious prick.

I'm watching *Tosh.O* on Comedy Central; commercials make me want to jam a lightbulb-shard into my ears, so I tend to remove my headphones during the whorish advertisements. joe, eyes locked on me, says, "At least the Celtics didn't get *swept* like the Lakers."

"Ooooh," I cry, "the Celtics got *one* whole game, that's sooo much better than none."

"Man, shutcho pussy ass up," bucktoothed joe says. "Ain't nobody talkin to you."

"I ain't a pussy, but I'd rather be a pussy than an ugly-ass bucktooth motherfucker!"

He charges me, murderous fury burning in his wide-eyed stare. p-funk, an oldtimer I'm cool with, rushes forward and jams his forearms into joe's chest, trying to hold him back. joe's ready to tear me down from the bunk and smash my face. "Punkass bitch!" he roars. "I'm'a fuck you up, muh-fucka, I'm'a tear yo ass up, white boy!"

Everything I've been going through has obliterated my rational sense. joe's got 100 lbs. of muscle and fat on me. He's scrambling closer and closer to my bunk. p-funk struggles to hold him back. joe frees one of his thigh-thick arms and claws for my leg. If it weren't for funk, joe'd yank me down onto the tiles now and stomp me into a coma. He snatches the sheet off my bed and then just barely misses my foot, tearing off its sock. "I'm'a get up in yo ass, punk! I'm'a fuck you up!"

"Come on then!" I cry. I'm up on my knees on the mattress. *Egging him on.* Let him beat the fuck out of me! Maybe I'll get a nice hospital bed for a couple days, and a shot of Demerol. Or not—I'm completely out of my mind right now. "Come on tough guy, go head 'n get up in my ass, I gotta fart right now! Get up in my ass so I can fart in your face!"

p-funk may be middle-aged, but he's done many years of hard time. He doesn't weigh as much as joe, but he's one strong sonofabitch. funk mana-ges to push joe all the way back against the far wall. *Talking him down. Shit ain't worth it fam, don't jag your bit, you know he cain't fight back!* Then, mercifully, it's over.

Later that evening, we're in the dayroom waiting for Medline; p-funk pulls me aside. Staring at me with intense seriousness. His skin is the color of bitter chocolate, with eyes so dark you can barely distinguish between iris and pupil. "You know I saved *both* yo asses, right?"

"Yes." Nodding. "I know you did. I'd'a got my ass kicked and he'd'a got in trouble."

"Thass right." Dark eyes boring into mine. That wasn't the first time he's broken up a near-fight in the room. A few months before I came here, joe got into it with a guy called eyes. They rushed one another, each bran-dishing an uncapped pen. funk got in the middle—and *he* was accidentally jabbed in the side with a pen, hard enough to break the skin. The guys who were present still crack up whenever it's mentioned.

"I appreciate what you did, funk. Thank you."

He's pissed at having to get involved. "Yer lucky, cali. Both'a y'all lucky."

"I know. Thanks, bro." I grasp his hand and pull him into one of those bro-ish halfhugs. It's funny how oldtimers—the most hardened prisoners among us—are often some of the nicest dudes. I think it's their age, and all the time they've served. They know how to do a bit without bothering anybody they don't *want* to bother!

One day I'm walking back from evening Medline near the very end of summer with this Turkish guy called Turnbo. I'm feeling especially miserable. It's almost eight o'clock, but still the sun hasn't fully set. A typical muggy Midwestern U.S. evening. My groin region is all slippy-slidey beneath my blue pants. I'm grabbing my shirt's chest every 20 seconds, flapping it up and down so puffs of cool air kiss my slick flesh. Turnbo's talking. I'm not really listening. But then I see a tiny spark of yellowish-white light in my peripheral. I turn to look, and there's another minute flash, this time over to the left. It's like those two individuals were signaling *all systems go*, because then the dazzling lights start popping all over, from dozens of sources in every direction, glowing for a split second then rapidly dimming. Fireflies! In 30 seconds flat, it went from scenic prison drudgery to sparkling like clean baywater on a cloudless sunny day. I adore them; fireflies, along with thunderstorms, may be the only things I truly love about the Midwest. So beautiful, so fascinating: To me, their ephemeral insect fire weaves along that fine and sometimes invisible line between chemistry and magic. Nature's glory, in one of its smallest naked-eye-visible manifestations. Turnbo's voice has faded to irrelevance with the arrival of these beloved nightsparklers.

Then he says, "Hey, lookit this!" He squats and sticks his hand down among the grass, index finger extended. We've halted on the gravel Walk. I don't see anything. But then he stands and holds out his hand. A tiny, brightgreen frog sits motionless in the center of his palm. Spotted with black dots like periods, small enough to fit inside a bottlecap. "Cute little guy, huh?" the muscular Turk says.

"Totally." I stare, grinning, and it's like an umbrella has opened over my head, giving reprieve from the cold, pounding deluge of my life. The fireflies flash their white magic all around. We, two convicts from different worlds, stand there admiring the frog. Others bounce around in the grass, but this one stays. As if knowing I *need* him right now. His whole body's about the size of a walnut. And yet he has a nearly 360° field of vision, a complex nervous system, intricate and unique vocalizations, hearing that greatly relies on electrical frequencies [whereas mammals' hearing is rooted more in physical vibrations], a beating heart, a brain . . . all of that and more in this tiny little vessel, a body anatomically very similar to the oldest known frogs from about 190 *million* years ago. Frogs—and other amphibians—serve as powerful "biological indicators" of an ecosystem's health. The reasons are myriad; their porous skin and general proximity to water being the biggest.

And amphibians are in serious trouble. Genetic mutations and defects, such as missing or extra limbs, have steadily increased as the human population and its industrialization has skyrocketed since the mid-1900s. There are several thousand known frog species in the world; about one-third [!] of them are threatened with extinction—that's <u>now</u>, and it's getting worse every single day. These little critters are canaries in the *global* coalmine. As such, they are further proof that so-called "civilized" humans are decimating the planet's very life-support systems, and that industrial society is careening toward massive collapse.

But none of that occupies my thoughts. I couldn't bear it. Just getting by right now is difficult enough. The Bureaucratic Machine has already stolen so very much from me. It'd be yet another terrible loss if I allowed their pathological workings to terrorize this moment, too. This morsel of happiness. So I forcibly expectorate, phlegmlike, everything but the *now* from my head. I'm not a member of the species causing a mass extinction— I'm not even in that world; I'm not in the Prison Vortex, either; I'm not jammed inside awful situations over which I have no control; I'm not even occupying four dimensions anymore! Just the three physical ones—I've willfully extricated myself from TIME and its insistence on perpetual change, motion. All that exists now is *me* and *this* frog and *those* fireflies, interacting on some level in a timeless state of enjoyment and respect and awe. I am happy. And I will hold onto this moment, place its character and connotations [made all the more precious by evanescent rarity] in that untouchable chamber of my mind where these things are kept, their joy and beauty cusped delicately, to be summoned whenever I need a reminder that things of such beauty *still exist*. Much like during the dead of winter— when I'd stare at snowflakes on my hands for a few seconds before they melted, and the snowdunes with their majestic windswept patterns.

These things are my rock-outcroppings, to be grasped at and gripped, ever so carefully, when I'm on the verge of falling. My tether to sanity— to <u>life</u>.

Turnbo sets the froglet back in the grass and he hops off. "Some of the young gangbanger punks here . . ." He pauses, reflecting. "I'd rather kill any one'a those niggers than hurt these lil critters."

Oh, for fuck's sake! Why'd he have to ruin such a lovely moment with ignorance and misplaced vitriol?!

keethan is the smartest guy I meet in prison. And he's like me: intelligent by nature, but also seeking further knowledge all the time. Exercising his *brain*—by far the most significant muscle. Yet it's largely neglected by the vast majority here. keethan reads a ton. Studies science textbooks from the library. He's also homicidally enraged at The System. No wonder we get along so well! Like my other good friend in 2A, the bible-defacing mike, keethan's a bisexual atheist. Based on his incarceration story, it sounds like he also got the ass-end of a shitty deal. Even worse than I did! He was charged with Possession of a Stolen Vehicle; a pretty low-level felony. But he's from Quincy County, a small rural area in west-central Illinois. There were apparently several dozen unsolved stolen-vehicle cases in the region. Seems like they wanted a scapegoat, and found their mark. The state only proved [sic?] he committed *one* theft—yet the Judge slammed him with the maximum sentence. As I showed pretty strongly in Inter-Mission 1B, Judges' and Prosecutors' careers innately <u>benefit</u> from convictions. A built-in bias that encourages them to mete out guilty verdicts or secure plea deals. The "Justice" System is bullshit, plain and simple. Undemocratic. Un*just*!

For stealing a single vehicle, keethan was sentenced to *six* years. Meanwhile, I'm confident you know there are people whose crimes produced a decimated psyche or a dead body—rapists and killers—who receive far less time than that.[103] I can tell keethan's ripe for some radical politicizing. I lend him the printed Januscript of my militant revenge-on-Monsanto novel *Orange Rain*. He loves it. [The book was eventually published in paperback by independent, progressive Trébol Press in July 2014.] He also reads Jonathan Safran Foer's *Eating Animals* after I'm done; it's a terrific, supercreative look at our treatment of nonhuman animals, which utterly blows keethan's world open—similar, it seems, to what my post-Katrina New Orleans relief work did for me.

---

[103] For an egregious & blatant recent example, see Stanford rapist Brock Turner, et [*so so many*] alia.

He's a goodlooking guy: short and neat auburn hair, a thin goatee, glacial blue eyes. When I find out he's bisexual, some . . . *strange thoughts* begin swirling through my mind. Now, I've long been comfortable telling people that I find particular men attractive. Not sexually attractive—I've never seriously considered banging a guy—but just physically, wherein I'll find myself admiring their faces and/or physique. When puberty party-crashed my life in middle school and these feelings began cropping up, they worried me. A lot. I was still your typical pubescent boy with that crazed hallmark obsessiveness for girls . . . yet we've all heard stories about men who marry and have kids, but then one day finally come to realize/accept they are in actuality gay or bisexual. Such thoughts caused me great concern. Who would *want* to be gay in this society?[104] Eventually—after a whole boatload of personal anxiety and soulsearching—I came to understand that I wasn't bisexual, but rather just simply . . . *going through puberty*, with all its attendant weirdness and penile-fixation and hormonal hurricanes. That I'm straight, but also confident enough in my sexuality to admit men can be physically attractive.

But. But but *but!* It seems prison, and yeah sure definitely keethan too, threw a monkeywrench into that whole notion. Tugging at the neat little bow I'd long thought my sexuality was wrapped in. All of a sudden I *understood* how legitimately straight men could have gay relationships in prison. The damned loneliness digs its sharp claws in, man, and it *hurts.* I've always been an exceedingly affectionate and tactile person—like, to a fault in many women's eyes. So now, here in the Vortex, I find myself yearning for physical intimacy. It grows into an actual bodily sensation, an aching jones in the heart and all the way down to the bonemarrow, to whatever's inside us that we call the soul. I've never felt such a piercing cry from my psyche for the touch, the closeness, the comfort of another warm body. Rikki would suffice. Rachel would obviously be best. It's been over six months since I grasped her hands in mine, since our lips met. The ache is deep—but sometimes it's also right on the surface, in the gooseflesh of my skin. That's when it hurts the most. And when, I imagine, people of a certain mental or emotional state begin to consider satisfying that yearning ache through . . . whatever means happen to be available.

---

[104] All jokes aside—like e.g. how much easier life would be if we didn't have to court women.

Of course, the prospect of merely holding hands and/or cuddling [the only things I'd even be interested in considering] is completely out of the question. Especially at a cell-less joint like this one. So, like so many other feelings in here, I expunge that tactile ache with some strategically applied, targeted suppression. And that's that.

The <u>fluidity</u> of <u>desire</u>—something I *never* expected to encounter in my life.

keethan also happens to be a talented artist. I pay him $5 in writeouts and noodles to do a black-and-white drawing of Rikki that I can gift to Rachel. She absolutely *adores* it. This portrait remains posted on her refrigerator to this day, 5+ years after she received it:

18.

Early fall now. Feels like I'm getting very very close to finishing *The Liber-*
ators [relatively speaking—after all, we're talkin about a book so massive
that I end up splitting the thing into two still-long volumes]. As you know,
I've used a sweater-analogy multiple times to represent my life, which
sweater has long been unraveling thread by thread. But now—seemingly
right on cue, like somebody *knows* how close I am to completing the wildly
ambitious project [prison must be a paranoid's worst nightmare]—suddenly, it's as if the errant threads are lit on fire, fuse-like.

This scorching is ushered in

[*big surprise!*]

by a visit to Health Care. I'm scheduled to see the Psychiatrist one
morning in late September. When I enter the Telepsych room and take a
seat, there's a new face projected from the TV. The South African "Jew-
in-the-box" has been replaced by one Dr. Koko, with a bald, dark-chocolate
egghead. He's staring down at my chart. "I see you're taking . . . two milligrams of Klonopin a day. But you're already taking the Celexa, which has
anti-anxiety effects. So I'm going to be taking you off the Klonopin."

Goddamnit, no! No no NO! Not this shit again, *yet again*—especially
with my novel's finale in such close sight. This bastard didn't greet me;
even more asinine, he didn't even ask <u>how I'm doing</u>! Just went straight
from zero to demedicating. Unbelievable! even in the context of prison.
I'm no doctor—which by now you might've figured out somehow—but for
a psychiatrist to alter a new patient's medication dosage, before at the very
least inquiring as to their mental state, doesn't quuuiite seem like an appropriate psychiatric strategy. Right? [Yes, that's right . . . may not be a doctor,
but I have been around them all my life. Also helps that I'm not a complete
fucking stupendous moron. Generally not, at least.]

So then if he's not gonna ask how I'm doing, I'll just have to tell him—
somebody needs to perform the halfwit's job! "Well first off, sir, greetings!
Nice to 'meet' you. But I'm really not doing well. My anxiety is unbearable
here, and the pain in my knees is awful. Klonopin helps a ton with both.
Please don't reduce it."

"mr. smitowicz, this is not a medication for treating pain." He's dead
wrong—it most certainly helps *me*, and there's ample evidence that many
chronic pain-sufferers benefit from taking benzodiazepines—but I don't
even have a chance to point this out. "I think you are just addicted to the

Klonopin. This is a narcotic medication; I think all these pains are in your head only."

Really wouldn't have thought I even had a slackjaw left in my arsenal of facial expressions given all I've been through, but alas, here it is! So let me get this straight . . . "all these pains" are just in my head. And that's why he's taking me off Klonopin. Or is it because Klonopin doesn't do anything for pain [the pain that allegedly doesn't exist]? OR is it due to my already taking Celexa, which may have anti-anxiety properties, thereby nullifying the need for any benzos? Certainly can't be all three! They're almost as mutually exclusive as you can get; make up your damn mind, Kwacko! Maybe you should jot down all these assertions, so you can consult them and at least maintain *consistency* with all this excrement scooped from your ass and smeared across the appointment, and my soul. I really do want to know what he's thinking [sic?].

His non-thoroughness, to put it mildly, and general demeanor give the distinct impression that, if I were on fire, he *would* pee on me . . . not to extinguish the flames, mind you, but rather for the sheer glee that pissing on another human would likely bring a person [-ish] like him.

Back in the unit, I make a beeline for the phone. As always, Rachel tries to comfort me, but what could she really accomplish? How much could *anyone* do? I'm trapped inside the Machine, my mind/body/spirit/etc. are caught in its gnashing gears, and my knees are being crushed and mangled by it. First Dr. Fatbody cut my Tramadol dose in half, and now

Koko the African Fuckin Kwacko's Anti-Clonazepam Crusade [K.A.F.K.A.-C.C.]

has been initiated.[105] With a ferocity very much reminiscent of other historical crusades. Viz., he seems to be on a legitimate mission to reduce or eliminate *everyone's* psych meds in toto. This applies to ALL medicine-types. Even including antipsychotics and mood stabilizers. Having said [typed] that, he's clearly harboring a special fervor against one particular kind . . . Koko is forcing *every* *single* *person* here who takes Klonopin off it— and it's the *only* true anti-anxiety available for prescribing! The entire joint

---

[105] Clonazepam = the real actual drug name of that particular benzodiazepam-classed pharmaceutical. Vis-à-vis Klonopin, which is just a brand name of the same exact drug. And yes, that's right—I really did create [and actually decide to *use*, and PUBLISH] the contextually accurate acronym K.A.F.K.A.-C.C.! Eat yer heart out, Thomas Pynchon [just kidding, love you]!

will soon be a Benzo-Drug-Free Zone. This ain't just a small handful of inmates, either. I talk to a couple *dozen* guys he's launched the K.A.F.K.A.-C.C. on, many of whom have been taking Klonopin for five, 10, even 20 friggin years! You're hopelessly stupid and/or delusional if you think that not a single one of the 1,000 convicted felons here has anxiety severe enough to merit actual anti-*anxiety* medication. You are hopelessly stupid and/or delusional if you think that, anxiety-wise, that number $\neq$ so much as 1/1000. Aaaand finally, you are hopelessly stupid and/or delusional if you think that—if A_K equals people with anxiety deserving of Klonopin, and Jacksonville's population equals P—then A_K / P < 0.001. Fuck outta here with that bullshit! [which I'm well aware at least some of you, my Dear Readers, are surely thinking about *me*, your Humble Author, right meow after all that excessive [?] self-indulgency! Well aware. *C'est la* me, though—yah?]

I'm overwhelmed by all the helplessness. Again. Trapped in a Bureau-crazy only by a few degrees less clusterfucked than Stateville. *I don't want to live anymore*, I tell Rachel. This is simply too much to bear. The pain has once more begun slicing through my ability to concentrate, to write and hence feed my spirit. And it's gonna get that much worse with the decreased Klonopin. "Pieces'a shit, dude!" Rachel says. "I wish there was, like, some disability group I could call to report them or something. HOW can they get away with so much of this crap?"

Straight-up cannot fuckin handle this, I tell her. Been accomplishing so much great writing in my couple-few daily hours of mental productivity! Having now surpassed *1,000 pages* on the novel. Zooming toward its super-long climactic escape sequence. I'll need to summon everything I have left inside . . . drawing buckets from my well's very deepest depths . . . in order to complete the book. I *have* to keep working—to finish this massive undertaking. If I stop now, it feels like I'll forever lose some crucial core essence from the project. This thought is terrifying me, Rachel. What'll I do as my meds're further decreased? I'm already treading water here; treading way far out from shore. And getting exhausted. Don't know how much longer I can withstand so much suffering. It'd be better if I were never born; why didn't my mother get an abortion? I wish I could just POOF! simply cease to exist.

I don't want to live anymore.

Now I'm *seriously* driven to complete my novel as fast as I possibly can. It'll soon be utterly impossible to work—a matter of *when*, not *if*. At most, I have about two months to finish. Somehow I fling myself upon the story with even more ferocity. Stop going to Medical Gym during the week [james is only there on weekends now anyway] in favor of that extra 30 or 40 minutes of writing before lunch. Oftentimes, I'll now force myself to pick the legal pad back up after lunch, getting some extra work in before my obligate siesta. And I go even harder at night; no reading until my inner inkwell is unquestionably depleted.

This heightened regiment doesn't start immediately, though. I don't write a word for about five days after my Klonopin dose is halved—the detox/withdrawal process renders it impossible. By this time I've detoxed from pain meds numerous times. It's terrible, no doubt. But now I discover that, compared to benzo withdrawal, opiates are *easy*!

That initial devastating appointment with Kwacko Koko happened on a Thursday afternoon. Friday, I received the new cut-in-half dose. By about mid evening, the detox had begun. At that point I'd been taking 2 mg of Klonopin a day, every day without exception, for almost two years. My body had grown strongly habituated. When it stopped receiving that accustomed amount, it staged a violent protest as ferocious as any Latin American dictatorial upheaval. Vis à vis benzo withdrawals, getting off opiates is startlingly simple: I shit a lot and hurt even more than usual. That's pretty much it. Since my opiate use has been universally medical-not-recreational, I've never gone through anything resembling true junk-sickness—the kind of hellish nightmare withdrawals of e.g. an intravenous heroin addict, like craig described.

But man oh man! benzo withdrawals are a whole nother magnitude of horrific. So many goddamn symptoms! In fact, there were such a multitude of wretched detox-elements, I'll just present them in list format:

[1] *Excessive shitting, including but not limited to diarrhea*—

No explanation necessary . . . although a particularly egregious example will help you at least get an inkling of the process's severity, which process was made oh-so-much-worse by the engulfing circumstances. One night several days after it began in earnest, I was besieged with a bout of the shits even worse than usual. This began around eleven p.m. Lights were out and almost everybody asleep. Over the next hour I went through an *entire roll* of toilet paper, my last one. But it wasn't over. Not by a long shot. Every 15 or 20 minutes, the pressure and churning pain began roiling once more in my guts. Being vegan, I usually shat twice a day even *with* constipating meds, and so always bought an extra couple rolls a week [cost = one writeout]. But around midnight when I ran out, nobody was awake to trade with! Desperate, I shuffled into the Bubble and told the Officer I had really bad diarrhea but had no more T.P. How'd this lovely humanitarian respond? by grudgingly handing over a roll . . . of brown paper towels. As in the rough, difficult to tear, supercheap sort you'll find in the towel dispenser of public schools and gas stations. If you know what I'm talking about, you'll know that that stuff isn't even pleasant to dry your *hands* with—let alone your already chafed and sore asshole. He claimed not to have any actual toilet paper, but gimme a break! you and I both know that's a blatant lie.

Over the next two-plus hours, I revisited the Bubble—each time more and more incensed and, sadly, ashamed—literally at least *six more times* for those viciously roughtextured paper towels that were my sole recourse. You'd have a hard time convincing me he wasn't enjoying my misery and degradation at least somewhat. After all, case you haven't noticed, a comfortable majority of the Guards throughout my Prison Experience seem to take almost pornographic pleasure in our humiliation/suffering/inconvenience etcetera. I'll finish this too-long aside by simply inviting you to imagine what it felt like on my rawchafed, enflamed, pulsating, and yes, by then—it's true—*bloodied* asshole to wipe the region clean half a dozen times . . . using material much much closer on the softness-spectrum to sandpaper than Charmin. Imagine it, if you will . . . I'll wait . . . and please, at least with this, please grant me forgiveness for the woe-is-me bitching. Thank you.

[2] *Increased pain*—

Well by gawd, what do you know, I was right! Imagine that—the Klonopin *was* helping with my pain. As I failed to convince Kwacko Koko. I'd estimate that, with the reduction in dosage, my overall pain increases by about 15 to 20 percent.

[3] *Increased rage*—

As you may've noticed, this whole living-in-prison deal had already made me an extremely angry person. To the point where it's just plain unpleasant to have access [as I unfortunately do] to my thoughts and emotions. Now it's become *even worse*. I start feeling stabby over things that're even less annoying than ones I'd feel stabby over before. I begin imagining scenes of grisly, ultraviolent torture, often lasting several minutes.[106] And these thoughts will continue with joyous aplomb until I get distracted by something even more enraging, probably, and then I merely swap subjects in my gruesome fantasies; this may last an entire trip to and from Medline. It's . . . *unpleasant* to feel so damn mad so often.

[4] *Increased anxiety*—

This one's obvious, since Klonopin's main purpose is to reduce anxiety, but still bears mentioning. Because I really didn't have much anxiety In the World. I got stressed out, of course I did—especially given all my financial troubles, and the subsequent legal nightmare—but it was never fullblown anxiety like I've developed in prison, which is now far worse since I'm not as mellowed on chemicals. Now I'll be standing in line somewhere, or sitting for extended periods, and the obnoxious noise of my fellow inmates will be zapping my nerves like a Tazer gun, the chemical fire scorching through my knees, and my heart starts pounding, I'm shuffling my feet and yearning for whatever it is that's bothering me to stop—or for me to drop dead, whichever is more expedient—and my chest feels constricted I can't take a full breath, I try to inhale deep down into my lungs but the oxygen seems to get pluggedup halfway down as if there's coalblack tar solids gumming up the works and I'm sweating it feels like I'm about to shriek and start weeping and fall to the ground in a defeated fetal heap . . .

[5] *Skincrawling discomfort*—

This is the most complex symptom, and also the most unbearable. It's more or less constant for the first five days. Sometimes not all that bad; but then by mid evening, it's absolutely MADDENING. I've long experienced periods of unstoppable discomfort—yet normally I'm able to

---

[106] Similar to the ones I had for Officer Forkface-Cook after he railroaded me from the Drug Unit. Here's a still-recurring one about him: I have a bucket of fecal-contaminated saltwater & a rubber garden hose, & I use the hose to beat him—sometimes grasping two lengths of hose together & bashing him w/ the loop at the end, then some whipping action w/ the metal mouth, then back to the loop-beating, just wailing on him for 30 or 40 minutes on the forearms, hands/fingers, elbows, spine, buttocks, feet, kneecaps, skull, face, groin . . . then when he's cut & bleeding & screaming w/ many open wounds, I'll stick one end of the hose into the fecal saltwater & force him to suck on the other end, siphoning it, until the foul salty shitwater starts gushing out, & then I hose him down head to toe & then make him stand outside in the frigid central Illinois night, the chilly Lake Michigan breeze lashing & biting at his wounds, which are festering with the saltwater/excrement-contaminated fluid. Just an idea—one of so very many I've legitimately thought about a ton.

distract myself and get through it. This, though, is a pervasive, all-consuming unease. Impossible to ignore; my body demanding I get comfortable. Forcing me to shift positions, move around, flip over so I'm facing upward, squirm, shift, flip back onto my belly, squirm-shift-flip-squirm-stretch-trytrytry-nodontquit. It's kinda like, like uhm like thousands of insects no not quite insects no but rather the *ghosts* of insects are scurrying tiny phantom legs scuttling scurrying same thing whatever doesn't matter scuttlescurrying all over my body; at the same time it's like my flesh—all of it, the entire single organ that is my skin—is attempting to pull itself away, sever its attachment to the rest of my body. *Skincrawling* to whole new levels of perilous heights. I truly believe that these sensations, with their crazed unmitigable persistence, are the physical equivalent of slowly losing your mind. Going insane. That's the best way to describe it: Every square inch of your body growing frenetically, increasingly schizophrenic. A physical manifestation of complete and utter madness!

I could utilize further [numerals], but you get the point. Starting that week, I desperately want to torture and murder Dr. Koko. This is not hyperbole. At all. Those violent fantasies I wrote about? Half the time Dr. Koko is now their star. He, like Officer Forkface before, inspires my homicidal rage to intensify and swell and spiral upward to dizzying heights of heretofore unthinkable levels of horrific violence. Savage, barbaric fantasies of violence so vicious and detailed and gruesome they'd make David Lynch quiver in revulsion. Quentin Tarantino would lay a nervous sidelong stare of horror on me and suggest I maybe tone it down a bit there, buddy. That first week is consumed by the detox symptoms at their most intolerably severe, and the murderous fury they nourish.

We start hearing about prisonwide reactions to Koko's chemical assault; guys buggin up, having panic attacks and breakdowns, getting sent to the Naked Room for Suicide Watch . . . dudes losing their mellow from withdrawals and/or lack of appropriate meds and attacking people. A black muslim in 3-House who's had his 2 mg of daily Klonopin halved, he's standing above his prayer rug [or "flying carpet" as some furtively call them] one early dawn in front of the dormroom's window, hands pressed together in calm meditation, eyes closed. Guys begin filtering back into the room from breakfast. Two of them are talking boisterously. The debenzoed muslim halts his prayers, calmly walks over, and gutpunches one of them. The guy drops to the tile floor gasping for breath; muslim dude gets "cuffed and stuffed" into Seg.

I can hear it now—a prescience based not in psychic ability [per se], but in applied knowledge of a particular, and particularly large, subset of America's assholes. I hear it so clearly it's like a reverse-echo. Echo somehow arriving before the thing that creates it. Like that weird part at the end of Led Zeppelin's "Whole Lotta Love" when you hear Robert Plant's lyrics' echoing *before* he sings them. People would or will reply to this Koko-development with something to the effect of, *Who gives a damn? Y'all're felons! Why should we care what you deem appropriate medical care? That's the doctor's job* [sic, of course—that's not even close to prison Doctors' primary function—for tangible evidence, consult pgs. 1-422 of this memoir. Can you hear it, Dear Reader? I bet literally millions of Americans think just this way. So I'll provide a preemptive attack, or counterattack; or rather a *preemptive* counterattack, so the attack need not ever come.

In short [too late]: *Even if you only care about you and your own, I suggest giving a shit about how prisoners in your country are treated.* Because . . .

"Today's prisons are a blueprint for rage," as Sherman Manning—himself an activist-prisoner at the time—writes in *Creating Monsters*. And after the inmates are released, "many will exhibit behaviors resulting from the scars of fear, anger, and prison devastation—such as alcohol and drug abuse, child abuse, wife beating, and an escalation in their willingness to utilize violence as a first resort." Later in the same book, Manning beautifully delineates this ubiquitous, ceaseless tragedy: "The folks we are sending to prisons and jails are very often nonviolent" [like me and the *majority* of my fellow prisoners]. "Once prison guards get their hands on them, once hardcore criminals get their influence on them, once they get acclimated to the survival tactics and mechanisms of the prison subculture, they become monsters!" This all ties in perfectly with that earlier quote—about the tragicomic, awful shittiness of American prisons' rehabilitative antisuccess—from environmental "terrorist" and saboteur Jeff Luers.

In any case, you don't have to be in a prison with rampant gang activity and rapes and assaults to emerge fucked up. It happens to plenty of people, even in minimum security joints. I assure you. The Bureaucratic Machines—with engines that run not on fossil fuels, but rather on the *souls* of those caught inside—and their fundamental absurdity alone can drive you mad. As can simply living in their godforsaken petri dishes. Yet another way incarceration can produce the exact opposite of its [ostensible] intended effect is through abysmal treatment of prisoners' serious health issues.

How much injustice can one person withstand before snapping? I now believe recipients of prolonged, obstinate injustice can be psychologically/emotionally <u>destroyed</u> by it. Just like people suffering severe depression or PTSD who're stuck with woeful care. Hence, I also believe American prisons are breeding grounds that foster and facilitate this kind of breakdown. They are indeed *blueprints for rage*—as Manning so aptly stated in the above quote—but U.S. prisons are also blueprints for *irreparable mental harm*. This very likely feeds into the multitude of reasons for America's calamitous recidivism numbers.[107]

Before prison, these return-rates seemed moronic, incomprehensible. But now I understand. Like those ["autostereogram"] images made famous by the *Magic Eye* books—which initially appear as random configurations of shape and color, but when stared at long enough and with the correct perception, form a complex 3D image—this whole experience has similarly coalesced into understandable patterns that are easy both to see and to quantify.

Oh shit, wait . . . I think I hear another reverse-echo! Hold on, I'm listening . . .

Ah yes. *But Klonopin's a narcotic. Prisoners don't deserve narcotic medications—they're probably just using them to get high!* Well, that one's even easier to preemptively debunk. Goddamn, have you spent even a day in prison? These bureaucrat-cunts [BureauCunts?] should be prescribing *more* benzos and tranquilizers and mood stabilizers. There'd be fewer fights, less nerve-rattling uproar, less conflict with Guards and Administrators. Safer for everyone! Upon arrival, the Doctor should offer every single inmate some form of mellowing chemical; dope us up and everyone wins! Just an idea.

Besides, as I mentioned, Koko's not just engaged in a Clonazepam Crusade. He's messing with *everyone's* psych meds. Lowering and/or changing and/or ceasing guys' antidepressants, anti-psychotics, anything—everyone. The whole thing is pure insanity [NPI].

---

[107] Calamitous, that is, for *almost* everyone. DEFINITELY for society as a whole. Yet, for the megacorporations raking in obscene profits from America's Prison-Industrial Complex—and the calculatedly Tough on Crime politicians they $upport—recidivism isn't calamitous. **It's a fucking *goldmine*.** Like, just a slight shade away from literally owning actual moneyprinting machines! And it's truly all but impossible to find a large corporation that doesn't or wouldn't sabotage society, to limitless extents, in the name of profit.

I'm utterly befuddled. I complain to Mom and Jim, Rachel and james and keethan and xavier and p-funk and Dr. Camerer. Every business day for *two weeks*, Jim—having learned the futility of pleading with Sudbrink or the Assistant Warden—tries to reach the statewide overseer of all non-psychiatric medical issues: He calls IDOC HQ in Springfield and asks to speak with their Office of Health Services, viz. the Acting Chief. Each time . . . each call for two fucking weeks, including days with multiple attempts, at all different times in their alleged hours of operation . . . every single sonofabitching time—we're talking *dozens* of calls—the phone either rings on and on and on without an answer [one time he waits for a full *30 rings!*], or the system just bounces him back to the main menu. Am I alone in feeling it's at least a *tad strange* that it's totally impossible to reach their HEADQUARTERS' OFFICE OF HEALTH SERVICES? Which is far and away the most important bureaucratic edifice for IDOC medical issues?!

On my end, I compose and drop a detailed grievance letter. But that process is yet another giant charade. Just like the arbitration proceedings for disciplinary writeups, its primary function is to serve as deflective window-dressing: *Look, there's a process in place if an inmate feels wronged! We have ample checks and balances to ensure no foul play!* My grievance comes back the next week and Administrator Sudbrink signed off on it, writing that she reviewed the materials and concluded that I was seen by Dr. Koko a couple weeks ago and Dr. Camerer a week ago, and I'm being prescribed medication for "pain in my knee [sic—*knees*]," so everything is A-OK. Basically, Sudbrink justifies the K.A.F.K.A.-C.C. and everything else by saying that I take medication—*some* sort of medication—and I've visited their Doctors. Ergo I must be receiving adequate medical care! Ironclad logic, eh? [108] It's kinda like claiming an accused rapist must be innocent

---

[108] One time back when I moved to the Drug Unit, my mattress was woefully thin atop the bunk's steel slab; uncomfortable for my back, painful on the knees. I was told by the Doctor & a Nurse to write Laundry about getting a newer, more padded one. So I dropped a request slip; it came back with *Laundry* crossed out and *Clothing* written next to it; handwritten under **Remarks by staff** was, "No Mattresses issued w/out Health Care Unit and Major's Authorized [sic]." So I wrote to Sudbrink, citing that previous response. She returned the slip w/ "HEALTH CARE UNIT HAS ABSOLUTELY NOTHING TO DO WITH MATTRES-SES." It's like the entire prison is a giant Rube Goldberg machine, except nothing is produced or accomplished or excreted at the end [aside from broken manhusks of course]. I'd already figured out enough about bureaucrazies' madness when I

because he's been seeing a psychologist, and anyway he already had sex the prior week! More classic rubberstamping by a certified #*Yessir*.

Moving along. When it finally stops feeling like my entire fleshorgan is trying to squirm off my body, I heave all the friggin energy I have left into finishing *The Liberators*—and then somehow find it in me to push harder still. Close, so very close. I'm telling you: That damn book saved me from a catastrophic collapse. From revealing to the world that Dr. Camerer was bribed to model for Abilify's animated cartoon ads [which for some reason would send her into violent, fish-out-of-waterlike-floor-thrashing, tongue swallowing paroxysms of shame at the unwanted attention it'd bring]; from wielding a battery-stuffed sock like a medieval mace to cave Officer Forkface's skull in; from trying to strangle Dr. Koko through the TV.

"Man," p-funk—the accidental pen-stabbing recipient in my room who bruteforce-stopped joe from ripping off my foot—says one day after visiting the now-prisonwide-notorious Kwacko. "That muhfucka crazy, cal!"

"Wha'd he do this time?"

funk shakes his head, lips menacingly gnarled. "He a *fool-ass* nigga, cali. Tryin d' take me off my goddamn . . . Risperdal."

"Trying? He didn't take you off it?"

"Hell nah! They better hope he don't, too. Else I'm headin t' Seg." funk had previously told me he's been taking that common anti-psychotic med for some 20 years, inside prison and out.

"What happens when you go off it?"

He scoffs. "Start hearin voices. Trippin out, fightin 'n shit. Fuckin niggas up. I tol' that fool, 'n them muhfuckas're damn lucky he listened!"

"That's good, my man. I don't want you t'be 'fuckin niggas up.'" I give him a mischievous half-smile.

He stares at me for a brief moment, then bursts out laughing. Pushes me in the chest. "You crazy, cal." He chortles again. "Goofass!"

Soon . . . too soon, oh please earth deliver me from this madness . . . it's time for me to see Kwacko Koko again. Which means another halving of my Klonopin, down to just 0.5 mg in the morning. GAH! Yes, this has

---

was just 17 to write, in my first completed novel *High Society* [unpublished] that, "The right hand doesn't know what the left hand is doing, and they're both jerking off the cock in the middle anyway." That was at 17. Everything in my post-adolescent & then adult life has merely confirmed that assessment's accuracy.

apocalyptic overtones—but I can't stop thinking *The End Is Nigh, The End Is Nigh!* just what the hell that could even entail, though, is beyond my purview at the time. And yet I know it's true . . .

I spend all of two minutes in the Telepysch room. Man, that TV airs the WORST fuckin material imaginable! This month's episode of *Koko the African Fuckin Kwack's Anti-Clonazepam Crusade* succeeds, as ever, in reinvigorating my massive suicidal and homicidal/kokocidal urges. **The pain is all just in my head!** he maintains. I wonder if, when he tried to take p-funk off Risperdal, Koko told him, "I don't believe you're really hearing these voices. I think they are all just in your head." Ha![109]

xavier's cellie chris—a fat bearded balding white guy—loved smoking crack and getting in drunken barfights. And his outdate was only five or six weeks away. He had . . . interesting post-release plans. He explained them one night on the way to Medline. Grinning joyously at the thought. "Man, I can't *wait* to get out—gonna smoke some crack and hit the bar on the way home."

I stared at him in disbelief—was he *seriously* serious?

Yep! He'd worked it all out. He had a year of parole; if you violate, you get sent back to prison to serve half your remaining parole time. "Ain't no way I'm wait'n a damn year to hit the rock!" chris figured he could drop dirty [i.e. fail a urine test for amphetamines] at least once with just a warning. That it'd take a minimum of three months for them to violate him over it. At which point he'd have nine months of parole left, so he'd serve four and a half months and then leave—this time "without papers," meaning no more parole. Then he could get high with impunity and not have to worry about pissing dirty. "*Totally* worth it," he said, grinning. "Do a few more months in prison, then I'm done!"

"Then the party really starts," xavier said.

"The party where a shit-ton of crack is smoked," I said for clarification.

---

[109] [A chorus of *Booooos* erupts in the audience; some drunk guy blurts a slurred, "Take yer puns 'n stick em up yer ass sideways!" I plead w/ them: *Thomas Pynchon constantly makes pun of things! Even* Shakespeare! *One of the best teachers I ever had, Mrs. Young [11th grade Creative Writing], once said—after unhefting one of her deep trademark sighs that seemed to express* Woe-is-me-in-this-lowbrow-philistinistic-culture—*"Well,* Victor Hugo *did say, 'Puns are the droppings of soaring wits' . . ."* But my pleas fall on deaf ears; the boos only intensify.]

"Fuckin-A right!" Grinning wide enough to stick a glass pipe in his mouth, sideways. I thought it was a scandalous plan, that he was a maniacal raging beast, but what do I know? Never done crack in my life. Who am I to judge? He feels that two or three months of rock-smoking would be totally worth another three months in prison. If only more of us had that level of passion for the things we love! Especially if they're meaningful things, like the pursuit of social justice and an equitable world, or saving animals, or stopping industrial society from continuing to decimate the natural world until earth becomes uninhabitable for most life forms.

I salute him. May we all be inspired by chris's insatiable appetite for crack cocaine!

I had to deal with Dr. Fatbody's halved Tramadol dose for three weeks. One pill in the morning and one in the evening. Except—get ready for one of my most shocking experiences—there was a super sweet Nurse who worked nights; she doled out the evening meds three, sometimes four times a week. The first night after the dosage changed, she called my name and I walked toward the back; she stood on the other side of the counter. "Good evening, mr. smitowicz," she said with her oh-so-sweet smile. [Further description withheld to protect her anonymity—and possibly this author's laziness.] My meds sat in their tiny clear plastic cup. I expected the one green Klonopin and only one white round Tramadol. But there were *two* white pills. My gaze shot up at her, head cocked. My first instinct was to say nothing and just benefit from what I assumed was a mistake. But it seemed like honesty would be wiser. Especially if she later realized her error—and perhaps used it against me.

"Uhhhm. Is this right?" At least I had the sense to speak sotto voce; the waiting room and front desk's C.O. are about 20 feet back toward the entrance. "The dose for the Tramadol changed yesterday."

She gave me a transparently readable look. I understood immediately. She knew the dosage had been cut, but was instead giving me the normal amount that I'd been taking [and she'd been dispensing] for over a year. *Stop talking, swallow the pills, and move along,* the look said. *I'm putting my ass on the line bigtime here, so you better not do anything to raise suspicion.* Roger that, Nurse ____, loud and clear. I kept my eyes trained on hers, smiling, as I tipped the pills onto my tongue and swallowed them with a sip of water. I'm sure the stunned, unquantifiable gratitude shone from my face with just as much clarity as her *mum's-the-word* look. "Thank you."

"Have a good night, mr. smitowicz."

"I will, thanks."

And I did—because of her! Ever since the dumb porky heartless Doctor cut my pain meds in half, I'd been writing only three, maaaybe four pages a day. But pain wasn't a limiting factor that night. I managed to maintain sharp focus for several hours and banged out *seven* pages right then and there. Doubling, in the evening alone, what I'd been averaging on full days! Didn't even stop for dinner until 11 p.m.

Nurse ___'s actions were [1] outrageously helpful—transforming, on the three or four nights a week she was able to sneak an extra tablet, what would've been an evening of constant discomfort and little writing into several hours of *tolerable* discomfort that allowed me to write profusely; and [2] outrageously risky for her—hence even more meaningful and heartwarming.

I could never say this enough: BLESS HER HEART!! Thank you, Nurse ___. Your warmth and kindness was profoundly beautiful, yes even life-affirming, amid that cold and barren wasteland. Thank you.

x.

One morning at Medical Gym, james tells me there's a new Doctor here as we walk our laps around the basketball court. james saw this Dr. Hartman, and was extremely impressed with his thoroughness. Two Gym workers are shooting hoops. The basketball bounces off the rim, rolling toward us. "Ey, ball!" one of them called. But james doesn't play like that, remember? He swats it away and it goes *tunk* on the wooden floor and wanders off, away from the nonworking workers.

I chuckle, watching james's face. "You crack me up. Really stick to your guns with that."

He shrugs, grinning slyly. "I'm a handicapped old man, what're they gonna do?"

"Yer lucky. Wish I had protection like that!"

"Just one'a the great things about get'n old." He pauses, staring straight ahead. Deadpan: "And about stabbing your wife and trying to commit suicide with a butcher knife."

Gales of laughter from me, and then him in response. I love how he can joke about such a horrific event. "Well, that new Doc sounds awesome." I sign up for Sick Call right when I get back to the unit.

Later in the week, I get to see Dr. Hartman. And james was spot-on. *Thoroughness*, a word of perfect precision. Hartman actually spends some time in the office with me, looking through my chart. I planned to merely request he put me back on 100 mg in the morning. Instead, he does even better—returning my Tramadol dose to its original 200 mg/day! That's shocking enough. He also vows to further review my chart [!!] before the next checkup in six weeks. Unbelievable!

"Oh wow," I manage. Surely staring at him as if he'd rescued me from a burning car. This is unprecedented: a prison Doctor who actually seems to *care*. Who takes the time for a decent evaluation of his patients. A Doctor with integrity, with thoroughness. Is my health-care-nightmare finally over? Were we inmates finally going to receive the medical treatment we deserve? Was the heartless bastards' reign of terror over, at last? Truly an amazing development. I return to the unit with an irrepressible grin, phoning Rachel and then Jim to share the great news.

Dr. Hartman's gone before my next appointment. Replaced by Sudbrink with yet another incontrovertible Company Man—a *Yessir*. A Doctor, I'll come to find, *even worse* than all the others.

It's like they tantalized me with amazing Dr. Hartman—then dropped the bomb. Playing me the whole time like a friggin marionette. The dream's over and now I'm back to hideous reality. Back to fighting for my life over something that is, for them, a pittance, the crumb-sized pills about as costly as actual crumbs. Back to another shithead Doctor unwilling to spend even five minutes examining my medical history to see that every single little piece points

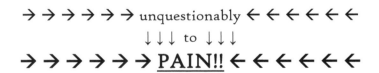

$$\rightarrow \rightarrow \rightarrow \rightarrow \rightarrow \rightarrow \text{ unquestionably } \leftarrow \leftarrow \leftarrow \leftarrow \leftarrow \leftarrow$$
$$\downarrow \downarrow \downarrow \text{ to } \downarrow \downarrow \downarrow$$
$$\rightarrow \rightarrow \rightarrow \rightarrow \rightarrow \rightarrow \underline{\textbf{PAIN!!}} \leftarrow \leftarrow \leftarrow \leftarrow \leftarrow \leftarrow$$

The new Doctor, in fact, is a primary factor that leads to my being transferred from Jacksonville to a medium-security "disciplinary prison."

When I'm awake and physically-mentally able, I'd rather be writing than doing *anything* else. So close; I'm getting so, so close to finishing. Due to my higher pain levels now that the K.A.F.K.A.-Clonazepam Crusade is in full swing, I've given up on exercise—like I said, I'm pouring *all* available energy into my novel now. Racing to finish the first draft before I'm off Klonopin completely, and effectively useless as a result. Almost 1,400 pages written now! I'm in the midst of the long, complex sequence where the main characters try to escape America through the desert into Mexico. It's so very difficult to write. I'll say it again: this project has a deadline, and it's rapidly approaching. I have to dig deep. Down to yet another inconceivable wellspring of strength that I never even knew existed. Relying more than ever on the incredible discipline and dedication I've fostered during this ferocious eight-month run—the craziest and fastest period of writing in my life. Just a little bit longer . . . almost done, almost there. Keep the pedal on the floor and don't dare let up until the final sentence is complete. *Then* come up for air.

19.

Toward the end of November, smitowicz finishes *The Liberators*. Total page count: 1,585 handwritten yellow sheets. It's bittersweet. The biggest accomplishment of his life—not just his writing life, but his *life*. Yet it's burdened by the crushing weight of the Prison Vortex's gravity; a type in constant flux, like the Earth's gravity in *Slapstick* by Kurt Vonnegut. Right now the Vortex's gravity is on a heavy swell . . . and yet it still hasn't reached its zenith [or rather *nadir*].

He finished the massively ambitious tome just in time, too. Literally just a few days before his last little pittance of Klonopin—0.5 mg in the morning—runs out and he's completely off it and it's torturous. He's unable to sleep more than a few hours a day for a couple *weeks* straight. Just like back in Stateville, awake all the way through each interminable, endless night. Yearning always for 2 a.m. That's when TBS plays a couple movies back-to-back, and sometimes they're not terrible. Surviving for almost four more months like this is unthinkable; if nothing changes, his suicidal depression will surely shift from this ambivalence-about-living to the ideation stage. The *yep-I-wanna-die-just-to-stop-this-suffering* mindset. Then something does change: **It gets even worse.** smitowicz receives a Health Care summons. His Tramadol prescription from Dr. Hartman, now long-gone, is about to expire.

Unaware of the terrible events to come, inmate smitowicz visits the new Doctor—term used loosely, and with a caveat: a person may be legally permitted to place the letters *M* and *D* after his name, but that does not make him a true caregiver! Dr. White is bald and very short, with glasses, pale skin, and whitish-gray hairtufts sprouting from his ears. He's convinced, or at least pretends to be, that smitowicz's knee pain stems from arthritis. Even though this has been ruled out by [1] smitowicz's orthopedic surgeon; [2] his rheumatologist; [3] his chronic pain specialist; and [4] Dr. Williams right here at Jacksonville, after examining the x-rays taken when he first arrived in June 2010. But Dr. White is gung-ho. *Then take new x-rays to see if there's any evidence for arthritis*, smitowicz suggests with a hint of demand. Nope! The Doctor wants to try smitowicz on 7.5 mg of Mobic, a common NSAID [Non-Steroidal Anti-Inflammatory Drug]. Even though smitowicz has tried, with zero effect on his knee pain, *four* other NSAIDs in the last few years: Ibuprofen, Aspirin, Naproxen, and Celebrex. He even developed severe stomach pain, commonly associated with long-term NSAID use. Probably an ulcer. White won't be dissuaded though; fuck that heap of silly "evidence"! smitowicz acquiesces: *Yeah, fine, whatever—I'll try* anything *that might help.* The Mobic doesn't, though. Doesn't have the slightest effect. smitowicz returns to Dr. White two weeks later to report back. Do you think this Doctor allowed that to convince him? Ha! He now wants to try smitowicz on 15 mg of Mobic. "I had a patient," White says, "who didn't respond to 7.5 milligrams, but when I increased it to 15, it helped tremendously!"

Did that patient's x-rays show evidence of arthritis? smitowicz asks.

"Oh, definitely. He definitely had arthritis."

But my x-rays don't *show evidence! How's that patient's situation comparable to mine?*

"I'd like to try you on 15 milligrams of Mobic."

Fine. If that'll make you happy—and help you rule out arthritis! I also need a refill on my Tramadol, please. It's especially important now that the Psychiatrist is taking me off Klonopin.

"Well. I'd like to see how you do on the 15 milligrams of Mobic, without any other pain medication."

smitowicz is enraged to yet another level [how many levels *are* there?! this is starting to seem reminiscent of the Great Stairway in *House of Leaves*]. First, Dr. White said if Mobic didn't work they could stick with Tramadol. Mobic didn't work, but instead of leaving things the way they've been for some 18 months, a way that's enabled smitowicz to function, White is taking away the medication that *works* and doubling down on one that *doesn't*. Can you see, Beloved Reader, how senseless, shitty, and facepalmingly moronic this is? I sure hope so. smitowicz can see it. I can as well. Can you?

smitowicz is unable to withstand any more of this. Being denied Klonopin was one thing; now he'll be getting *zero* pain meds, too? This is it—the big one. The moment smitowicz finally cracks, loses his shit, and unleashes on a Staff Member [emphasis on *Member*]. An eruption that's been building since day one.

"Are you a fucking *sadist*?" he says to the Doctor, voice clear and strong and loud. "Do you enjoy inflicting pain on people?"

The Doctor chuckles, shaking his down-tilted head.

"Do you keep little kittens at home so you can torture them whenever you like? Because you sure seem to enjoy torturing your patients here at the prison!"

He says that that's ridiculous.

"This is a terrible, idiotic plan. You're a shit Doctor. A sadist. Quack."

smitowicz is vaguely aware this will likely bring huge trouble, but he's acting on Anger Autopilot. The Doctor closes smitowicz's file and stands up. Says he'll see smitowicz in a couple weeks.

smitowicz steps down to the tile floor from the vinyl-cushioned exam table, knees stiff, and follows the Doctor out. "Fucking *sadist*," he growls. "Fucking HACK!"

inmate smitowicz marches straight to the front desk and requests to please speak to Ms. Sudbrink, the by-now-far-more-familiar-than-we'd-like-her-to-be Health Care Administrator. Becky Sudbrink takes smitowicz into an exam room and asks what the problem is. He sits on the table and tells her about the Doctor's asinine plan, and how it amounts to complete medical neglect. "It says in our Orientation Manual that 'Health care is a right, not a privilege,'" he tells her. "This is not health care. This is *sadism*."

"I can't prescribe you any medication, and I can't force the Doctor to do anything," she says.

"I know that. But can't you ask him to review my chart, and perform another x-ray to see whether there's actually any evidence for arthritis?" smitowicz speaks calmly, pleading his case. He's not demonstrating the slightest anger or aggression toward Sudbrink.

"He's the Doctor, and there's nothing I can do about his decisions." She begins walking out.

"Then you need to find another Doctor, because this one is a pitiful quack."

Sudbrink shoots a glance back at smitowicz with what'll prove to be prophetic abhorrence.

The Doctor must've reported smitowicz's angry tirade, because after lunch, a Lieutenant walks into his room. "Pack up," he tells inmate smitowicz. "Yer goin t' Seg." He handcuffs smitowicz in the Bubble. Then on the Walk, yanking smitowicz alongside, he snarls, "Hurry up."

"Bad knees. I'm walking my normal speed, Sir."

"Walk faster, or I'll drop yer ass t' the ground 'n drag you."

The Segregation wing is part of the same building as Health Care; smitowicz somehow finds a way to appreciate this irony. The Lieutenant stuffs him into an unoccupied cell after a full strip-search. This is it—the culmination of a year and a half of frustration, helplessness, mistreatment, and hopeless anger . . .

In truth, though . . . .

for what it's worth . . . .

smitowicz is surprised he didn't get sent to Seg a *lot* sooner!

PART 4

The Final Stretch
[*Goin Home Goin Home Holy Shit Am I Really Actually Going* <u>*Home*</u> *Holy Sh . . .*]

I.

Two weeks later, I'm once more wearing a ridiculous Big Bird jumpsuit. Sitting on a bus, about to be sent on a "Disciplinary Transfer" to Logan Correctional Center. Thank Earth it's only about an hour's drive! To be sure, my stomach is knotted in trepidation—going to a medium-security facility, especially with only three months and change left on my sentence, poses a whole new set of difficulties. But I've learned to take this nightmare not even day-by-day, but *problem-by-problem*. The rest is just details.

My two weeks in Jacksonville's Segregation were bad, but could've been a *lot* worse. [That's become, like, the benchmark for notable experiences within the Prison Vortex, hasn't it? I.e. *This is awful, but at least it's not* ____ *!*] Seg was comprised of six two-man cells in a single row. With a shower stall at the front end—available M-W-F—and a door that opened into the Seg-exclusive "Yard" at the far end, to which we had access for up to an hour every weekday. To call the "Yard" pathetic, and to wrap the word in quotation marks, are patent understatements. It was nothing more than a 15' by 15' concrete block. Enclosed in its own chainlink fencing. A netless basketball hoop stood near the door, looking slouched in depressive neglect. The ball weathered to a smooth, pitiful thing in a cracked and faded rust-orange. And also borderline worthless, the ball—limp and sluggish from extreme underinflation. I went out for 15 to 30 minutes every day it wasn't raining, and one day that it was, so I could at least inhale some fresh air and be outside the cell and get some dim semblance of exercise. Walking in short little loops—and once again wearing those thin ole canvas Karate Joe shoes that feel like you're clomping on the concrete with nothing but a tanktop wrapped around your feet. The best day outside was the day it was raining, strangely. It felt nice; a superfine drizzle more like fast-moving dew than actual rainfall. This happened to be on Xmas morning. Not that the holiday means anything to me anymore.

Aagh, this is too much information [TMI], too many specific details, for a quick summation of my time in Seg. Let's switch to a rapidfire recount. First, some of the shittier parts . . .

[1] Reading material. Or more like lack thereof; since they take away your property boxes while you're in Seg, you can only read what they have up front in the control room. There were no more than 15 books to choose from, and a few issues each of half a dozen magazines. I read *three* Dean Koontz novels during my time "In the Hole," and anyone who knows me knows I fucking despise Koontz and his cookie-cutter, write-by-numbers, terrible-prose-filled books.[110]

[2] Seg is Seg, and Seg always tests your threshold for boredom. Especially with nothing good to read, no electronics, etc. It got so excruciatingly boring that I actually *tried to perform fellatio on myself*. Simply to break up the monotony. And, to answer a question you almost certainly don't want to think about, No—my attempt was not successful. [Must you legitimately suck yourself to completion for autoerotic-fellatio enthusiasts to label it successful? or is it sufficient to merely stretch your cock into your mouth and bob once or twice?]

---

[110] I even created a Venn diagram demonstrating the absurd, laughable repetitiveness of certain themes in his oeuvre's 60+ book titles, which [if you so choose] you can chortle and shake your head at in bemused disbelief on my Author Blog here: www.jansmitowicz.com/blog/2016/10/15/terrible-dean-koontzs-terrible-book-titles/

[3] Stress. The stress of not knowing my fate, since you spend a good couple-few days in Seg before even receiving your disciplinary violation writeup copy—see below—and then another several days before meeting with the Major Infraction Hearing Committee to plead your case and learn what your punishment will be. This part was especially bad for me, as the charges turned out far more serious, overwhelmingly serious, than I'd expected even the worst case scenario to be.

See, for the first couple days, I assumed the *Doctor* wrote me up on an Insolence charge for badmouthing him. But no; turns out it was actually that Health Care Administrator Sudbrink asshole who wrote my ticket— and she trumped up the charges *even more* than Officer Forkface ever did! Something I might've thought impossible. That scumbag-lady wrote me up for Insolence and INTIMIDATION/THREATS; as you can probably guess, that is some serious, *serious* shit. We're talking potential time- added-to-your-sentence bad! First the truth. What happened in reality— the Prison Vortex's kaleidoscopically skewed version of reality, anyway— is that Sudbrink and I were in the exam room. I was sitting on the vinyl table in a hunched, benumbed posture, simply making an impassioned plea against Dr. White's idiotic plan. That's it. Go back a few pages to the scene if you want; just like with Officer Forkface the Fuckface, I rendered everything precisely as it happened to the best of my ability. Said ability being pretty damn accurate, because I wrote about it in great detail to Rachel and kept those letters for just such an occasion. But Sudbrink had grown increasingly weary of my presence. I'm certain she'd been yearning for some time to get rid of me; fed up with my ceaseless resistance to their neglectful medical bullshit, steadfast assertion of my civil rights, outside supporters—especially Dr. Jim—calling on my behalf, and, perhaps most of all, the ways I helped/encouraged *other* inmates to know their rights and not hold back in demanding them. This incident just sent her over the edge. Pissed her off enough to finally take aggressive action. It also prov- ided a convenient opportunity for her to utilize Staff Members' greatest weapon against us, a her-word-vs.-mine situation wherein she could play the terrified cowering little victim and railroad me out of her life for good.

So you already have the truthfully depicted scene from me. Ready for her laughably over-the-top version? In the ticket writeup, she harped again and again on how she felt <u>physically threatened</u>.

[*Is this bitch seriously ferreal?* I thought with increasing horror, sitting there in my cell reading her insane chickenscratch.]ᴵᴵᴵ

She wrote that I was being extremely intimidating in the exam room; viz., "His body language was very tense with fists balled up and become [sic] more and more red and tense and keep [sic] yelling at me and arguing"—

[*oh gawd please no let this nightmare end*]

And that she "was scared and feel [sic] extremely intimidated because his body language I thought [huh?!] inmate smitowicz was going to hit me"—

[*shitfire hellbastard I'm FUCKED! As if my remaining three months weren't gonna be agonizing enough already, I'm lying on my stomach in Seg reading this vile cunt's halfwit-ramblings growing more and more shellshocked, heart hammering breaking out in a cold sweat as the Black Dread tightened its crushgrip on my entire being . . .*]

And finally that, "he walked extremely close behind me continuing to yell and make threatening remark [sic] as he followed right behind me all the way back into the waiting room."

These jawdropping and ludicrous claims left me with multiple interminable Segregation-days of gutcramping anxiety. Front and center in every waking moment until at last I met with the two-person Major Infraction Committee. I beseeched them: the Psychiatrist recently took me off my anti-anxiety meds, I'm in terrible pain, I may've been insolent but I was *absolutely NOT* yelling at her—if anything, my tone was more *bitchy* than threatening! "Just please," I implored, "please please don't add time to my sentence!" The Committee responded with shocking sympathy, assuring me I wouldn't be punished *that* severely—but that it'd probably be best if I were to leave Jacksonville. Their final verdict: One month in Seg, two months' C-grade, and a disciplinary transfer to a medium-security facility. Whatever man, I only have a few months left!

A final eye-rolling absurdity came out of this. I saw Dr. Camerer one last time before the transfer to Logan. Turns out they'd hired an actual

---

ᴵᴵᴵ In fact, the initial ticket she wrote was so incredibly illegible—like to the point where fully 90% of it could've been some Slavic language minus those zany pronunciation/accent marks, and the remaining 10% was wild guesswork—so bad that they made her rewrite the ticket. *Even the second one,* for which she was expressly directed to write legibly, was still very difficult to decipher. Kinda hilarious, despite the terrifying circumstances.

onsite Psychiatrist to replace Koko. "Oh, that's good for my friends here," I told Camerer. "Because that guy was an awful, *awful* Doctor!" No longer giving the slightest fuck what she thinks of me. But then she made a startling admission; she said, "Yeah, he was a . . . problematic Doctor. Messed up a lot of people's mental health care." Wait, WHAT?! I can still feel the unhinged *clunk* from my jaw. Eyes and mouth all wide open. How nice of her to admit Koko was a terrible quack who put many dozens of us through utter hell—*after* the damage had already been done! When I dropped a grievance letter like the day after his Kwacko Crusade was initiated, she signed off on Sudbrink's response. Writing that there was nothing at all wrong with Koko's medical treatment. Like a good little bootlicking #*Yessir* shill. NOW she would concede that he wreaked havoc on inmate psyches prisonwide, when it no longer made a goddamn lick of difference! Well, but hey . . . at least she gave me that whiff of satisfaction, tainted though it was by the whole situation's absurdity and futility and indignation. My only real joy from her concession comes in knowing that *she knows* she willfully helped sabotage her patients' mental health—to, like, truly agonizing levels of anguish and torment—and she did it merely for the unconscionable purposes of protecting the Bureaucratic Machine! Rubberstamping the actions of a Doctor she *knew* was causing active harm. Was it worth it, *Frau Doktor*? Does it feel good knowing you defended the morally reprehensible? That you strongly aided the torturous Koko the African Fuckin Kwack's Anti-Clonazepam Crusade [K.A.F.K.A.-.C.C.]? Man, I really hope this book reaches a huge audience. It'd make all my anguish oh-so-worthwhile to expose all of you fucking crooked-ass liars, sadists, hypocrites, and dipshit Podunk halfwit losers! That's one reason I chose—for the scummiest cunts I encountered—to use real names. Officers Cook and Batterson and Patton [*Forkface, DoucheBeast, and balding Ms. Piggy*, respectively], Sergeant Johnson [gross old creep with the smarmy mustache], Major Robinson at I.A., Dietary's [T]watson, Drs. Camerer and Koko, Health Care Admin Becky Sudbrink . . . You all deserve to be called out and exposed at the very least. I only wish I could remember more of the bastards' real names! Elitist, powerdrunk, despicable fucking idiots in every way; fleshy mounds of human excrement. Fuck you, and everyone like you. Please die a slow and relentlessly agonizing death!

Sorry, my Dear Beloved Reader[s]. Hope I didn't lose any of you—I simply **HAD** to get that out of me, and more importantly out into the world! So . . . uhhm . . . ah yes, Seg! I do believe that's where I veered scandalously off course. Despite its overwhelming shittiness, I must admit that there were *some* pleasant aspects to being in Segregation:

[1] Privacy, real extended privacy, for the first time since like my one day spent alone at Stateville before craig arrived. Can you imagine what full-on privacy feels like after having had NONE for 18 months?! I do get placed in another dude's cell for a few days; he's incredibly obnoxious, e.g. smacking his head several times an hour—*thwap! thwap! thwap! thwap!* From a letter to Rachel: *I'm bored outta my mind, and hurting damn bad. My cellie is a black guy who farts all day and breaks into terrible, misogynistic monotone rapping, and uses his palm to loudly and vigorously smack his head all day, **hard**, instead of scratching—because "It pulls the hair out t'scratch."* Luckily, an empty cell becomes available and they let me switch.

[2] A few of the nights, that lovely Nurse _____ is the one who comes by to dole out meds, and each time she manages to include a Tramadol pill; with the hellacious pain from having my Klonopin *and* Tramadol taken away, this is yet again phenomenally helpful, providing a few hours of slight yet still oh-so-precious relief.

[3] Food. For some reason, the meals delivered to our cells in Styrofoam boxes thrice a day are loaded with literally double the normal amount of food.

Other than that, Seg is shit and it's a huge relief when I'm sent off on my disciplinary transfer to Logan.

Now, I could go into painstaking [emphasis on *pain*] detail about my last three months. Hell, if you've read this far, you know I could produce an entire book about my time at medium-security Logan! But I won't put you—US—through that. Won't go into tremendous, soulwrenching detail about my incarceration's final stretch. Know why?

You've heard it all before.

There are plenty of disparities between Jacksonville and Logan. Yet the main differences are fairly minor details. Like how I now reside in a four-man cell instead of those 20-man dorms, and Logan has twice the inmate population [≈2,000], and the Vegan Trays are absolute guttertrash compared to J-ville's. Though still of course better than the animal-flesh-and-secretion-based meals! Also, Logan's scenery is breathtaking and lovely, especially after suffering Jacksonville's utter barrenness. The closest actual tree at J-ville was several hundred yards beyond the fences. Visible only as colors and ambiguous shapes. But Logan contains *dozens* of trees, lining the sidewalks that run throughout its grounds. Being right up close to them after all this time is almost *revelatory*. A sort of homecoming, in the titular words of a U2 song. My new unit sits in Logan's extreme southwest corner—which is surrounded by scattered copses of oak and other hardwoods! Far more nonhuman neighbors here, too: I see four or five feralish cats on a regular basis; raccoons skulk all over the place; various avian species occupy the trees and bushes; there's even a family of deer that lounges on a hillside not 50 yards from my unit; heading to and from Medline, we see them almost every night. Here's a satellite image of said prison-corner, with my new unit on the far left [Logan's much too sprawling for an adequate all-encompassing shot; but notice all the winter-spindly trees in this small chunk alone—and then compare it to the overhead view of Jacksonville inserted just after Rachel's visits at the beginning of *Part 3*]:

So *that's* pretty damn wonderful. In the ways most substantial, though, Logan and J-ville operate on the same general frequency—except Logan's dial is notched up a little higher in volume and intensity. Interpersonal disputes tend to be more serious, with legit fights breaking out on a regular basis. Lot more of the sketchy stuff going on here, too: drugs, tattoos, all the usual higher-security-prison fare. A natural extension of the much greater privacy inherent to having cells rather than populous, open dorms. One night I unwittingly return to my old ways of trafficking illicit substances; in this case, improvised tattoo ink [typically produced by igniting Styrofoam under a [steel] bedframe or toilet, then scraping off the black residue and mixing it with soap]. This comes about when a friend at Medline asks me to deliver a miniature shampoo bottle to someone in my unit; I conceal it under my jacket's cuff, assuming it's nothing more than, y'know, *shampoo*. But then he informs me what it really is—woops! dude, so much for plausible deniability!

Aaand this should surprise not one of my Dear Readers: The Doctor here is utter shite, just like 90 percent of the other derelict turds. Except this dickhole's stoic disregard and lack of compassion is perhaps second only to Kwacko Koko! He refuses to prescribe *anything* for my pain. Asserting that under no circumstance will they provide opioids for more than a few days following a dramatic injury. However, you stupid fuck [the Dr., not you, Dear Reader!—I'd *never* disparage someone intelligent and judicious enough to read me! *winks*], you must be a real goddamn idiot if you think anything will remain a secret among prisoners! A guy we go to Medline with—name withheld, because I *can* keep a secret—has a fractured collar bone and receives Codeine every night for at least *two months*. And apparently the injury's not too severe; dude plays table tennis every week. And apparently the medication's not too necessary for him; the dude often secretes it under his tongue to sell back in the unit! So fuck you too, DR. OBASI, you lying garbage-sack of sewage. Yehhp—I'm putting him on blast with his real name. Just like others of his despicable ilk [see Seg-tangent above]. Isn't it just fabulous, and so very unsurprising, so very *me*, that somebody who clearly doesn't need opioids manages to get them prescribed, while I'm in unrelenting anguish but cannot get them? Pretty sure now that ≈99.72% of Staff Members in prison have their heads jammed so far up their own assholes that they're in danger of disappearing up there . . . just *POP!* flashing out of existence. And also that they're fuckin unfathomable morons, like borderline retarded except without the innocent sweetness, and also massive criminals who deserve like quintuple life sentences with no possibility of parole. And also they are massive cunts. I'm sure of it!

As it turns out, my final three months are mentally gobbed together in a changeless stretch of anguished waiting. Whereas I wrote the 1,585-page Januscript of *The Liberators* in nine months—averaging seven pages per day [!!]—aside from a handful of scribbled missives, I write precisely ONE page my entire 90-plus days at Logan [a hilarious poem about the benefits of getting a vasectomy, which you can find on my website's blog]. And believe me, that lack of writing is *not* for lack of trying! Just too much pain and resultant inability to concentrate. From a letter to Rachel during the period:

Christ, it's like I can't even <u>think</u> when I'm undermedicated like this. It's a most subtle and yet exquisitely malicious form of psychological warfare. There aren't too many more wretched things you could do to a self-styled intellectual and writer than hinder their ability to form and maintain complex mental threads. To <u>concentrate</u>!

As I'm now far removed from the hideous experience, I can look back and at least appreciate the silver lining in four months' living without medication. Sometimes people begin taking narcotic pain meds for a legit injury, but end up becoming addicted. It's actually a tiny percentage— recall my 988/12 analysis and discussion rooted in *The Pain Chronicles*—but it *does* happen, and Murphy's Law seems like one of the few laws that apply well to my life. For those unfortunate few, their subsequent feelings of pain are just the body's sly *creation of reason* for them to continue medicating. Given certain cultural myths and misconceptions and prejudices, I naturally couldn't help but worry that might've been the case for me. All that unbearable time without meds, though, proved valuable in the long run. Because my pain-severity the week I was forced to stop remained identical *12-plus weeks later!* I underwent detox; then all opioid remnants that'd accumulated in my fat cells gradually sloughed away. Facilitating then a perfect, objective evaluation of my pain levels. After that, never again could anybody [including myself!] claim with any legitimacy that my pain was mere illusion. A figment of addiction lodged in my brain for the sole purpose of maintaining pharmaceutical intake. Nope—this maniacal bitch of a condition was and is still the real deal. Now that I've healed from those harrowing months of torture, distant reflection allows me to feel gratitude that at least *something* positive sprouted from all my overwhelming misery.

It goes without saying—but you know how I am, Dear Reader, so you know I'm of course gonna say it anyway: At the time, it DAMN SURE didn't feel worthwhile! Or that anything useful could possibly result! The pain → anxiety → *pain* → depression → **pain** cycle didn't become more tolerable over time, either. In fact, it got *even harder* to bear! The stress and torment and helpless feelings just piled up, more more more, growing heavier by the day . . . crushing my spirit and psyche under an ever-accumulating weightload, until eventually I sunk into suicidal yearnings. Well . . . maybe *suicidal* isn't the best term; I never quite had the full-on desire to kill myself . . . but I most certainly did not care to live anymore. [The difference may seem negligible, or even merely semantic, but not for me; I experience the two as noticeably distinct feelings.]

Without my meds' welcome bowel-regulating effects, and with Logan's barely edible meals that were starch-dominant and perilously low in fruits and veggies, I was shitting three, four, sometimes *five times a day*. For unknown reasons, my bathroom shitting-time was always prime territory for the death-urges. While I layered the seat with toilet paper before sitting down, a mantra would run ceaselessly, uncontrollably through my head every damn time: *Please kill me gawd please kill me gawd please, please kill me, why am I still alive, I don't even believe in you so if you DO exist I totally deserve to be killed for constantly shitting* [NPI] *on you and even more so on religion! so what the hell, fuckin kill me dude, stop being such a pussy cuz I'll never stop shitting on religion so you should execute me NOW, please kill me gawd please kill me gawd please, take my life right now, RIGHT NOW GODDAMNIT, I'm not remotely kidding, please kill me please kill me please please please kill me kill me* **kill me fucking KILL ME***!!!* No hyperbole—that exact stuff tore through my mind like a learned Tasmanian Devil geeked outta his skull on bathtub crank. Every time. Constantly. Then I'd take yet another shit within an hour or two, embarking on the walk of shame from my end-of-the-row cell to the long hallway's extreme opposite side . . . guys laughing and making snide remarks about me and my bowels' mind-boggling hyperactivity, and about veganism [the only thing I bothered to speak out in defense of during these times] . . . and then get roasted *again* by the ubiquitous dozenish guys playing cards/chess/whatever in the hallway as I returned all the way back to its far end . . . mocked and laughed at on both sides of my suicide-obsessive toilet occupancy . . . only back in the peaceful cell would that speedfreak-mantra subside [such thoughts still present though, constantly, just reduced to a muted din; or, when I was lucky, sometimes dwindling to a spot *juuuuust* north of my subconscious mind]. Then I'd gain a measure of reprieve from those odd and inexplicably geospecific death-yearns, a pleasant degree of remission . . . until, of course, my next inevitably soon trek to the bathroom.

2.

Every day's the same. You're wrenched from dreams of the Free World. [Those familiar, painful images that'll *soon!* become reality again: among magical Humboldt's towering redwoods with your sweet pittie and your soon-to-be wife, fog rolling in to nasally reveal its secret relation to the sea, my body and hers drawing together, close enough to share oxygen . . .] Torn away from it by your friend and bunkmate emad: *Yo cellie—Medline! Let's go!*

You toss on your blues—wincing at the achiness already present in your knees and lower back too—and a jacket and beanie because it's February and that frigid Midwestern wind, whipcracking outward from the Great Lakes across hundreds of flat-terrain-miles . . . man, can that wind ever *bite*. Mutter your bed number to the sleepy-eyed Guard as you slip out the door. You catch up to your cellie on the sidewalk and notice then that nighttime bestowed him with a bulbous whitehead in the blurry-skinned notch where his nose cuts an angle into his cheek. The pimple looks poised to burst in suppurating glory and you just wanna reach out and pop the damn thing; it's discomfiting and gruesome, you're itching to get it over with. This is what your life has become? Oh, but don'tcha dare pause to dwell on *that* one, buddy. Trust me here.

You pass in twos through the Health Care unit's glass doors. ID card unclipped from your collar, you hand it to the front desk Guard. Then corral yourselves into the glasswalled waiting room—claustrophobe's nightmare—with seating enough for about 24 people. But there are what like 60 people inside? and someone farts jeezus they *rip ass* in that tiny cramped room. Come on; really dude? Stink spreading like mustard gas, the descriptive word that comes to mind is . . . *gamey*. Hear the groans ripple out in a wavelike pattern. Guys clutching beanies over their faces' bottom halves. You groan too, pulling up your t-shirt collar to rest over your nose. Smelling your own bodily funk; didn't have time to apply deodorant before leaving "the crib," but your own B.O. is infinitely better than the sausagefart now threatening to get at your nostrils through the shirt's thin cotton fabric. Your eyes actually *water*. As you thought before—like fuckin mustard gas. Last night's cock-in-the-sock tray recalled via that vile sausagefart. The Officer on duty is sick of hearing the inmate brouhaha of groans and angry muttering, so she shoves closed the hinged door. Now there's *no* ventilation. Awesome.

emad's talking. You're half-listening, but largely focused on watching someone else.

Cellie. g-dog, man, I don't know how much longer I can take that guy.

Your friend mikey is lined up outside the fartbox now, standing against the white brick wall leading to the counter where they dispense little plastic thimblecups containing each inmate's medication.

He's pushin me, cellie. I gotta put a stop to it. No matter what could happen. You dig? I wanna write down my parents' information in case somethin happens you can let em know.

mikey is next in line. He's a scrawny, bald junkie of 30-plus years; his blue jacket is an XL, which is at least two sizes too big and so the jacket sleeves hang down past his fingernails. He has a glazed-over look in his eyes—probably intentional, as he's trying to grift the System by convincing them he's a paranoid schizophrenic so they'll give him drugs and also free state housing when he gets released. A long-running scheme going back as far as Stateville, where he apparently tried to climb out of the cell through its 1'x6" chuckhole—somehow managing to get an entire leg outside before Staff arrived to find him shrieking in [mock-] terror that his cellmate was planning to kill and eat him.

Will you do that for me, cellie? If I hafta fight g-dog 'n go to Seg, will you please contact my parents so they know I'm okay when they don't hear from me?

Your knees are killing; it's like you weigh 400 pounds, the twist-grinding clamp cinching tighter and tighter; every minute it's like you've gained another 30 pounds and the pressure's commensurately intensifying. That's why you're laser-focused on mikey. He **might** be able to help this unspeakable hurt that invades your world's every nook and quarter. Terrorizing down to the hour-minute-*second*. It's been two months now since *Herr Doktor* Koko and *Herr Doktor* White abolished your pain medications in toto. NO SENTIENT BEING, human and nonhuman alike, should have to endure these levels of pain; nor should they be forced to suffer so much, for such an extended duration. No matter their health insurance-status. No matter if they're in prison.

But you have zero non-fleeting recourse. *Herr Doktor* Obasi cannot be reasoned with. Nor can anybody else with any modicum of power. Your outside supporters can't do a thing without further jeopardizing your release! [recall Major Robinson and his threats—exquisitely ironic threats, now that you think about it—of charging *you* with Extortion.] Your *sole* potential for relief lies in that scrawny, middle-aged junkie: His simple human decency, his empathic kindness, his concern for your suffering. All of which surpass—by motherfucking light years—whatever iota of perfervidly suppressed concern **may be** present in ALL the Prison-Industrial

Complex's #*Yessirs* combined! So very much depends on mikey's skillful execution there at the Medline counter. An utterly staggering amount of dependence! Indescribable, unfathomable even by you! The value of a little relief . . . no matter how temporary . . . is impossible to express. Impossible also to overstate. Greater than the sum of its individual elements; like, dizzyingly so. I mean, look at it this way—what on Earth *wouldn't* you give to stop the ruthless torture of your dearest, most beloved pet or buddy or partner? Even if you knew straightaway that their reprieve would only last a few hours . . . what price wouldn't be worth paying just to end their screaming agony?! There. That's the clearest portrait I'm capable of painting right here and now. Hopefully you can at least discern the shapes and colors existing therein, and hopefully that's sufficient. I did my best.

First thing mikey does is pluck out the three orange Neurontin pills from the Nurse's proffered cuplet; there's still a Celexa tablet sitting inside, but he's instituted a wellplanned strategy here that all feeds into his yearlong grift to establish credible behavioral patterns that'll land him his coveted official label of "paranoid schizophrenic." The dude is ridiculously committed—it's not quite like anything you've ever witnessed. See, he's worked hard for several months now to convince his Psych Doctors that he truly believes it's poisonous to swallow more than one type of medication simultaneously. He will never ever take all his meds in one shot. Not only does this aide the Doctors' and Nurses' desired perception, it allows him to take some pills there and save others for later. You happen to have the inside track on this crazy [NPI] but brilliant scheme; so you know he likes to secrete the Neurontin—an anti-seizure med also used for nerve pain, which you also take—beneath his tongue and hide them in his cell, eventually ingesting like 12 or 14 at once because it fucks him up. Gives him the closest thing to a heroin zonk he's found in here [other than the *actual* heroin that occasionally somehow makes its way into the prison— more on that shortly]. You also know that, as he tilts his head back and raises the little plastic cup, he's pressing tongue-tip up against soft palate. Now when he flips the pills into his mouth they tumble right into the convenient hiding space under his tongue. Then he sips from the cup of water they provide and makes an ostentatious show of swallowing, *gulp!* and so but when he opens his mouth to show the Nurse, she thinks he's indeed swallowed the pills. After he for-real-takes the Celexa, it's finally time for what you've been waiting and waiting on—*his* **Klonopin**. Yyyyehp, *he* gets Klonopin . . . except it's actually legitimate in this case because he has epilepsy; they only prescribe it here to help prevent seizures [supposedly anyway!] He receives two 2 mg tablets a day; but he insists that just one is sufficient. Summing it up with, *You need it way fuckin more than I do, brother!* He can spare each day's morning dose—*if* he successfully pulls his sleight-of-tongue trick, that is.

Cellie, will you do that? Please man, I don't want my parents to be worried if they don't hear from me.

The Nurses' standard protocol is to crush up meds like Klonopin—ones that have value as intoxicants—into a fine powder to discourage inmates from tonguing such pills and later selling them.

Cellie?

Hold on, I finally tell him. *We'll talk back in the dayroom, okay? Promise.* It's my turn to exit the fartbox and I get in line at the dispensary station just as mikey is tipping the cup and its powderized Klonopin mouthward. My nerves buzz. Blood coursing throughout my body with what seems like hypervascular throbbing—if such a thing does indeed feel the way I feel it'd feel. You feel me?[112] *Please let him get away with it. Please, Nurse, PLEASE don't ask to see under his tongue!*

mikey takes a couple dainty sips of water and opens his mouth for the Nurse, tongue no doubt gently pressed against bottom inner lip. Then he shuffles outside. [His every movement and mannerism while in or near Health Care have been pondered at length and then carefully selected for optimal chances of success in his grand scam! He always affects that glazed, only-sorta-with-it mien, which the dude's mastered to the point where—among our little crew of dark-humored Medliners—*we* can't even always be sure if it's just that purposeful put-on, or if maybe he's blitzed outta his skull on a fistful of Neurontin or whatever the hell else he manages to get his junkie hands on! Sometimes, in the waiting room [first making sure it'll be witnessed by at least one Nurse or Staff Member], he'll engage in angry, ultraconspicuous verbal confrontations . . . *with his own blurred reflection* in the glass windows. And so on. Every last little minutia of his intentional madness is juicy, uproarious stuff. Providing some of my few truly joyful moments of escape during those final—and of course interminable, overwhelming, torment-drowned—few months.]

---

[112] [*Ed. note: Rec'd removing that one altogether*] *NOTE: REMEMBER TO CUT FROM NEXT DRAFT!*

mikey halts outside the entrance, bending over to tie his shoes. He is indeed waiting for me—but why? Does he merely want my company on the walk back, or is he also planning to bestow upon me the chemical fruits of his sly efforts? Could go either way. So I'm still anxious as ever. Dying to just find out already, good or bad. I slam my Celexa and Neurontin— which latter I'm almost certain does nothing for my actual pain. It does help me fall asleep though, so I'll continue taking it for now. As you saw in Stateville—and, to an even greater [plus much much longer] extent during those final, bad-acid-trip-like, de-Klonopinned and -Tramadolled several weeks at Jacksonville—sleeping difficulties only further intensify my suffering.

I catch up with mikey on the sidewalk. His index finger's crammed two-knuckle-deep under his tongue. He's digging and gathering, pushing everything in there together to form a single mudlike clump. "Ah gah oo!" he exclaims as we walk. "Hole ahn." YES! HE SUCCEEDED!! Mental relief utterly engulfs me at once. My eyes moisten with joytears—or maybe they're just simple old tears of relief—and I have to legit struggle not to break down crying at my imminent liberation from this misery. The chemically/mikey-induced mercy will only last till about mid-afternoon; but, given the Dumpster-fire that is my life these last three months at Logan, being granted a few hours of pain-reprieve seriously feels like I've received an unexpected pardon from the firing squad. Dostoevskyesque? Absolutely! But remember: By this point, I've largely willed myself to occupy a carved-out niche of mental existence wherein life progresses not so much in a smooth and linear continuum, but rather in a series of herky-jerky fits and starts from one obstacle to the next. Trying—with all my might, and all my mighty cultivated powers of agony-suppression—not to glance more than a few hurdles at a time into the future. So yes, oh yes indeed: Within this purgatorial darkness I now hobble around in from one miserable day to the next, *two or three* **hours** of comparatively wholesale escape/relief DOES feel like being pardoned from a horrible death!

Little by little, mikey scoops all the #Klonopaste out from the underside of his tongue and smudges it onto my palm. Then I scrape off what I can with my teeth, artichoke-like, and lick up the rest. Gross? Sure. Dangerous from a variety of angles? Definitely. Paradoxical behavior, given my mild germophobia and overall revulsion at sharing anything—let alone *saliva!*— with eaters of animal carcasses and pus/blood-tainted bovine mammary secretions and unfertilized menstrual products from chickens? You bet yer ass it's an outlandish behavioral paradox! But does the #Klonopaste's sub-sequent effects render all those issues totally inconsequential? Yes. Yes indeed it does, very much so. At this point I couldn't care less about the riskiness, grossness, etc. Some people will no doubt label me a hopeless pill-popper [first the Stateville snorting-routine, now this]. That's fine though. Label me all you want—if you've come this far down the rabbit hole with me, seeing everything I've been through and dealt with, and you nonetheless believe with all your heart that I'm no different from a junkie, said heart is functioning poorly, with a regrettable dirth of empathy. And NOTHING will change your mind; nothing short of personal experience and/or witnessing the relentless soul-hole-fucking of my own medical history enacted on someone you love [i.e. your mindset will remain narrow and incorrect, trapped in the status quo's highly limiting box, until or unless you become capable of feeling *intense empathy* [an emotion that may well be the single most underrated human emotion among the whole lot of them]!].[113]

Once the Klonopin kicks in a half hour later, for the next three hours I'm blissfully relaxed. Concerned about nothing. Sprawled out in my bed until Chow—but instead of watching TV, I'm actually able to read! Blazing through over 100 pages on a Dave Eggers book, whereas I'd normally have trouble slogging through 20 at once, even in the least uncomfortable of

---

[113] Isn't it sad—terribly, tragically sad—that so damn many humanoids seem incapable of compassion & understanding . . . *until the issue affects them* **personally?** I see it all the time! A couple prominent & stark examples may help clarify, viz. [1] Dick Cheney: it was against gay marriage until its daughter came out as a lesbian, and *only then*—when it had a personal loved one negatively affected by antigay sentiment—did it start feeling [sic?] that its disgusting position on the issue was inappropriate; so basically, it didn't give a shit about gay rights until it felt [sic?] a personal connection. That's textbook cunty self-centeredness, folks! [2] Much more generalized than the first example, it irritates me to no end when people are apathetic and don't give a shit about promoting good causes . . . like, say, helping children with cancer . . . until such an issue affects *them*. All these anti-cancer warriors—where were they before *their* child got cancer? I'm gonna hazard a guess that they were willfully oblivious. Of course it's great they're advocating for a meaningful cause, but how bout we participate in social advocacy because it's the right thing to do, without first needing the whole self-interest deal to kickstart it? Ugh. That's one reason I so love animal rights activists & Earth liberationists. Fighting for causes that don't even directly impact you per se— that's TRUE heroism!

times. I still have pain of course; but the medication I should've never been taken off in the first place renders that pain distant, of little concern or consequence. A wonderful reprieve.

mikey is a true hero. Wiping the paste onto my hand on the post-morning-Medline walk every time he's able to get away with it, amounting to three or four times per week. The reprieve this brings doesn't just last a few hours, either. Stressors and depression in prison is accumulative. So it makes the *entirety* of my time easier to deal with.

Except this sadly only lasts about a month. Then my release date seems to finally appear imminent. When I'm left with around six or seven weeks on my sentence, it feels *close*, and the reality starts sinking in. It *really is* gonna happen! Rachel and my family and friends are increasingly excited and anxious with every passing day. The relief—no matter how unspeakably precious—just becomes harder and harder to justify, given its huge inherent risk. I mean, my release could be pushed back if we get caught! So I feel no choice but to stop. Obligated to everyone who cares about me. *You can just stop trying to save it for me*, I tell mikey—with no small regret. *Sell it back in the unit if you want, whatever, but I can't take it anymore.* I expressed my appreciation to him countless times. But I want to do so in writing: thank you, buddy. You helped me get through one of the shittiest stretches more than you even know. *Thank you.*

3.

Most of my time at Logan is spent staring at the TV or hanging with one/both of the two guys who become truly good friends [I'd spend way more time with mikey and ryan and big will, our little Medline crew, but they're in a separate unit and so only chillable for that short time each day]. One is a Pakistani who, while intelligent and sensitive and funny, is also an unfortunate narcissist and compulsive self-aggrandizer. We receive definite solace in our mutual disdain for nearly everyone here, and our misanthropy in general. So we spend many hours together. Just chatting about life as we lounge in the dayroom—or in my cell where I can lie down and be less miserable. Life, philosophy, books . . . the imbeciles whose imbecility torments us . . . whatever we can find to kill the monotony. In a wonderful kindhearted gesture, he convinces his girlfriend to orchestrate a three-way call so I'm able to *speak to Rachel* on her birthday! I'm still on C-grade at the time. Unable to use my telephone account. My poor sweet darling is elated by the surprise contact; it's *so* lovely to hear each other's voices and talk in real time after many many weeks with no verbal communication!

My other good friend here is oddly similar to james back at Jacksonville. james, my Christian friend who was—and presumably still is—actually *Christ-like*. His name's emad: an Iraqi immigrant with strong Christian beliefs. Quite the enigma. Our narrow-minded fellow inmates have a hard time reconciling emad with their preconceived notions about Middle Easterners ["A-rabs," as they're referred to here]. He often passes for white, with his light skin and blue eyes and Christianity, aka non-Muslimness. But he has a chunky accent and speaks Arabic. He moves into my cell a couple weeks after my Logan residency begins and we hit it off almost immediately.

Sometimes I'm in so much pain I don't even want to get out of bed and walk a hundred yards to the Chow Hall for dinner. On such occasions, emad collects about four to six potatoes and secretes them in his pockets and jacket-arms, giving several to me. We'll eat noodles with plain beans and lukewarm potatoes. Once I'm finally off C-grade and able to shop at Commissary, I purchase a Y-cord so we can both plug our headphones into my TV or Walkman. We start listening to the local classic rock radio station every night as we drift off to sleep. It's one of the only aspects of daily life right now that provides any modicum of joy.

emad and I have very similar senses of humor, cracking each other up throughout the days. Again, much like james at Jacksonville. Except emad and I are *cellies*! So we get to hang out all the time, all day. One of our running jokes concerns the energy-sapping depression we both feel. I'll say something and then, seeking affirmation, follow it up with "You dig?" Then he'll respond, "Ya cellie, I dig—gonna *dig a hole* and get th' hell outta here!" This never fails to produce gales of laughter. Same with another fun trick we often pull; usually in the dull midday when our other two cellies are out at Yard. emad will start singing hymns in Arabic, loud enough to echo down the 50-yard hallway of cells. Even though ours sits at the very far end. I then try to mimic his singing, and it's atrocious. Top of our lungs, sputtering off and on to giggle like teenage girls. It's great. Even though guys think we're freaks, and "fags." We don't care. The shit is hysterical to us, and that matters infinitely more than what the troglodytic knuckle-dragging halfwits think.

emad saber "shawarma"—buddy, you may be a Christian, but I can't hold that against you! You helped me get through that awful period so damn much. Even found a way to make me *smile*-smile, and laugh uproarriously, despite my agonizing pain. Thanks pal. Shine On, You Crazy Diamond!

Opposite page—

Here's the final image of me inside a "Correctional" facility, taken just one day before my release; note my defiant smirk, stylish "fauxhawk" haircut, and, below the camera's purview but definitely implied, my joyous hardon for the six thousand-plus things I'm yearning and preparing to eat-hug-kiss-fuck-watch-listen-xxx-xxx-etc. *Peace out, assholes—I'm physically unable to run, but I'll STILL find a way to leave a trail of dust in my wake!*

EPILOGUE

Gone and Also Hopefully Able to be Forgotten at Least Eventually Anyway

[By That I Mean Prison—Hopefully I'm Able to Forget Prison, Although I'm Not Exactly Making it Easy on Myself by Writing and Publishing this Memoir Now Am I?]

A.

April 1, 2012—

MY RELEASE DATE!!

—at last rolls around, coming as it did in starts and stutters and blasts of acceleration and stalls and grinding apparent halts and, for the last few weeks especially, with the unbelievable-yet-long-known-inevitability of a Doctor's appointment at Jacksonville if I'd been staring at the clock unwaveringly for the final half hour, seconds c r a a a w l i n g into minutes and somehow, eventually, turning into hours-days-weeks-months. To be precise, 22.5 months. You assume such staggering moments of long-awaited expectation will, when they finally arrive, burst into your life like

Hiroshima. But that's not always the case. Sometimes your anticipation's focal point creeps up on you and then just sorta . . . happens. "Anticlimactic" doesn't even *begin* to delineate this feeling's outer edges; to describe escaping the Prison Vortex; but it may be the [pitiable] best word we have. That's what the actualization of my release is like.

It certainly doesn't help that—when an Officer comes to my cell at six a.m. to collect me and I bid my cellies goodbye: *See ya guys good luck stay free!* and then a much-deserved hug for the wonderful emad, then the Officer takes me outside to a waiting small transport truck they use to drive around the streetlined grounds and I stand at the back of the cargo area, door open, clutching tight to the freezing metal handbar as I watch my prison corner recede in the distance in the unfurling dawn, a chilly fogwisped spring morning that's strangely reminiscent of the one 22.5 months ago with Rachel on the way to S.F. International that began this narrative—*even then, I* **still** *don't know* if they're sending me home, or to a halfway house [which could be anywhere in the state], or what. My total ignorance as to where I'm going next . . . *Will I be back in California with Rachel & Rikki tonight? tomorrow? or will I spend weeks in blueballed gawdawful limbo, lingering in some shite-area of this shite-state—which I've heard, from numerous sources, has happened to tons of guys as they waited for their Interstate Parole paperwork to go through—one last Haha-fuck-you from the insane Prison-Industrial Bureaucrazy, a final parting gift of psychological warfare out of the now-clearly endless variety at its disposal* . . . this all serves to heighten the tragically withered sense of feeble anticlimax on what **should** be an unfettered celebratory day of glorious, even unprecedented glee.

It's just not right. Not fair. This is supposed to be MY DAY! My release date, finally finally at long everlasting long fucking last *finally* HERE! How can I let them ruin this for me? This *too*, after E.V.E.R.Y.T.H.I.N.G ELSE they've ruined?

. . . I can't. That's the answer. I can't let them ruin it!—not completely anyway, because, unless I go home today or at least find out *when* I'll be going home, an "anticlimactic" buzz will linger around my head no matter what. Nonetheless, I can do my best to enjoy bursting forth from the Vortex onto the other side of the fences; that alone is worth celebration. Yes, yes! *Out of the Vortex!* An innately joyous occasion; for, no matter where I end up laying my head to rest tonight, it'll be somewhere *other than* prison. That's a big, BIG leap forward. Even if I can't yet leap all the way to California.

And so, as I sit and sometimes stand and pace in a room in the prison's central control building for a couple hours, waiting for whatever outtake [rather than intake] procedures need to occur before I can leave to go ahead and *occur* already. Those last bits of paperwork and red tape. Thankfully, I'm now—through that sheer brute-willpower alone—eager to move on no matter where I'm headed, buzzing with kinetic excitement to embark on the very last stages of this wild odyssey.

After more than two hours of final interminable waiting, it's time. A Guard comes to collect me and a young black kid who's also being released with no one there to pick him up and we head for the front . . . for those gates . . . so close . . . a couple last signatures required, and then they give me a box with my meager belongings . . . and then oh gawd oh hell yes, then we're walking toward the gate . . . will the paved distance leading up to it stretch to near-infinity? Or maybe, no actually this makes way more sense, maybe approaching the gate I'll suddenly find myself sucked back by the Vortex's stupendous gravity, the gate acting as event horizon to the black hole of prison! . . .

NOPE—I'M OUT! OUT!! AHHHH OH YES I'M OW-OW-OUT!!! ☺

It's true. I made it. Omygawdyes MADE IT! Words can't even . . .

The Guard drives to the local Amtrak station and we wait in the DOC vehicle until the train arrives; he needs to ensure we get on the right train, and just *get on* period. I take a seat and it begins creaking forward and, just like that, I'm officially out of custody. I'm a free man.

More or less, anyway; turns out that [big surprise] my Interstate Compact hasn't been approved yet, so I'm being sent to a "Christian Men's Shelter" for the interim. It's about 150 miles away, in Rock Island—County and city—which is a mere ten miles from where I got arrested, the next county west of Henry. Just before exiting Logan, they gave me a printout with instructions on getting to the shelter via public transit, along with train and bus fare and the $170 or so left on my books. Cash money! a strange thing to see after 22.5 months during which funds only existed as either a nebulous figure in the computer system, or in the form of writeouts and noodles.

I learn before we've even climbed to full speed that there's a snack bar at the front of the train, and so I grab a wad of cash and hustle through several cars to hit it up. Hoping they have—yep, they sure do!—some kind of booze available, despite how it's not even ten a.m. yet. I'm not a fan of alcohol; not back then and especially these days, wherein I haven't had so much as a drop of liquor for months! But long-distance travel on public transportation is no cakewalk; and of course with my pain condition and no meds it's particularly awful. Not to mention the positively stupefying amount of time it'll take to get where I'm being sent. Per my printed itinerary sheet: I ride this train for about a half hour, then have a *five-hour* layover in the town of Normal, then bus an hour to Peoria [which I'm mildly interested in seeing, as it's my beloved Richard Pryor's hometown], another half hour of waiting, then finally a different bus for two-ish hours to Rock Island. Why *wouldn't* I want a little numbing alcohol buzz, early morning or not? So I order a vodka-cranberry juice and some pretzels and potato chips. The black woman behind me in line kindly offers to pick up the $12 tab. "You jus got outta prison, didn't you?" she says with a little smile.

"How'd you know?!"

"My lil nephew did a bit recently. I know how it is—you get out'n they jus send you on into the world with a few bucks, 'Good luck!'"

[Random black woman, the first person I speak to after getting out, has a close relative who's also done time. SHOCKER! But not really, of course—you read the statistics I gave, and saw my resultant nifty-though-staggering visual from Inter-Mission 2, right?] I beam at her.[114] "That's really really sweet of you, but I had plenty of funds left on my books, so I'm good. Thanks anyway! If you wanna help someone who truly needs it, there's a young black kid a few cars up I got out with . . ." She's all for it. So on the way back to my seat, I tell the dude he's got free snacks waiting for him, and he hurries off with a quick *Thanks mah dude.*

Know what? This is all fine and good, you and I both know damn well I could painstakingly describe every little step and stumble on my way home. Does anybody really want/need that though? Doubt it. So then, let's do narratively what I wish could've been done in real life, which is spend very little time in this bullshit lingering limbo-period that should've never had to happen in the first place. And *wouldn't* have happened . . . if not for the fact that, ostensibly, every last bureaucratic halfwit involved with my

---

[114] Turns out I'm gonna be one of those inexplicable ex-cons who tells like pretty much everyone in the world that they were in prison, from new acquaintances to cashiers innumerable to literally random people on the street.

California transfer-process, no matter how minor or brief, seems to have their heads planted deep in the sand, with both thumbs simultaneously crammed palmdeep into their own asses in a double-thumbs-up [-the-butt]. As if to congratulate themselves with a celebratory gesture of yet another job well fucked. I should hope that, this late in the memoir, my Dear Readers require no analysis or additional explanation as to my exact meaning with regard to the head-ass-thumbs Bureaucrazy-imagery.

So then . . . The trip to Rock Island sucked, but not nearly as much as anticipated. The endless five-hour layover in Normal was actually kinda cool, because I got to swing by its University of Illinois campus, where one of my favorite writers—David Foster Wallace, who tragically killed himself in 2006—taught various literary and writing classes for a time; also, I managed to get ahold of my wonderful longtime family doctor back home. She knew all about the medical purgatory I'd been stuck in, and had the awesome kindness and decency to phone a Tramadol prescription in to a CVS Pharmacy near the train station, so I had a glorious bit of relief for the arduous journey . . . The Christian Men's Shelter wasn't nearly as bad as I thought it would be and as it sounds; it was clean and mellow, and a guy in my dormroom [yehp, yet another bit of dorming-with-strangers] loaned me his library card and I got to read some stuff I'd been looking forward to . . . Sadly, not only were their communal meals not vegan-friendly, they somehow almost seemed *anti*-vegan; like, for example, stick-ing pigflesh "bacon" in the damn green beans—so I just ate Subway Veggie Delights every day. Even worse, all residents were required to attend a kind of church service-lite each weekday evening [again, so much for that alleged separation of church and state!], during which I just zoned out as much as possible . . .

Guess how long I ended up having to stay there, waiting, wondering every single day if that'd be the day my transfer *finally* went through. Five days? A week? Two weeks? No. That would've been bad enough. But no: I HAD TO STAY THERE FOR AN ENTIRE BLOODY *MONTH*! My gawd, you can't imagine—and I sure-shit don't wanna try conveying—just how un-goddamn-*bearable* those four weeks were.

It SUCKED. Let's just leave it at that.

Then it came. Finally, *finally* came: My transfer went through! I could now go home! Literally within five minutes of signing the Interstate Com-pact paperwork my Illinois parole agent brought to the shelter, I bought a plane ticket home; he came in the early afternoon, and I was on a plane by five p.m. [This trip involved one last whirlwind of painful, unbearable transport; here's my travel itinerary: catch a bus around the corner → Quad Cities Airport [yehp, the same one Mom and I flew into and out of, back between my arrest and incarceration] → Denver International → S.F. Int'l → RACHEL & RIKKI & NORCAL!!]

↓↓↓↓↓↓↓↓↓↓↓↓↓↓↓↓↓↓↓↓↓↓↓↓
GOIN HOME GOIN HOME GOIN HOME I'M GOIN HOME HOME HOME RACHEL & RIKKI & NORCAL

RACHEL RIKKI NORCAL
O GAWD SO EXCITING!!
↑↑↑↑↑↑↑↑↑↑↑↑↑↑↑↑↑↑↑↑↑↑↑↑

Honestly, we're almost to the end and I can't—or don't want to, more likely—do any more than say our feelings are exquisitely typified, in a perfect microcosmic representation, by this video Rachel took. It shows the very first few moments of me and Rikki together again after 23.5 months' utter separation. It's a carefully orchestrated and executed reunification that speaks volumes. And thank Earth for that, because I'm damn tired of writing as voluminously as I have been throughout this narrative. Here it is [**friendly warning**—you might wanna turn your volume down before watching due to Rachel's highpitched gleefulness]:

Alternatively, here's the direct link:
https://www.youtube.com/watch?v=O4pzhcWojHc&t=5s

B.

I'm back among my beloved redwoods, in Humboldt County—*the* redwoods, the North Coast, which has far and away the biggest, best, and greatest quantity of redwood forests and individual trees remaining after 95-plus percent have been annihilated by logging. California, where I belong and always have. Humboldt, where I belong and always have. We live here now—my wife and I, and of course our goofball pittie angel.

It's a fine spring day, sun shining bright in a picturesque cloudless sky. Redwoods tower all around us; you have to crane your neck way way back just for a distant glimpse of the nearly infinitely complex canopies, countless secondary trunks jutting out from the main boles and shooting up toward the sunlight in all these ancient giants. Creating scraggled proliferating masses of branches trunks cones rogue ferns cross-sections and graygreen needles and who knows what-all else, descending in size and visibility all the way down to salamander eggs, specks of dirt, water particles in the form of dewdrops clinging as if in suspended animation to the thirsty endpoints of commalike needles, and then down to the microscopic and atomic level. Each oldgrowth tree endlessly variable, no two even remotely the same—you could rightly say that these amazing lifeforms are very much like snowflakes, scaled up to maximal immensity. Snowflake-level complexity and individuality, but, compared to any living land mammal, like elephant legs soaring up from an ant's perspective. In this unbelievable uniqueness . . . this marvelous complexity incomprehensible to anyone but the subjects themselves . . . here this morning, eyes scanning the upper forest in jawdropped awe, I'm imagining this place's dominant residents as . . . as *talismanic living embodiments* of books, or really any ambitious works of "art." Each book developed with identical basic elements [diction, syntax, punctuation, pacing, etc. etc.] . . . and yet coming to full final bloom with infinite variability, from grand sweeping themes all the way down to individual words and even letters. In this book, I've tried—though it wasn't necessarily always a conscious attempt until very well into its seven-year composition, from the first tiny spores of inchoate musing to defenseless new seedling to sturdy but still vulnerable proper trunk, carrying on through storms and floods and lightning and dangers uncountable, to something resembling the sui generis giants here surrounding us—I've tried to produce a narrative [an *experience*] wholly unlike anything before it. As unique and proliferatingly complex, maybe, in its very best moments *maybe*, as these redwoods. As nature itself—always and forever my greatest muse and inspiration. Perhaps I've achieved nothing remotely close to this . . . yet sometimes, I think the grandest magic in human endeavor reveals itself not through straightforward successfulness in simple, easy tasks—but rather via the tangible odyssey of *attempting to grasp the unreachable*. To my mind, it's far better and more meaningful to fail magnificently at a project of wild, nonimitative ambition than to succeed, no matter how triumphantly, at things that've *already been done* ad nauseum.

Hey—if nothing else, watching the attempt unfold is often entertaining as hell. Sometimes *that's* enough.

I'm throttled out of my inward-spiraling navalgazing by the soft call of my beautiful wife. *What's up, Buttercup?* she sotte voces. As if in [apt] reverence for the quiet majesty all around us. "Nothin," I say, smiling. "Just methinks."

Our dogger flits by on the dirt path, and then dashes off just as quick. We chuckle at her. Our goofy canine queen. A mass of fog has begun to seep into the woods, as is so common in this region, with these trees. After all, starting up here in northern Humboldt, it's classified as temperate rainforest. My wife wraps me in her arms. The fog creeps forward to envelop us, ever so slowly, bringing with it a faint briny trace of the Pacific. We're staring into each other's eyes, close enough . . .

close enough to . . .

to *share oxygen* OH MY GAWD HOLY SHIT it's my dream! My recurring dream from prison, the one from which I'd awake and keep my eyes closed and try against all rational decorum to *will into being*. That unforgettably detailed dream—no not just that, not just a dream, but also it turns out a VISION . . . *it's come to life!* I **did** succeed, ultimately, **in willing it** *to fruition!*

EXCEPT! there are a couple, well, not-so-minor differences . . .

This is *not* Rachel, here in my arms with our bodies pressed together and faces close enough to share oxygen. And this is *not* Rikki, either, here in the woods blasting through the vegetation. It turns out my *real* dream girl is a woman named Andria . . .

Six months or so after my prison release, Rachel and I broke up. No details, sordid or otherwise, are necessary here. Suffice it to say that we merely realized we weren't quite right together. As partners. Sadly, it took two years of pining for one another, yearning in tragic lonesome misery, for us to [eventually] realize it. But Rachel regrets none of it. I can't express how happy this makes me. "If everything we went through was the price of having Rikki in my life, then it was all worth it," as she smartly summarized the whole big mess. "No question." That's right: Rikki's no longer part of my life. Rachel moved to a different state, and Rikki went with her. Why? Well, *I* was the one who ultimately chose to end our relationship. So—despite my "legal right" to keep Rikki [obviously we don't view her, or any ani-mals, as property; we [that's royal-we, meaning all of us] should consider ourselves *guardians* for our nonhuman *companions*; NOT the *owners* of our *pets*]—I didn't even consider exerting that right. My only concerns were: [1] the best outcome for Rikki; and [2] the best thing for Rachel, though this was admittedly far less important.

They formed a profound bond while I was away. Rikki became Rachel's granite rock; sometimes she was the sole reason Rachel managed to drag herself out of bed in the morning. I simply did not have the heart to sever that connection. Breaking up with Rachel was agonizing enough; trying to also keep Rikki was plainly not an option for me. And it really was the best thing for Rikki. So I did what was right. Not because I wanted to [I didn't] and not because it'd make me feel good about myself [it really didn't, and doesn't still], but because it was undeniably just *the right thing to do*—that alone should be sufficient reason.

I served two years' parole; after breaking up with Rachel, I moved back down to the L.A. area and bounced all over Southern California. Mostly, though, I spent my time in Big Bear up in the San Bernardino Mountains, a couple hours inland from L.A. The same place—if you'll recall—where my passport was stuck in blizzard-hell during my first stint in County Jail. Things have a funny way of coming full circle, don't they? Very soon after moving to Big Bear, I visited the local animal shelter and met a gorgeous, sweet black pit bull-labrador mix. Mom didn't want me to get a dog—I was staying at her cabin—but when the sweet girl was slated for euthanasia [the dog, not Mom], I couldn't turn away. I'd become emotionally inves-ted, thereby forming what felt to me like a moral obligation. Luckily my mother is a wonderful person, as you must know, so I managed to con-vince Mom to let me adopt her [the dog, not Mom] in early 2011. With her jetblack fur and big brown eyes and her ears' tendency to flare way out to the sides and remain like that at length, she totally resembled a bat. So I tried out the name *Batty*. In addition to her appearance, she's also a wild frenzied beast, a crazed ball of uncontainable frenetic energy. In other words, she even *acts* rather batty! It's the perfect name for her. Also, it serves as an originally-unintentional-but-now-presented-as-intentional homage to maybe the most important kids' movie ever, *FernGully: The Last Rainforest*. In it, Robin Williams [another heartwrenching artist-suicide] voices a bat who escaped a vivisection laboratory-prison and suffers PTSD from the terrible experiments—and also has the same name as my baby girl! So again, a perfect name. Rikki may be the best dog ever, I admit it. Yet my newer dogger Batty is damn close! Right on Rikki's white-splashed heels.

For the entire post-Rachel 18 months I was shackled by parole, I yearned to be in Humboldt. *Painfully* yearned. In fact, on literally the very first day I'd ever spent there—way back in 2006—I decided that I *had* to live in Humboldt some day. One thing or another though was always getting in the way. Like finances and relationships and, you know, the whole *prison* thing, etc. But then, after being released from parole in April 2014, I knew there'd never be a better opportunity. It was also an excellent occasion for me to have a fresh start. To finally go live where I yearned to live, and where I knew I belonged. No more excuses!

In the couple months leading up to my release from parole—to my *real* freedom—I began seeking to make a friend or two online with people already living in Humboldt, so that I wouldn't be completely alone once I moved up there. That's how Andria and I first "met." Via OKCupid.com, of all places. We fell in love almost immediately. Madly in love: I drove 700 miles, 12ish hours straight through the night, in February [two months before my parole release-date] to meet and spend time with her. We had a total blast; an unforgettably fantastic week together. She's marvelously sweet, mellow, gorgeous, caring, compassionate, understanding, hilarious, and on and on. We have an absurd amount in common. And our flaws are such that they basically cancel each other out, making us utterly *perfect* together. My amazing, vegan, childfree-by-choice Humboldt stoner-girl sweetheart! We got engaged after six months together, finally marrying in June 2016. Our friend/partnership has continuously grown more and more special and joyous all the time. Andria . . . a literal dream [vision?] come true.

Maybe this doesn't seem like a Happy Ending to you, after everything Rachel and I went through together. Inside and outside this book. But it very much *is* a Happy Ending, unequivocally and absolutely; trust me. Rachel found an amazing man who's perfect for her, and whom I trust with Rikki's life. I've found my soulmate. So it's all good, all around, through and through. And it's not just a Happy Ending—it's the RIGHT ending. The *true* and *proper* end to my Prison Saga—at least insofar as such a traumatic and transformative experience could ever fully be over [it can't].

If nothing else, I know one thing for certain after all we've been through together. After all the outlandish bureaucratic absurdity and hellacious suffering and triumphant survival detailed herein. And, I feel compelled to add, after the excrutiating difficulty I had in *writing* my story. Here it is—the one thing I'm most certain about after all this: Words and language are *everything*. What we say, how we say it, when and where we are, the contextual circumstances surrounding our choice of expression . . . everything. All of it matters so very much. This goes for prison and its macrocosmic "Free" World counterpart, it goes for health care and int-erpersonal relationships and the kind of people we choose to be and the human decency of our actions, it goes for navigating any and all Burea-crazies, for marriage, and it goes for writing a highly ambitious and long [and inflammatory] narrative nonfiction book; the means with which we choose to express ourselves is one of the most important decisions we ever have to make amid our existence as human animals in this demented, ludicrous, fucked up society. What else is there, really? Without words, all we have left is

REBEL HELL

Connect with Jan Online

www.JanSmitowicz.com
www.Facebook.com/JanSmitowiczWriting
YouTube: www.bit.ly/2p1Kmry
www.Twitter.com/JanSmitowicz

If you enjoyed *Rebel Hell*, reviews are very much appreciated on Amazon, Goodreads, et al. Thank you so much for reading!

~Love and Liberation~
Jan, June 2010—April 2017

Partial Bibliography and
Recommended Further Reading

Soledad Brother, George Jackson

A Prayer for Owen Meany, John Irving

Green is the New Red, Will Potter

Drug Crazy, Mike Gray

Creating Monsters, Sherman Manning

Welcome to the Machine, Derrick Jensen & George Draffan

The Culture of Make Believe, Derrick Jensen

The Pain Chronicles, Melanie Thernstrom

All Things Censored CD, Mumia Abu-Jamal

In a Pig's Eye CD, Ward Churchill

Rant in E-Minor CD, Bill Hicks

Long Walk to Freedom, Nelson Mandela

High Society [unpublished], Jan Smitowicz

The Monkey Wrench Gang, Edward Abbey

www.mysterium.com/extinction.html

Still Life with Woodpecker, Tom Robbins

www.Erowid.com

National Institute of Justice:
www.nij.gov/topics/corrections/recidivism/pages/welcome.aspx

"Civil Disobedience," Henry David Thoreau

"Judge Sentenced . . . ," *Blue Nation Review*:
www.bluenationreview.com/judge-sentenced-selling-kids-profit-prison/

www.ThinkProgress.org

Orange Rain, Jan Smitowicz

Angela Davis: An Autobiography, Angela Davis

The Sixth Extinction: Biodiversity and its Survival, Leakey and Lewin

Under a Green Sky, Peter Ward

www.worldometers.info/world-population/

Human Rights Watch,
www.hrw.org/legacy/backgrounder/usa/incarceration/

United Poultry Concerns, www.upc-
online.org/chickens/chickensbro.html

ADAPTT [Animals Deserve Absolute Protection Today and
Tomorrow], www.adaptt.org/killcounter.html

www.deepgreenresistance.com/en/deep-green-resistance-
strategy/decisive-ecological-warfare

"Rick Santorum Wants Pope Francis to Stop Talking About Climate
Change," The Huffington Post,
http://www.huffingtonpost.com/2015/06/02/rick-santorum-pope-
climat_n_7498768.html

Assata, Assata Shakur

Deep Green Resistance: Strategy to Save the Planet, Aric McBay and Lierre
Keith

Endgame, Volumes 1 & 2, Derrick Jensen

Free the Animals, Ingrid Newkirk

Strong Hearts: The Liberators, Volume 1, Jan Smitowicz [forthcoming]

Better Never to Have Been: The Harm of Coming into Existence, David
Benatar

The Species Barrier Podcast, www.thespeciesbarrier.podbean.com/e/the-
species-barrier-35-antinatal/

The Huffington Post, www.huffingtonpost.com/2013/09/17/racial-
disparity-drug-use_n_3941346.html

Stanford Law & Policy Review: "Race, Drugs, and Law Enforcement in the
United States," www.journals.law.stanford.edu/stanford-law-policy
review/print/volume-20/issue-2-drug-laws-policy-and-reform/race-
drugs-and-law-enforcement-united-states

Made in the USA
Lexington, KY
30 May 2018